Arata
THE LEGEND

23

WE ARE MAN, BORN OF HEAVEN AND EARTH,
MOON AND SUN AND EVERYTHING UNDER THEM.

EYES, EARS, NOSE, TONGUE, BODY, MIND...

PURITY WILL PIERCE EVIL AND
OPEN UP THE WORLD OF DARKNESS.

ALL LIFE WILL BE REBORN AND INVIGORATED.

APPEAR NOW.

STORY & ART BY
YUU WATASE

Arata
THE LEGEND

CHARACTERS

EH?

NASAKE
Although Zokusho of Ameeno, one of the Six Sho, he serves Arata Hinohara.

BLUMP

BLUMP

WHAT THE DEVIL'S HAPPENED TO ME?!

ARATA HINOHARA
A high school student from modern Japan. In Amawakuni, he is chosen by the famous Hayagami, Tsukuyo, and becomes a Sho. Due to circumstances, he has been transformed into a girl.

KANNAGI
One of the Twelve Shinsho, he wields the Hayagami Homura. Like Arata Hinohara, he has undergone a gender change.

YATAKA
Shinsho of the Hayagami Zekuu. He has also been transformed into a girl.

YII! EVEN MY VOICE IS CHANGING!

ORIBE

A young girl in the modern world who possesses the Amatsuriki power of the Hime Clan.

AMEENO

One of the Six Sho and perhaps Arata Hinohara's deadliest foe.

MASATO KADOWAKI

A classmate of Arata Hinohara. He has pursued Arata to Amawakuni and is the Sho of the Hayagami Orochi.

ARATA

Youth belonging to the Hime Clan who came to the modern world when he switched places with Arata Hinohara.

HARUNAWA

One of the Six Sho who switched places with Kadowaki and is now in the modern world. Seeks to kill Imina Oribe.

KOTOHA

A young maiden of the Uneme Clan who serves the Hime Clan. She is currently a boy.

MIKUSA

Swordswoman of the Hime Clan. She is currently a boy.

THE STORY THUS FAR

Arata Hinohara, finding himself in Amawakuni, a land in another dimension, is chosen as the successor to the legendary Hayagami Tsukuyo. In order to stop the fighting that ensued after Princess Kikuri's collapse, he continues his journey to make all the Sho submit and unify the Hayagami.

Arata and company enter the territory of Ikisu, one of the Six Sho. But another of the Six Sho, Ameeno, appears and a battle ensues between him and Ikisu. Ameeno wins and forces Ikisu to submit, then leaves in his airship. Arata and the others commandeer Ikisu's airship and go in pursuit, but due to the effects of a "scent sphere" on board, everyone's gender is switched. Meanwhile, in the modern world, Harunawa, an invading Sho, demonizes all the students at Hinohara's school and sends them to attack Arata of the Hime, with whom Hinohara had switched places, and his classmate Oribe.

23
Arata
THE LEGEND

CONTENTS

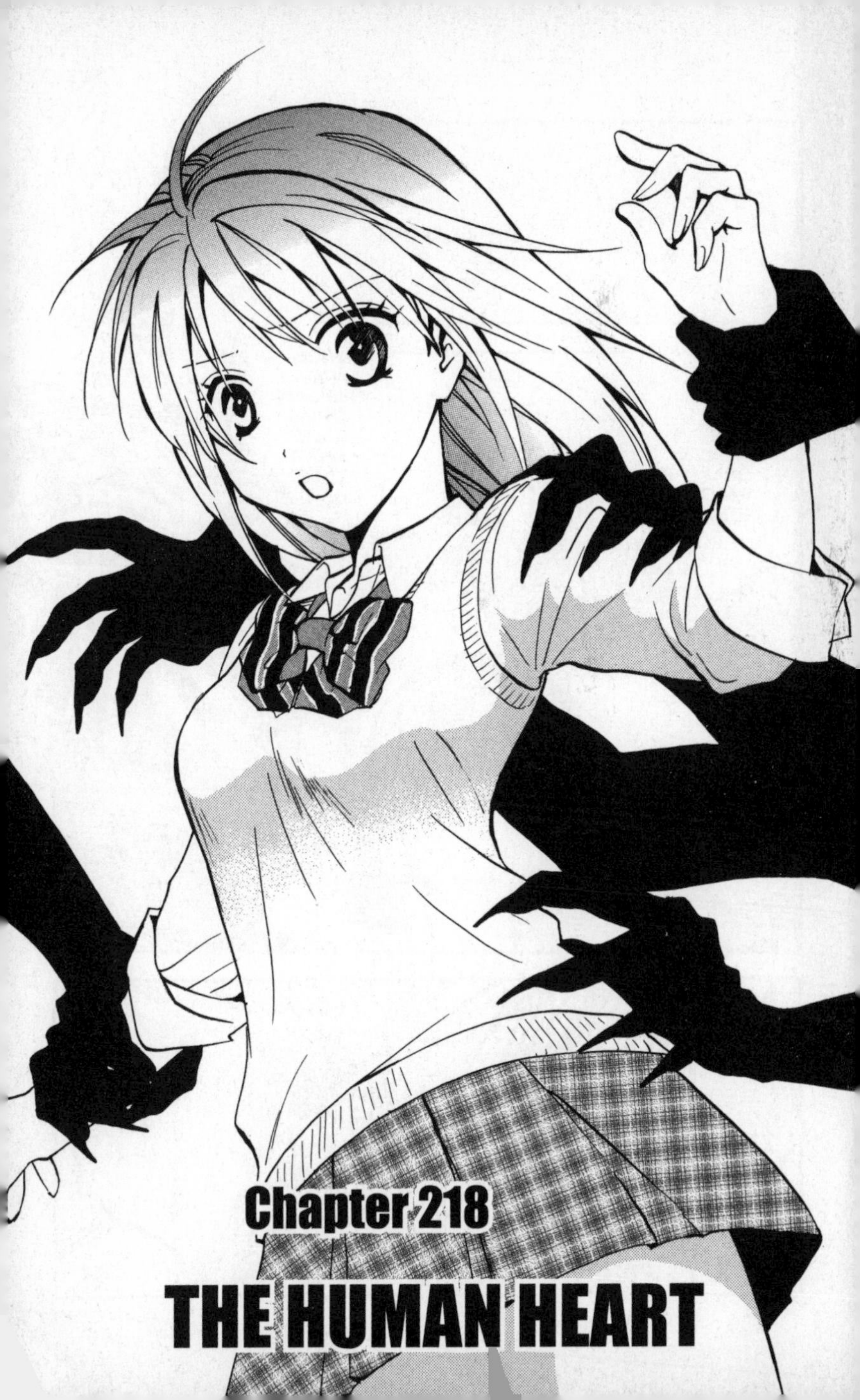
Chapter 218
THE HUMAN HEART

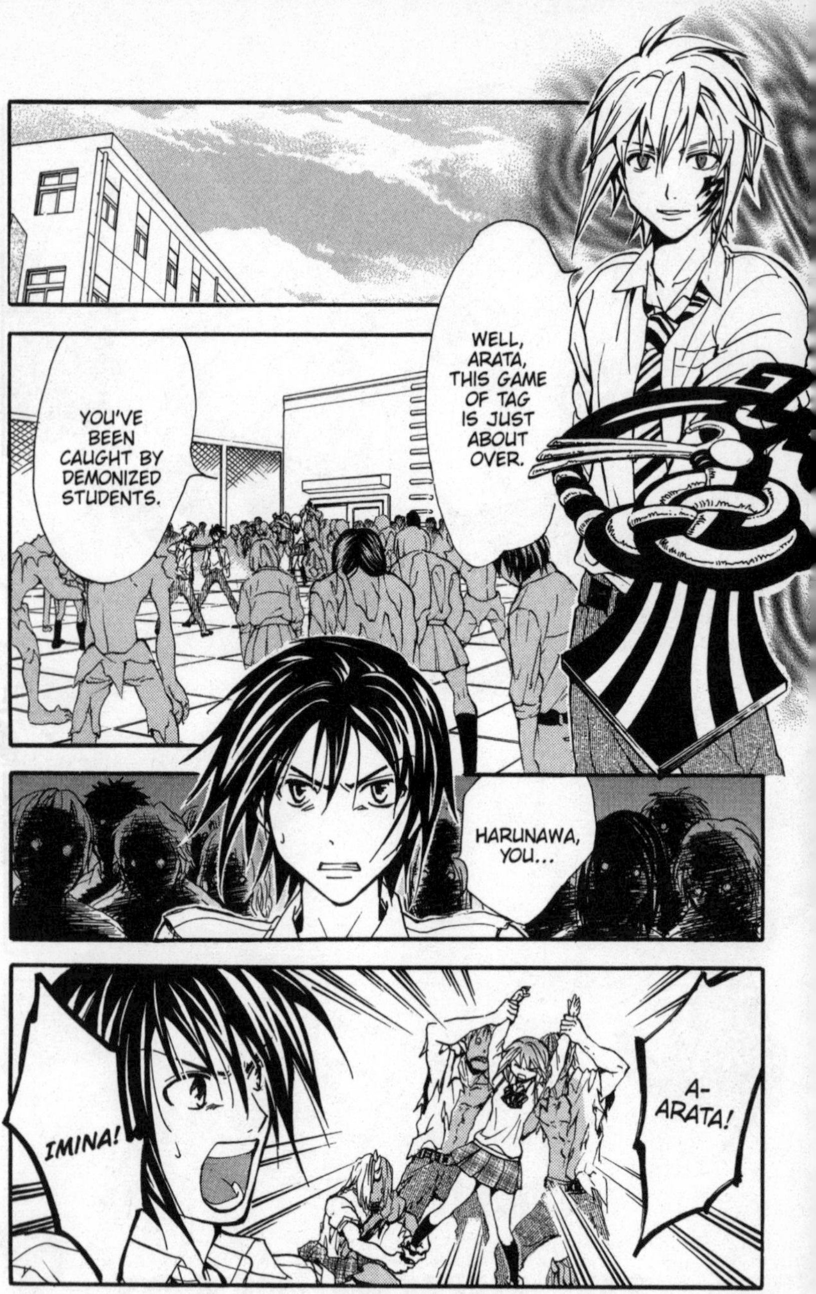
WELL, ARATA, THIS GAME OF TAG IS JUST ABOUT OVER.
YOU'VE BEEN CAUGHT BY DEMONIZED STUDENTS.
HARUNAWA, YOU...
A-ARATA!
IMINA!

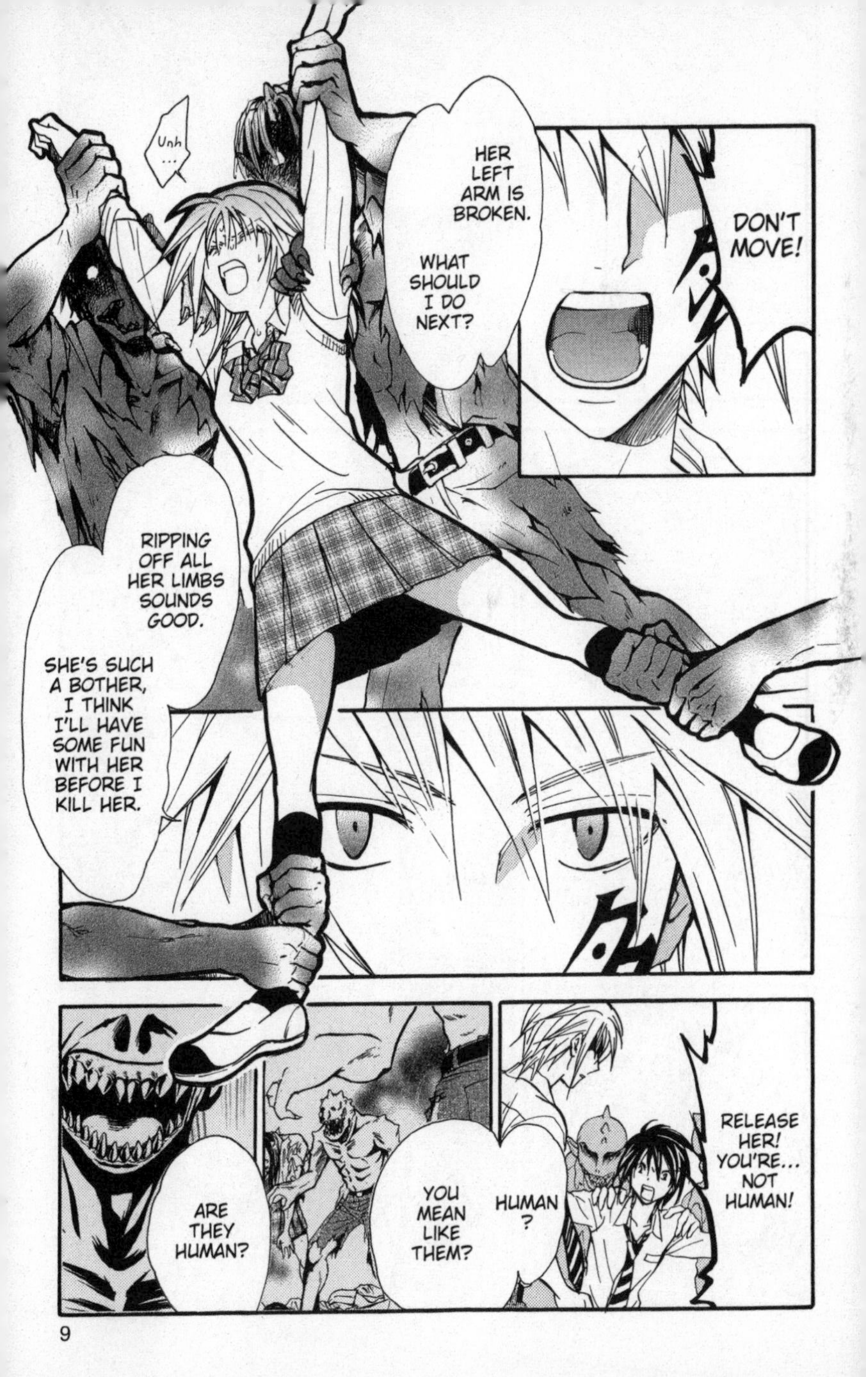
DON'T MOVE!
HER LEFT ARM IS BROKEN.
WHAT SHOULD I DO NEXT?
Unh ...
RIPPING OFF ALL HER LIMBS SOUNDS GOOD.
SHE'S SUCH A BOTHER, I THINK I'LL HAVE SOME FUN WITH HER BEFORE I KILL HER.
RELEASE HER! YOU'RE... NOT HUMAN!
HUMAN?
YOU MEAN LIKE THEM?
ARE THEY HUMAN?

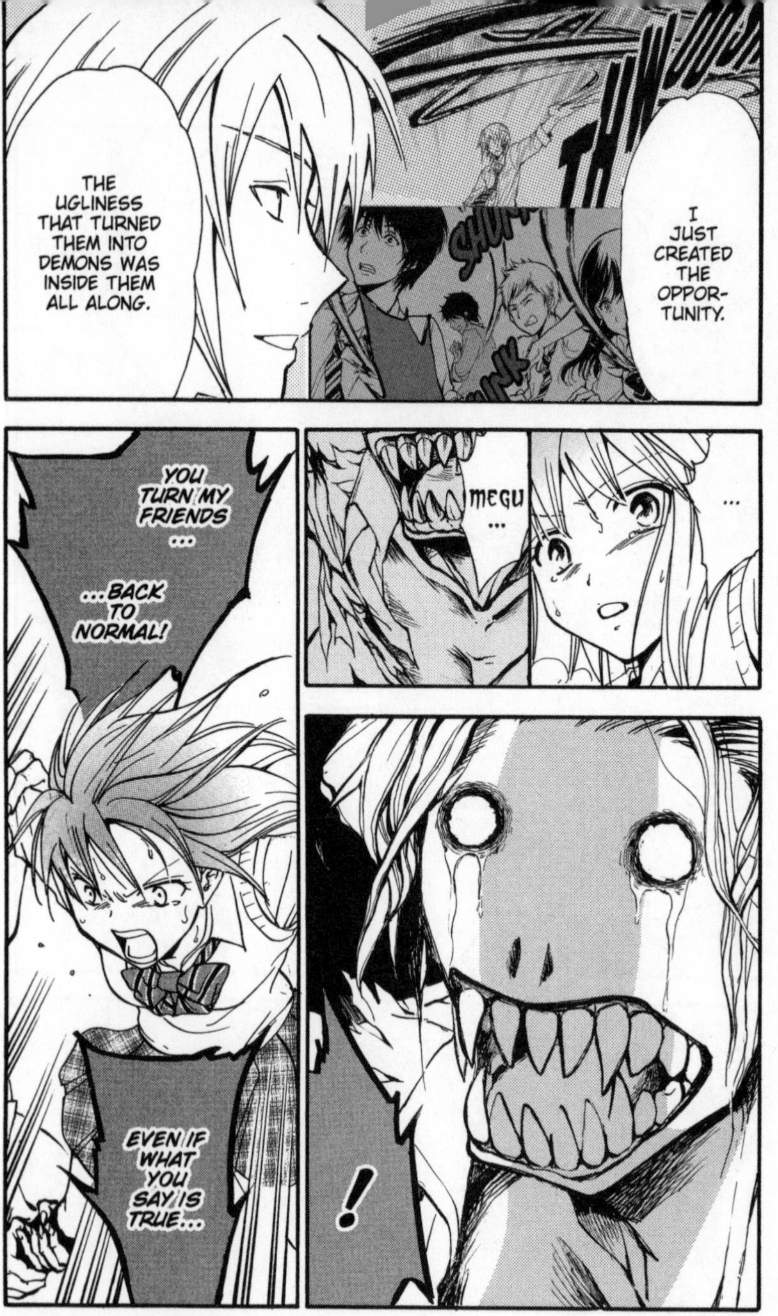
I JUST CREATED THE OPPORTUNITY.
THE UGLINESS THAT TURNED THEM INTO DEMONS WAS INSIDE THEM ALL ALONG.
...
MEGU ...
!
YOU TURN MY FRIENDS ...
...BACK TO NORMAL!
EVEN IF WHAT YOU SAY IS TRUE...

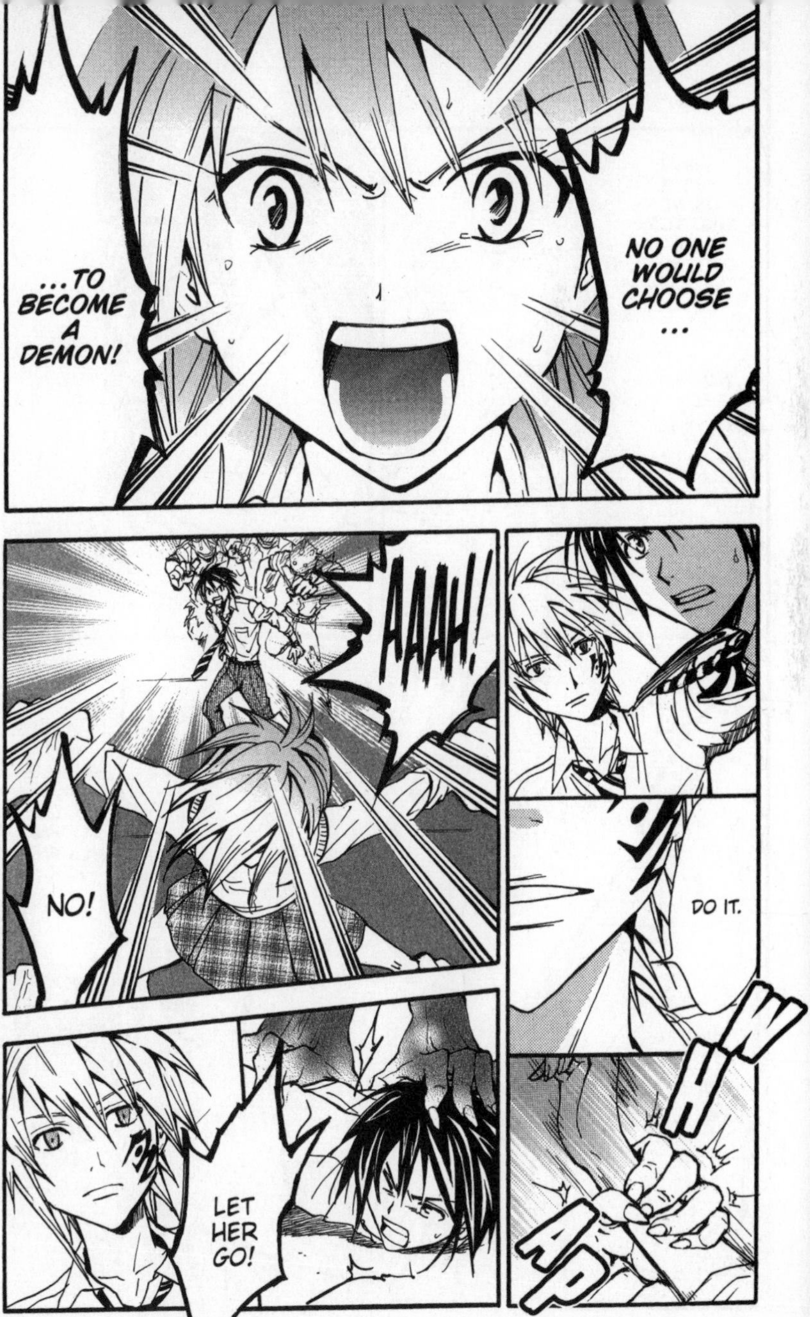
NO ONE WOULD CHOOSE ...
...TO BECOME A DEMON!
DO IT.
AAAH!
NO!
WHAP
LET HER GO!

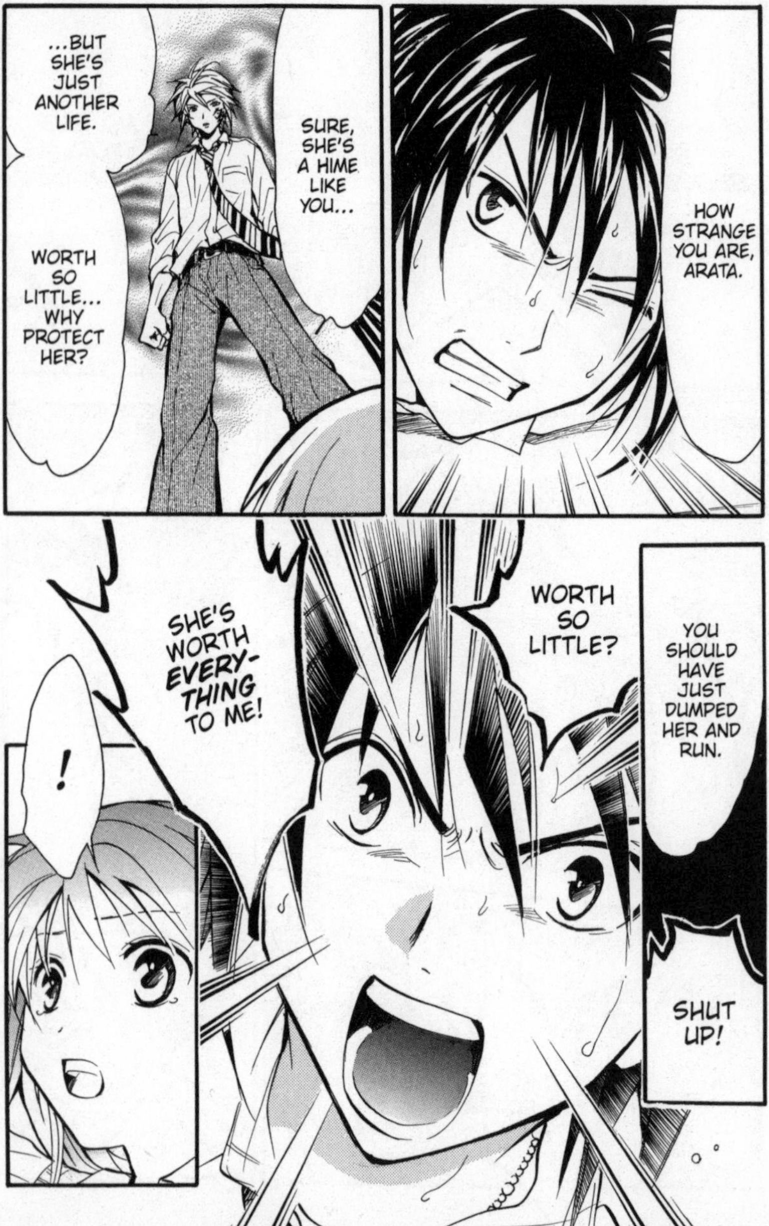
HOW STRANGE YOU ARE, ARATA.
SURE, SHE'S A HIME LIKE YOU...
...BUT SHE'S JUST ANOTHER LIFE.
WORTH SO LITTLE... WHY PROTECT HER?
YOU SHOULD HAVE JUST DUMPED HER AND RUN.
SHUT UP!
WORTH SO LITTLE?
SHE'S WORTH EVERYTHING TO ME!
!

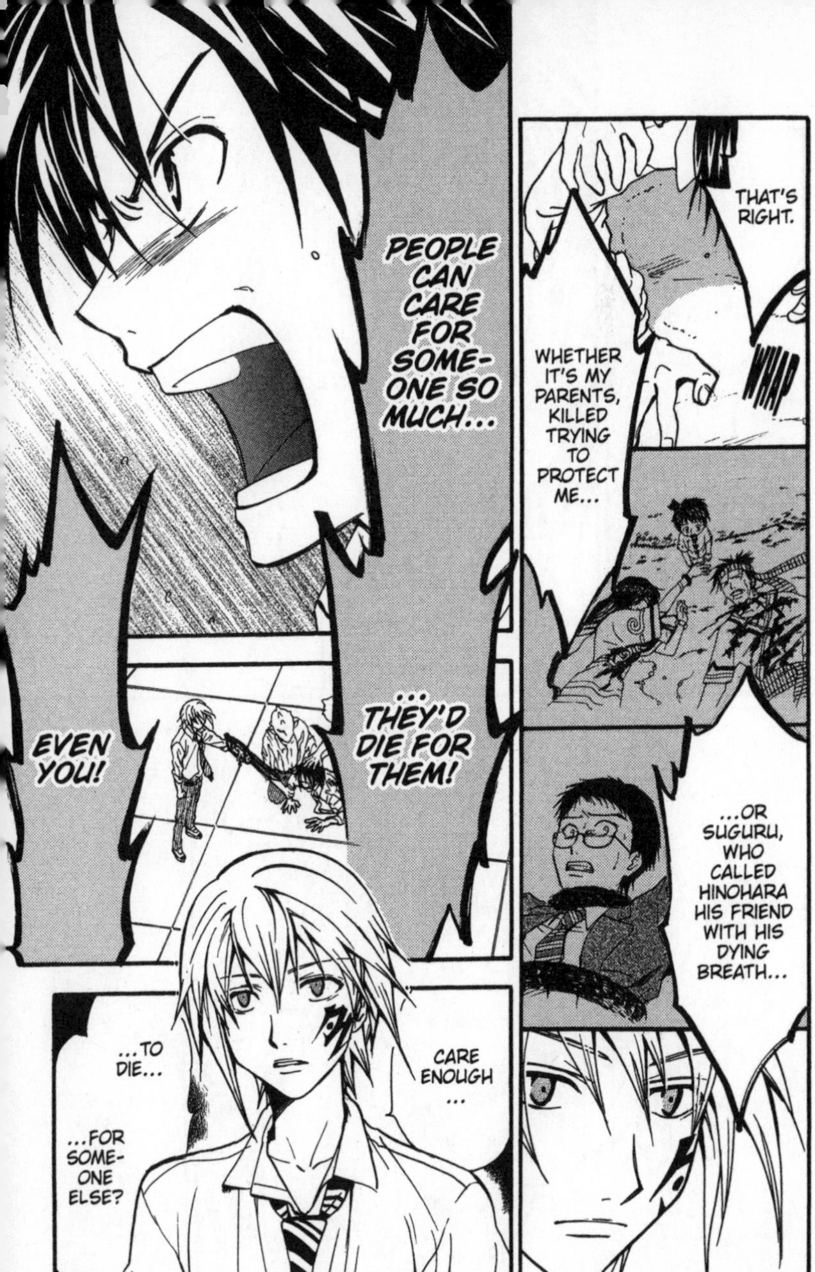
THAT'S RIGHT.
WHAP
WHETHER IT'S MY PARENTS, KILLED TRYING TO PROTECT ME...
...OR SUGURU, WHO CALLED HINOHARA HIS FRIEND WITH HIS DYING BREATH...
PEOPLE CAN CARE FOR SOME-ONE SO MUCH...
...THEY'D DIE FOR THEM!
EVEN YOU!
CARE ENOUGH ...
...TO DIE...
...FOR SOME-ONE ELSE?

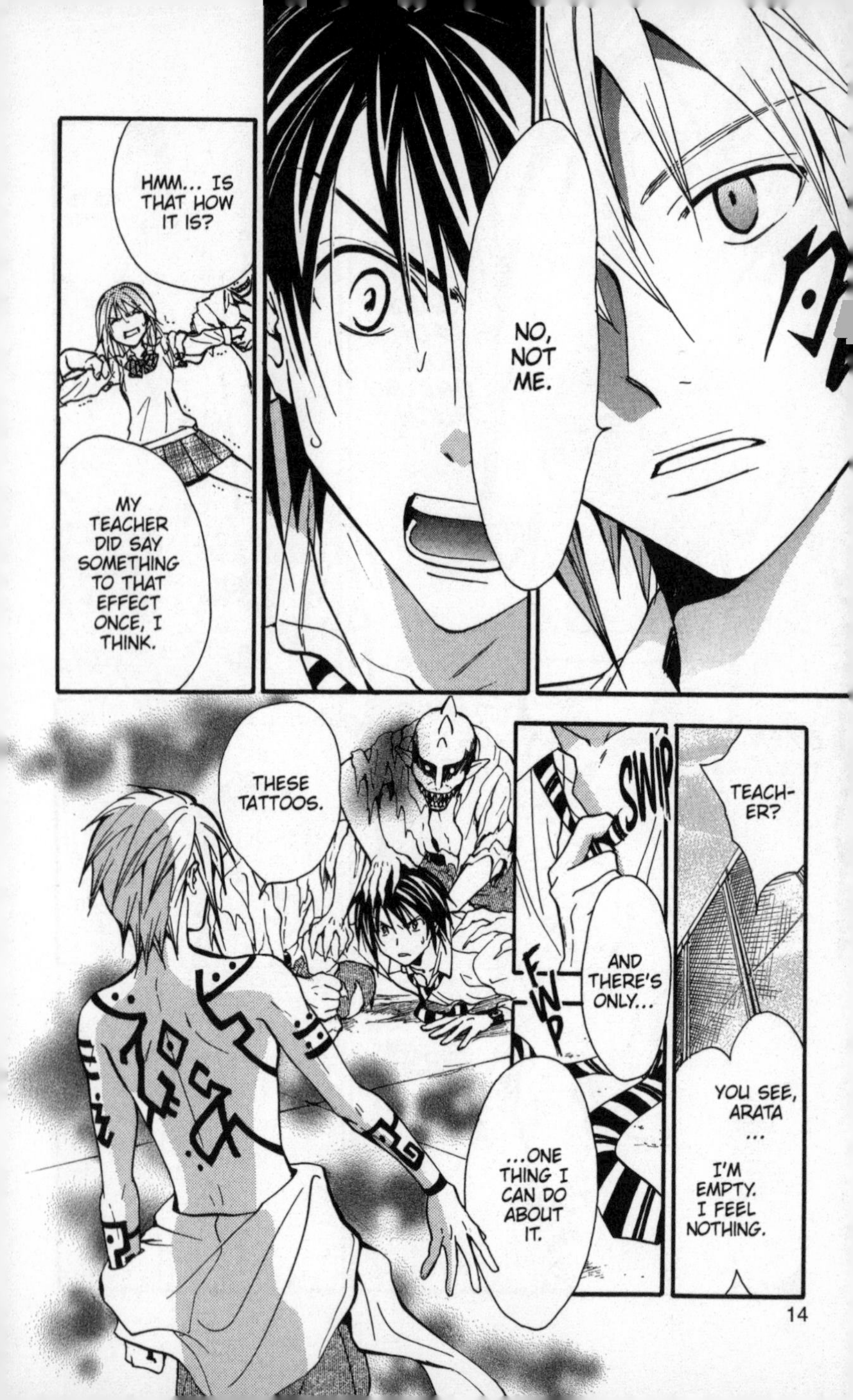
NO, NOT ME.
HMM... IS THAT HOW IT IS?
MY TEACHER DID SAY SOMETHING TO THAT EFFECT ONCE, I THINK.
TEACHER?
YOU SEE, ARATA ...
I'M EMPTY. I FEEL NOTHING.
SWIP
AND THERE'S ONLY...
FWP
...ONE THING I CAN DO ABOUT IT.
THESE TATTOOS.

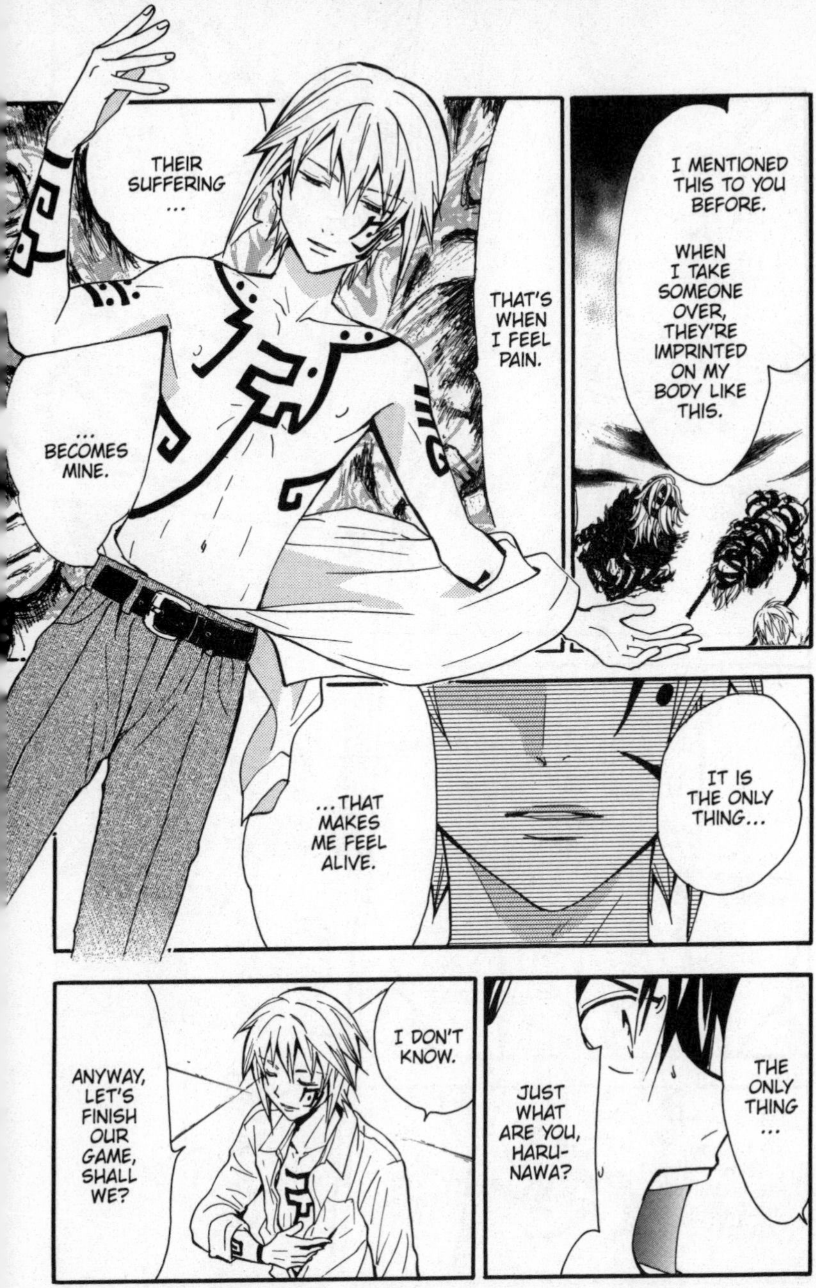
I MENTIONED THIS TO YOU BEFORE.
WHEN I TAKE SOMEONE OVER, THEY'RE IMPRINTED ON MY BODY LIKE THIS.
THAT'S WHEN I FEEL PAIN.
THEIR SUFFERING ...
... BECOMES MINE.
IT IS THE ONLY THING...
...THAT MAKES ME FEEL ALIVE.
THE ONLY THING ...
JUST WHAT ARE YOU, HARU-NAWA?
I DON'T KNOW.
ANYWAY, LET'S FINISH OUR GAME, SHALL WE?

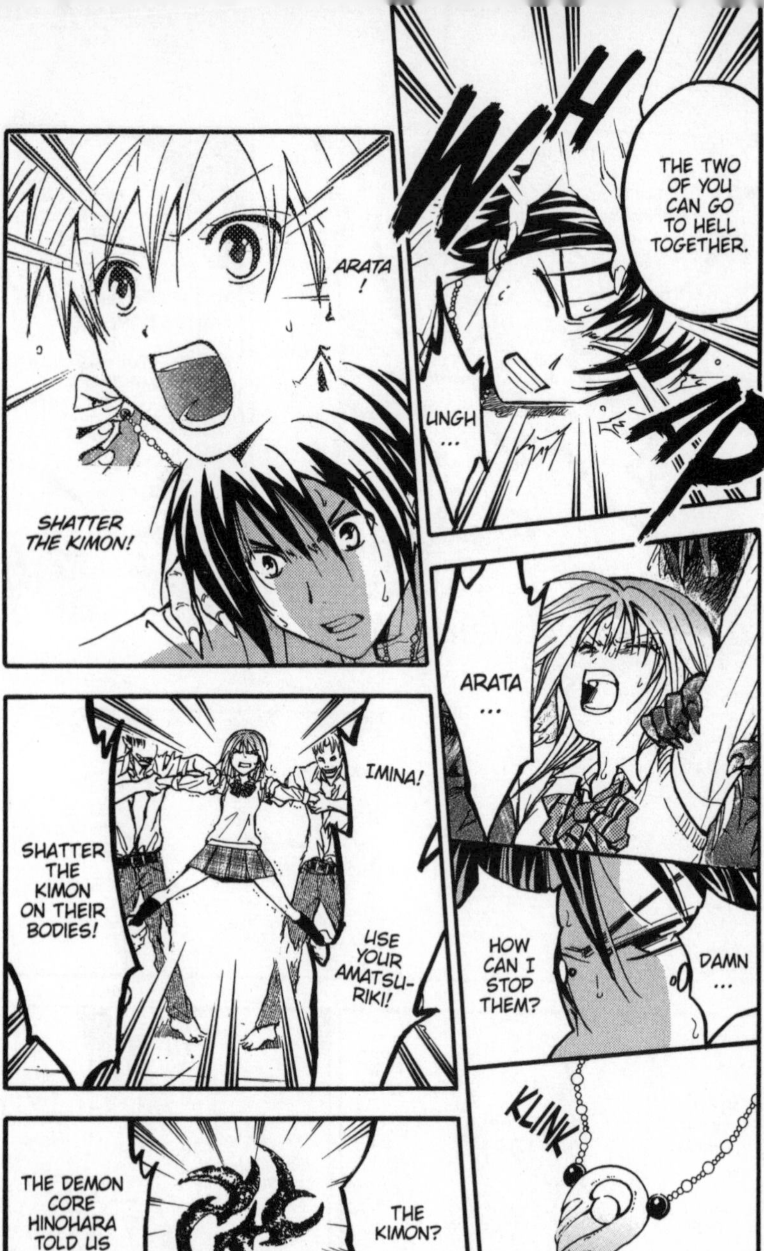
THE TWO OF YOU CAN GO TO HELL TOGETHER.
WHAP
UNGH ...
ARATA!
SHATTER THE KIMON!
ARATA ...
DAMN ...
HOW CAN I STOP THEM?
IMINA!
USE YOUR AMATSU-RIKI!
SHATTER THE KIMON ON THEIR BODIES!
KLINK
THE KIMON?
THE DEMON CORE HINOHARA TOLD US ABOUT!

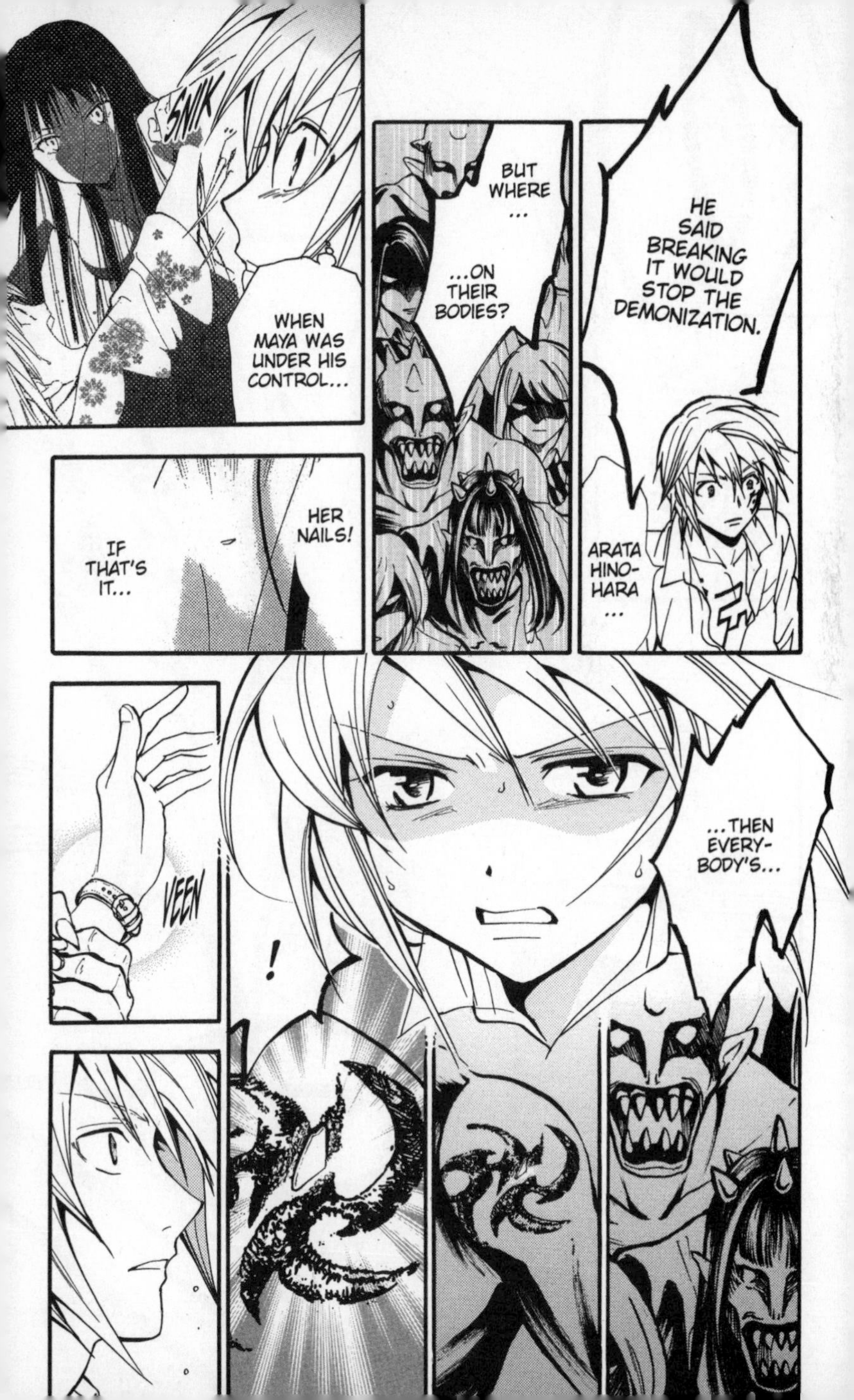
HE SAID BREAKING IT WOULD STOP THE DEMONIZATION.
ARATA HINO-HARA ...
BUT WHERE ...
...ON THEIR BODIES?
SNIK
WHEN MAYA WAS UNDER HIS CONTROL...
HER NAILS!
IF THAT'S IT...
...THEN EVERY-BODY'S...
!
VEEN

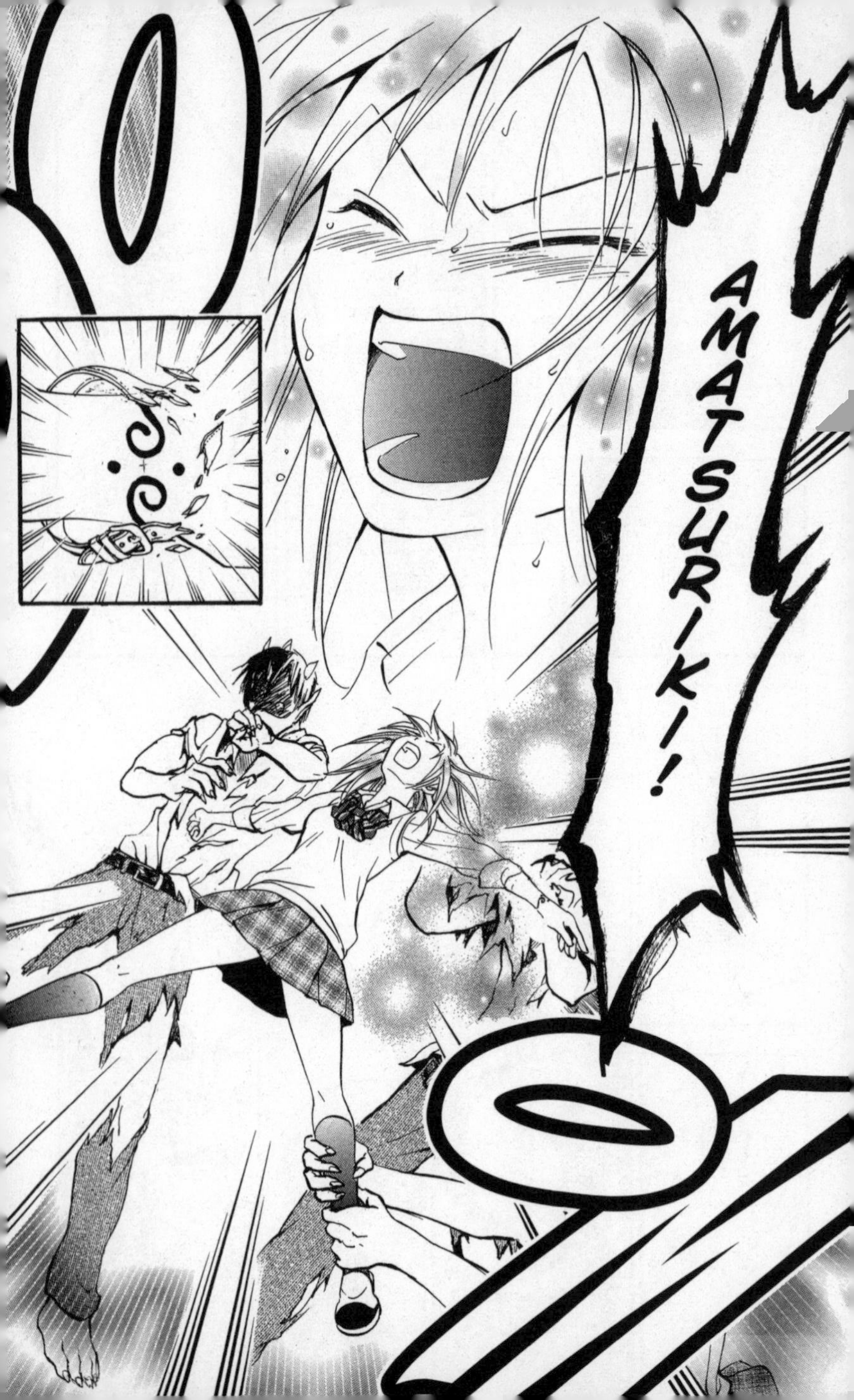
AMATSURIKI!!

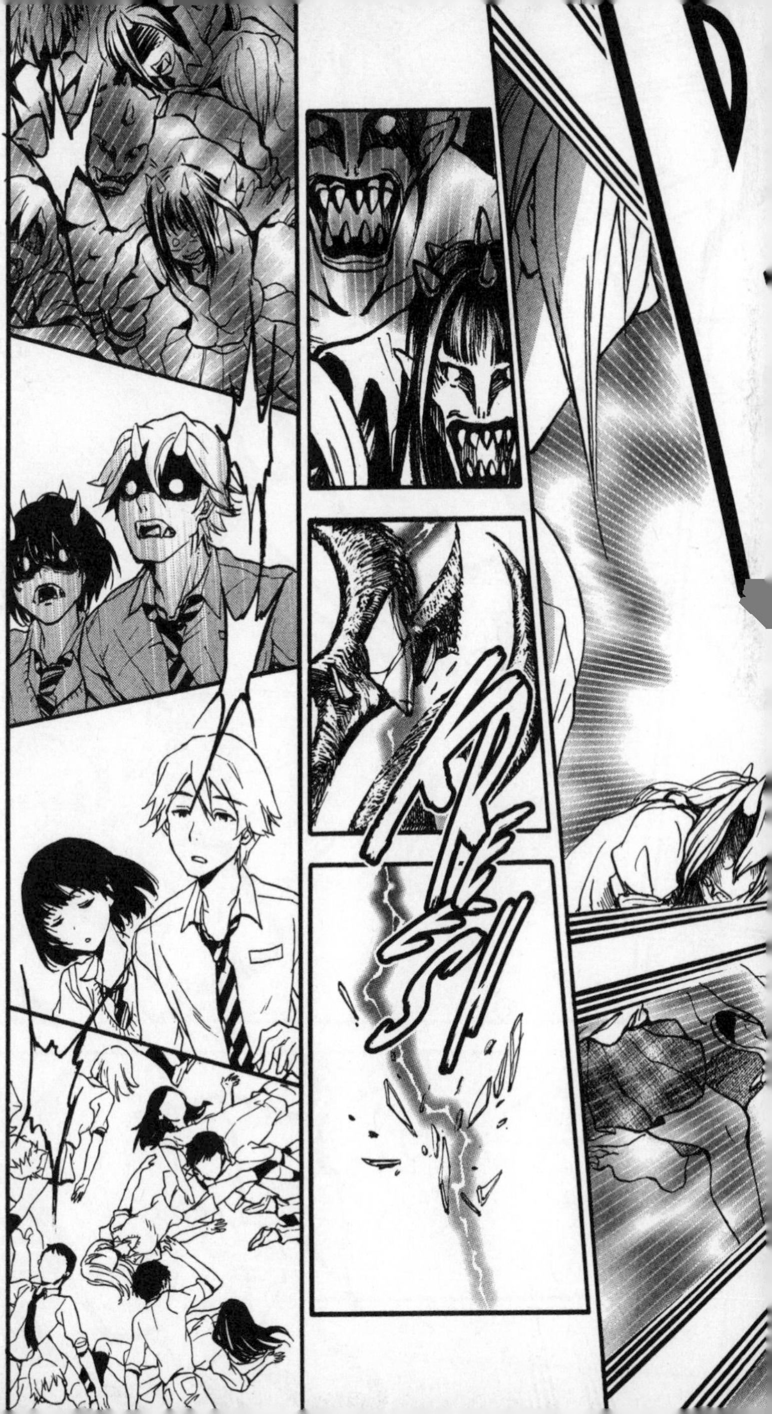

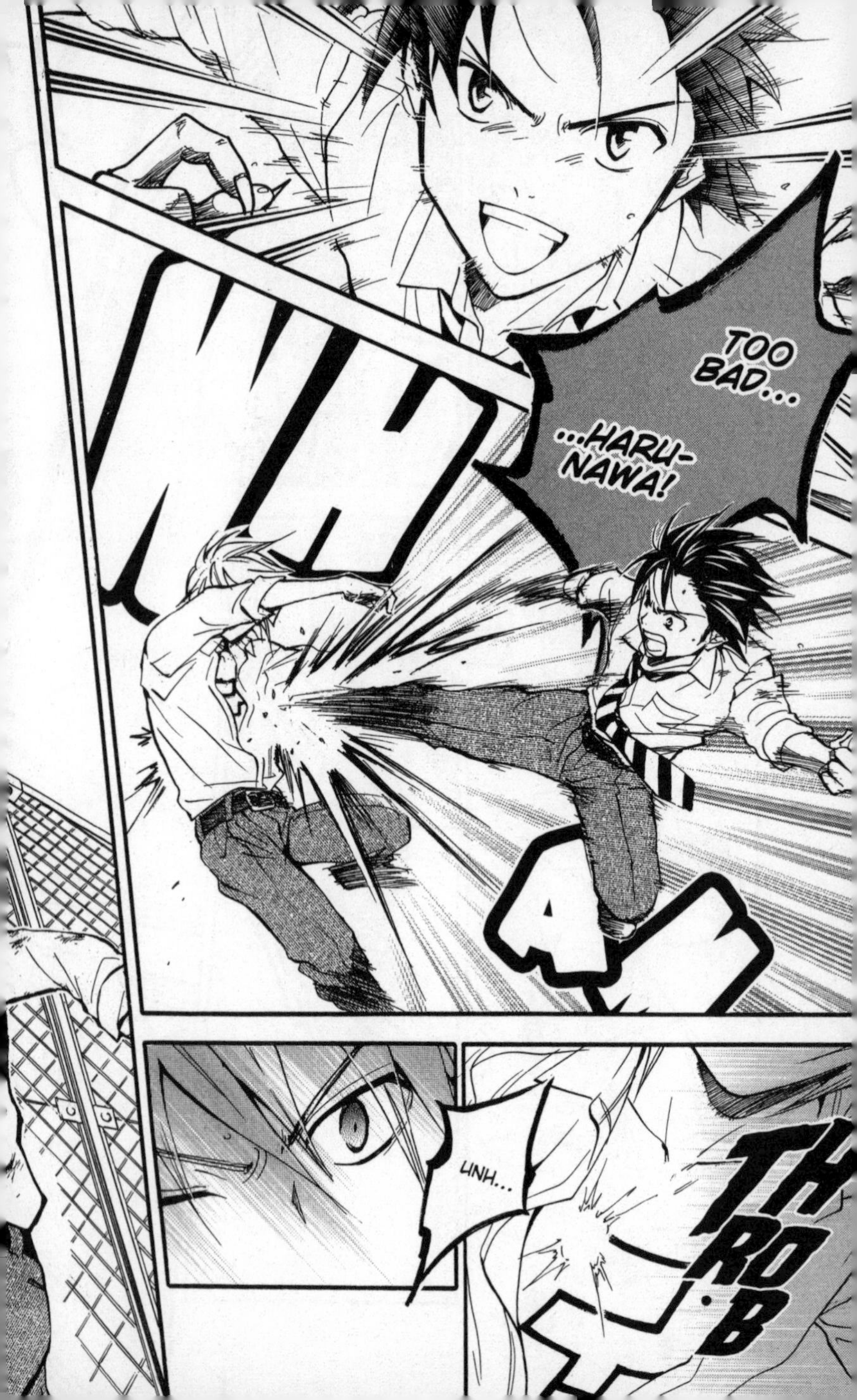
TOO BAD...
...HARU-NAWA!
WHA
THROB
UNH...

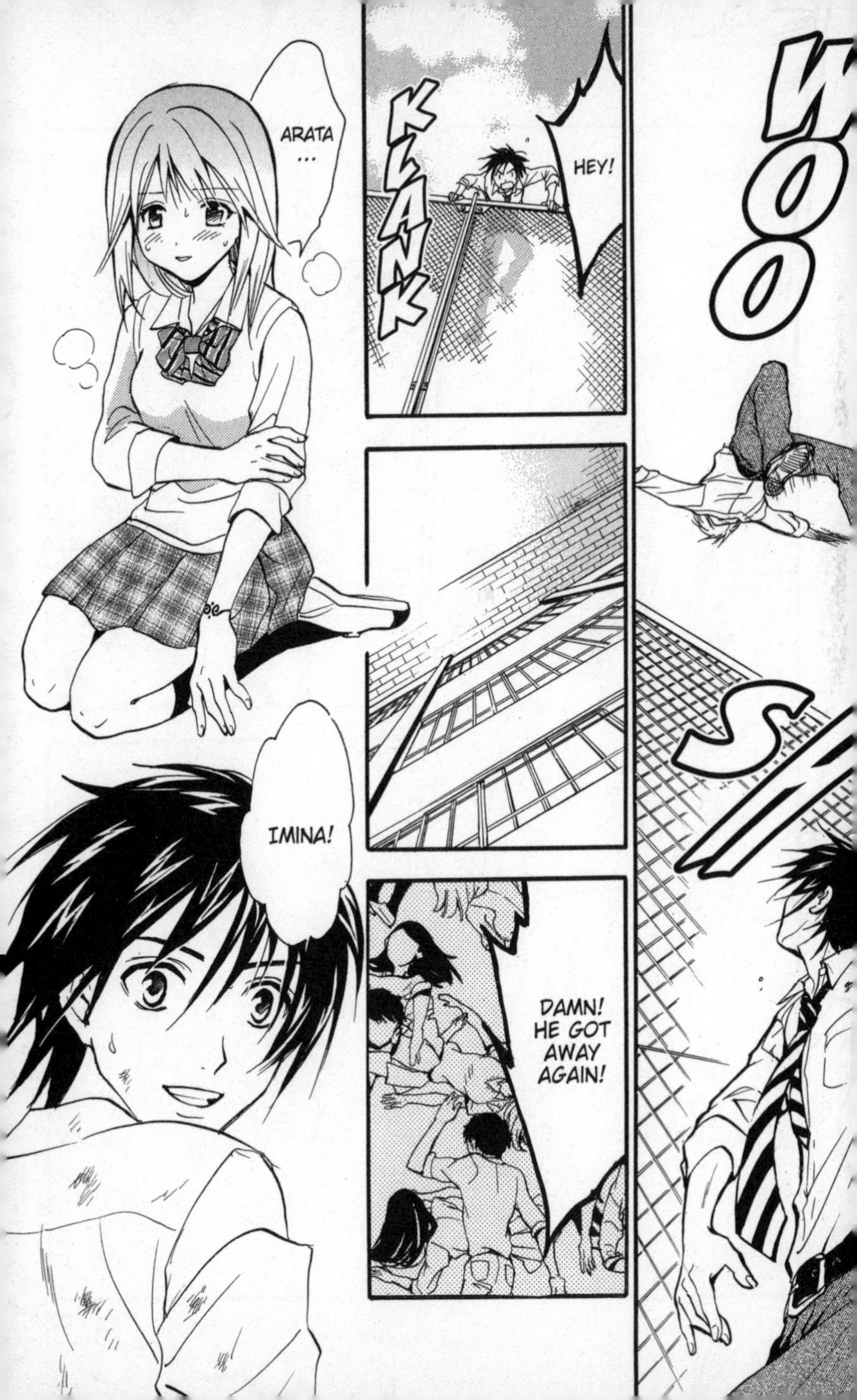
WOOO
S
HEY!
KLANK
DAMN! HE GOT AWAY AGAIN!
ARATA ...
IMINA!

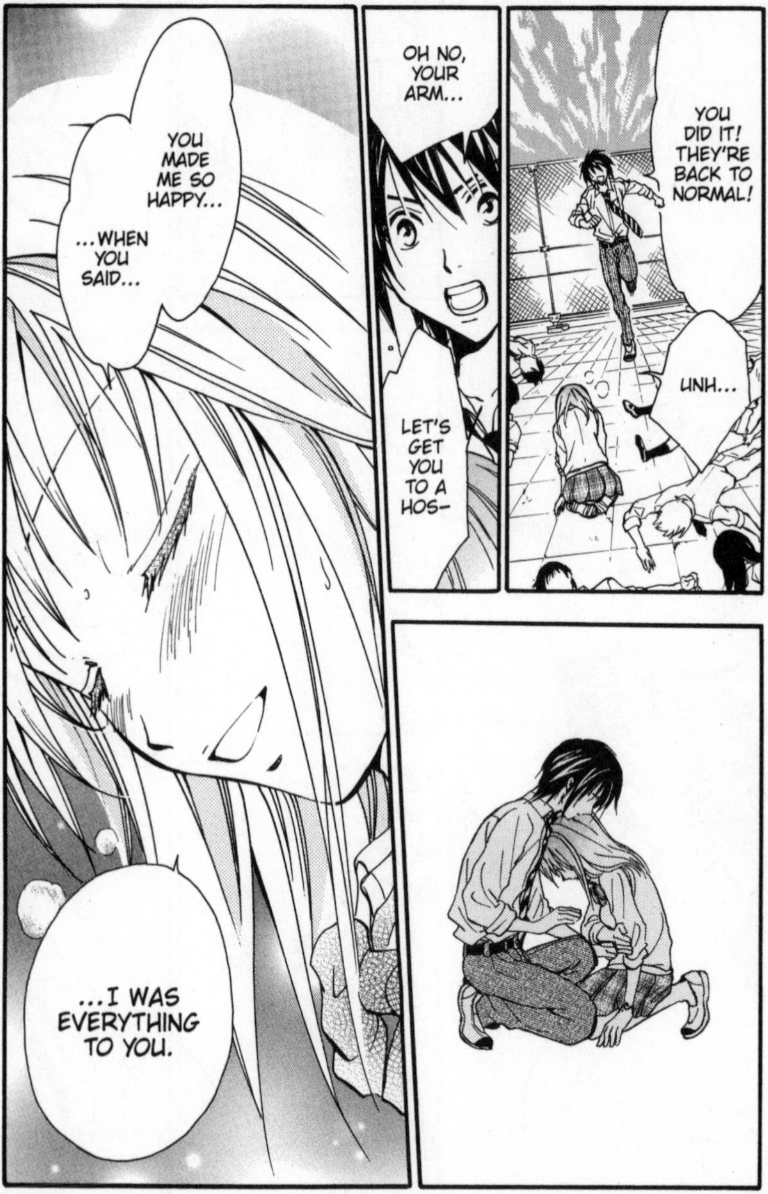
YOU DID IT! THEY'RE BACK TO NORMAL!
UNH...
OH NO, YOUR ARM...
LET'S GET YOU TO A HOS-
YOU MADE ME SO HAPPY...
...WHEN YOU SAID...
...I WAS EVERYTHING TO YOU.

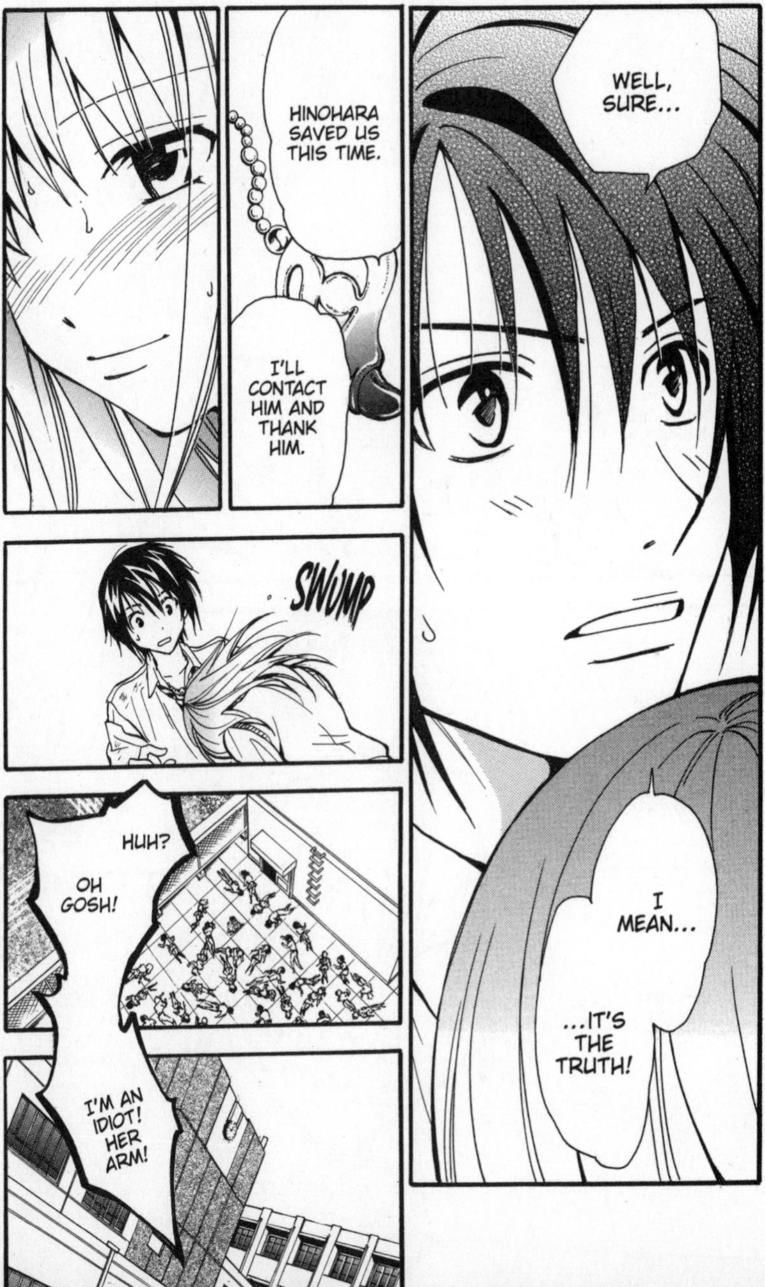
WELL, SURE...
I MEAN...
...IT'S THE TRUTH!
HINOHARA SAVED US THIS TIME.
I'LL CONTACT HIM AND THANK HIM.
SWUMP
HUH?
OH GOSH!
I'M AN IDIOT! HER ARM!

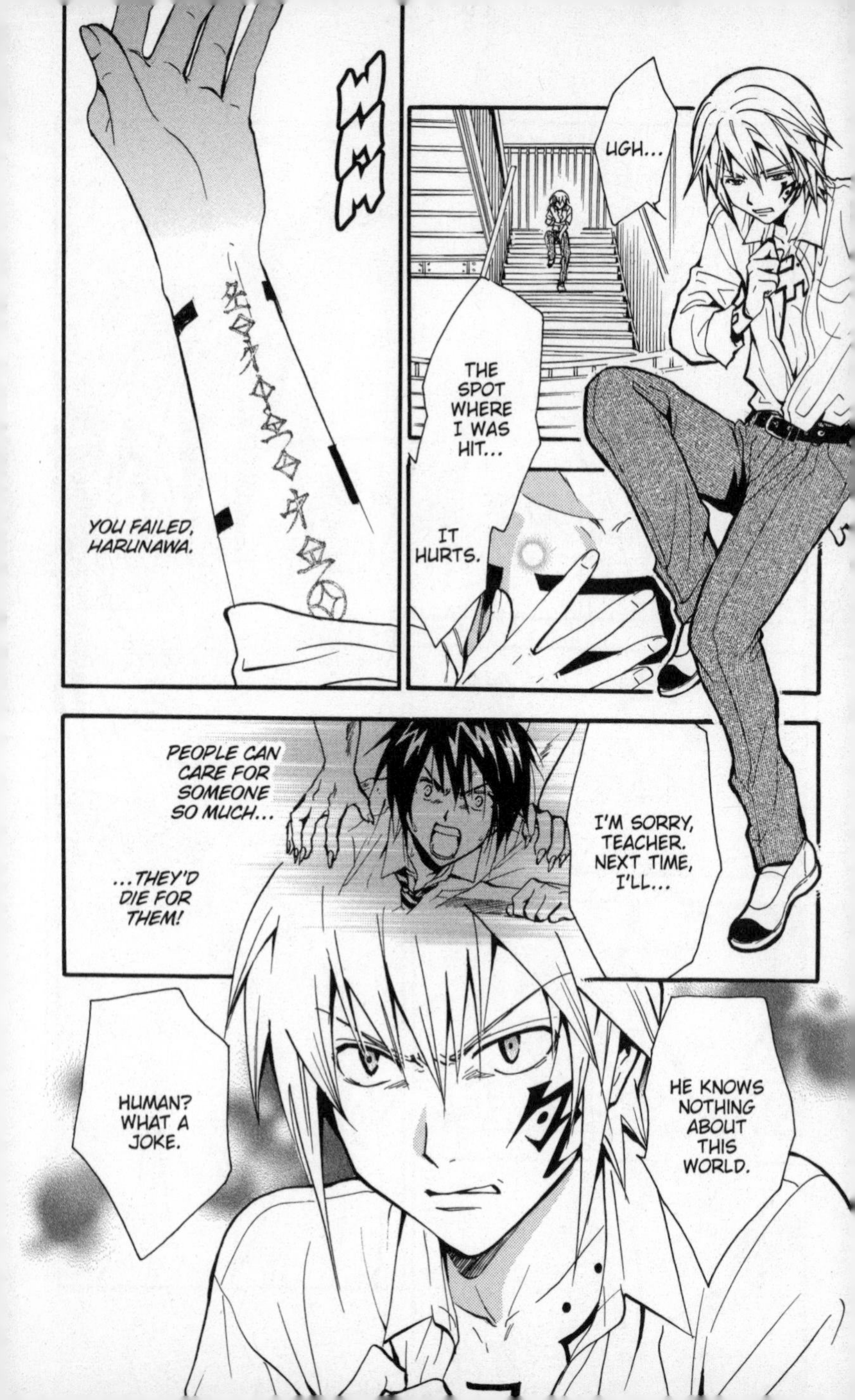
UGH...
THE SPOT WHERE I WAS HIT...
IT HURTS.
YOU FAILED, HARUNAWA.
I'M SORRY, TEACHER. NEXT TIME, I'LL...
PEOPLE CAN CARE FOR SOMEONE SO MUCH...
...THEY'D DIE FOR THEM!
HE KNOWS NOTHING ABOUT THIS WORLD.
HUMAN? WHAT A JOKE.

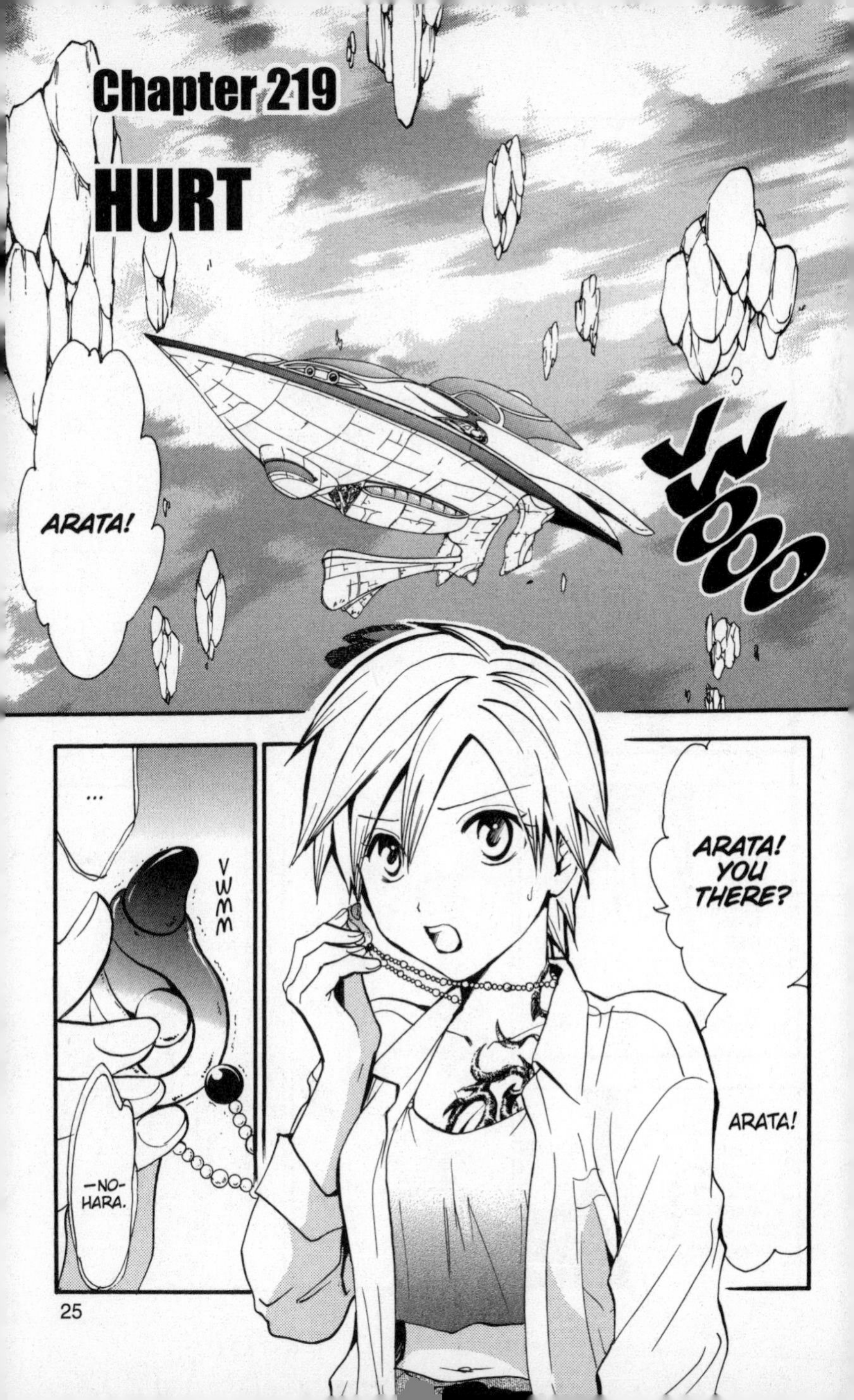
Chapter 219
HURT
ARATA!
ARATA! YOU THERE?
ARATA!
...
VWMM
—NO-HARA.

ALL THE PEOPLE HARUNAWA DEMONIZED...

...ARE BACK TO NORMAL!

HINOHARA?

ARATA!

YEAH! YOU OKAY?

MORE OR LESS, I GUESS!

HINOHARA, THERE'S A SONG OVER ON YOUR SIDE.

OH YEAH!

UNH...

BUT HOW DID YOU KNOW?

WE BROKE THE KIMON LIKE YOU SAID.

UMM... IT STARTS OUT, "THE MASTER OF TSUKUYO AND AMAWAKUNI..."

SONG?

SORRY, HINOHARA! GOTTA GET IMINA TO THE HOSPITAL.

WELL...

26

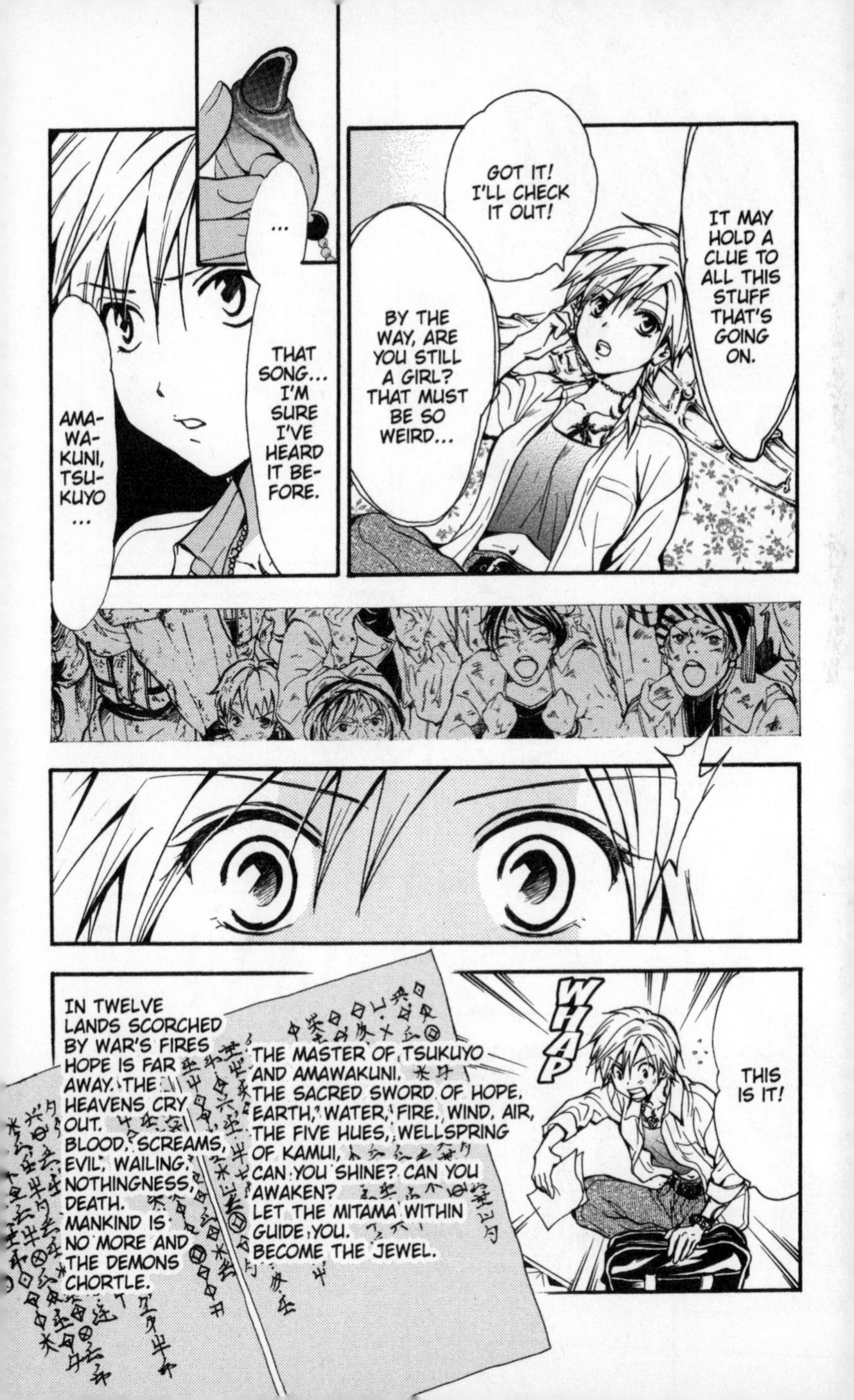
GOT IT! I'LL CHECK IT OUT!
IT MAY HOLD A CLUE TO ALL THIS STUFF THAT'S GOING ON.
BY THE WAY, ARE YOU STILL A GIRL? THAT MUST BE SO WEIRD...
...
THAT SONG... I'M SURE I'VE HEARD IT BEFORE.
AMAWAKUNI, TSUKUYO...
WHAP
THIS IS IT!
THE MASTER OF TSUKUYO AND AMAWAKUNI. THE SACRED SWORD OF HOPE. EARTH, WATER, FIRE, WIND, AIR, THE FIVE HUES, WELLSPRING OF KAMUI, CAN YOU SHINE? CAN YOU AWAKEN? LET THE MITAMA WITHIN GUIDE YOU. BECOME THE JEWEL.
IN TWELVE LANDS SCORCHED BY WAR'S FIRES HOPE IS FAR AWAY. THE HEAVENS CRY OUT. BLOOD, SCREAMS, EVIL, WAILING. NOTHINGNESS, DEATH. MANKIND IS NO MORE AND THE DEMONS CHORTLE.

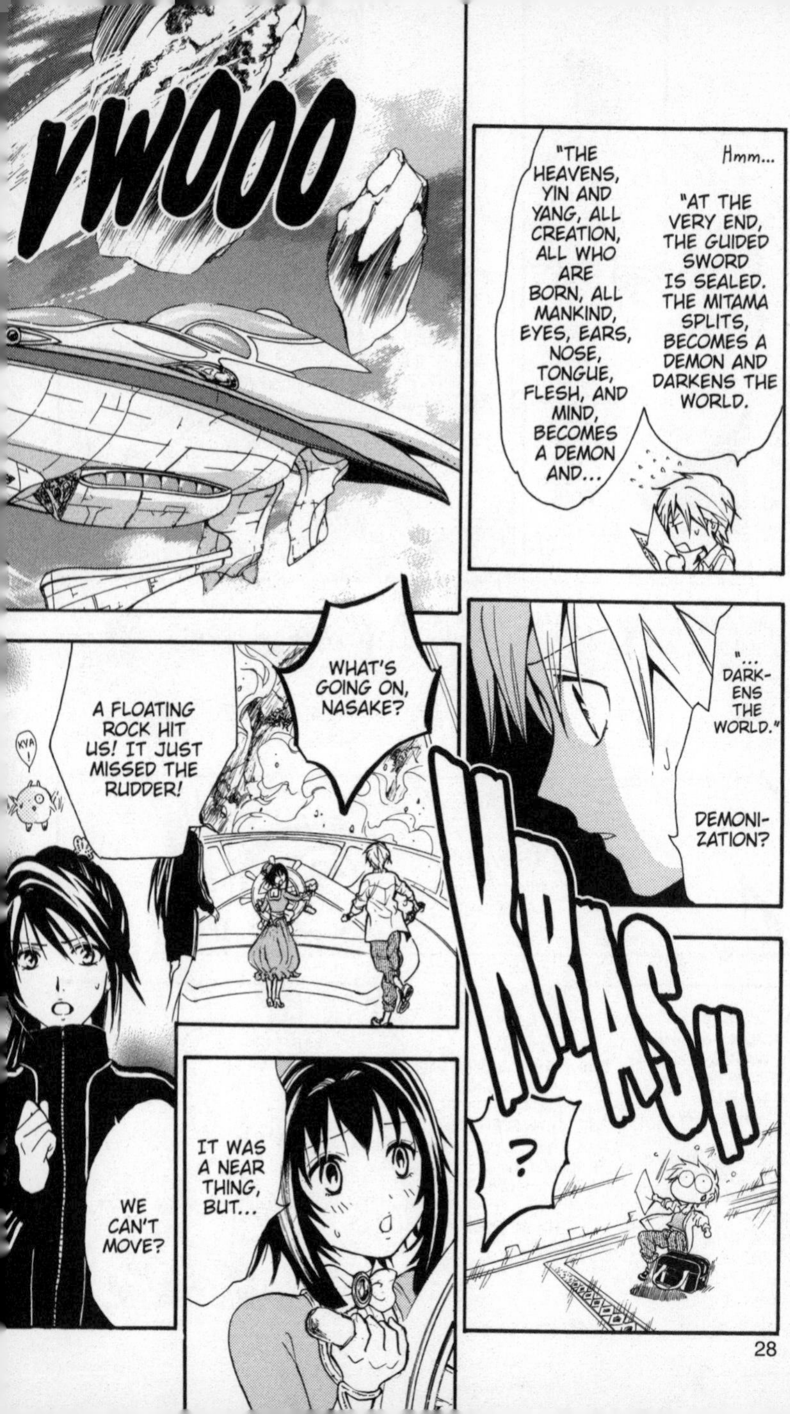
Hmm...
"AT THE VERY END, THE GUIDED SWORD IS SEALED. THE MITAMA SPLITS, BECOMES A DEMON AND DARKENS THE WORLD.
"THE HEAVENS, YIN AND YANG, ALL CREATION, ALL WHO ARE BORN, ALL MANKIND, EYES, EARS, NOSE, TONGUE, FLESH, AND MIND, BECOMES A DEMON AND...
VWOOO
"... DARKENS THE WORLD."
DEMONIZATION?
WHAT'S GOING ON, NASAKE?
A FLOATING ROCK HIT US! IT JUST MISSED THE RUDDER!
KYA!
KRASH
?
IT WAS A NEAR THING, BUT...
WE CAN'T MOVE?

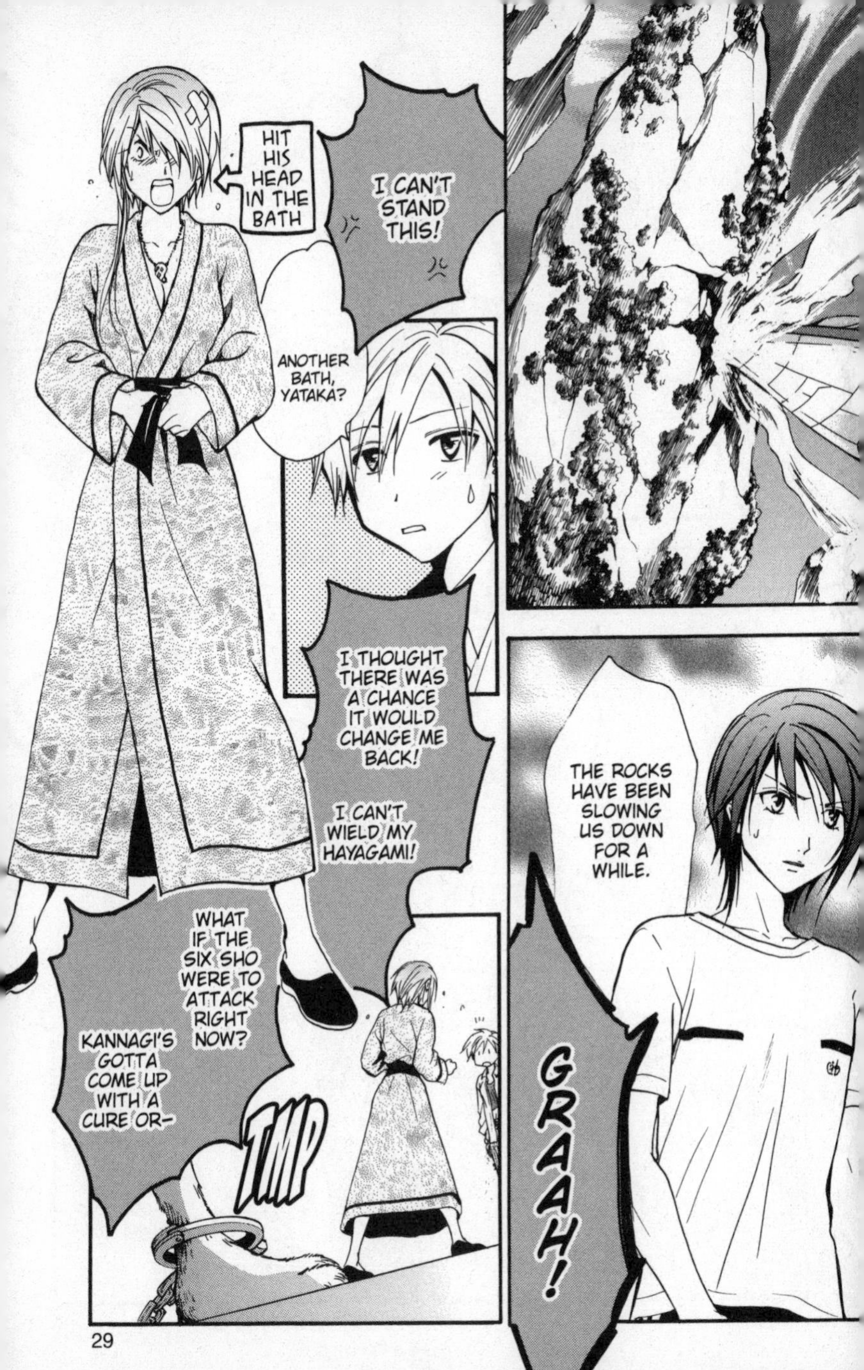
THE ROCKS HAVE BEEN SLOWING US DOWN FOR A WHILE.
GRAAAH!
I CAN'T STAND THIS!
HIT HIS HEAD IN THE BATH
ANOTHER BATH, YATAKA?
I THOUGHT THERE WAS A CHANCE IT WOULD CHANGE ME BACK!
I CAN'T WIELD MY HAYAGAMI!
WHAT IF THE SIX SHO WERE TO ATTACK RIGHT NOW?
KANNAGI'S GOTTA COME UP WITH A CURE OR-
TMP

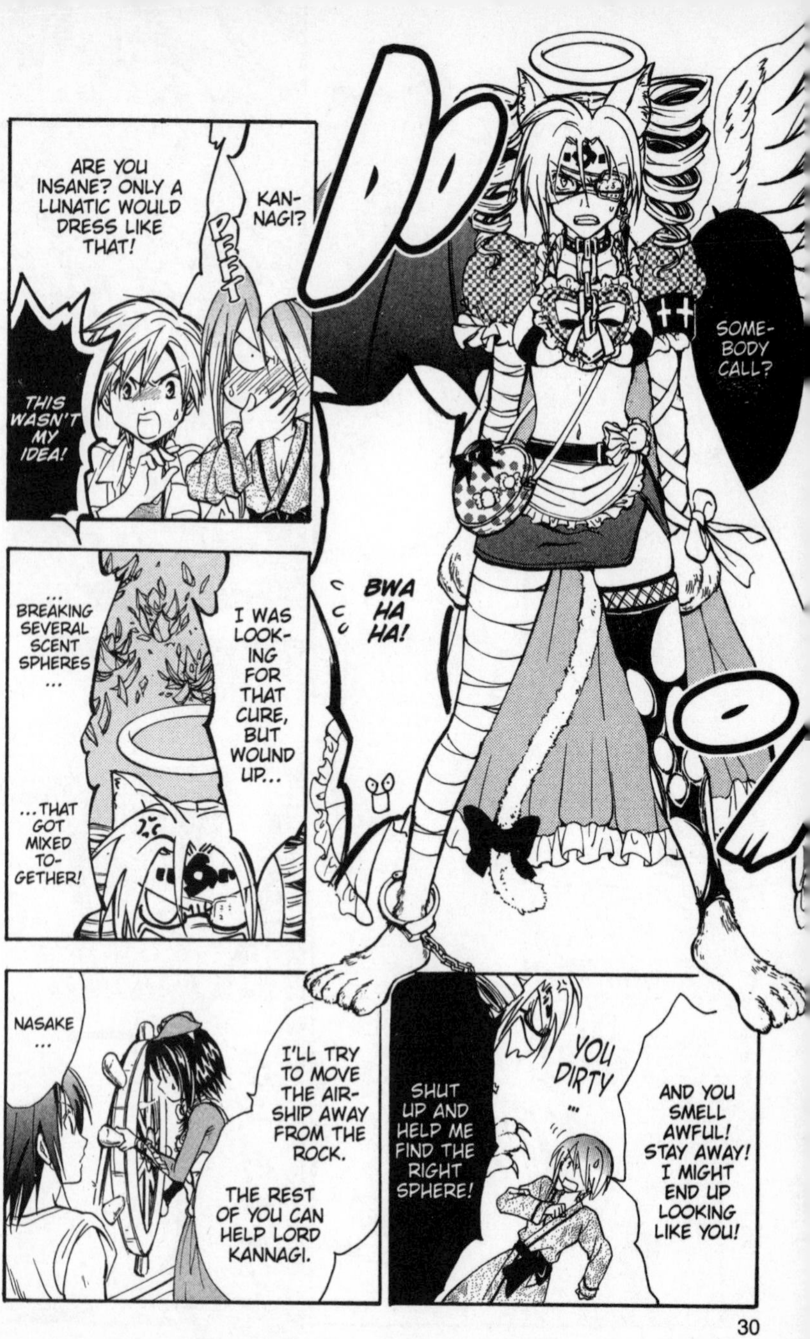
DO
O!
SOME-BODY CALL?
BWA HA HA!
KAN-NAGI?
PFFT
ARE YOU INSANE? ONLY A LUNATIC WOULD DRESS LIKE THAT!
THIS WASN'T MY IDEA!
I WAS LOOKING FOR THAT CURE, BUT WOUND UP...
...BREAKING SEVERAL SCENT SPHERES...
...THAT GOT MIXED TOGETHER!
YOU DIRTY...
AND YOU SMELL AWFUL! STAY AWAY! I MIGHT END UP LOOKING LIKE YOU!
SHUT UP AND HELP ME FIND THE RIGHT SPHERE!
NASAKE...
I'LL TRY TO MOVE THE AIRSHIP AWAY FROM THE ROCK.
THE REST OF YOU CAN HELP LORD KANNAGI.

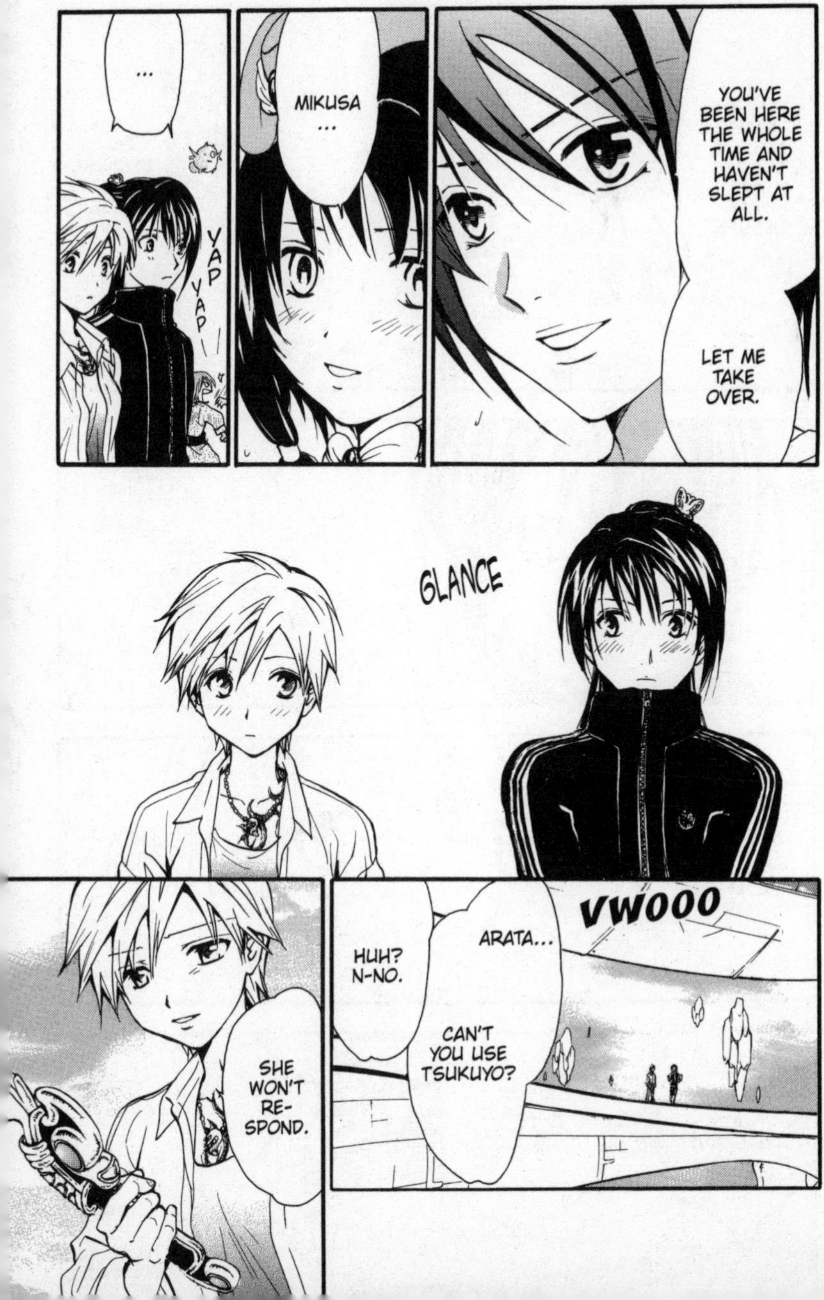
YOU'VE BEEN HERE THE WHOLE TIME AND HAVEN'T SLEPT AT ALL.
LET ME TAKE OVER.
MIKUSA ...
...
YAP YAP
GLANCE
VWOOO
ARATA...
CAN'T YOU USE TSUKUYO?
HUH? N-NO.
SHE WON'T RE-SPOND.

THEY CAN SENSE A SHO'S DOUBTS AND WEAKNESSES.

THE GODDESSES ARE VERY STRICT.

...

I'M NOT SURE.

BARRIER

I SEE. IS IT BECAUSE YOU'RE A GIRL NOW?

I THINK TSUKUYO...

...IS UPSET ABOUT THE LAST TIME I DEMONIZED.

HEY, KOTOHA...

SLIP YOUR TOP DOWN AND LET ME HAVE A LOOK.

WHAT?

WHAT FOR? NO WAY!

C'MON, YOU'RE A GUY NOW. IT'S OKAY.

WELL... THAT'S IRRELEVANT!

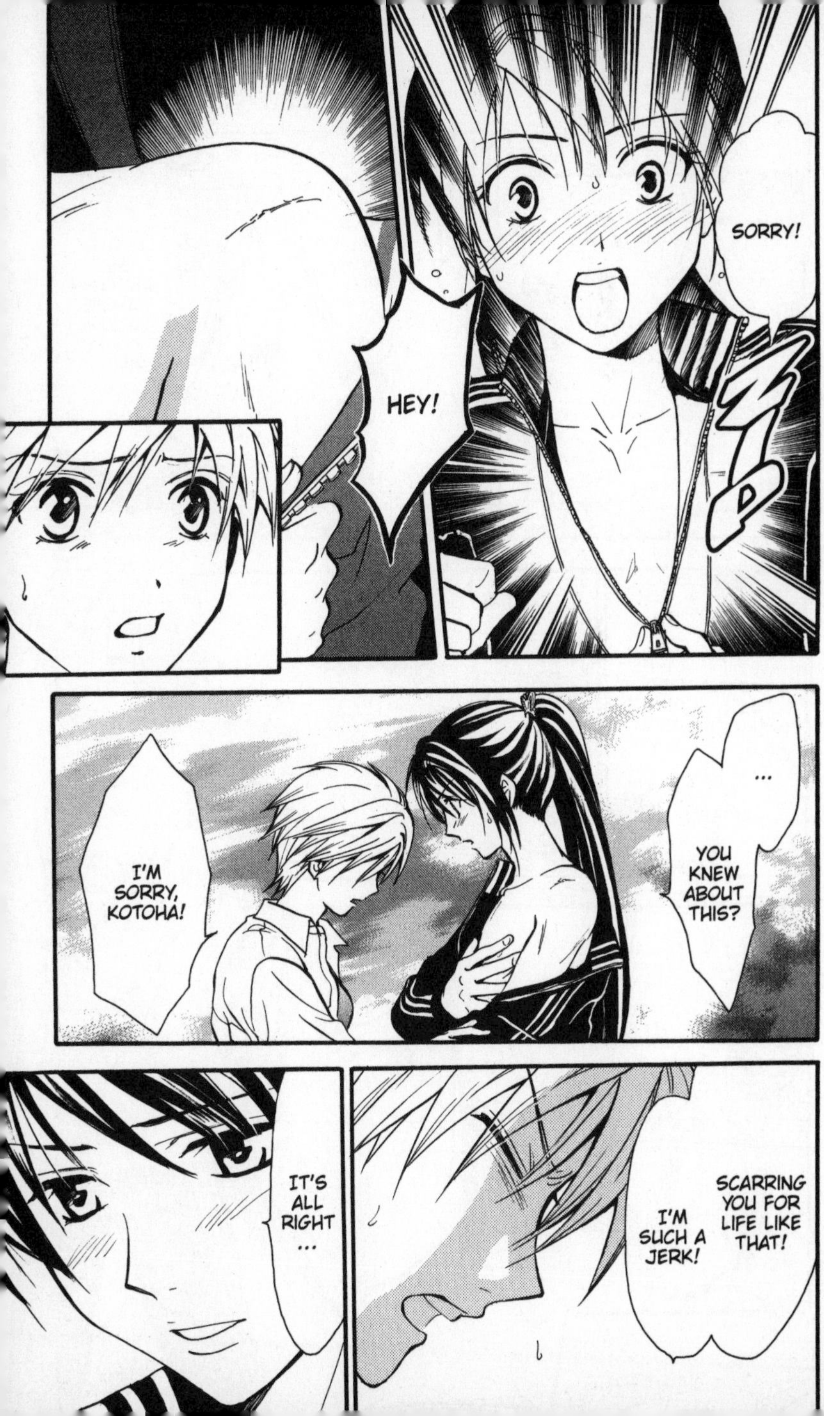
SORRY!
HEY!
...
YOU KNEW ABOUT THIS?
I'M SORRY, KOTOHA!
SCARRING YOU FOR LIFE LIKE THAT!
I'M SUCH A JERK!
IT'S ALL RIGHT ...

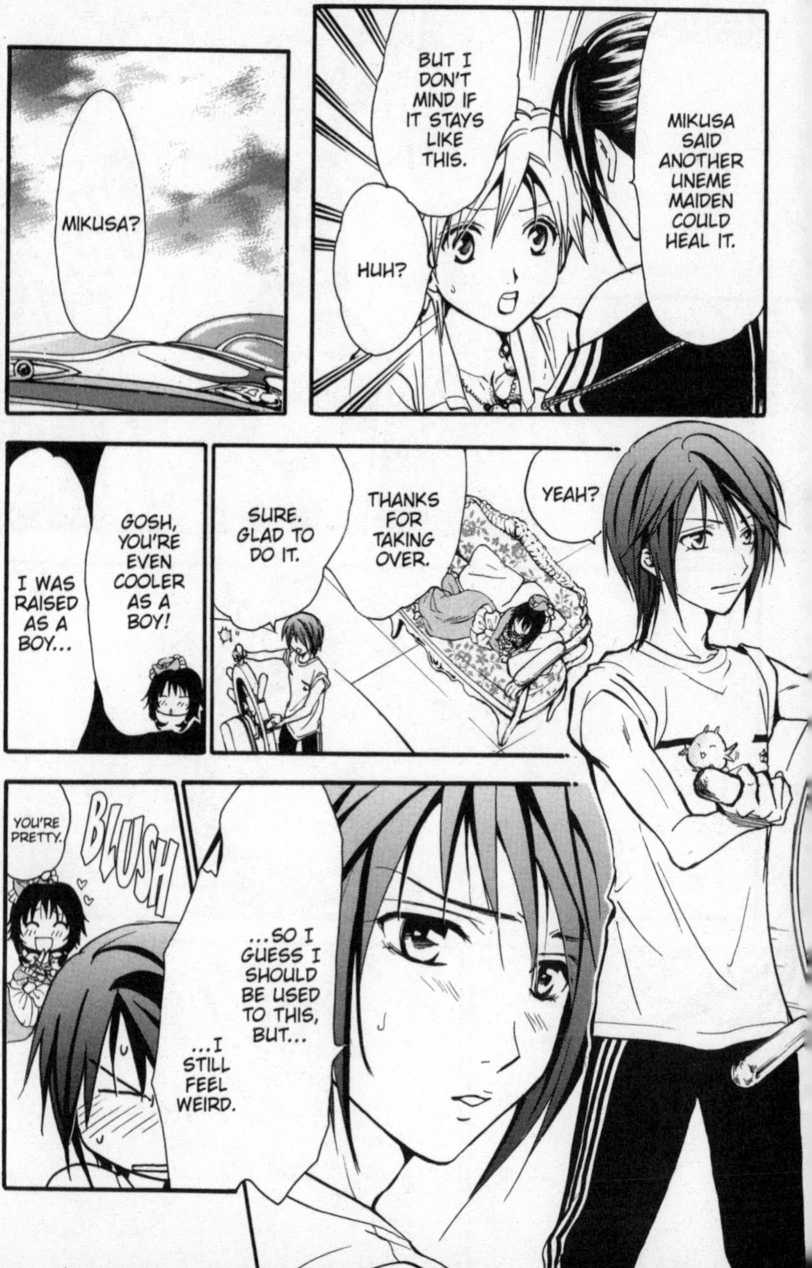
MIKUSA SAID ANOTHER UNEME MAIDEN COULD HEAL IT.
BUT I DON'T MIND IF IT STAYS LIKE THIS.
HUH?
MIKUSA?
YEAH?
THANKS FOR TAKING OVER.
SURE. GLAD TO DO IT.
GOSH, YOU'RE EVEN COOLER AS A BOY!
I WAS RAISED AS A BOY...
...SO I GUESS I SHOULD BE USED TO THIS, BUT...
...I STILL FEEL WEIRD.
BLUSH
YOU'RE PRETTY.

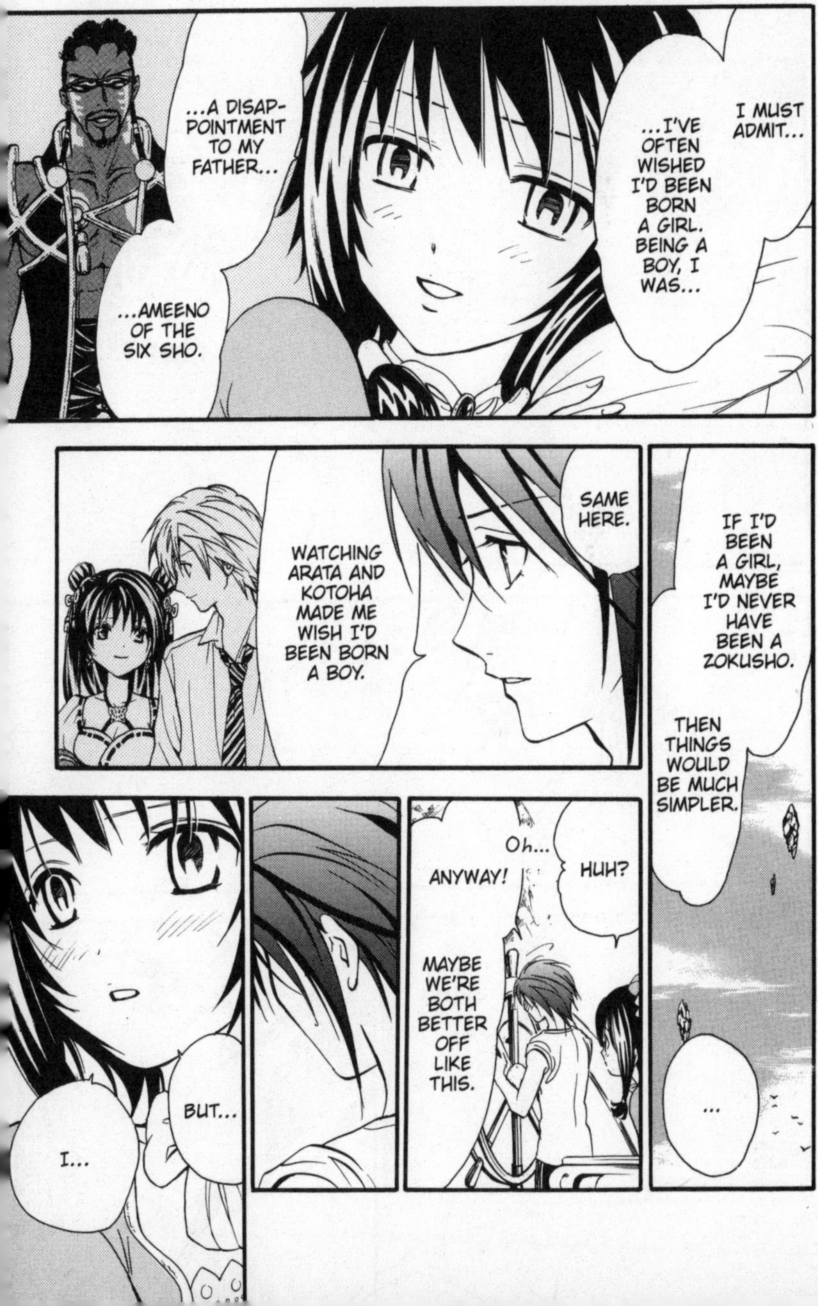
I MUST ADMIT...
...I'VE OFTEN WISHED I'D BEEN BORN A GIRL. BEING A BOY, I WAS...
...A DISAP-POINTMENT TO MY FATHER...
...AMEENO OF THE SIX SHO.
IF I'D BEEN A GIRL, MAYBE I'D NEVER HAVE BEEN A ZOKUSHO.
THEN THINGS WOULD BE MUCH SIMPLER.
...
SAME HERE.
WATCHING ARATA AND KOTOHA MADE ME WISH I'D BEEN BORN A BOY.
HUH?
Oh...
ANYWAY!
MAYBE WE'RE BOTH BETTER OFF LIKE THIS.
BUT...
I...

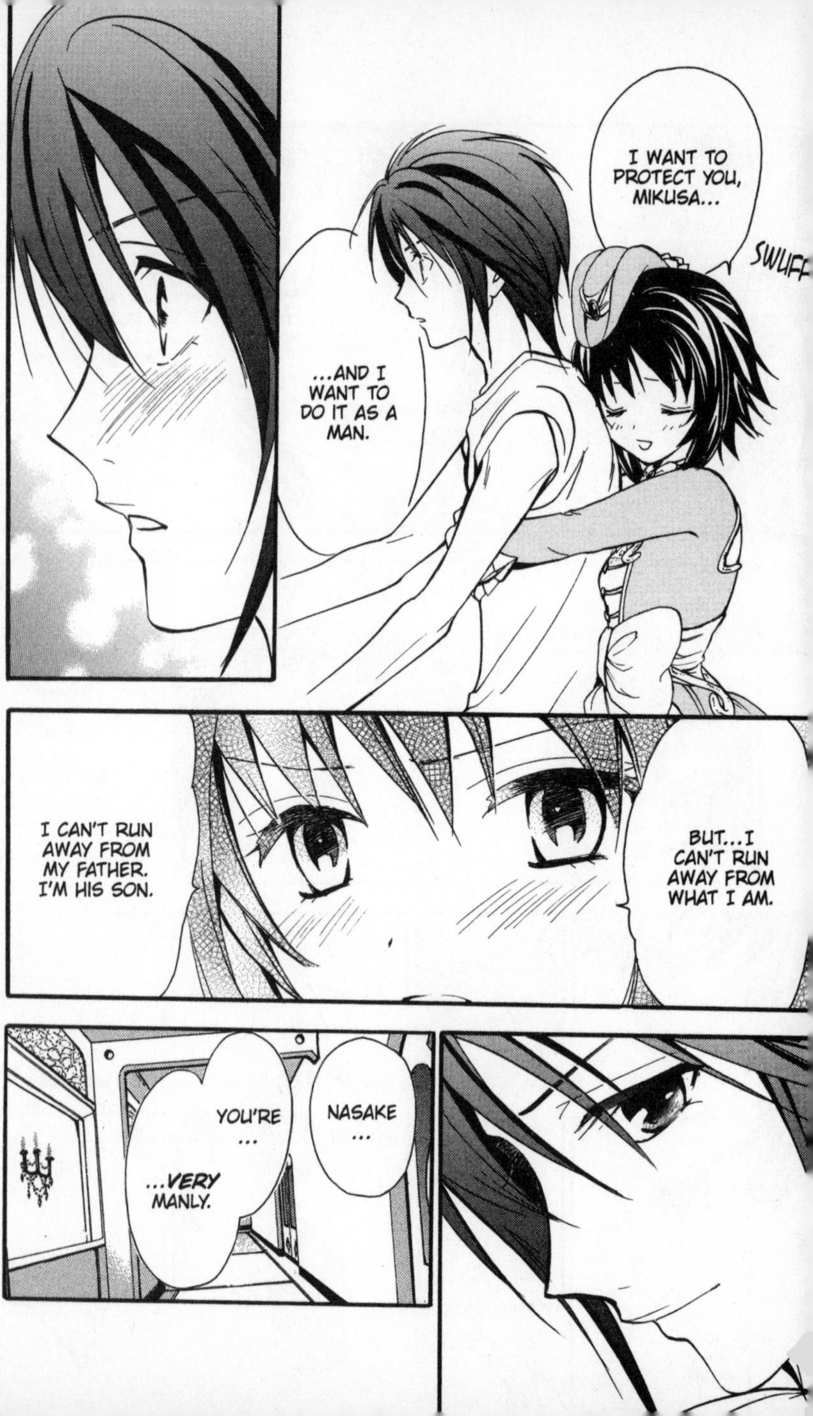
I WANT TO PROTECT YOU, MIKUSA...
SWUFF
...AND I WANT TO DO IT AS A MAN.
BUT...I CAN'T RUN AWAY FROM WHAT I AM.
I CAN'T RUN AWAY FROM MY FATHER. I'M HIS SON.
NASAKE...
YOU'RE...
...VERY MANLY.

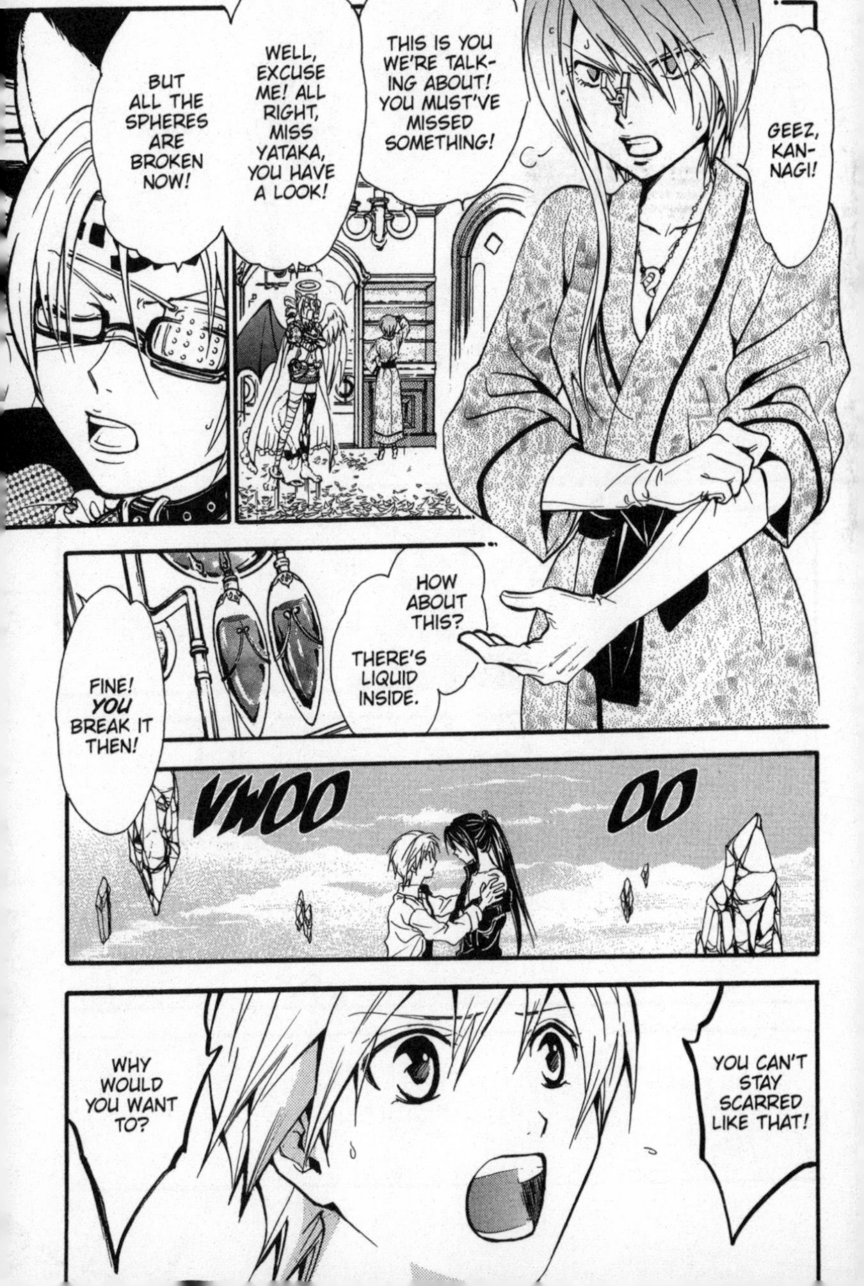
GEEZ, KAN-NAGI!
THIS IS YOU WE'RE TALK-ING ABOUT! YOU MUST'VE MISSED SOMETHING!
WELL, EXCUSE ME! ALL RIGHT, MISS YATAKA, YOU HAVE A LOOK!
BUT ALL THE SPHERES ARE BROKEN NOW!
HOW ABOUT THIS?
THERE'S LIQUID INSIDE.
FINE! *YOU* BREAK IT THEN!
VWOO OO
YOU CAN'T STAY SCARRED LIKE THAT!
WHY WOULD YOU WANT TO?

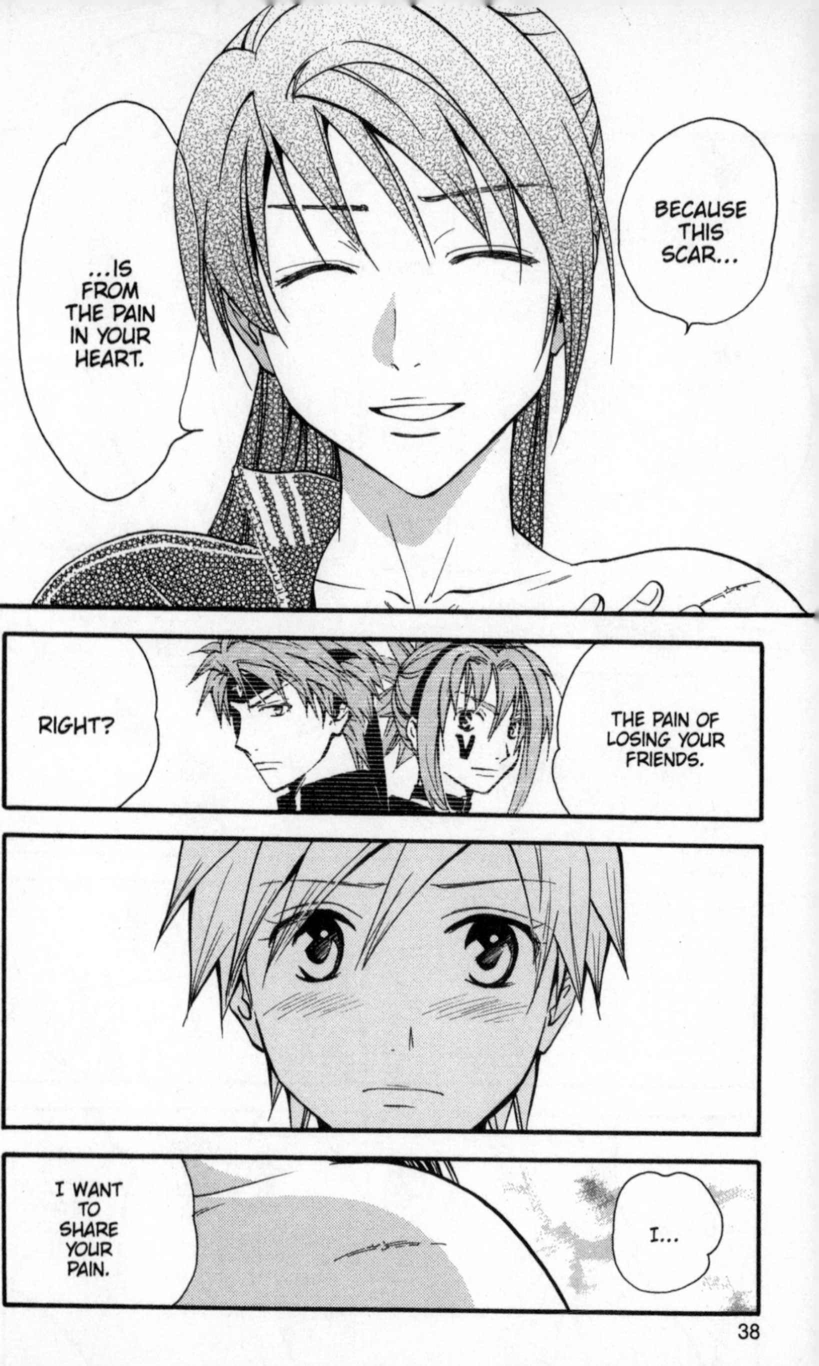
BECAUSE THIS SCAR...
...IS FROM THE PAIN IN YOUR HEART.
THE PAIN OF LOSING YOUR FRIENDS.
RIGHT?
I...
I WANT TO SHARE YOUR PAIN.

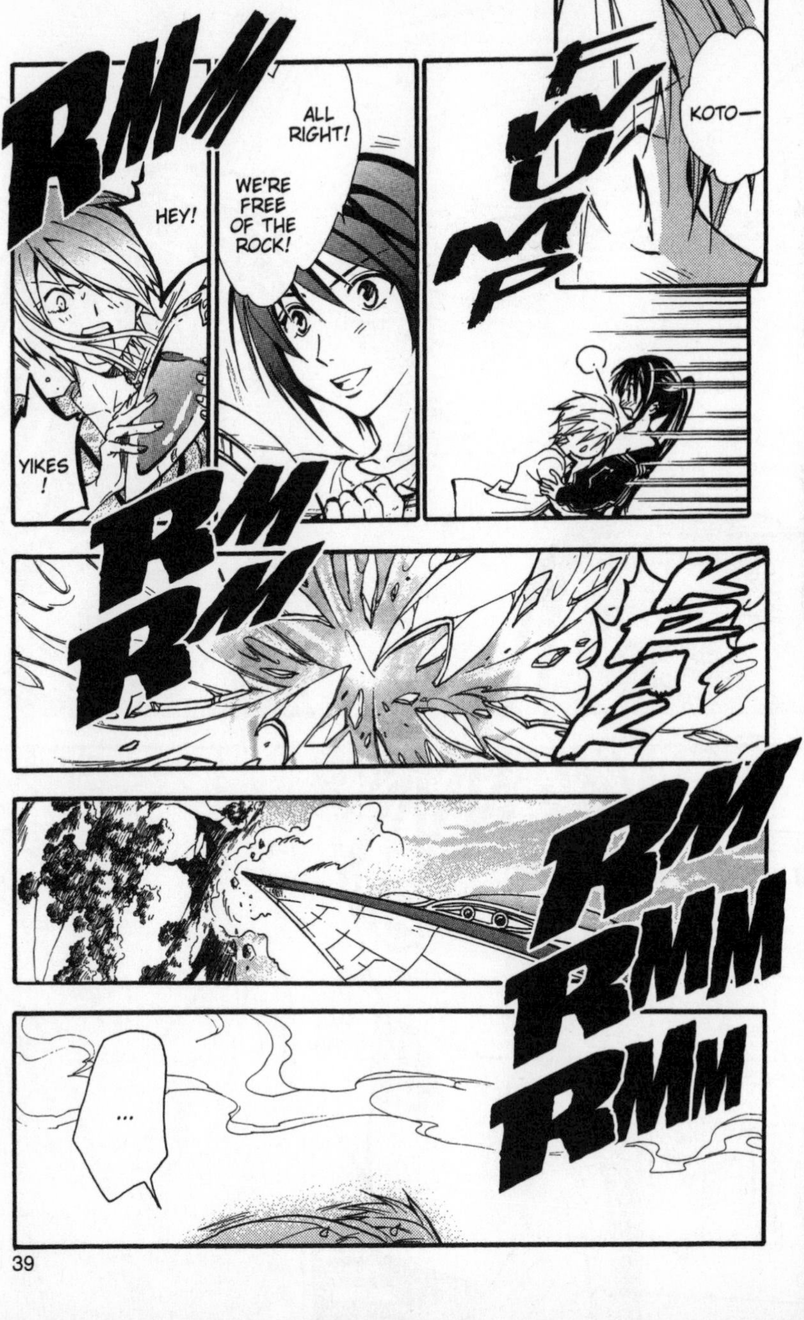
KOTO—
THUMP
ALL RIGHT!
WE'RE FREE OF THE ROCK!
RMM
HEY!
YIKES!
RM RM
RM RMM RMM
...

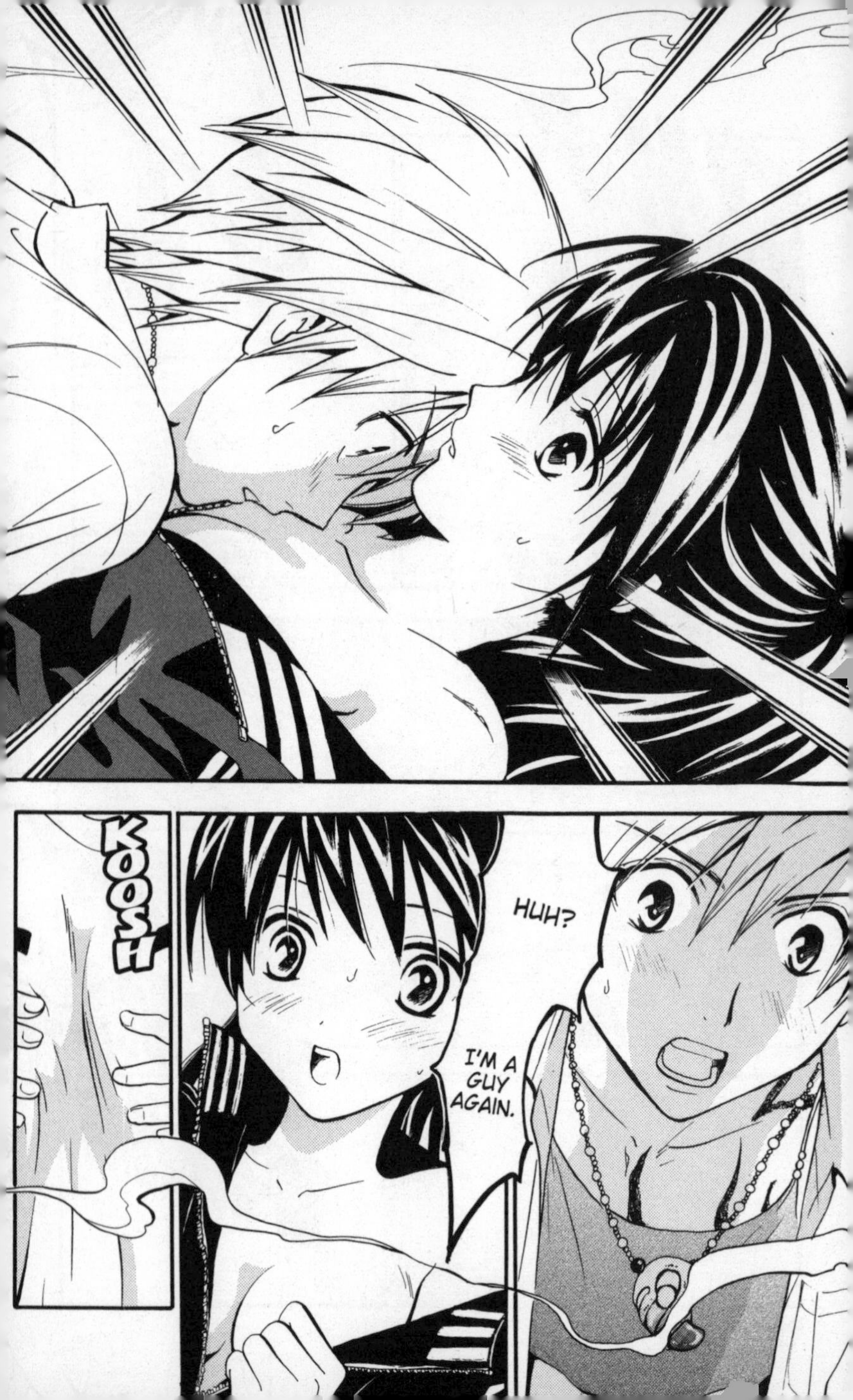
HUH?
I'M A GUY AGAIN.
KOOSH

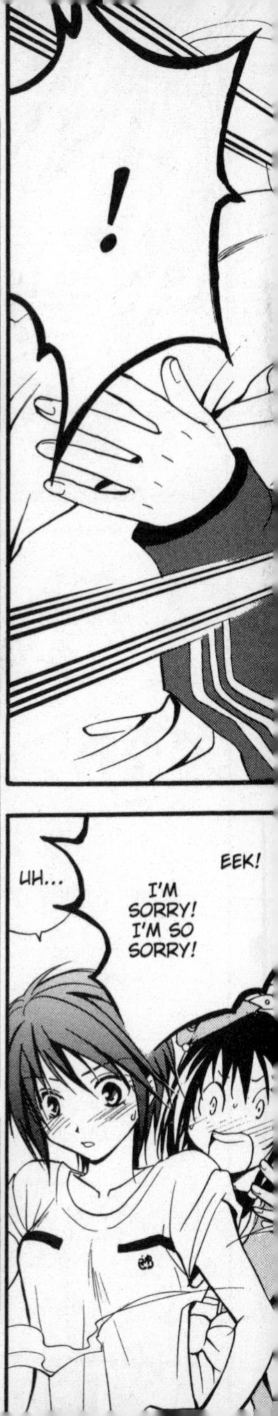
!
EEK!
I'M SORRY! I'M SO SORRY!
UH...
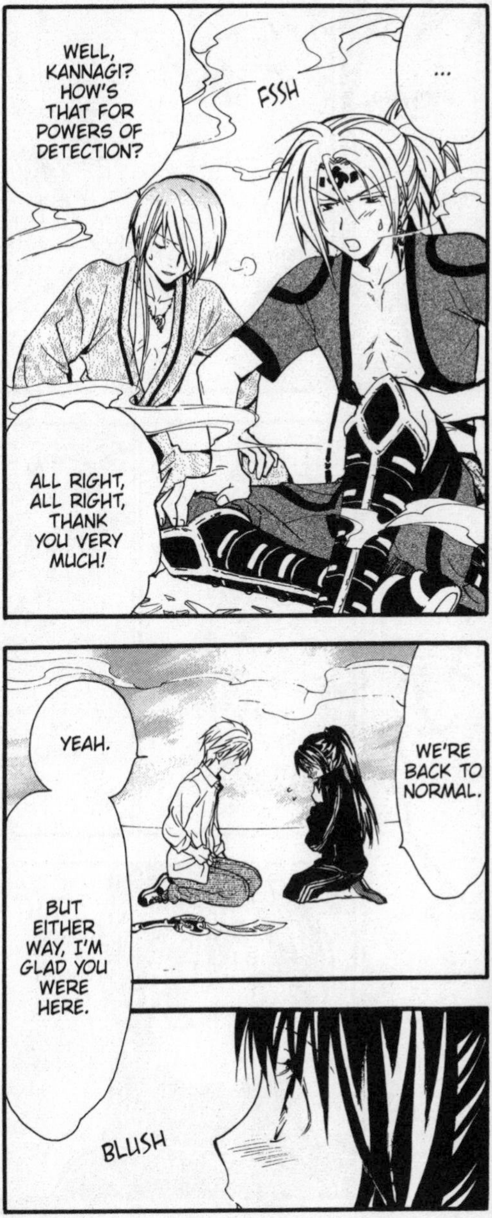
...
FSSH
WELL, KANNAGI? HOW'S THAT FOR POWERS OF DETECTION?
ALL RIGHT, ALL RIGHT, THANK YOU VERY MUCH!
WE'RE BACK TO NORMAL.
YEAH.
BUT EITHER WAY, I'M GLAD YOU WERE HERE.
BLUSH

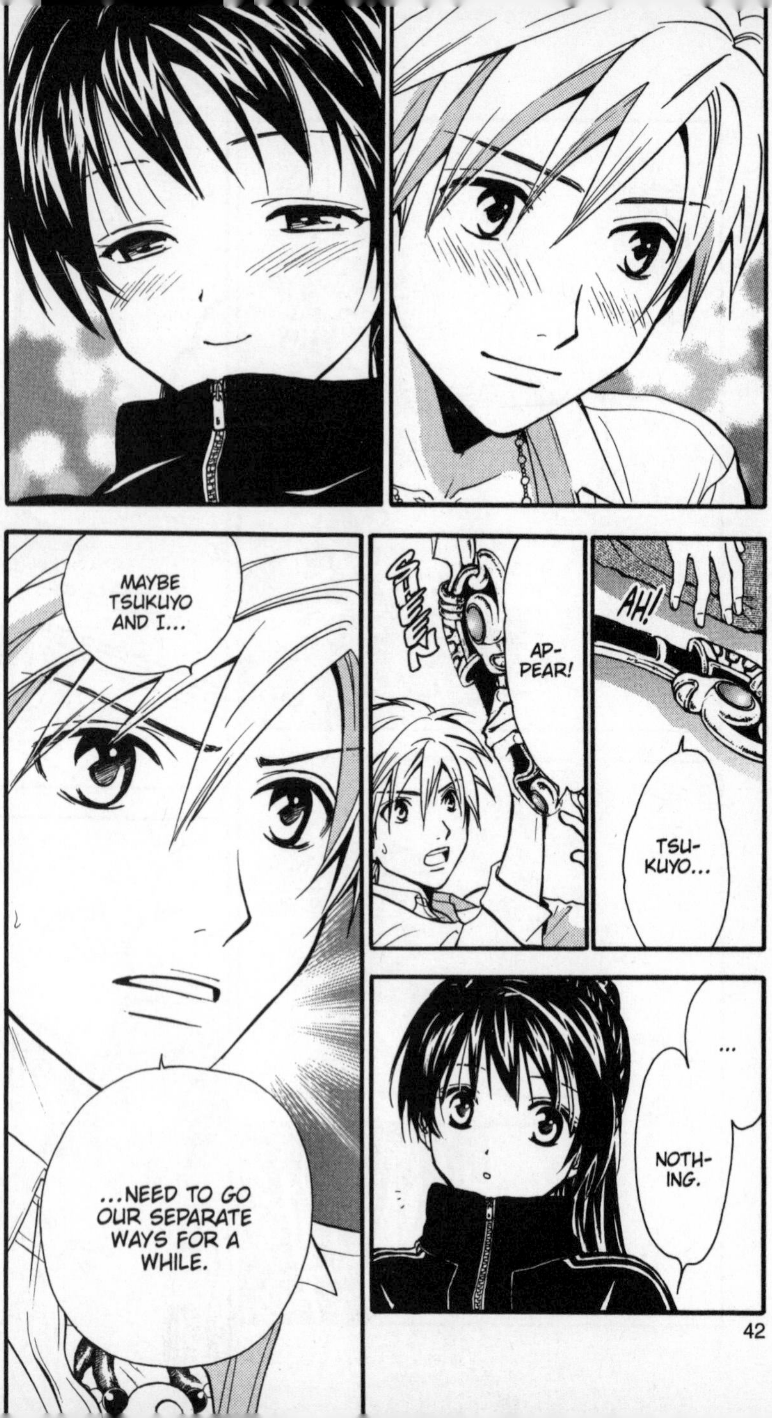
AH!
TSU-KUYO...
AP-PEAR!
...
NOTH-ING.
MAYBE TSUKUYO AND I...
...NEED TO GO OUR SEPARATE WAYS FOR A WHILE.

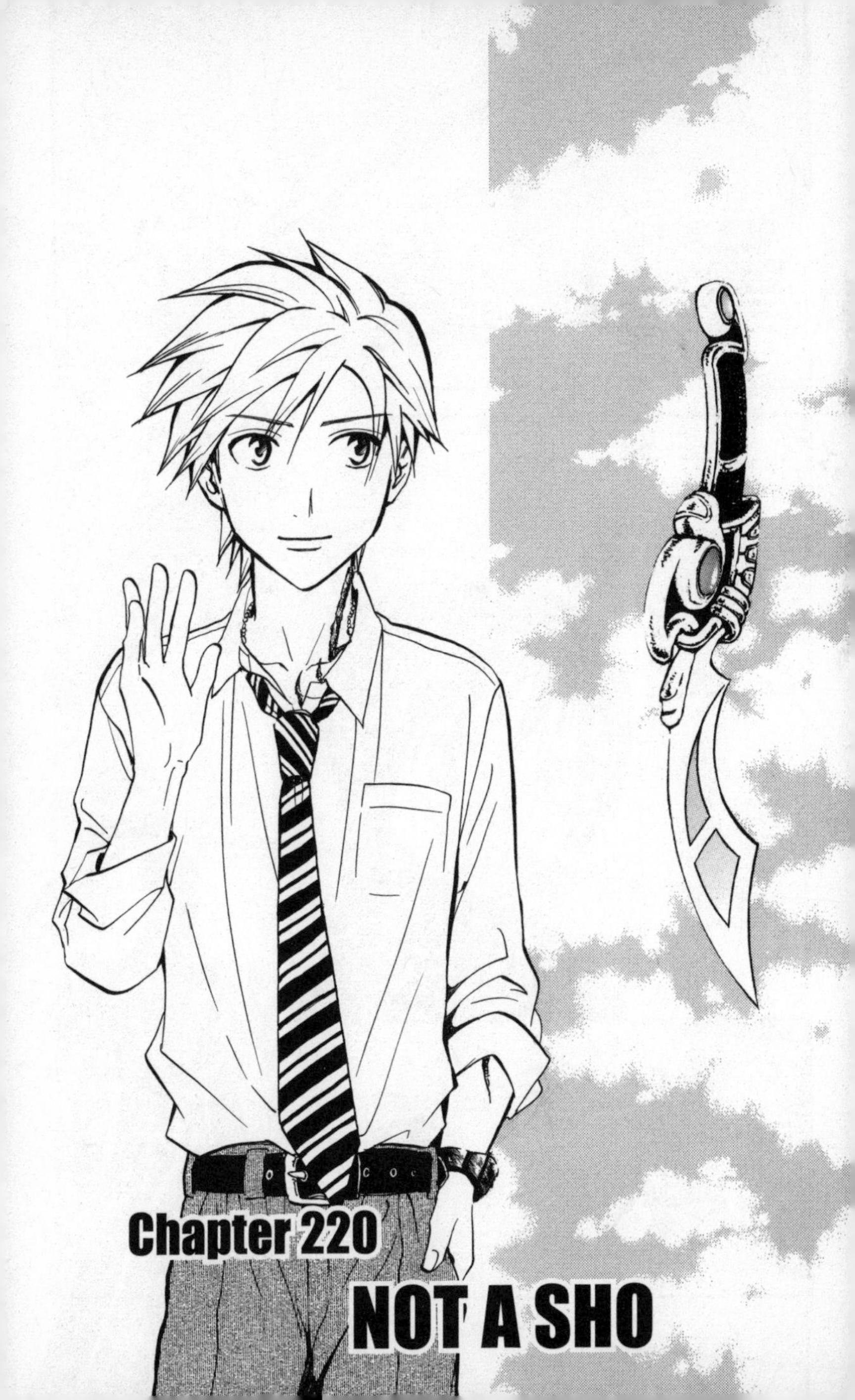
Chapter 220
NOT A SHO

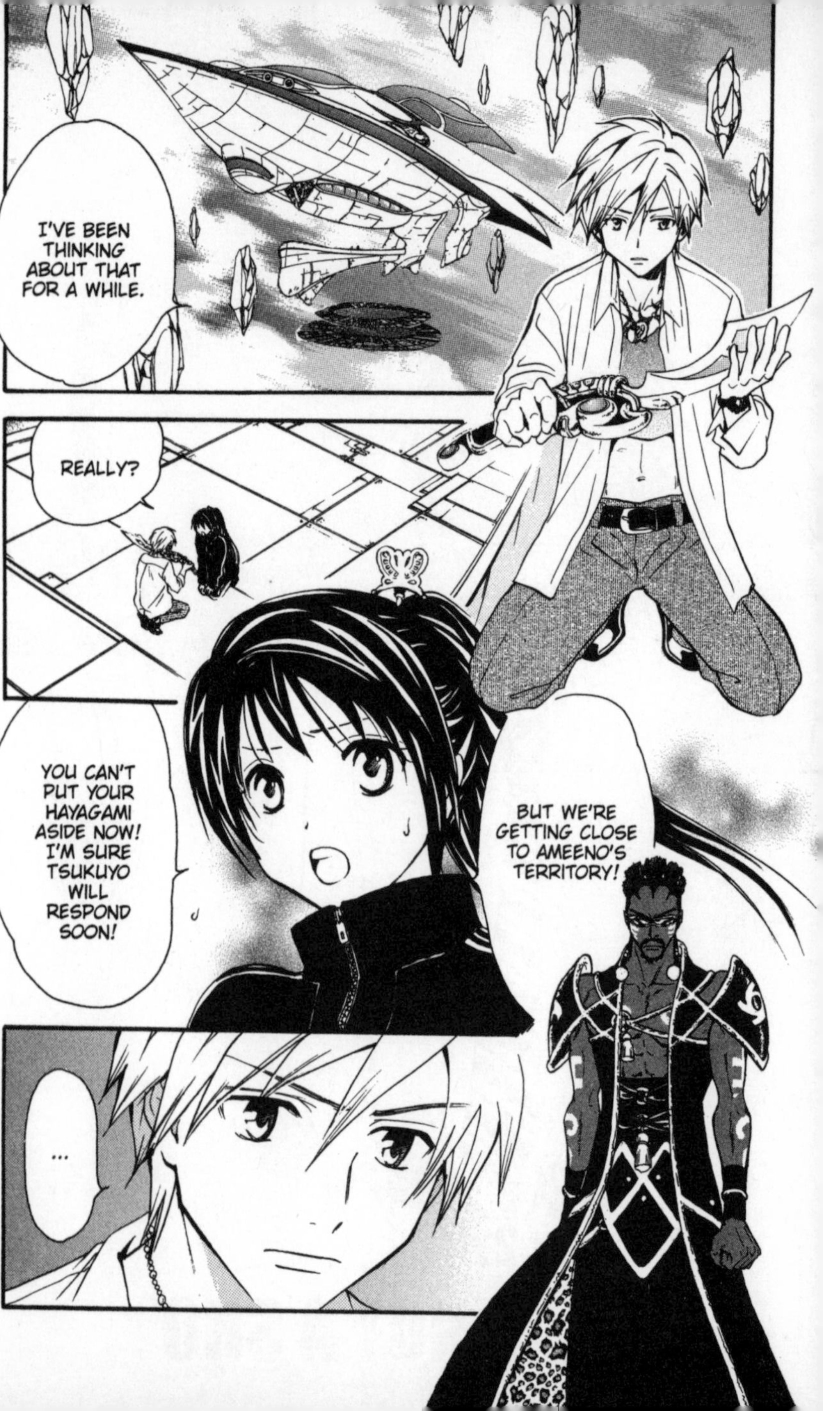
I'VE BEEN THINKING ABOUT THAT FOR A WHILE.
REALLY?
BUT WE'RE GETTING CLOSE TO AMEENO'S TERRITORY!
YOU CAN'T PUT YOUR HAYAGAMI ASIDE NOW! I'M SURE TSUKUYO WILL RESPOND SOON!
...

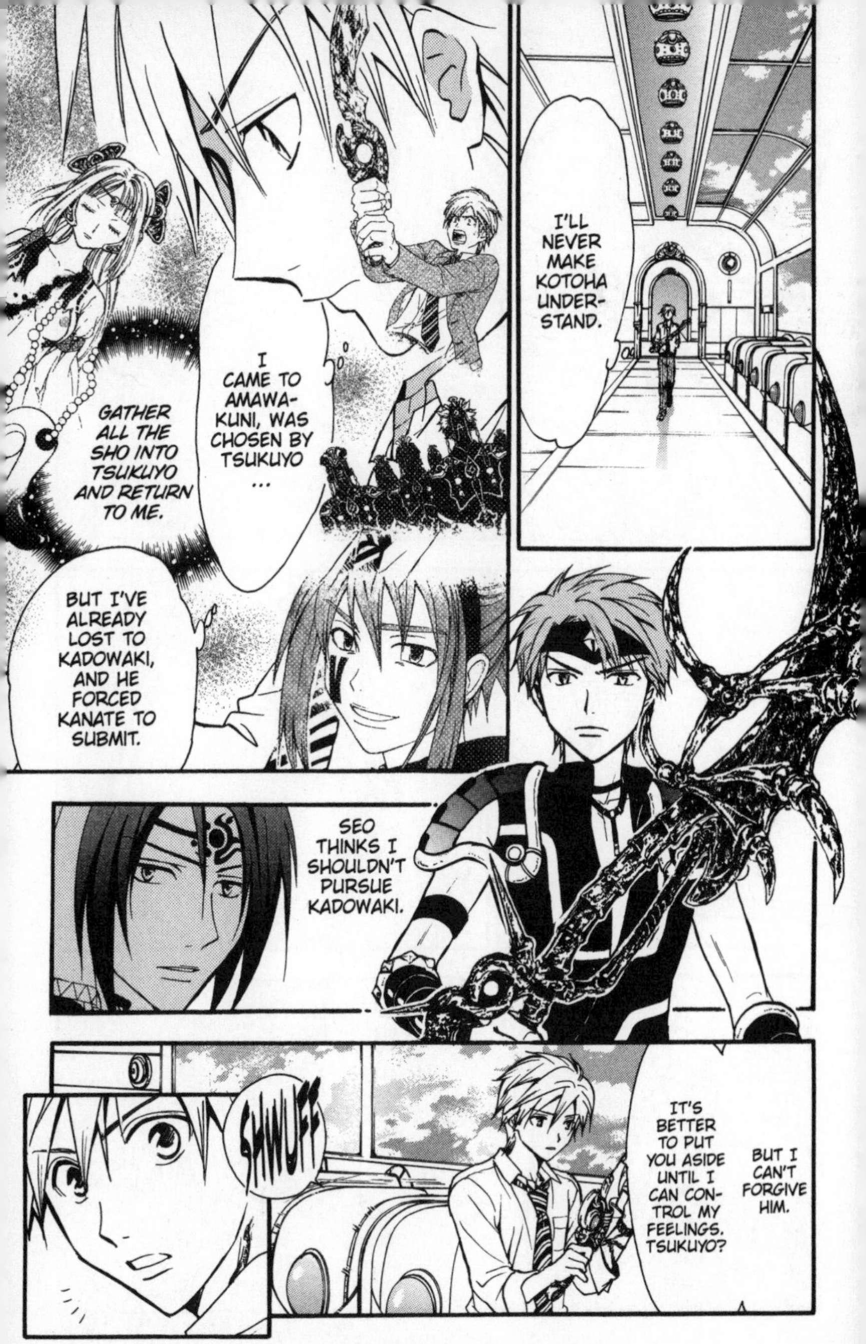
I'LL NEVER MAKE KOTOHA UNDER-STAND.
I CAME TO AMAWA-KUNI, WAS CHOSEN BY TSUKUYO ...
GATHER ALL THE SHO INTO TSUKUYO AND RETURN TO ME.
BUT I'VE ALREADY LOST TO KADOWAKI, AND HE FORCED KANATE TO SUBMIT.
SEO THINKS I SHOULDN'T PURSUE KADOWAKI.
BUT I CAN'T FORGIVE HIM.
IT'S BETTER TO PUT YOU ASIDE UNTIL I CAN CON-TROL MY FEELINGS. TSUKUYO?
SHWUFF

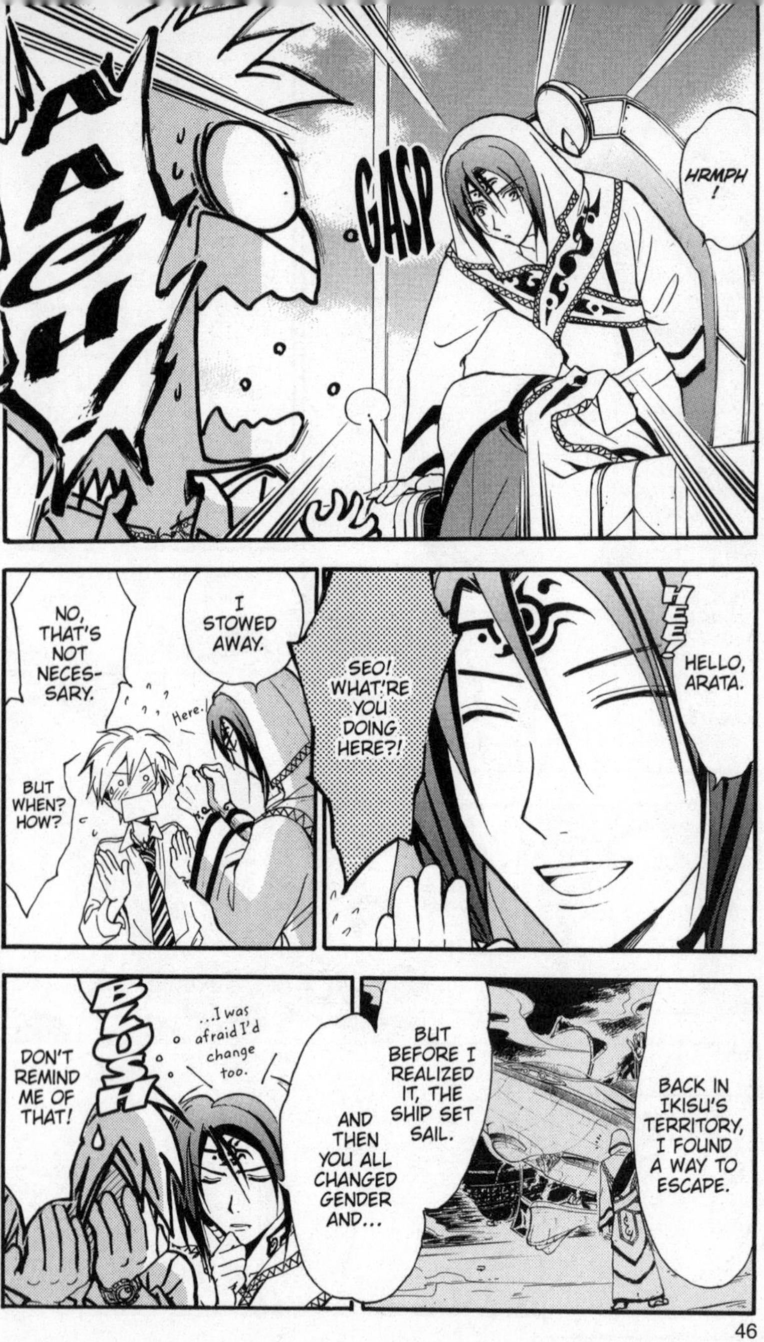
HRMPH!
GASP
AAGH!
HEE!
HELLO, ARATA.
SEO! WHAT'RE YOU DOING HERE?!
I STOWED AWAY.
Here.
NO, THAT'S NOT NECES-SARY.
BUT WHEN? HOW?
BACK IN IKISU'S TERRITORY, I FOUND A WAY TO ESCAPE.
BUT BEFORE I REALIZED IT, THE SHIP SET SAIL.
AND THEN YOU ALL CHANGED GENDER AND...
...I was afraid I'd change too.
BLUSH
DON'T REMIND ME OF THAT!

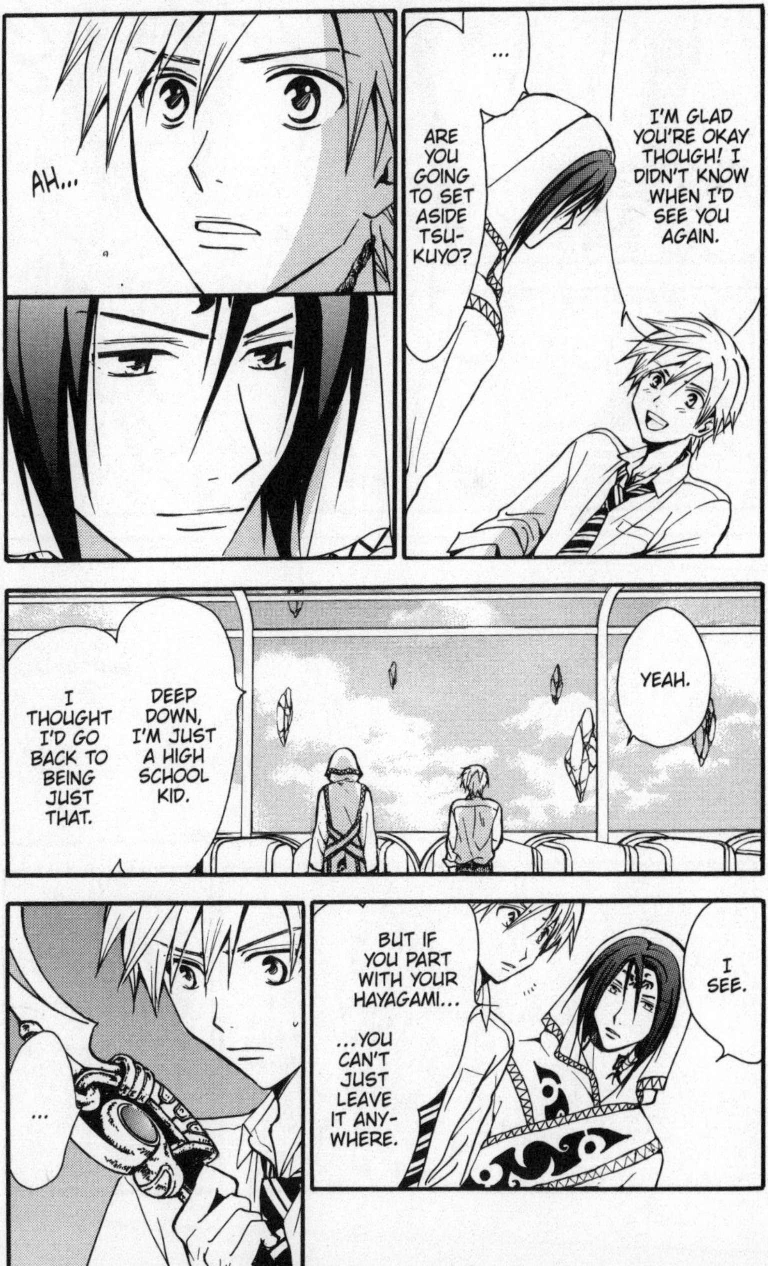
I'M GLAD YOU'RE OKAY THOUGH! I DIDN'T KNOW WHEN I'D SEE YOU AGAIN.
...
ARE YOU GOING TO SET ASIDE TSU-KUYO?
AH...
YEAH.
DEEP DOWN, I'M JUST A HIGH SCHOOL KID.
I THOUGHT I'D GO BACK TO BEING JUST THAT.
I SEE.
BUT IF YOU PART WITH YOUR HAYAGAMI...
...YOU CAN'T JUST LEAVE IT ANY-WHERE.
...

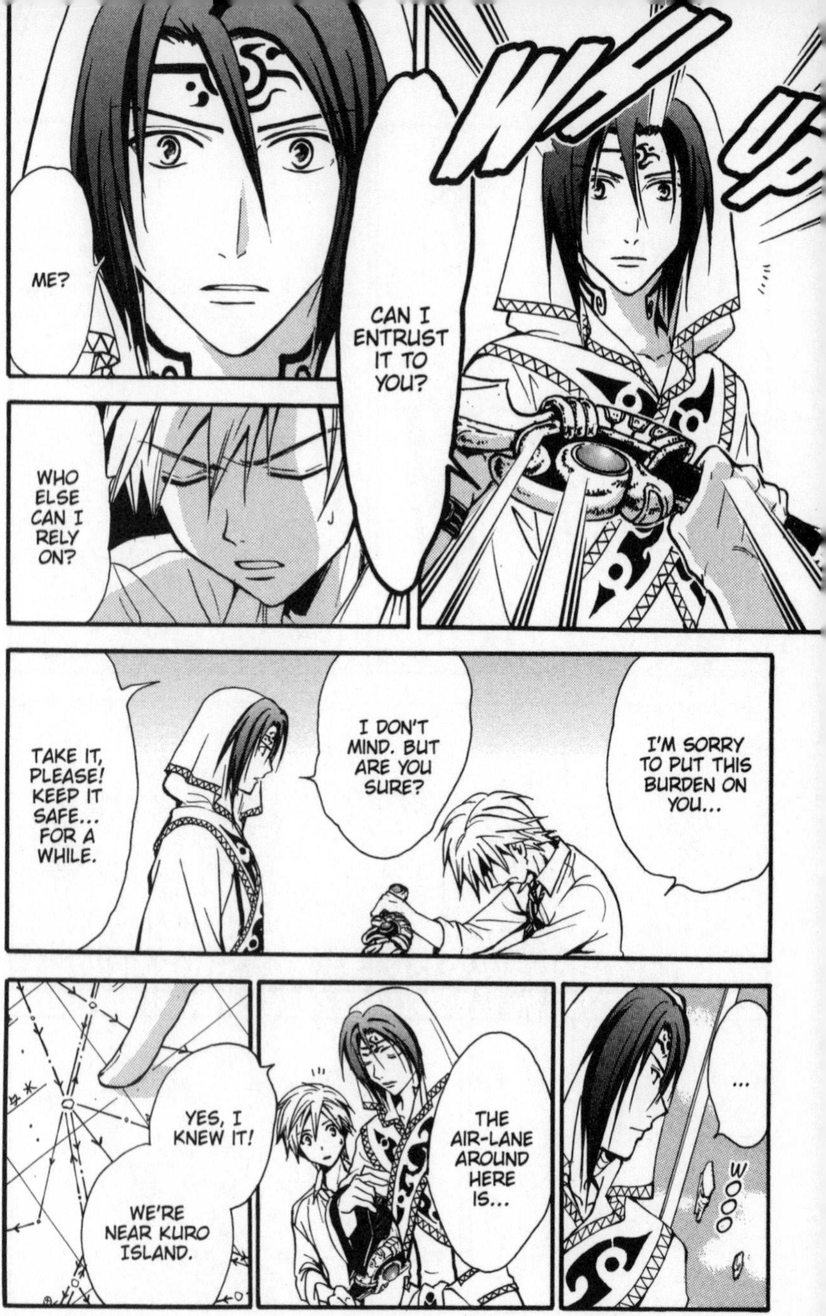
WHUP
...
CAN I ENTRUST IT TO YOU?
ME?
WHO ELSE CAN I RELY ON?
I'M SORRY TO PUT THIS BURDEN ON YOU...
I DON'T MIND. BUT ARE YOU SURE?
TAKE IT, PLEASE! KEEP IT SAFE... FOR A WHILE.
...
WOOO
THE AIR-LANE AROUND HERE IS...
YES, I KNEW IT!
WE'RE NEAR KURO ISLAND.

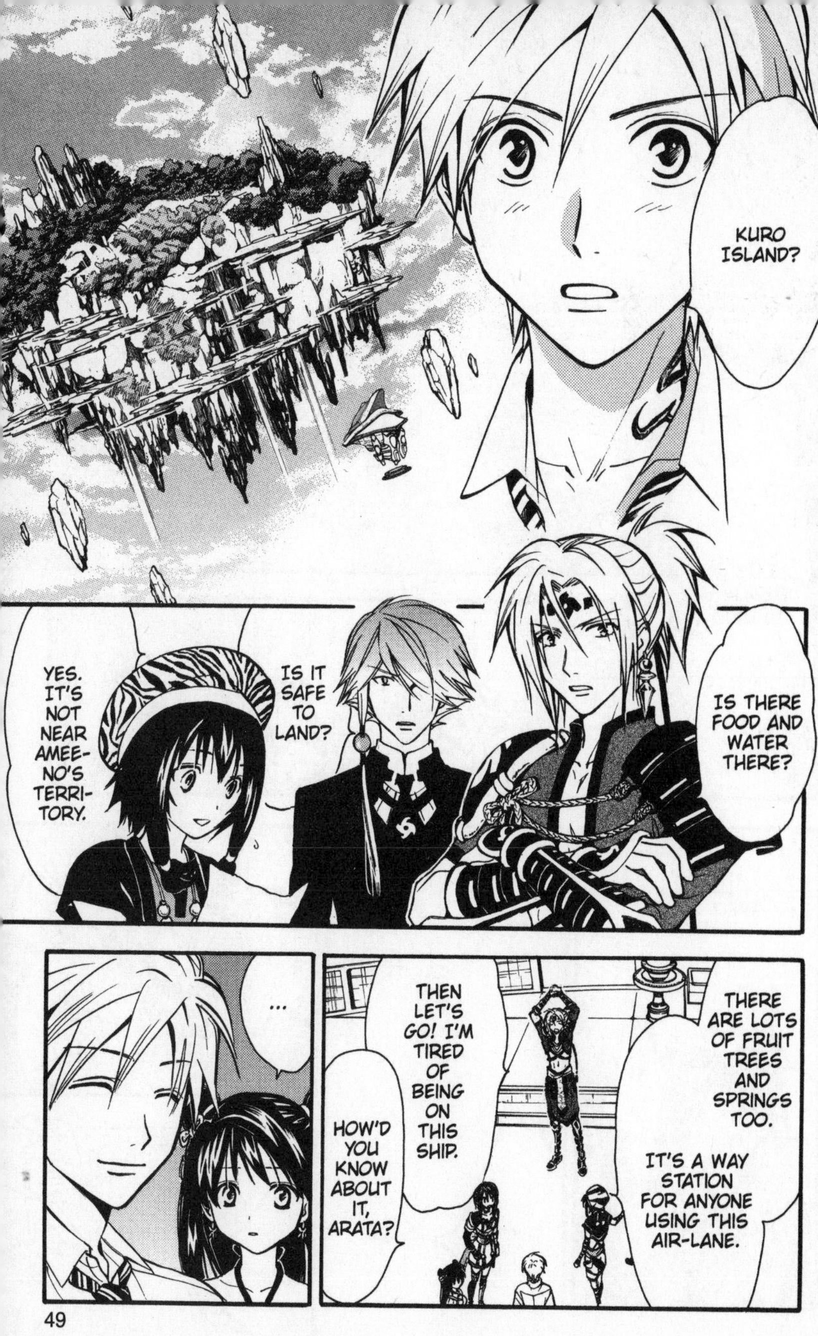
KURO ISLAND?
IS THERE FOOD AND WATER THERE?
IS IT SAFE TO LAND?
YES. IT'S NOT NEAR AMEE-NO'S TERRITORY.
THERE ARE LOTS OF FRUIT TREES AND SPRINGS TOO.
IT'S A WAY STATION FOR ANYONE USING THIS AIR-LANE.
THEN LET'S GO! I'M TIRED OF BEING ON THIS SHIP.
HOW'D YOU KNOW ABOUT IT, ARATA?
...

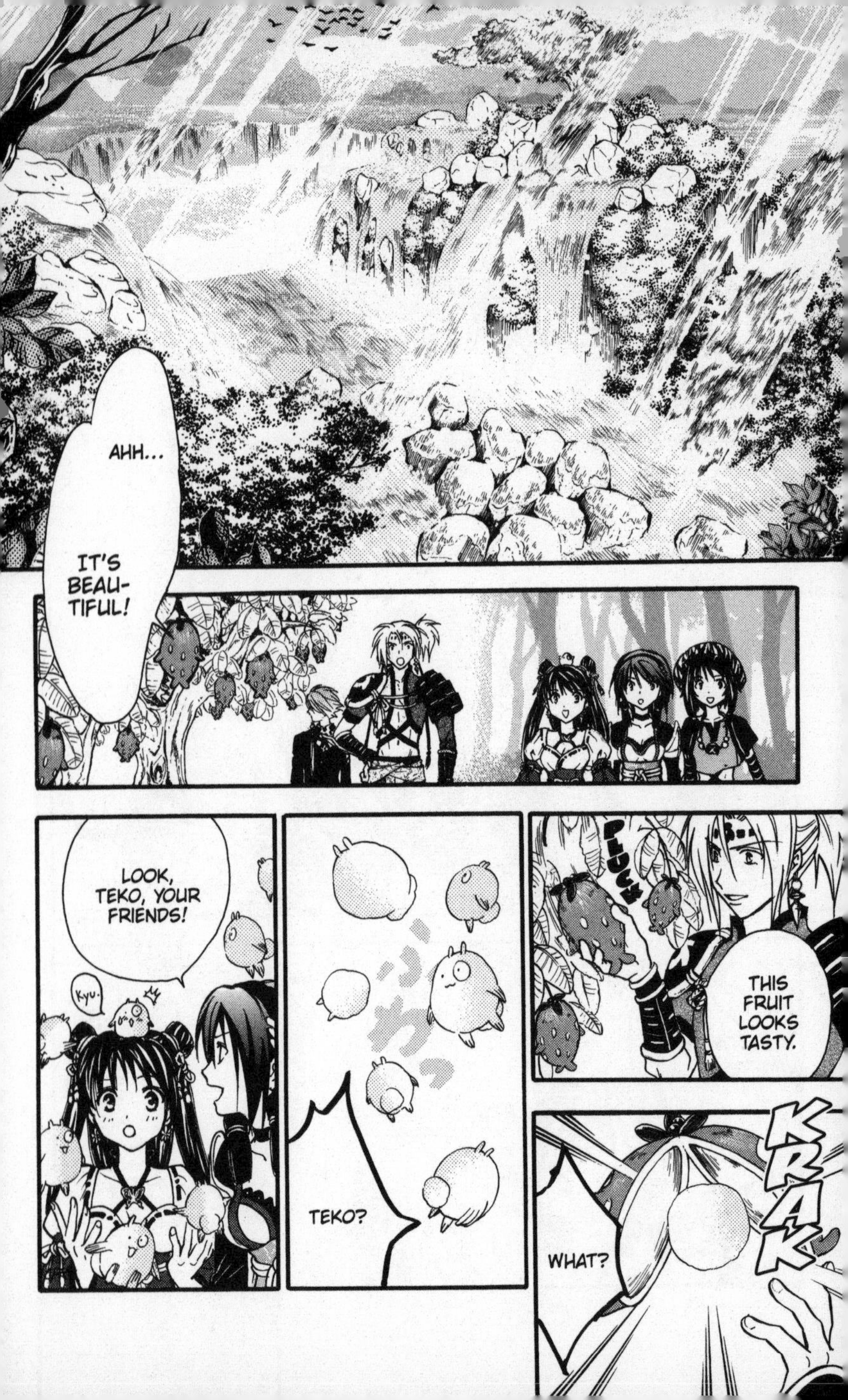
AHH...
IT'S BEAU-TIFUL!
PLUCK
THIS FRUIT LOOKS TASTY.
KRAK
WHAT?
TEKO?
LOOK, TEKO, YOUR FRIENDS!
Kyu.

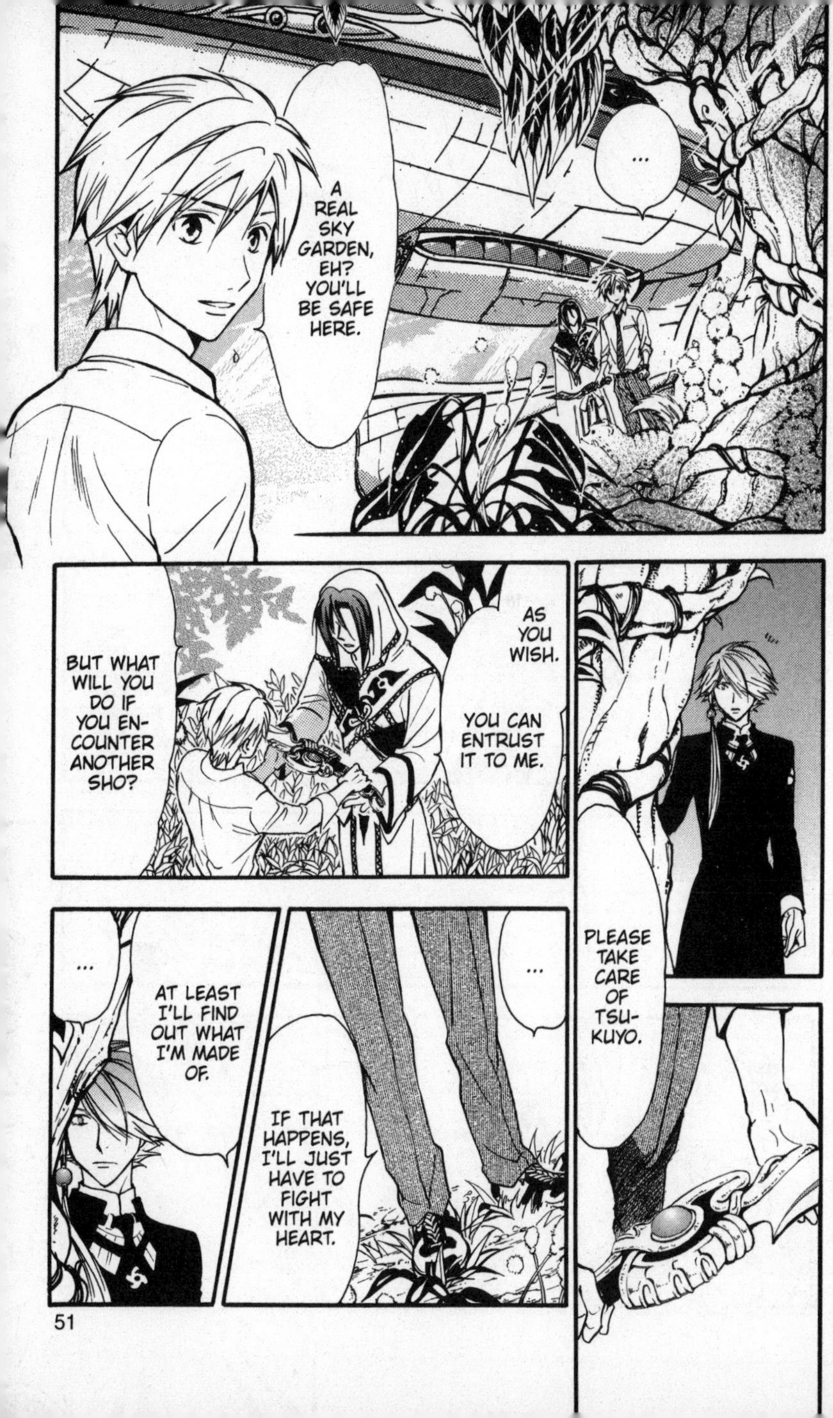

...
A REAL SKY GARDEN, EH? YOU'LL BE SAFE HERE.
PLEASE TAKE CARE OF TSU-KUYO.
AS YOU WISH.
YOU CAN ENTRUST IT TO ME.
BUT WHAT WILL YOU DO IF YOU EN-COUNTER ANOTHER SHO?
...
IF THAT HAPPENS, I'LL JUST HAVE TO FIGHT WITH MY HEART.
...
AT LEAST I'LL FIND OUT WHAT I'M MADE OF.

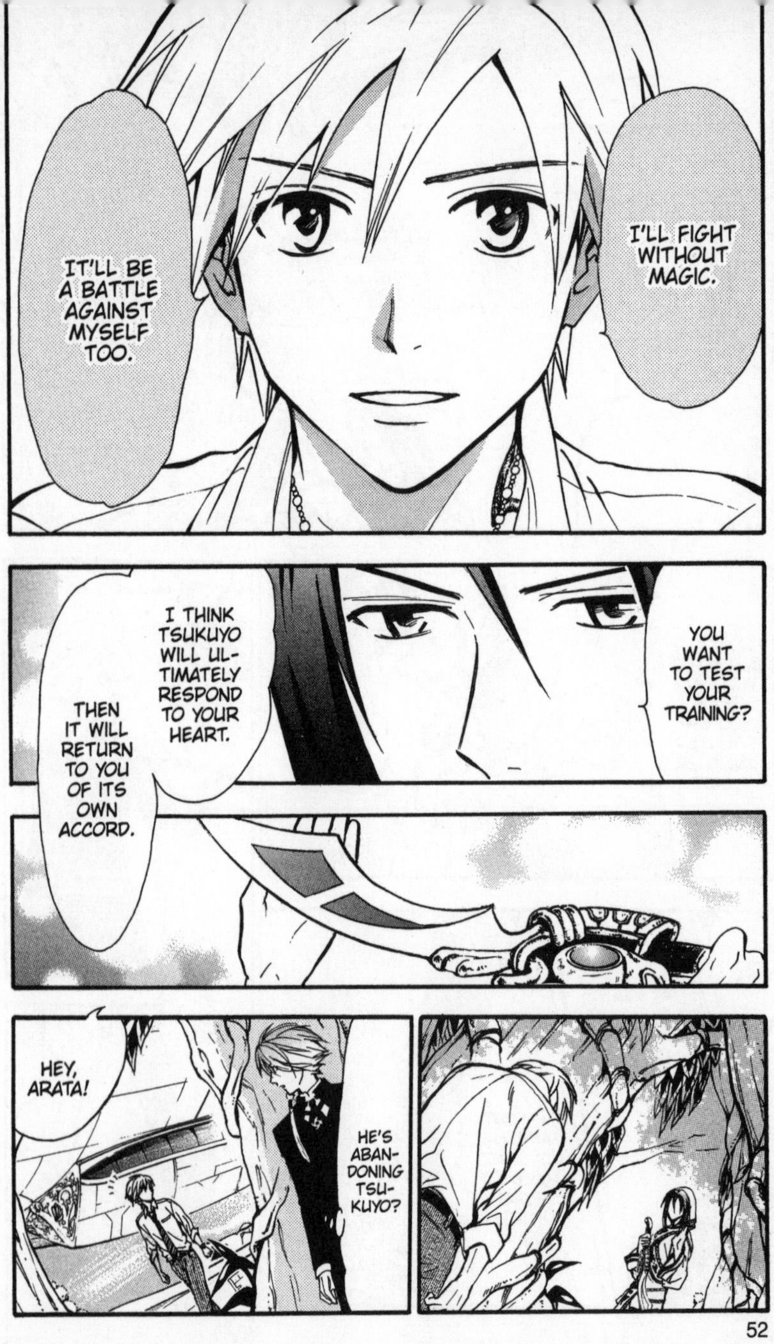
I'LL FIGHT WITHOUT MAGIC.
IT'LL BE A BATTLE AGAINST MYSELF TOO.
YOU WANT TO TEST YOUR TRAINING?
I THINK TSUKUYO WILL ULTIMATELY RESPOND TO YOUR HEART.
THEN IT WILL RETURN TO YOU OF ITS OWN ACCORD.
HE'S ABANDONING TSUKUYO?
HEY, ARATA!

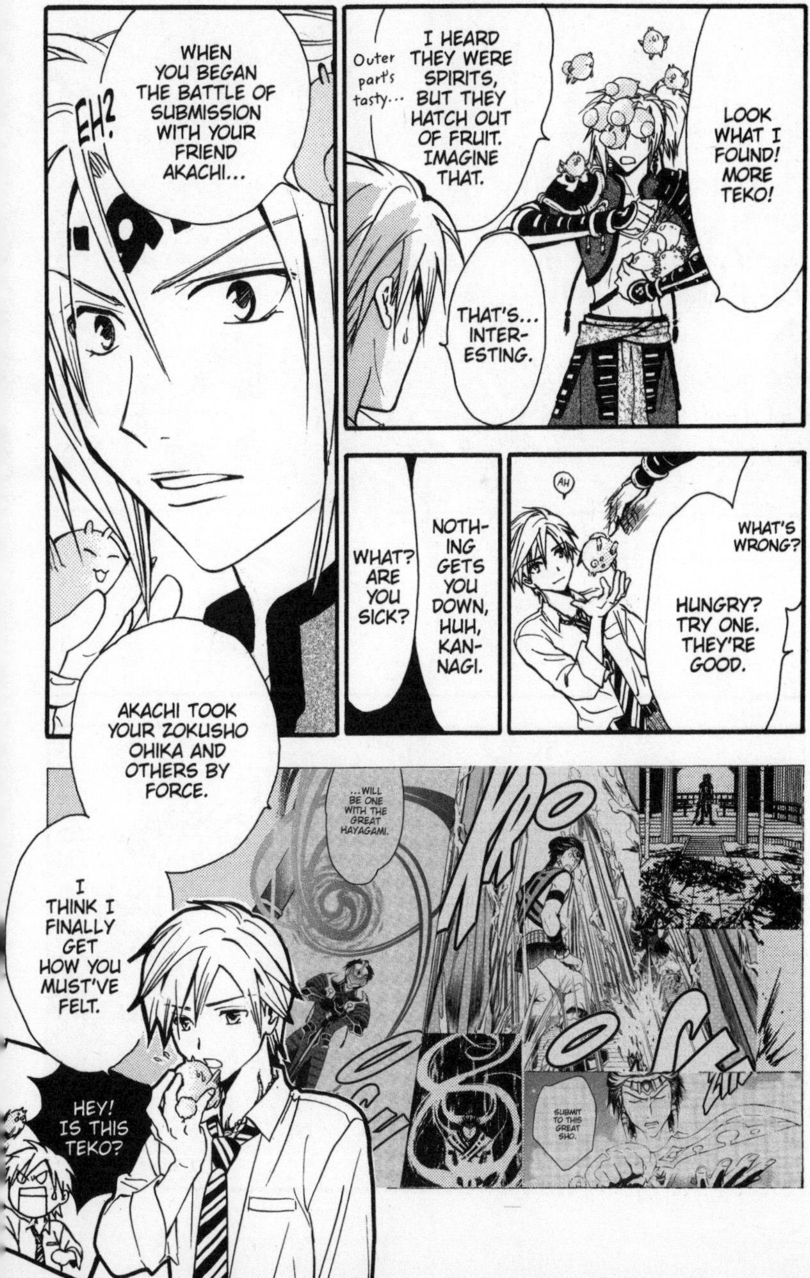
LOOK WHAT I FOUND! MORE TEKO!
I HEARD THEY WERE SPIRITS, BUT THEY HATCH OUT OF FRUIT. IMAGINE THAT.
Outer part's tasty...
THAT'S... INTER-ESTING.
AH
WHAT'S WRONG?
HUNGRY? TRY ONE. THEY'RE GOOD.
NOTH-ING GETS YOU DOWN, HUH, KAN-NAGI.
WHAT? ARE YOU SICK?
EH?
WHEN YOU BEGAN THE BATTLE OF SUBMISSION WITH YOUR FRIEND AKACHI...
AKACHI TOOK YOUR ZOKUSHO OHIKA AND OTHERS BY FORCE.
SUBMIT TO THIS GREAT SHO.
...WILL BE ONE WITH THE GREAT HAYAGAMI.
I THINK I FINALLY GET HOW YOU MUST'VE FELT.
HEY! IS THIS TEKO?

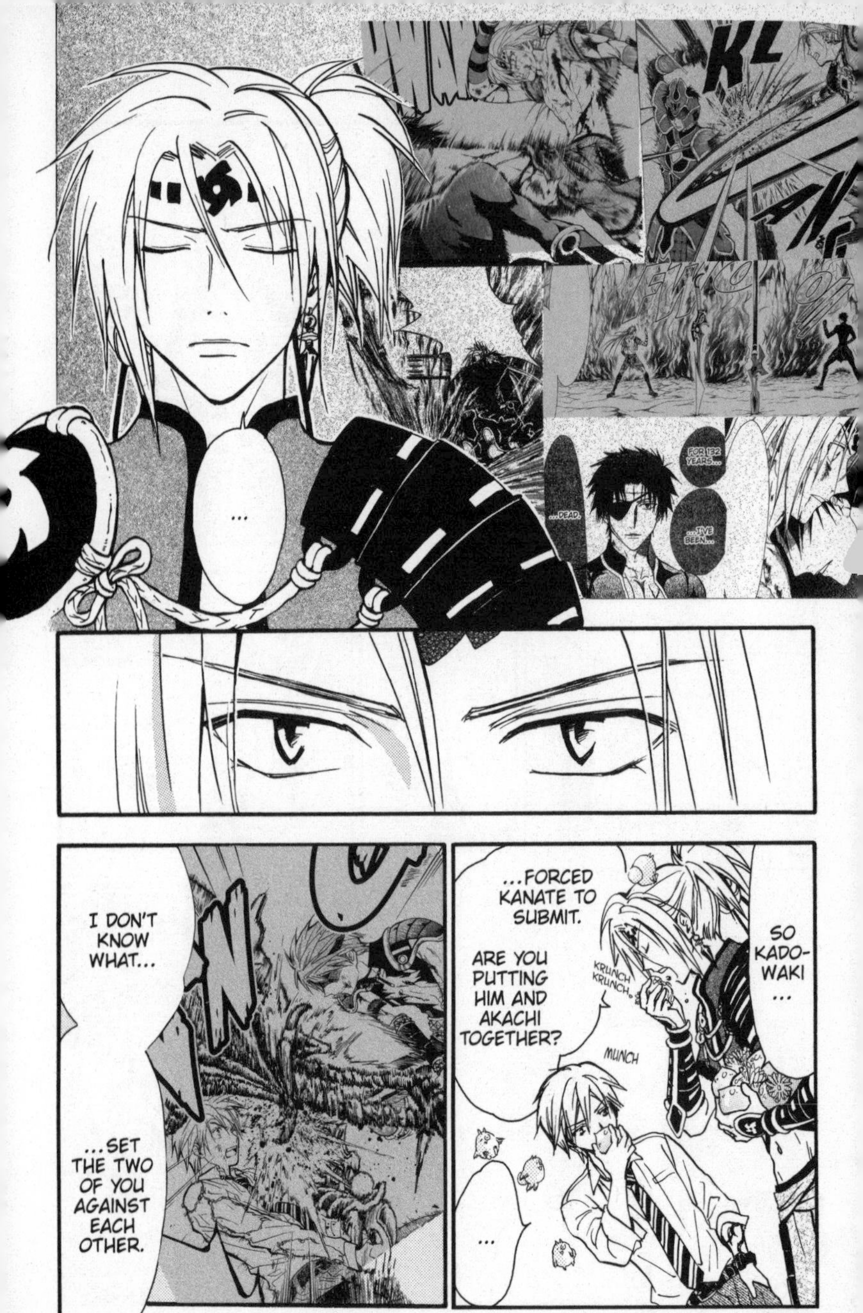
FOR 132 YEARS...
...I'VE BEEN...
...DEAD.
...
SO KADO-WAKI...
...FORCED KANATE TO SUBMIT.
ARE YOU PUTTING HIM AND AKACHI TOGETHER?
KRUNCH KRUNCH
MUNCH
...
I DON'T KNOW WHAT...
...SET THE TWO OF YOU AGAINST EACH OTHER.

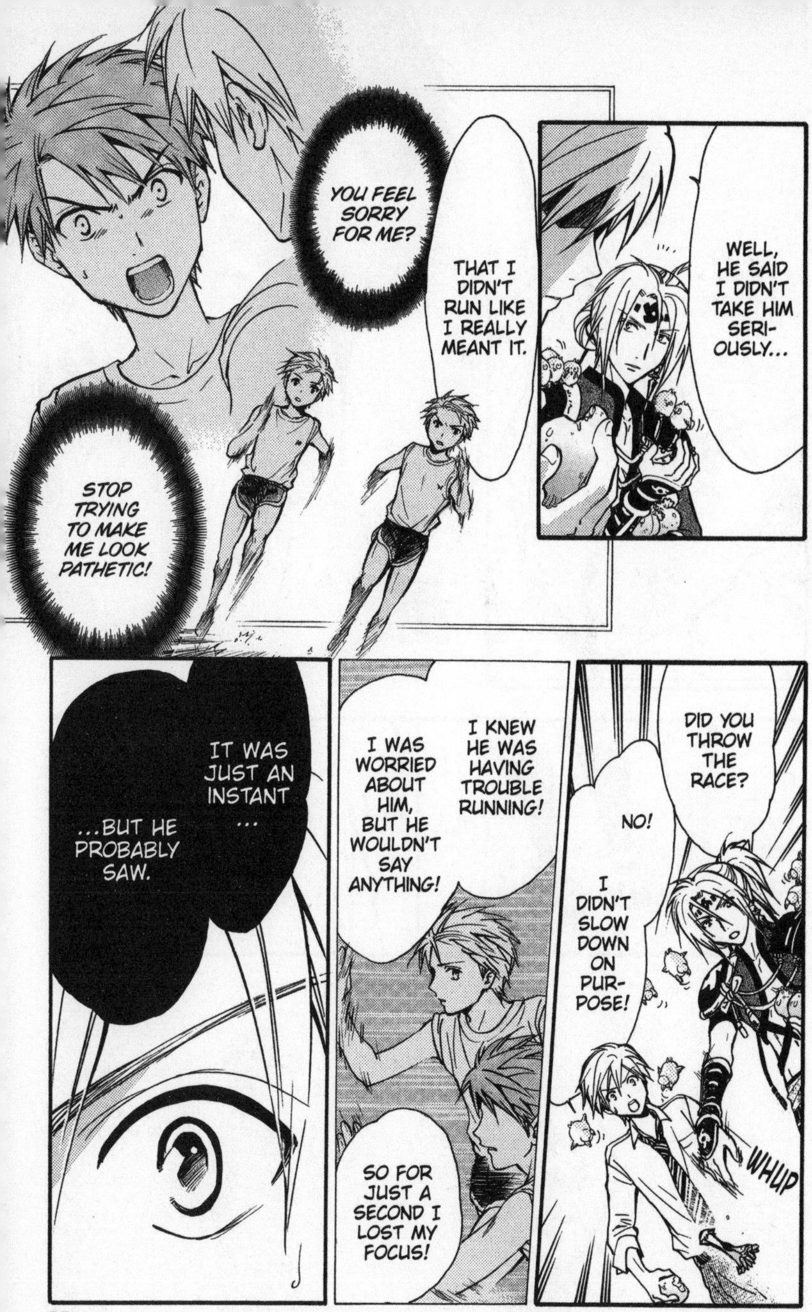
WELL, HE SAID I DIDN'T TAKE HIM SERI-OUSLY...
THAT I DIDN'T RUN LIKE I REALLY MEANT IT.
YOU FEEL SORRY FOR ME?
STOP TRYING TO MAKE ME LOOK PATHETIC!
DID YOU THROW THE RACE?
NO!
I DIDN'T SLOW DOWN ON PUR-POSE!
WHUP
I KNEW HE WAS HAVING TROUBLE RUNNING!
I WAS WORRIED ABOUT HIM, BUT HE WOULDN'T SAY ANYTHING!
SO FOR JUST A SECOND I LOST MY FOCUS!
IT WAS JUST AN INSTANT...
...BUT HE PROBABLY SAW.

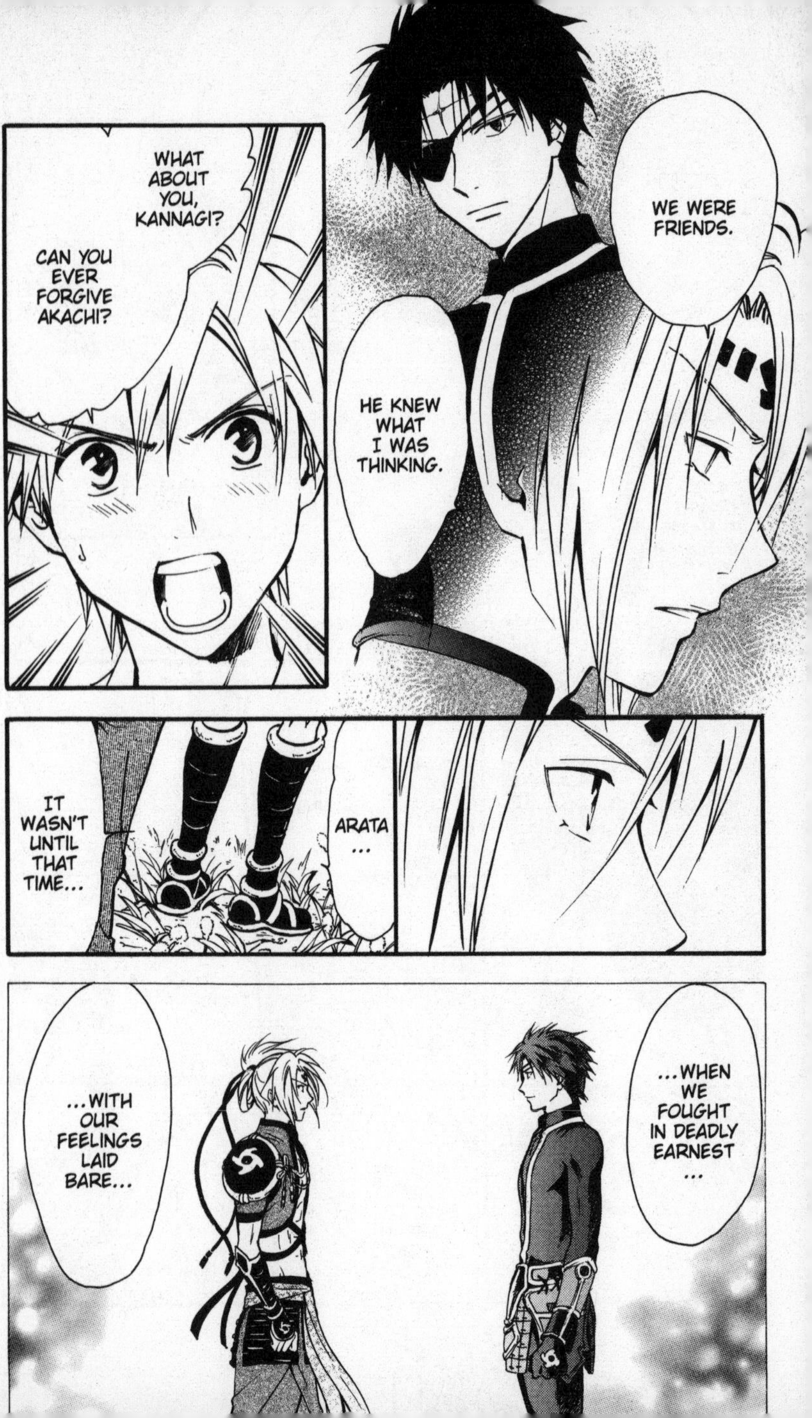
WE WERE FRIENDS.
HE KNEW WHAT I WAS THINKING.
WHAT ABOUT YOU, KANNAGI?
CAN YOU EVER FORGIVE AKACHI?
ARATA ...
IT WASN'T UNTIL THAT TIME...
...WHEN WE FOUGHT IN DEADLY EARNEST ...
...WITH OUR FEELINGS LAID BARE...

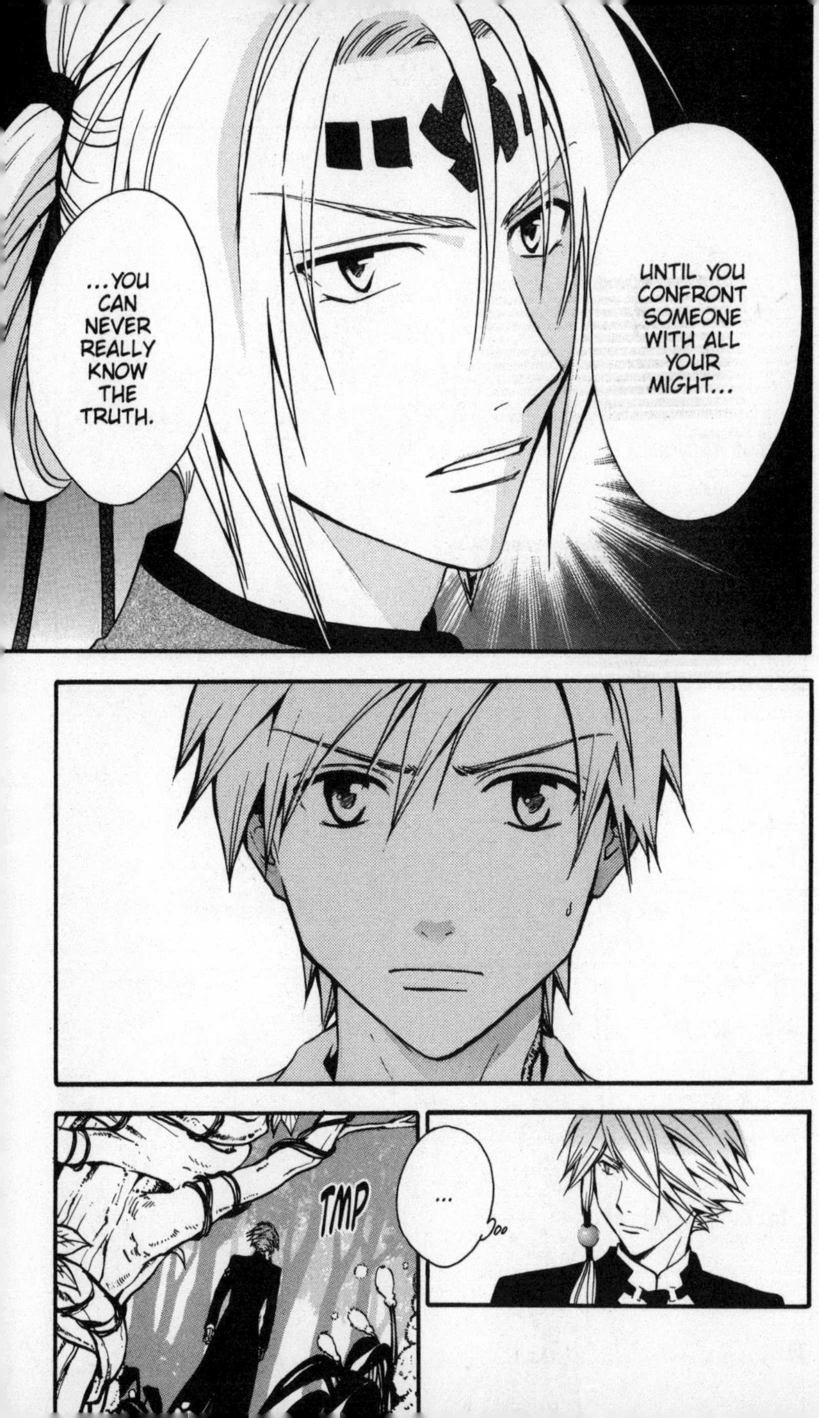
UNTIL YOU CONFRONT SOMEONE WITH ALL YOUR MIGHT...
...YOU CAN NEVER REALLY KNOW THE TRUTH.
...
TMP

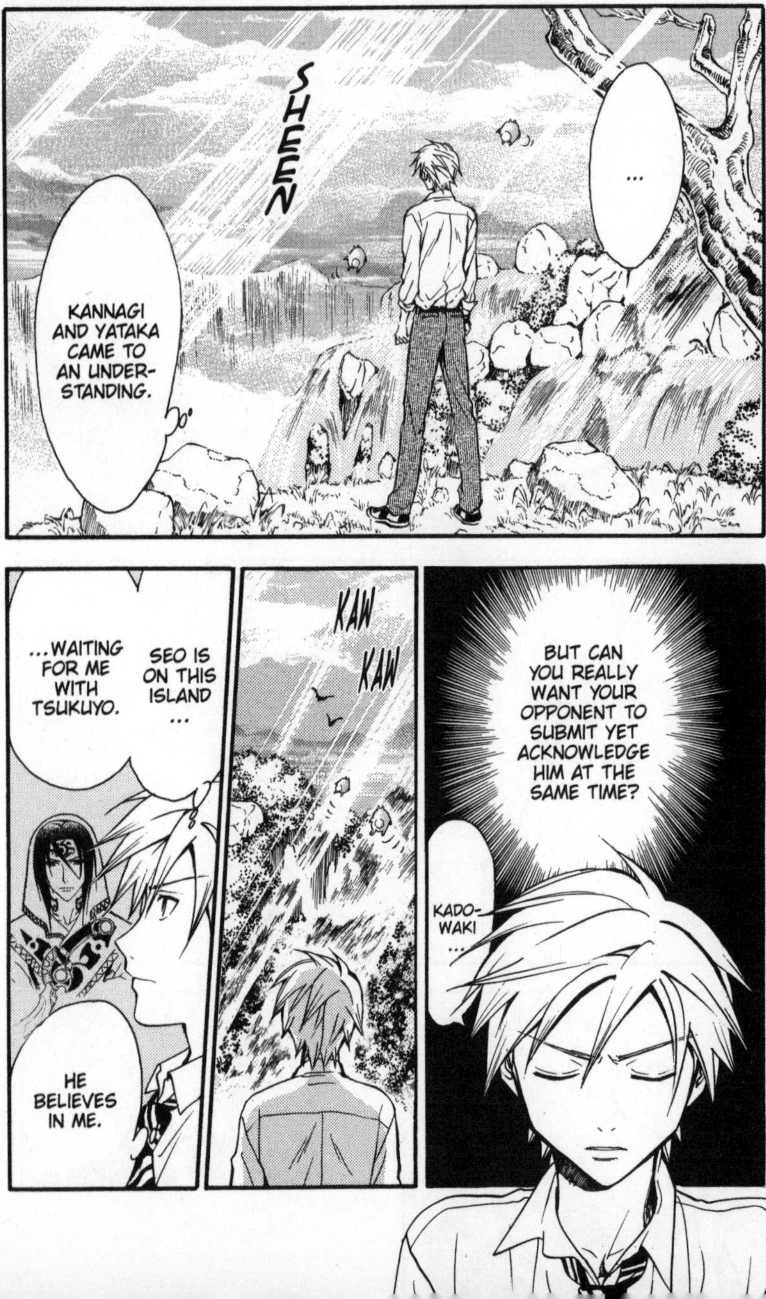
...
SHEEN
KANNAGI AND YATAKA CAME TO AN UNDER-STANDING.
BUT CAN YOU REALLY WANT YOUR OPPONENT TO SUBMIT YET ACKNOWLEDGE HIM AT THE SAME TIME?
KADO-WAKI ...
KAW KAW
SEO IS ON THIS ISLAND ...
...WAITING FOR ME WITH TSUKUYO.
HE BELIEVES IN ME.

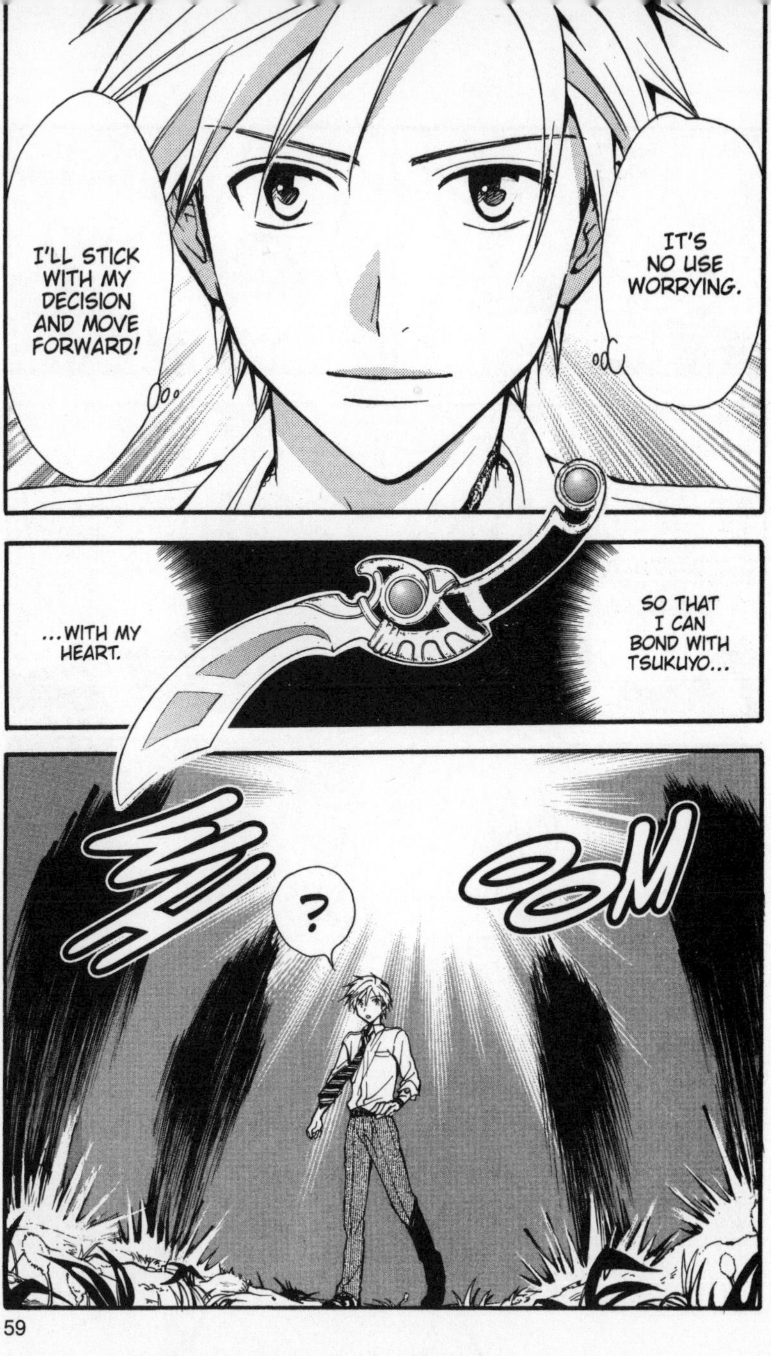
IT'S NO USE WORRYING.
I'LL STICK WITH MY DECISION AND MOVE FORWARD!
SO THAT I CAN BOND WITH TSUKUYO...
...WITH MY HEART.
WHOOM
?

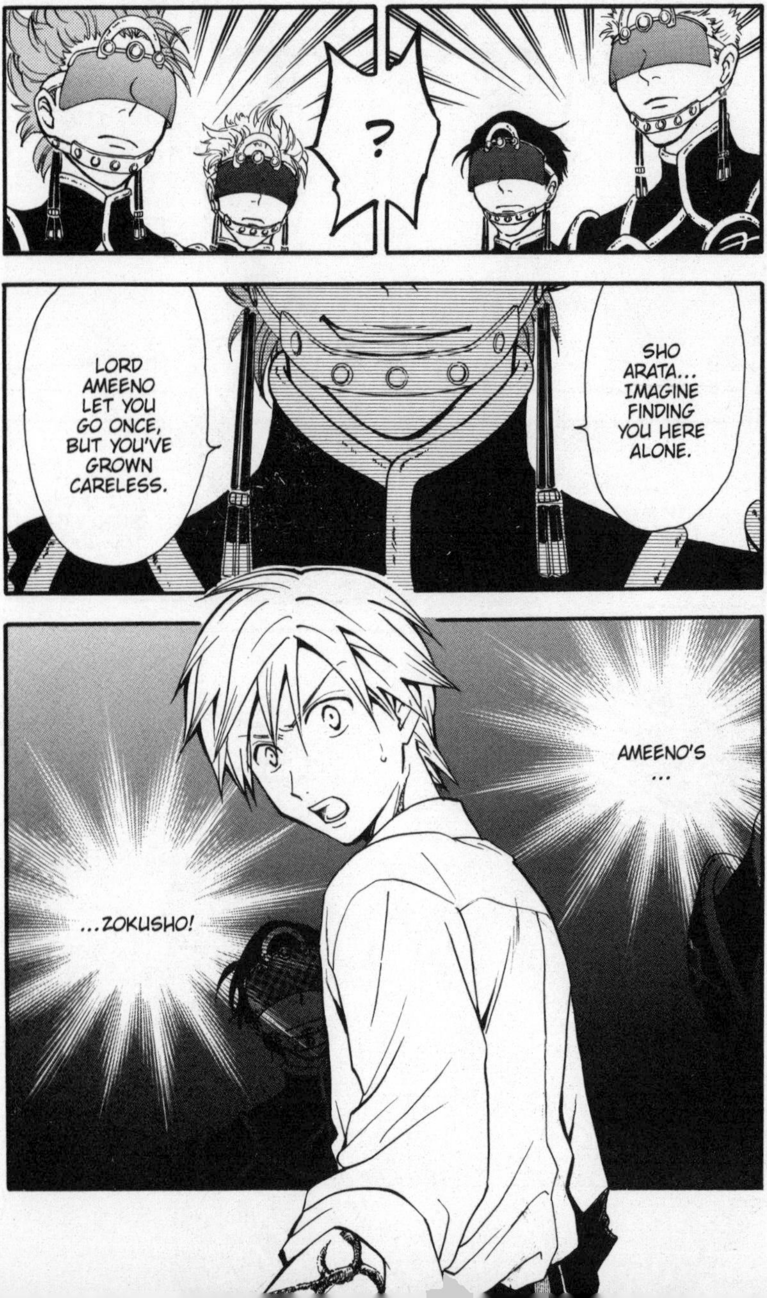
?
SHO ARATA... IMAGINE FINDING YOU HERE ALONE.
LORD AMEENO LET YOU GO ONCE, BUT YOU'VE GROWN CARELESS.
AMEENO'S ...
...ZOKUSHO!

Chapter 221
CHIWAYA

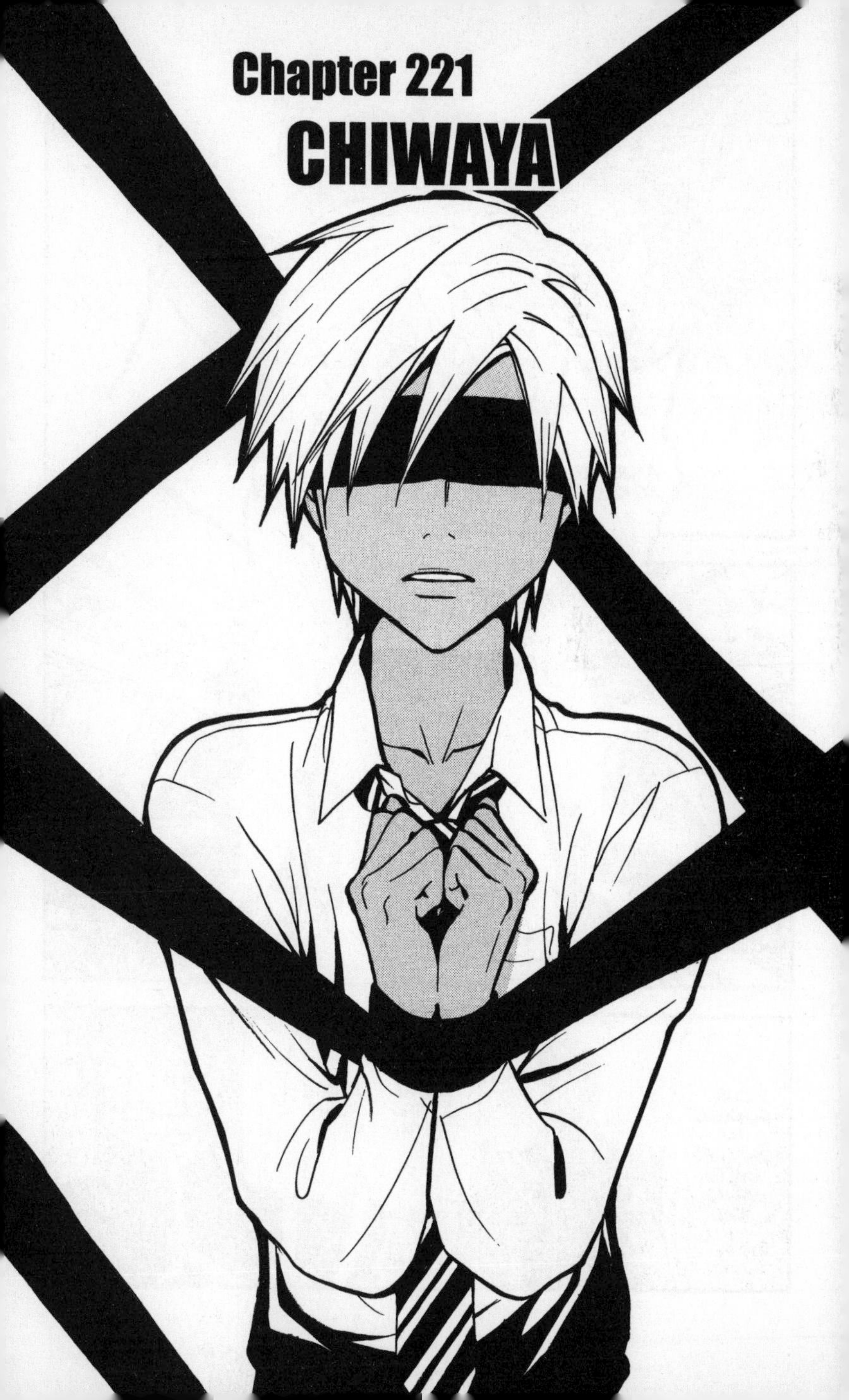

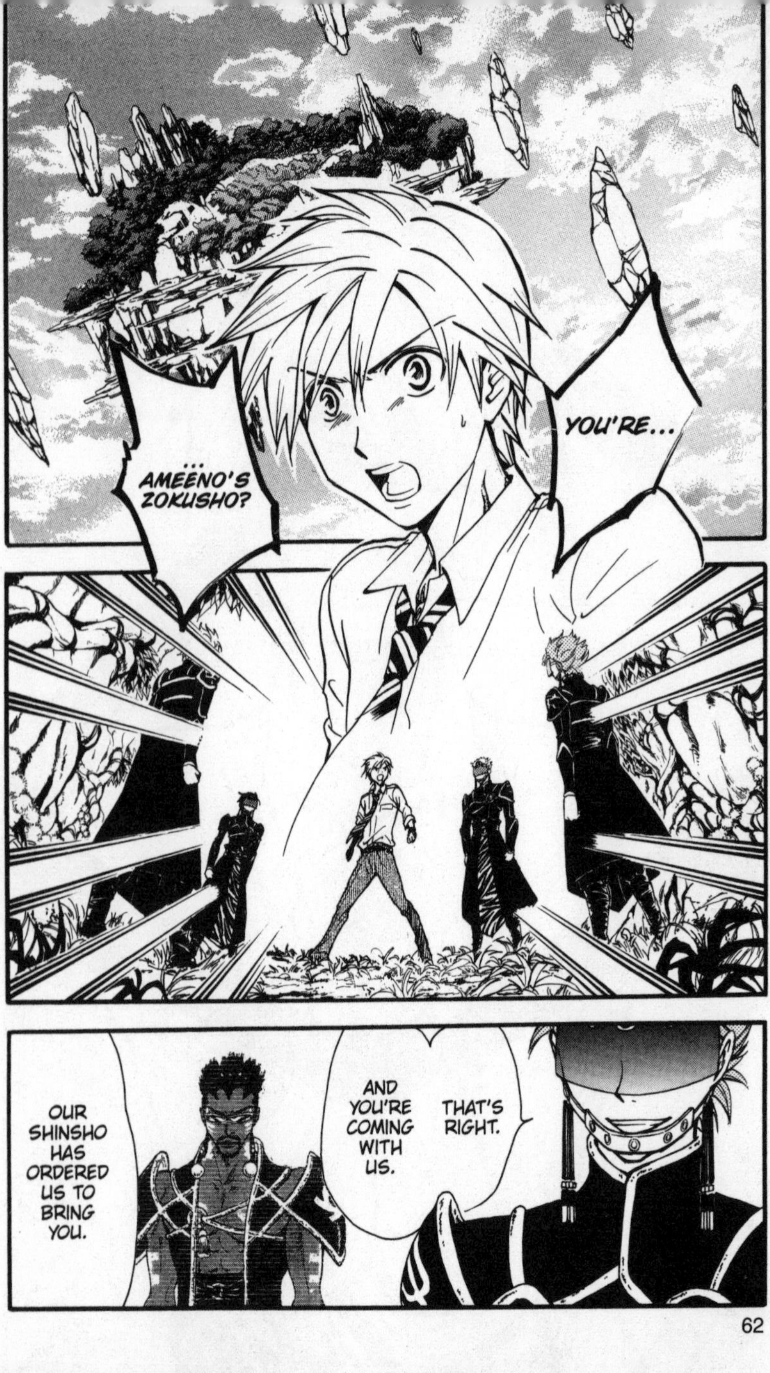
YOU'RE...
...AMEËNO'S ZOKUSHO?
THAT'S RIGHT.
AND YOU'RE COMING WITH US.
OUR SHINSHO HAS ORDERED US TO BRING YOU.

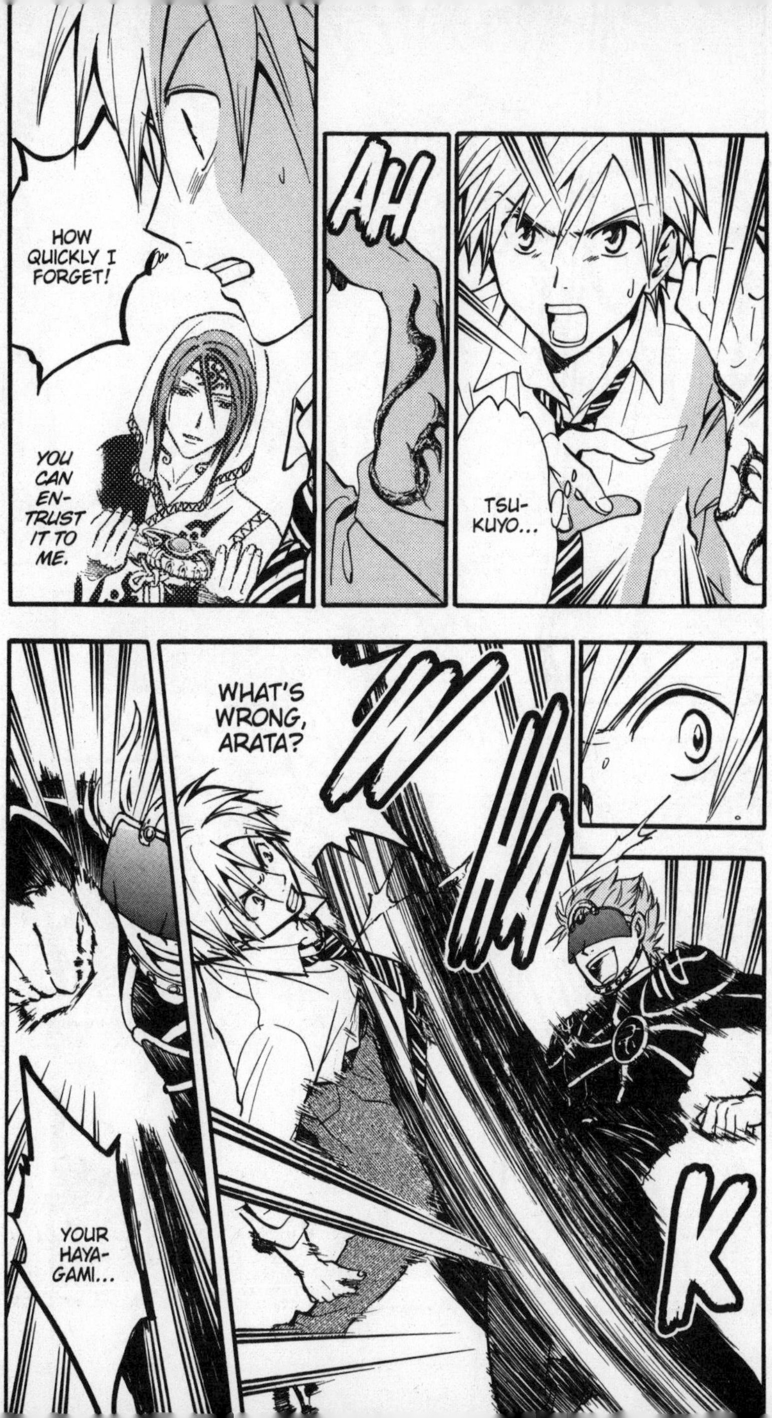
TSU-KUYO...
AH
HOW QUICKLY I FORGET!
YOU CAN EN-TRUST IT TO ME.
WHAT'S WRONG, ARATA?
WHAK
YOUR HAYA-GAMI...

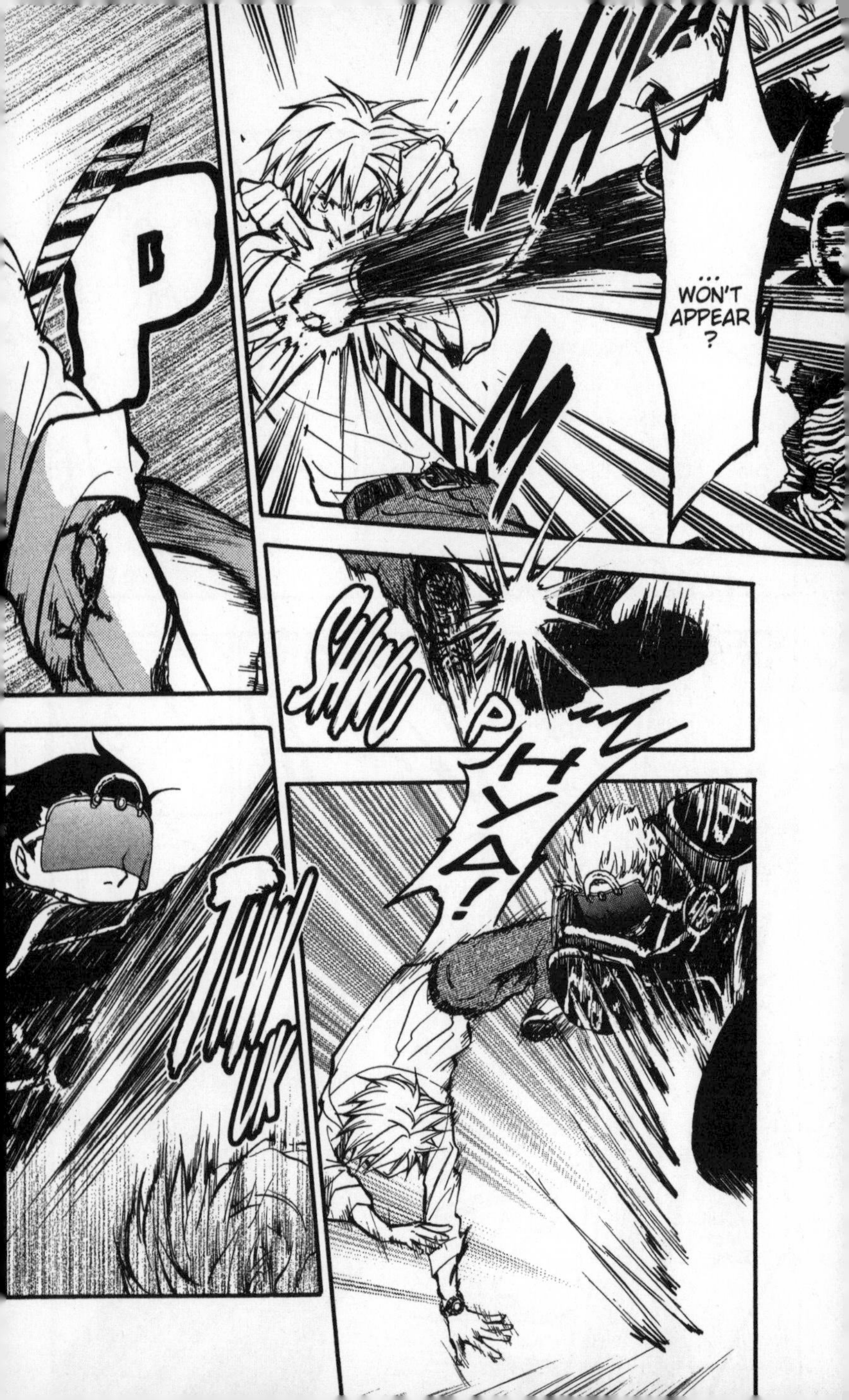
... WON'T APPEAR?
PHYA!

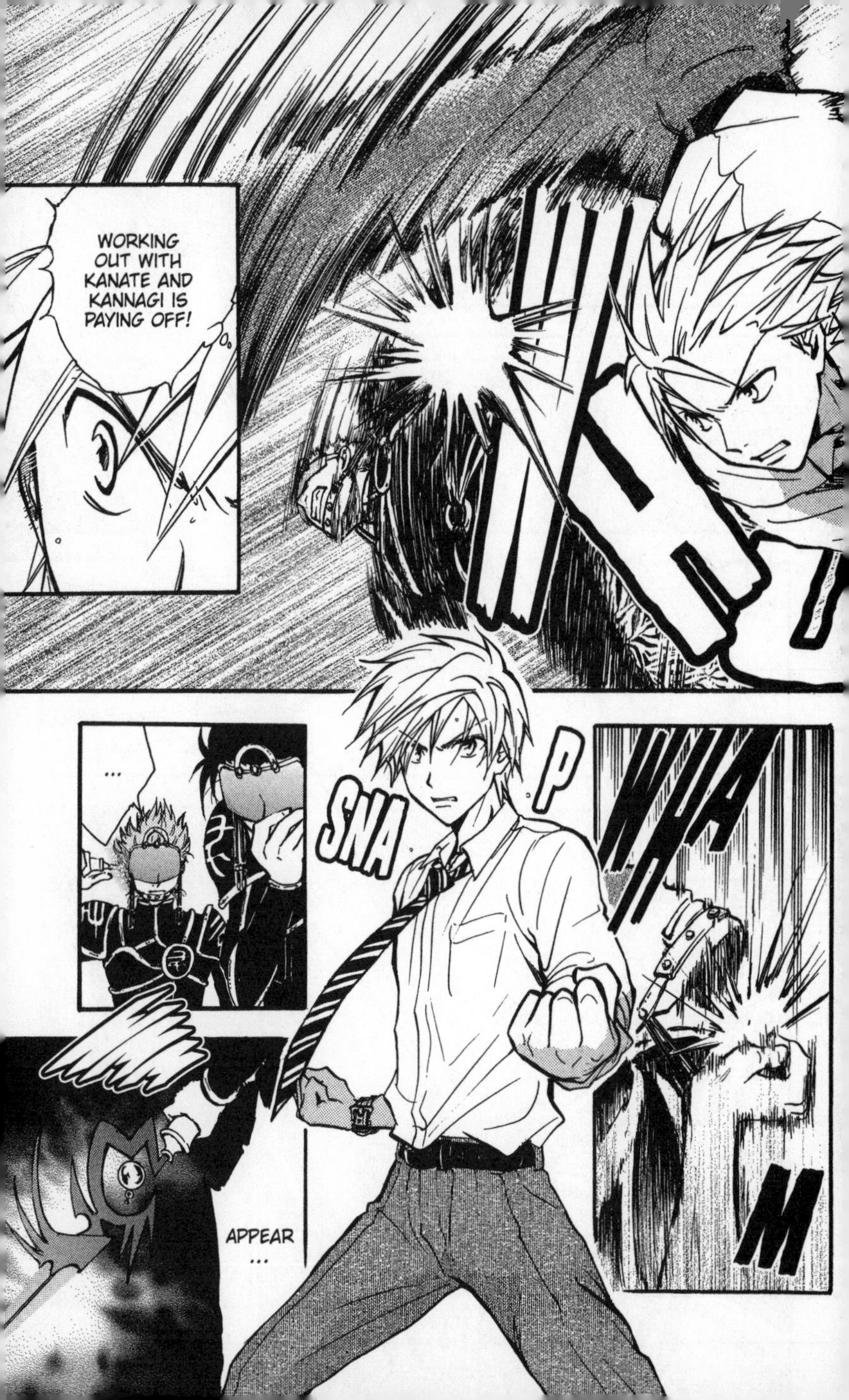
WORKING OUT WITH KANATE AND KANNAGI IS PAYING OFF!
WHAM
SNAP
...
APPEAR ...

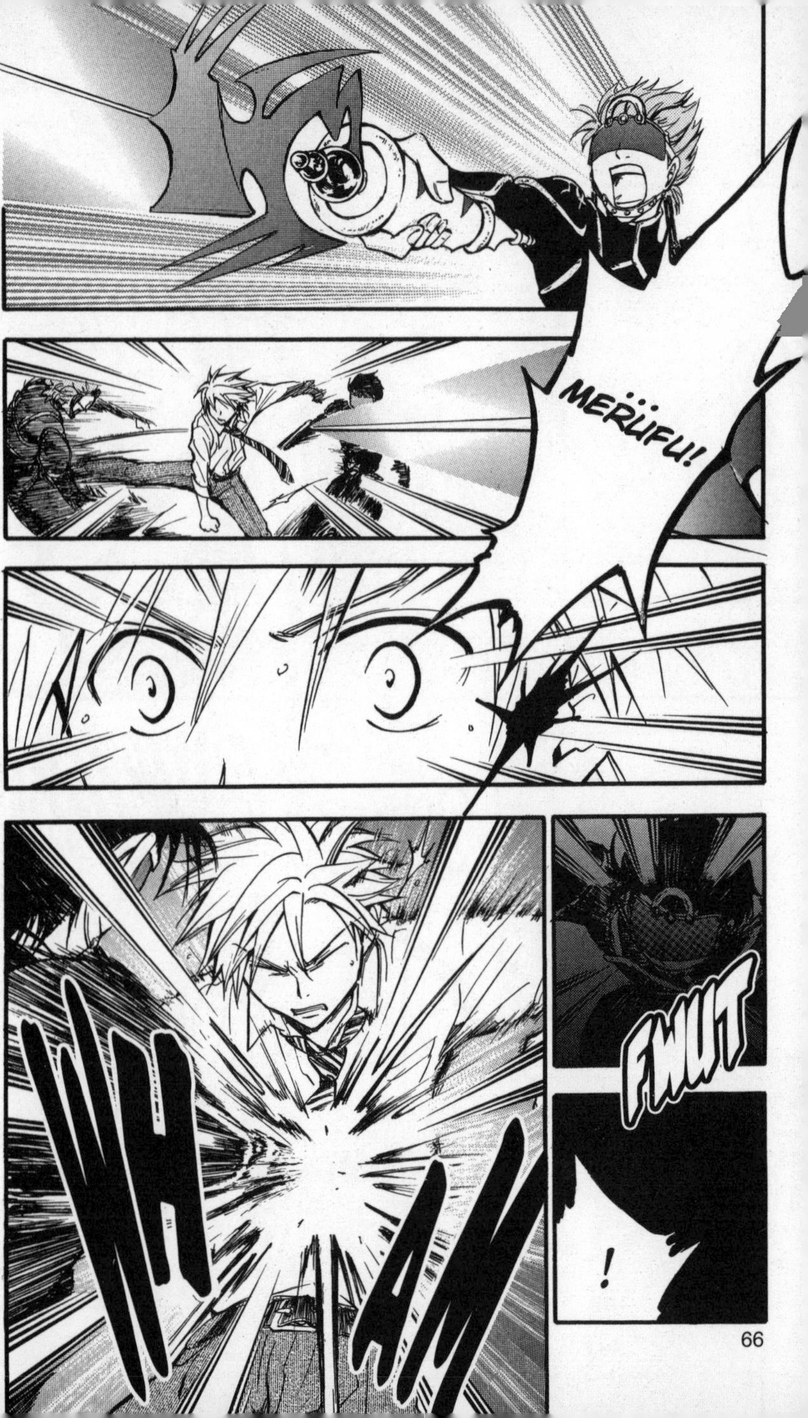
MERÜFU!
FWUT
!
WHAM

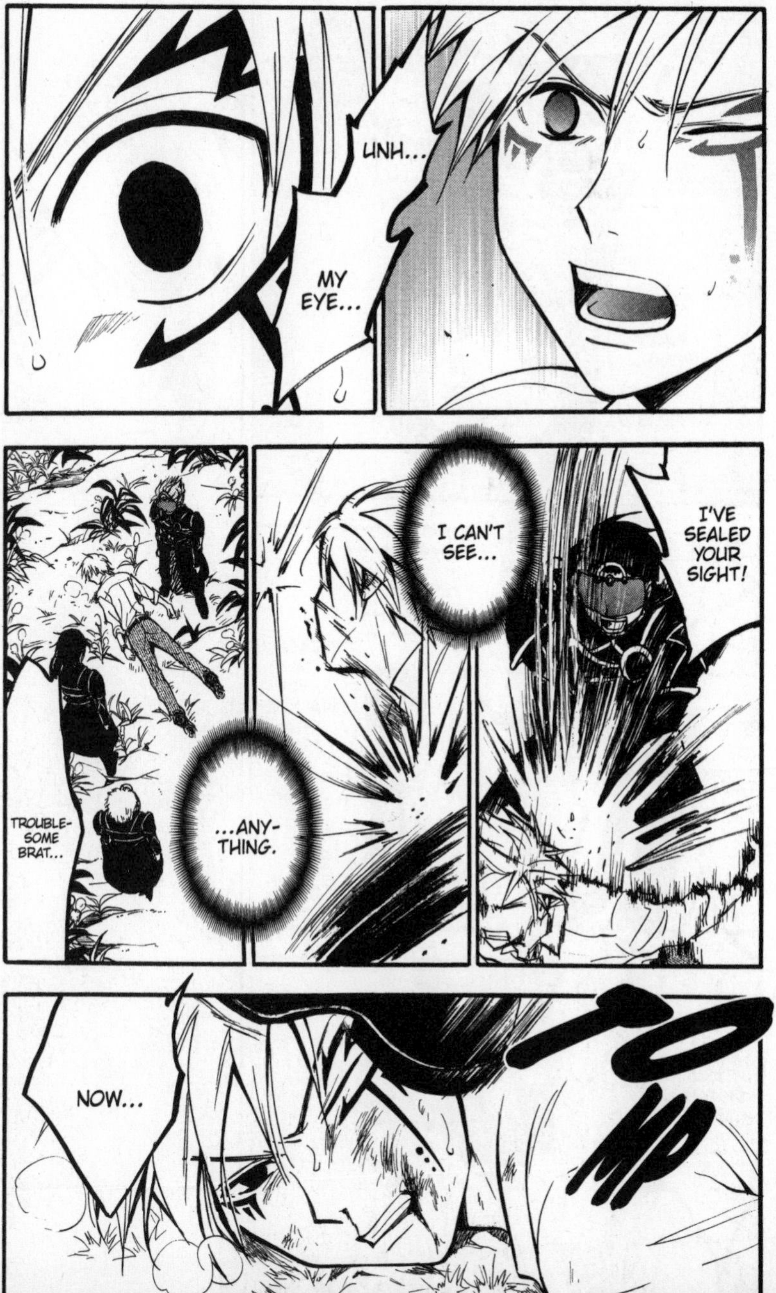
UNH...
MY EYE...
I'VE SEALED YOUR SIGHT!
I CAN'T SEE...
...ANY-THING.
TROUBLE-SOME BRAT...
TOMP
NOW...

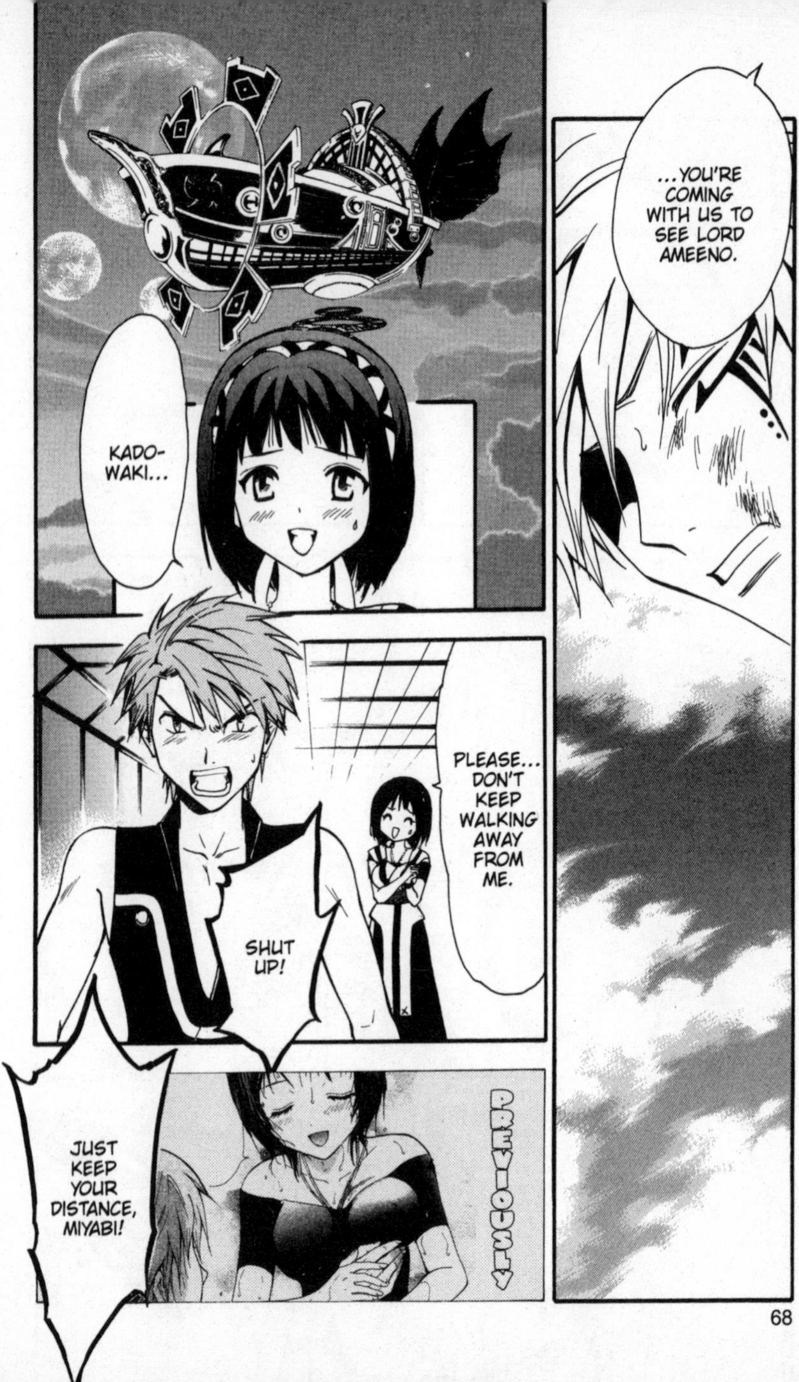
...YOU'RE COMING WITH US TO SEE LORD AMEENO.
KADO-WAKI...
PLEASE... DON'T KEEP WALKING AWAY FROM ME.
SHUT UP!
PREVIOUSLY
JUST KEEP YOUR DISTANCE, MIYABI!

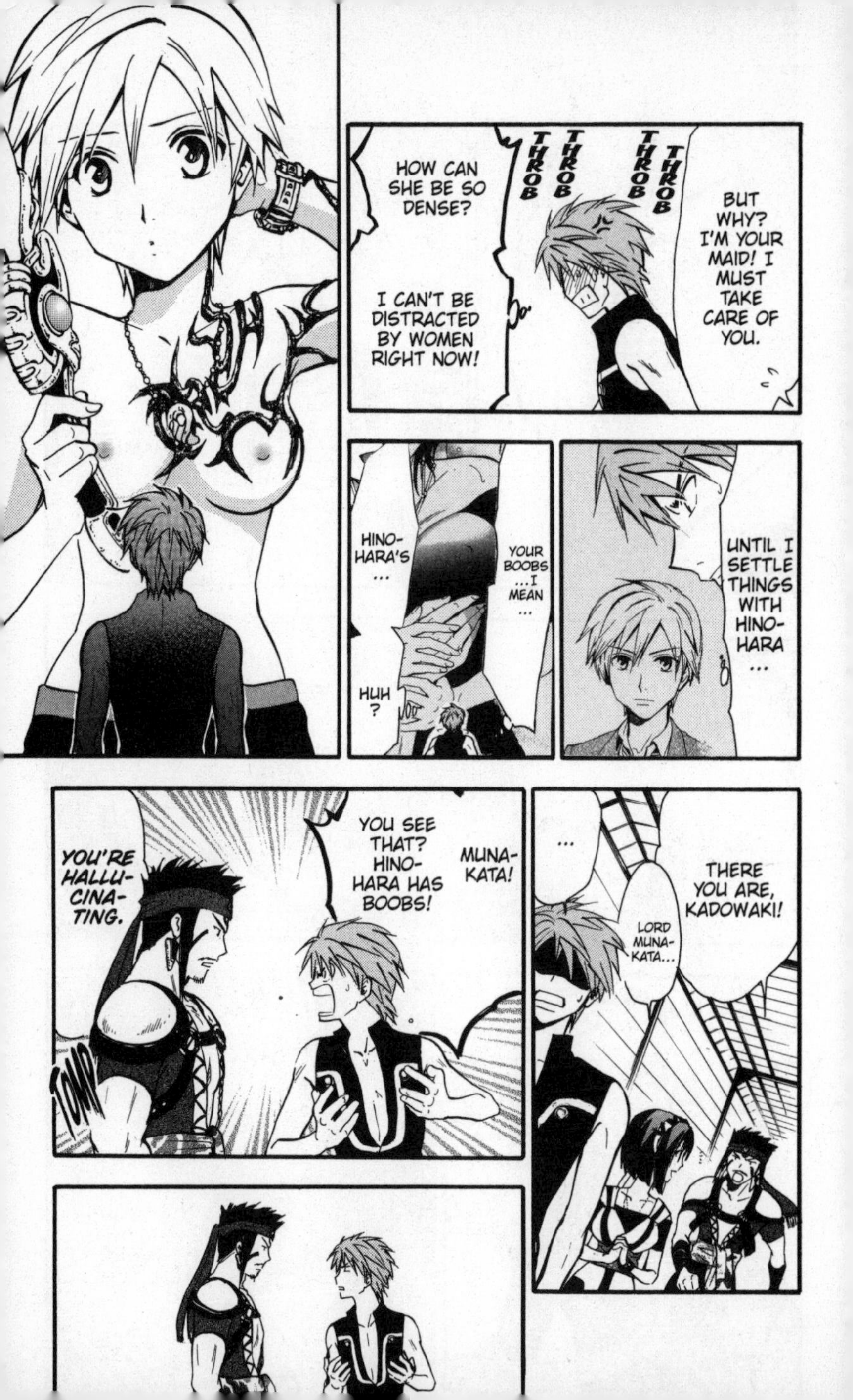
BUT WHY? I'M YOUR MAID! I MUST TAKE CARE OF YOU.
THROB THROB THROB THROB
HOW CAN SHE BE SO DENSE?
I CAN'T BE DISTRACTED BY WOMEN RIGHT NOW!
UNTIL I SETTLE THINGS WITH HINO-HARA...
YOUR BOOBS ...I MEAN ...
HINO-HARA'S ...
HUH?
THERE YOU ARE, KADOWAKI!
LORD MUNA-KATA...
...
MUNA-KATA!
YOU SEE THAT? HINO-HARA HAS BOOBS!
YOU'RE HALLU-CINA-TING.
TOMP

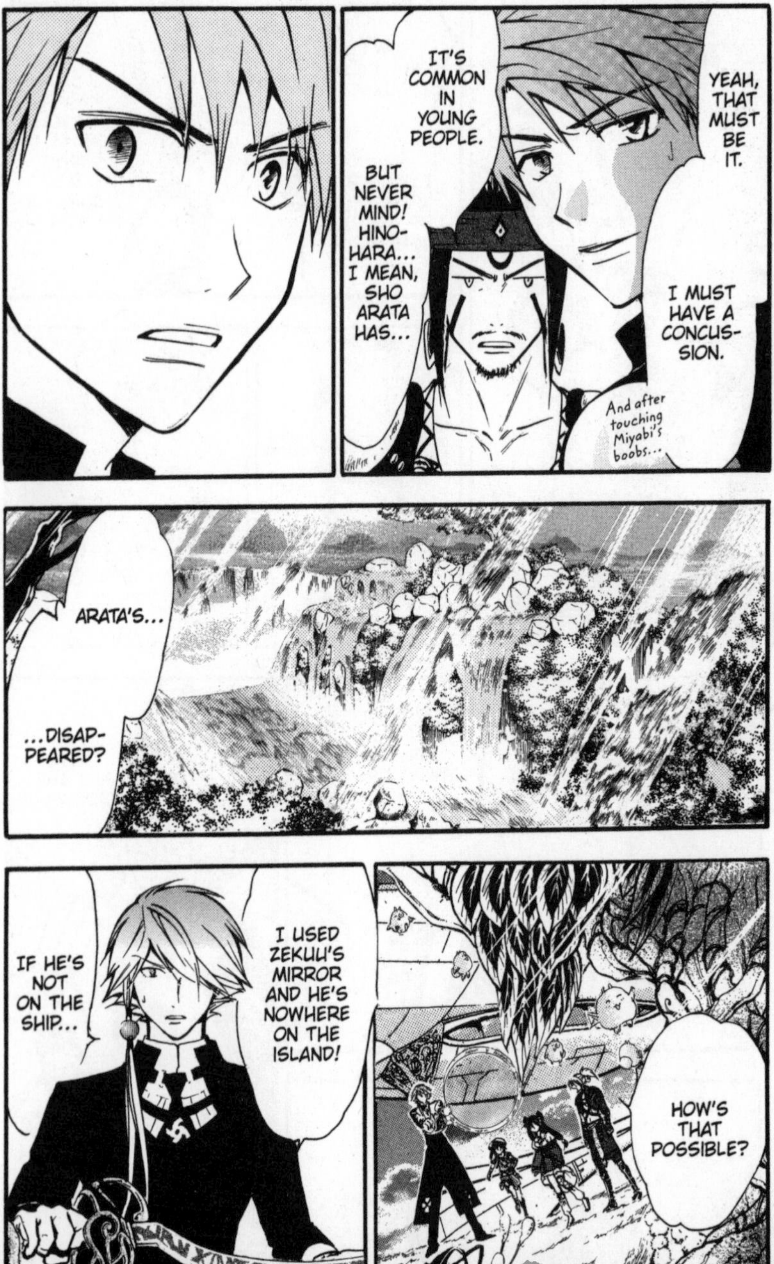
YEAH, THAT MUST BE IT.
I MUST HAVE A CONCUS-SION.
And after touching Miyabi's boobs...
IT'S COMMON IN YOUNG PEOPLE.
BUT NEVER MIND! HINO-HARA... I MEAN, SHO ARATA HAS...
ARATA'S...
...DISAP-PEARED?
HOW'S THAT POSSIBLE?
I USED ZEKUU'S MIRROR AND HE'S NOWHERE ON THE ISLAND!
IF HE'S NOT ON THE SHIP...

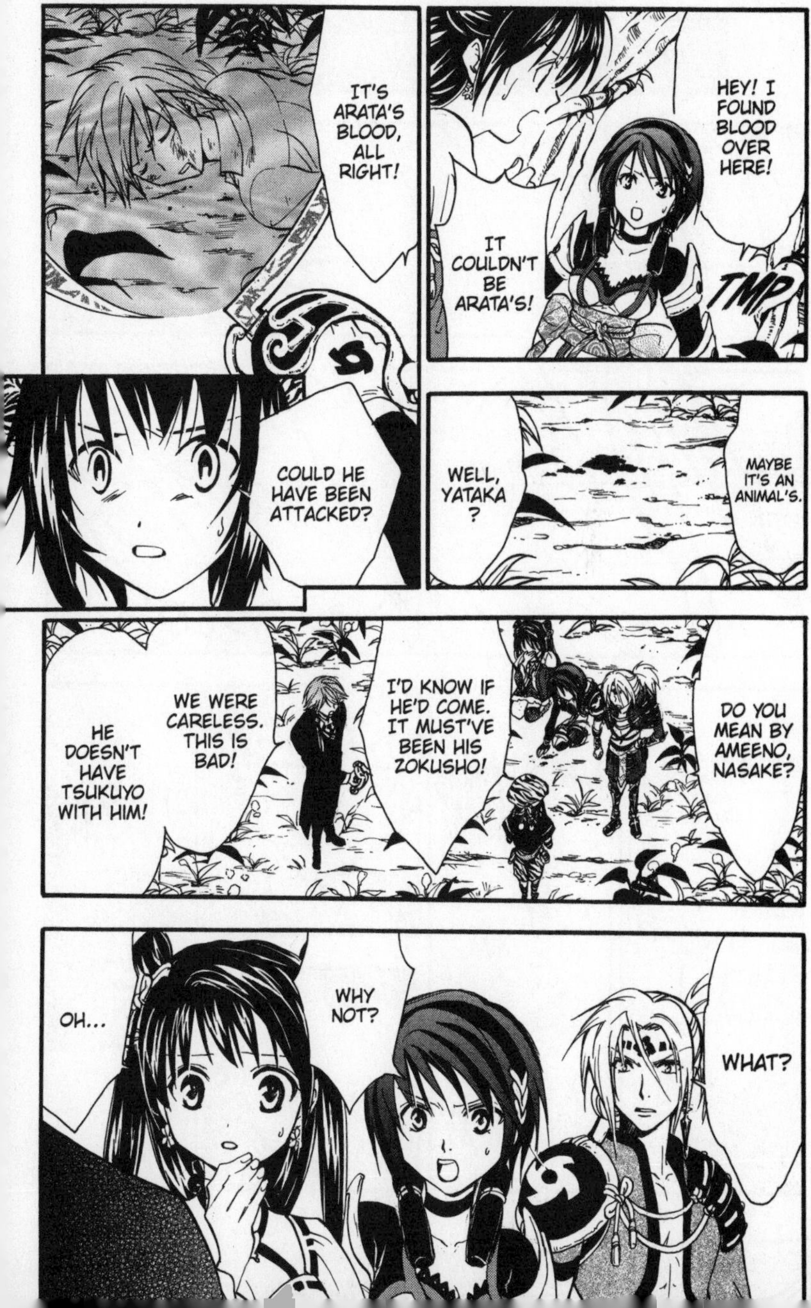
HEY! I FOUND BLOOD OVER HERE!
TMP
IT COULDN'T BE ARATA'S!
IT'S ARATA'S BLOOD, ALL RIGHT!
MAYBE IT'S AN ANIMAL'S.
WELL, YATAKA?
COULD HE HAVE BEEN ATTACKED?
DO YOU MEAN BY AMEENO, NASAKE?
I'D KNOW IF HE'D COME. IT MUST'VE BEEN HIS ZOKUSHO!
WE WERE CARELESS. THIS IS BAD!
HE DOESN'T HAVE TSUKUYO WITH HIM!
WHAT?
WHY NOT?
OH...

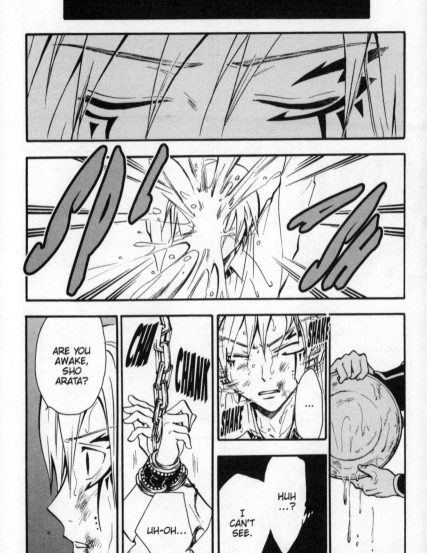

ARE YOU AWAKE, SHO ARATA?

CHA CHANK

SHAKE SHAKE

...

UH-OH...

I CAN'T SEE.

HUH ...?

72

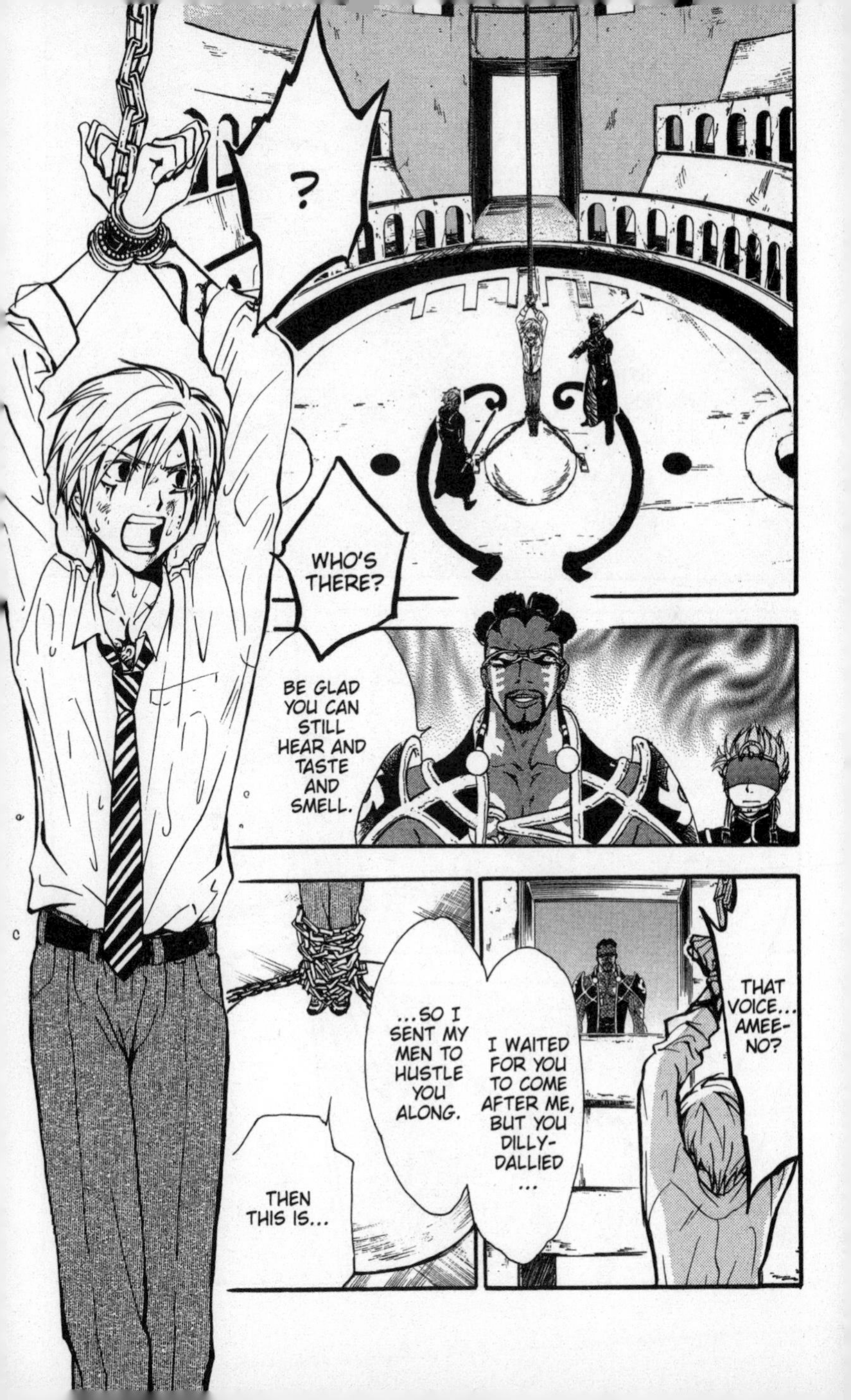
?
WHO'S THERE?
BE GLAD YOU CAN STILL HEAR AND TASTE AND SMELL.
THAT VOICE... AMEE-NO?
I WAITED FOR YOU TO COME AFTER ME, BUT YOU DILLY-DALLIED...
...SO I SENT MY MEN TO HUSTLE YOU ALONG.
THEN THIS IS...

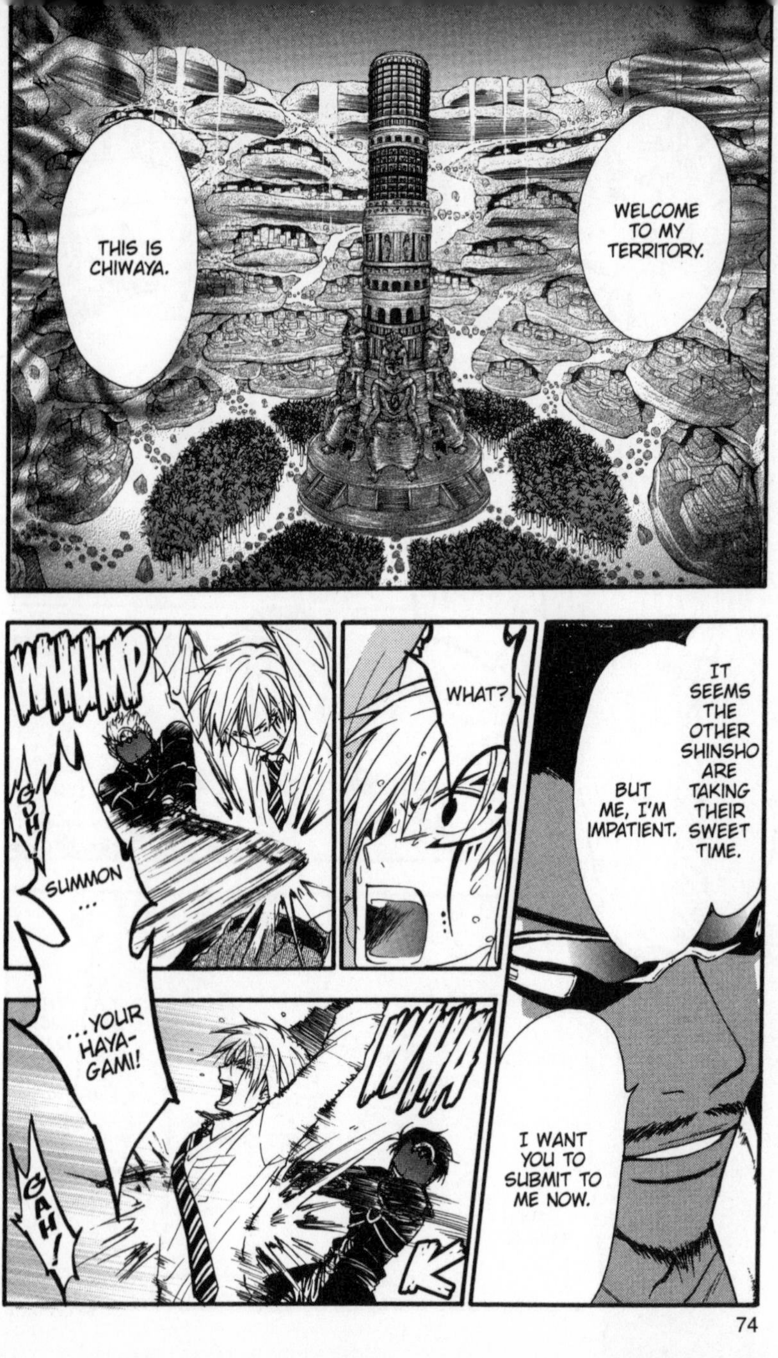
WELCOME TO MY TERRITORY.
THIS IS CHIWAYA.
IT SEEMS THE OTHER SHINSHO ARE TAKING THEIR SWEET TIME.
BUT ME, I'M IMPATIENT.
I WANT YOU TO SUBMIT TO ME NOW.
WHAT?
WHUMP
GUH!
SUMMON ...
...YOUR HAYA-GAMI!
WHA
K
GAH!

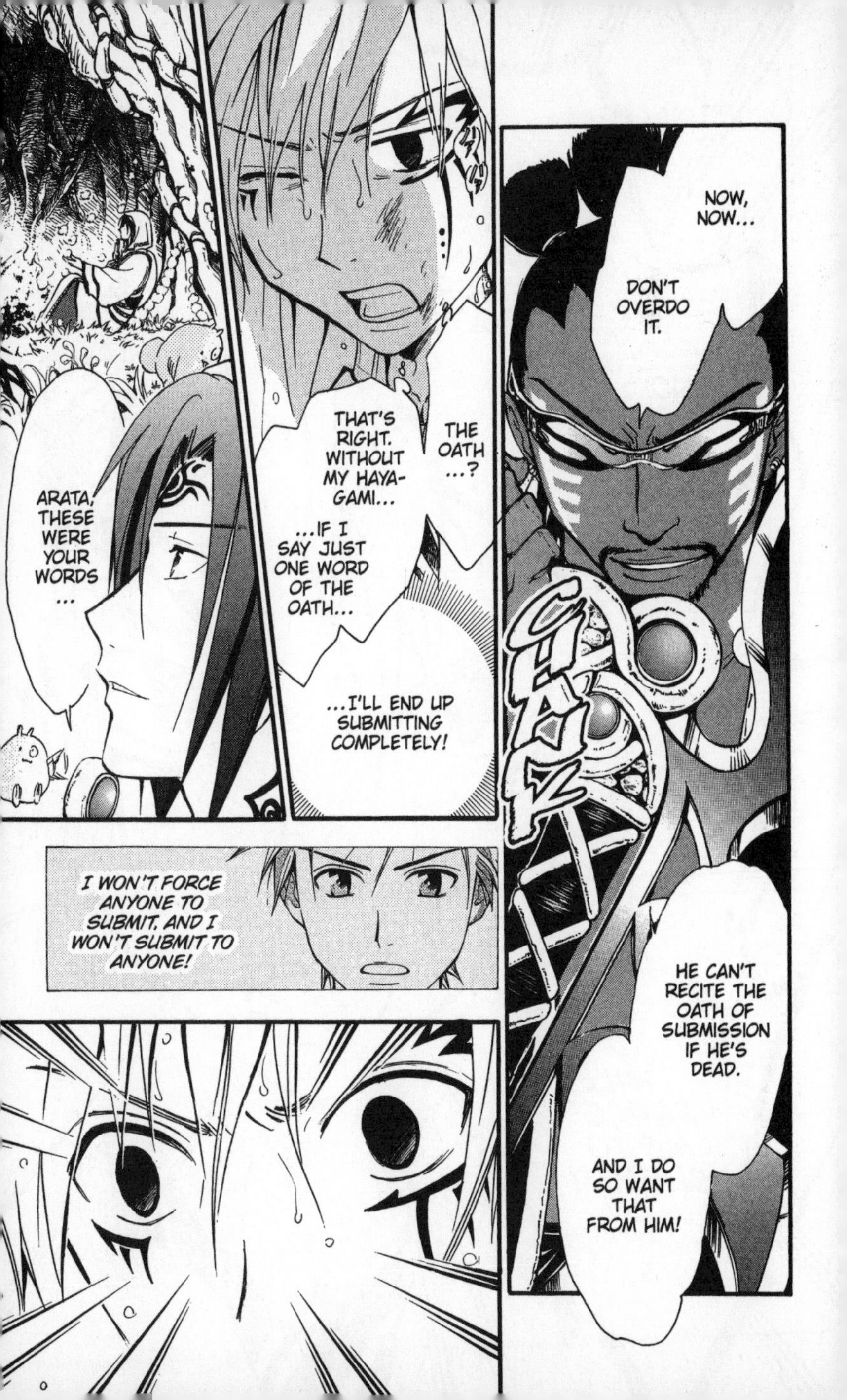
NOW, NOW...
DON'T OVERDO IT.
CLICK
HE CAN'T RECITE THE OATH OF SUBMISSION IF HE'S DEAD.
AND I DO SO WANT THAT FROM HIM!
THE OATH ...?
THAT'S RIGHT. WITHOUT MY HAYA-GAMI...
...IF I SAY JUST ONE WORD OF THE OATH...
...I'LL END UP SUBMITTING COMPLETELY!
ARATA, THESE WERE YOUR WORDS ...
I WON'T FORCE ANYONE TO SUBMIT. AND I WON'T SUBMIT TO ANYONE!

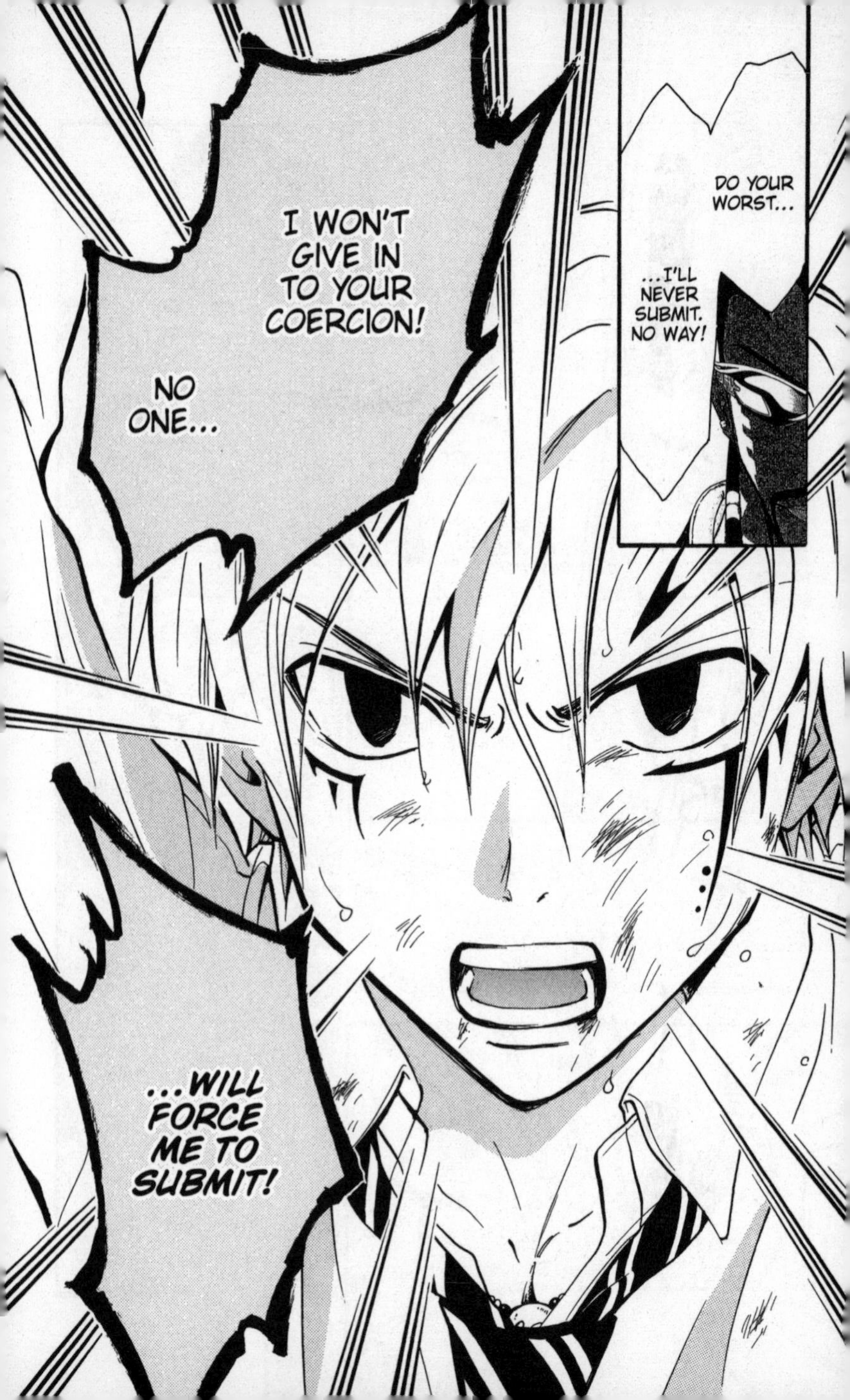
DO YOUR WORST...
...I'LL NEVER SUBMIT. NO WAY!
I WON'T GIVE IN TO YOUR COERCION!
NO ONE...
...WILL FORCE ME TO SUBMIT!

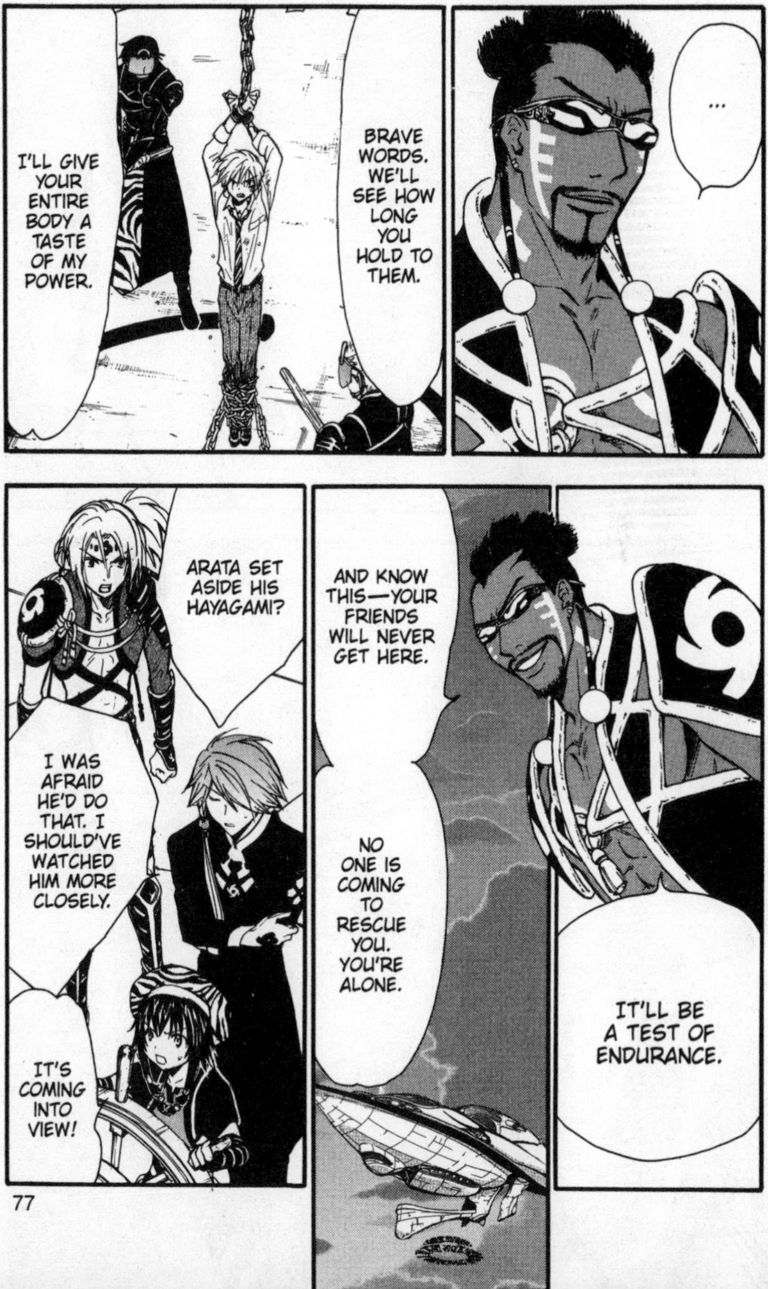
...
BRAVE WORDS. WE'LL SEE HOW LONG YOU HOLD TO THEM.
I'LL GIVE YOUR ENTIRE BODY A TASTE OF MY POWER.
IT'LL BE A TEST OF ENDURANCE.
AND KNOW THIS—YOUR FRIENDS WILL NEVER GET HERE.
NO ONE IS COMING TO RESCUE YOU. YOU'RE ALONE.
ARATA SET ASIDE HIS HAYAGAMI?
I WAS AFRAID HE'D DO THAT. I SHOULD'VE WATCHED HIM MORE CLOSELY.
IT'S COMING INTO VIEW!

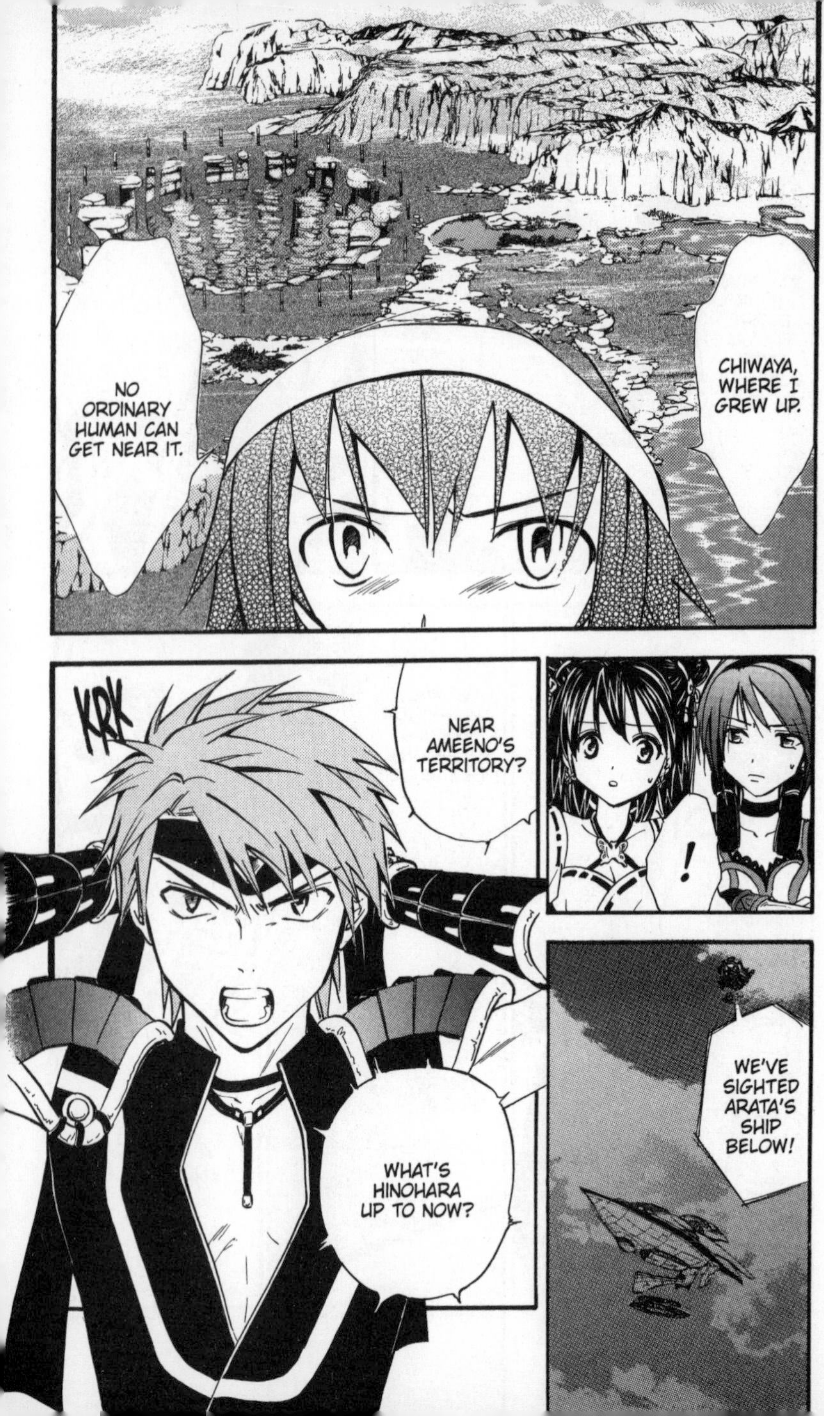
CHIWAYA, WHERE I GREW UP.
NO ORDINARY HUMAN CAN GET NEAR IT.
!
WE'VE SIGHTED ARATA'S SHIP BELOW!
KRK
NEAR AMEENO'S TERRITORY?
WHAT'S HINOHARA UP TO NOW?

Chapter 222

CITY OF SAND

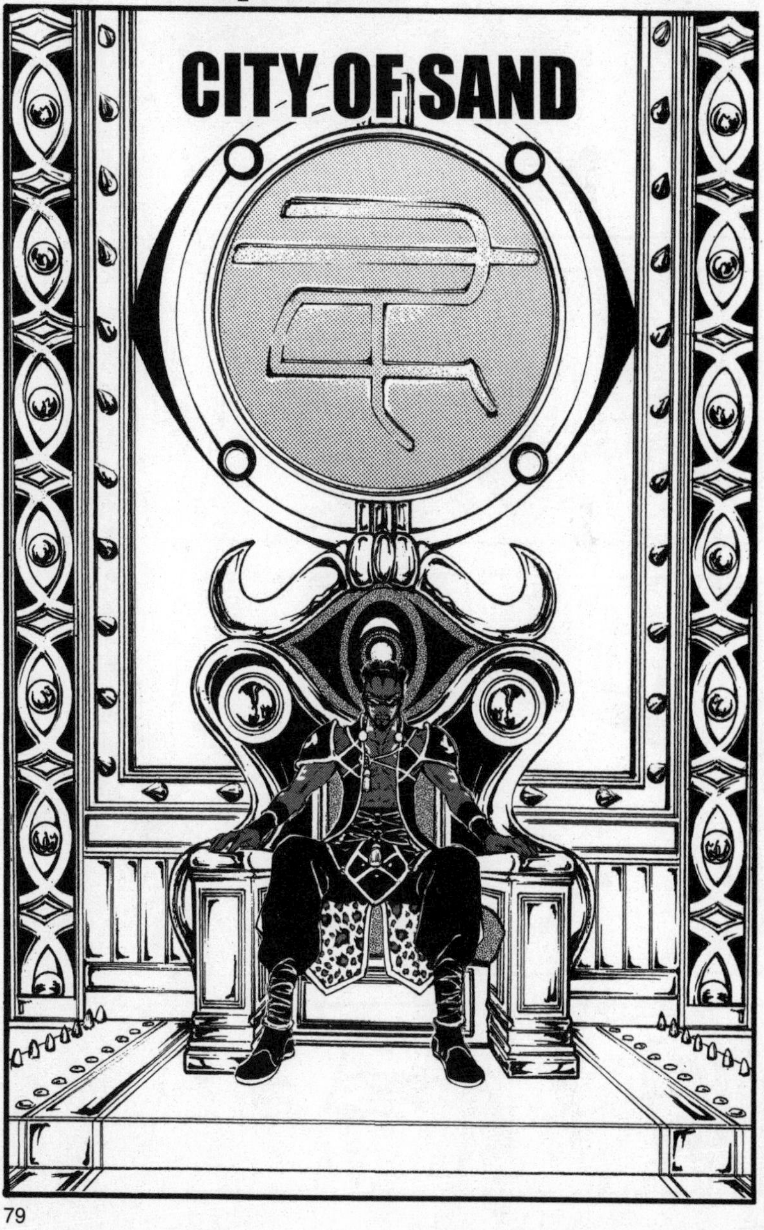

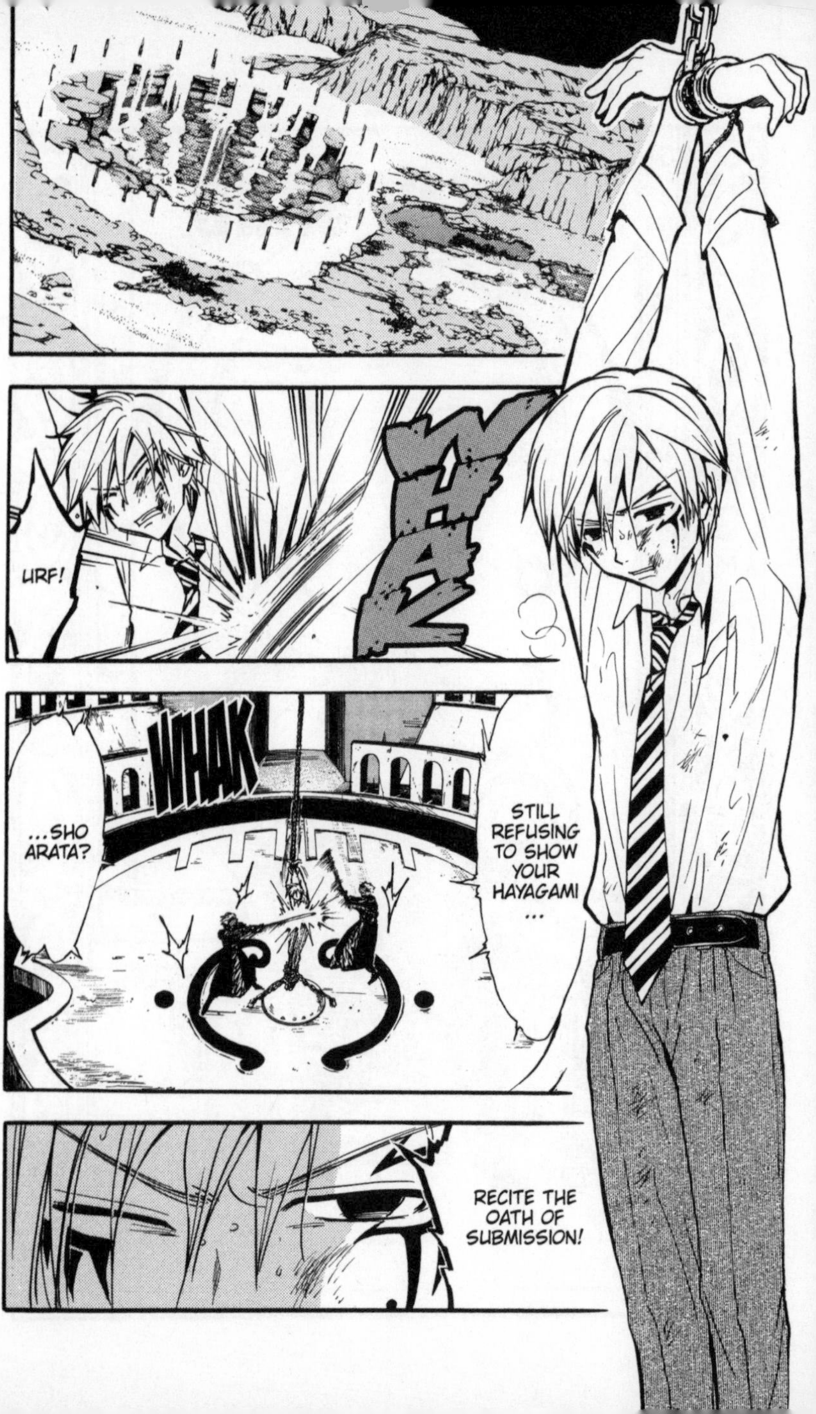
URF!
STILL REFUSING TO SHOW YOUR HAYAGAMI ...
WHAK
...SHO ARATA?
RECITE THE OATH OF SUBMISSION!

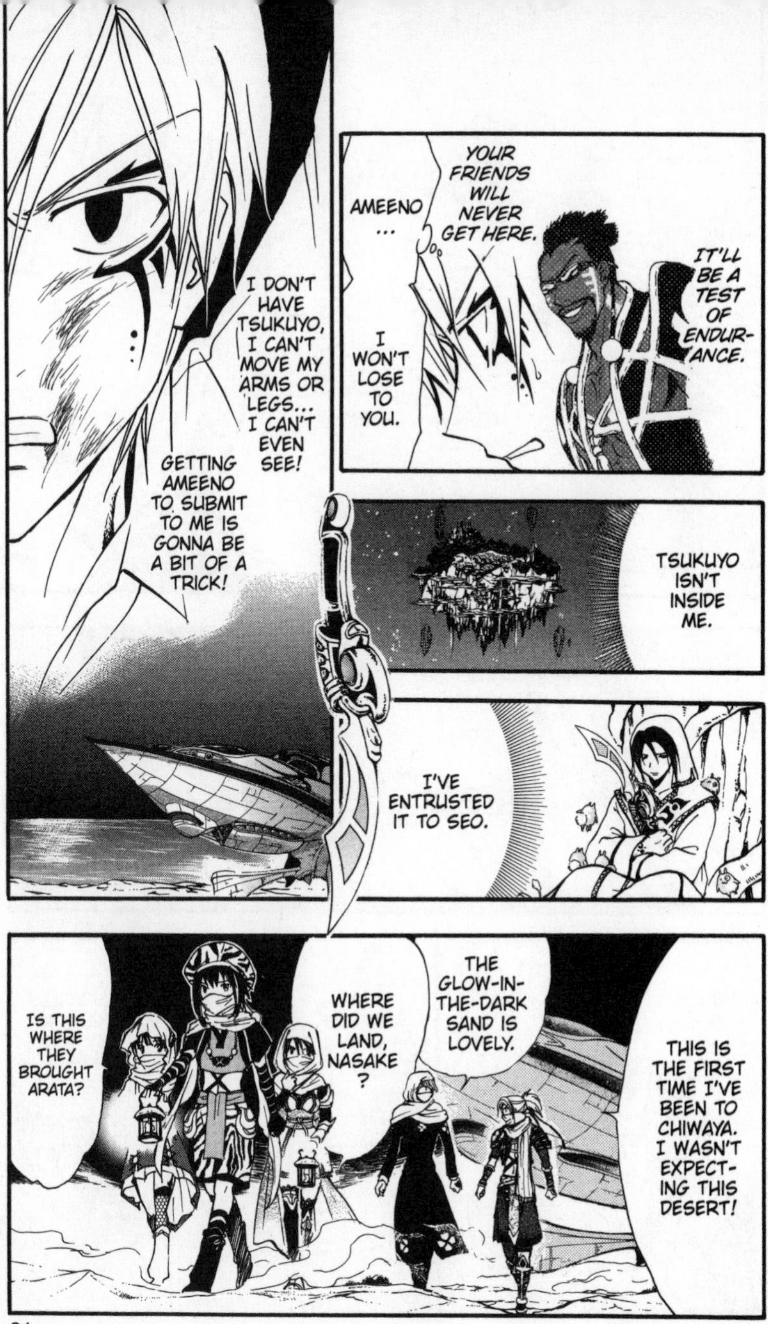
YOUR FRIENDS WILL NEVER GET HERE.
IT'LL BE A TEST OF ENDURANCE.
AMEENO...
I WON'T LOSE TO YOU.
TSUKUYO ISN'T INSIDE ME.
I'VE ENTRUSTED IT TO SEO.
I DON'T HAVE TSUKUYO, I CAN'T MOVE MY ARMS OR LEGS... I CAN'T EVEN SEE!
GETTING AMEENO TO SUBMIT TO ME IS GONNA BE A BIT OF A TRICK!
THIS IS THE FIRST TIME I'VE BEEN TO CHIWAYA. I WASN'T EXPECTING THIS DESERT!
THE GLOW-IN-THE-DARK SAND IS LOVELY.
WHERE DID WE LAND, NASAKE?
IS THIS WHERE THEY BROUGHT ARATA?

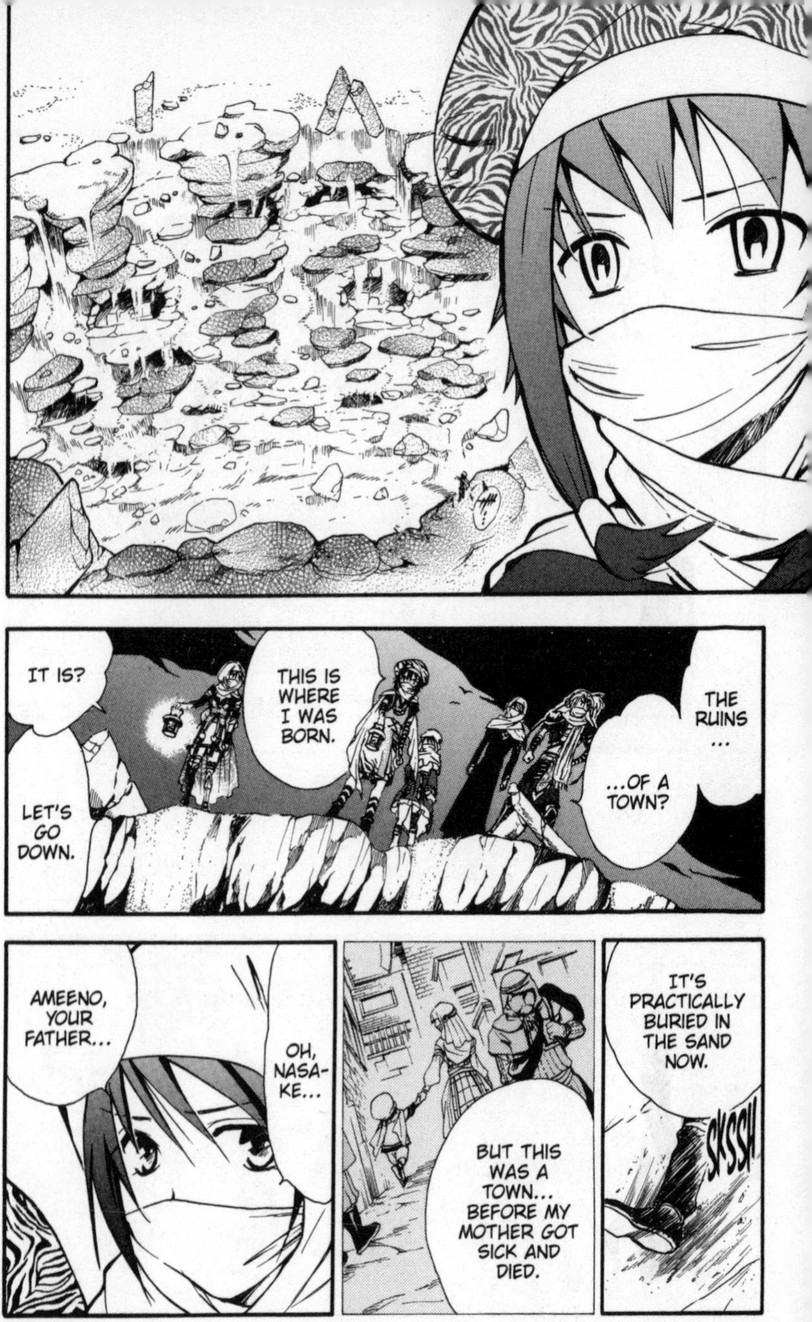
THE RUINS ...
...OF A TOWN?
THIS IS WHERE I WAS BORN.
IT IS?
LET'S GO DOWN.
IT'S PRACTICALLY BURIED IN THE SAND NOW.
SKSSH
BUT THIS WAS A TOWN... BEFORE MY MOTHER GOT SICK AND DIED.
OH, NASA-KE...
AMEENO, YOUR FATHER...

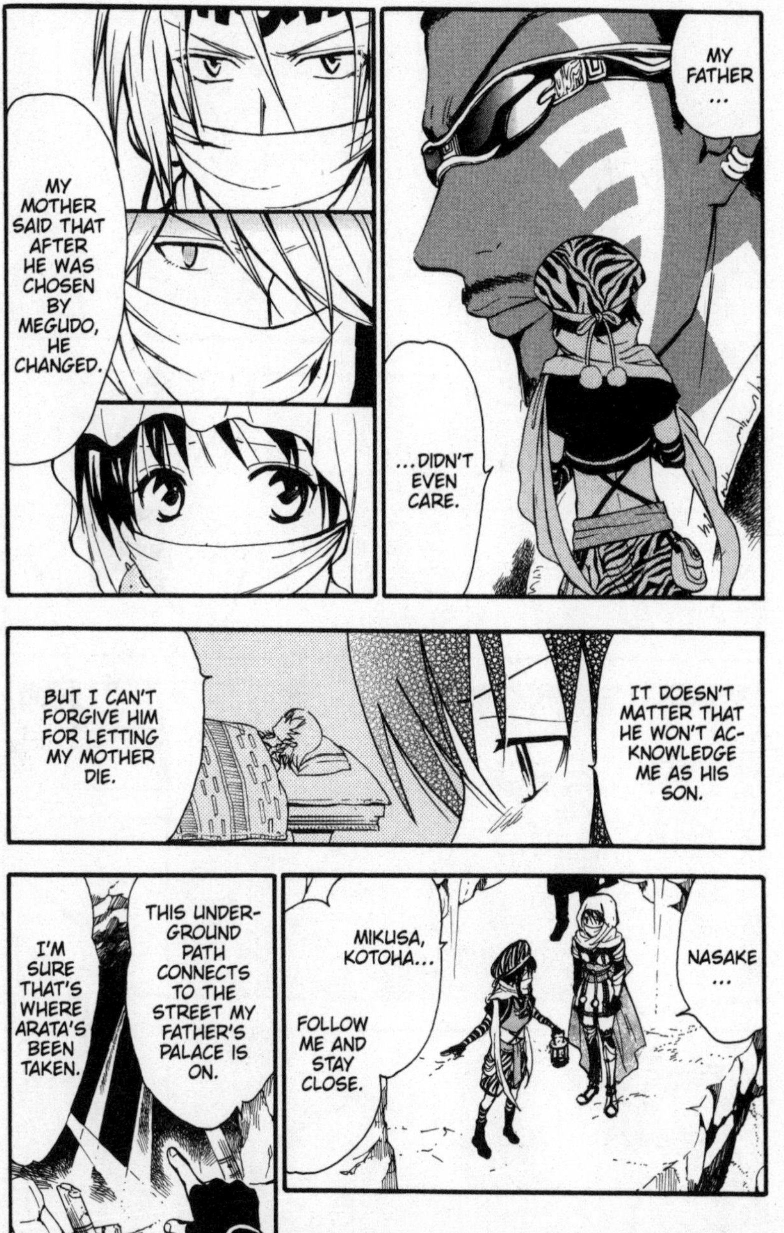
MY FATHER ...
...DIDN'T EVEN CARE.
MY MOTHER SAID THAT AFTER HE WAS CHOSEN BY MEGUDO, HE CHANGED.
IT DOESN'T MATTER THAT HE WON'T ACKNOWLEDGE ME AS HIS SON.
BUT I CAN'T FORGIVE HIM FOR LETTING MY MOTHER DIE.
NASAKE ...
MIKUSA, KOTOHA...
FOLLOW ME AND STAY CLOSE.
THIS UNDERGROUND PATH CONNECTS TO THE STREET MY FATHER'S PALACE IS ON.
I'M SURE THAT'S WHERE ARATA'S BEEN TAKEN.

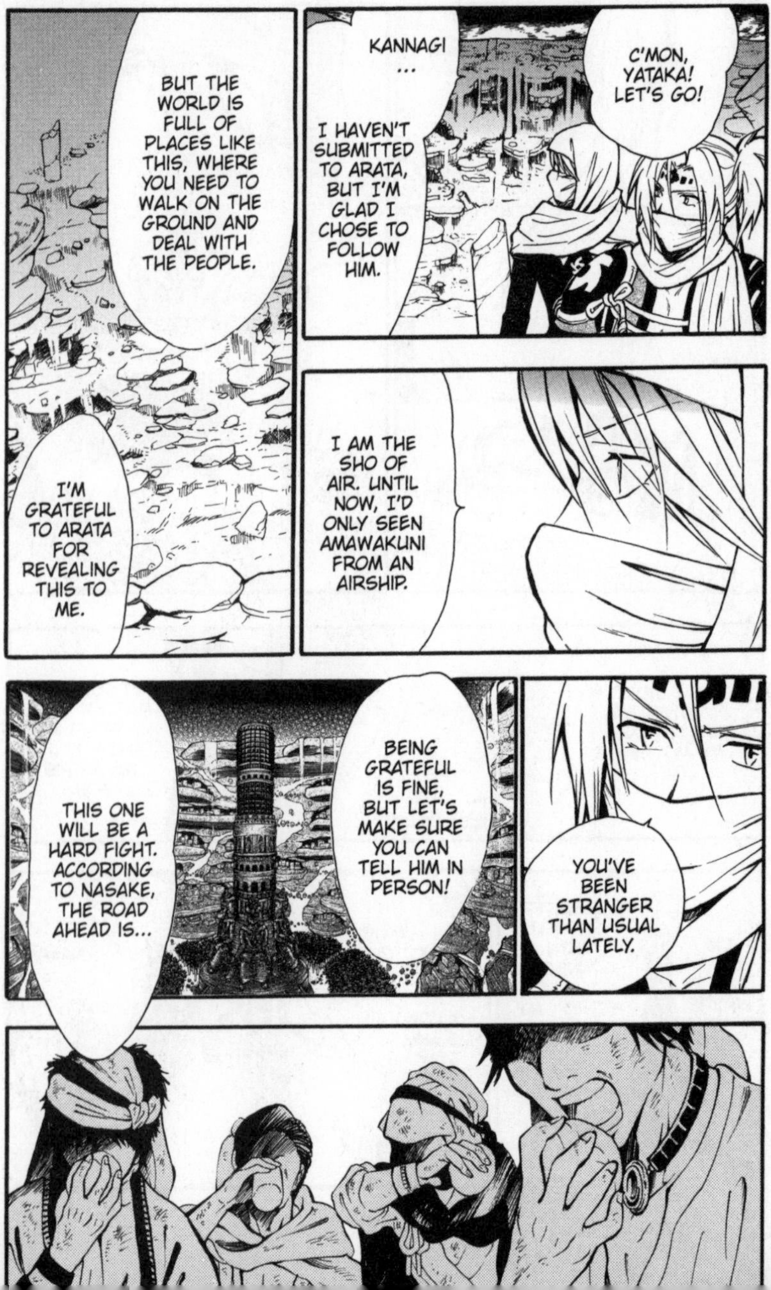
C'MON, YATAKA! LET'S GO!
KANNAGI...
I HAVEN'T SUBMITTED TO ARATA, BUT I'M GLAD I CHOSE TO FOLLOW HIM.
I AM THE SHO OF AIR. UNTIL NOW, I'D ONLY SEEN AMAWAKUNI FROM AN AIRSHIP.
BUT THE WORLD IS FULL OF PLACES LIKE THIS, WHERE YOU NEED TO WALK ON THE GROUND AND DEAL WITH THE PEOPLE.
I'M GRATEFUL TO ARATA FOR REVEALING THIS TO ME.
YOU'VE BEEN STRANGER THAN USUAL LATELY.
BEING GRATEFUL IS FINE, BUT LET'S MAKE SURE YOU CAN TELL HIM IN PERSON!
THIS ONE WILL BE A HARD FIGHT. ACCORDING TO NASAKE, THE ROAD AHEAD IS...

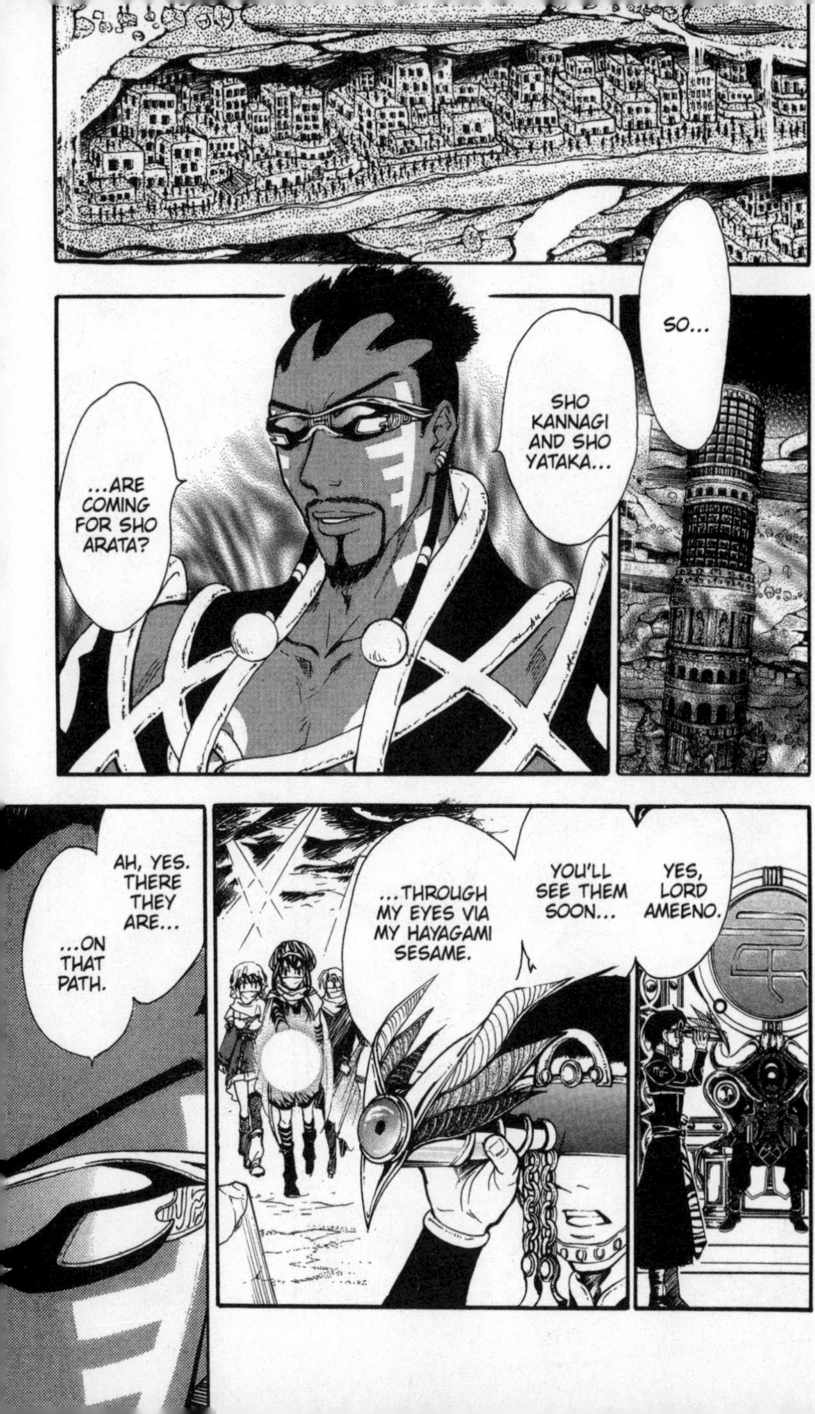
SO...
SHO KANNAGI AND SHO YATAKA...
...ARE COMING FOR SHO ARATA?
YES, LORD AMEENO.
YOU'LL SEE THEM SOON...
...THROUGH MY EYES VIA MY HAYAGAMI SESAME.
AH, YES. THERE THEY ARE...
...ON THAT PATH.

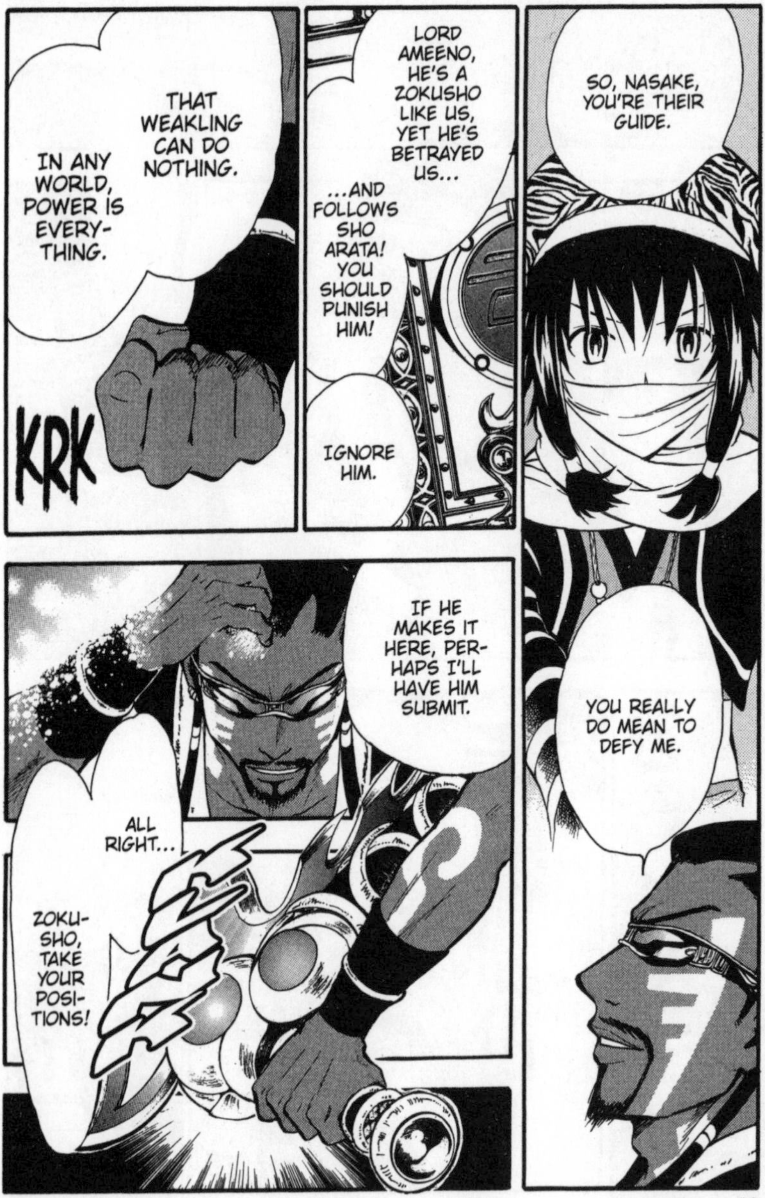
SO, NASAKE, YOU'RE THEIR GUIDE.
YOU REALLY DO MEAN TO DEFY ME.
LORD AMEENO, HE'S A ZOKUSHO LIKE US, YET HE'S BETRAYED US...
...AND FOLLOWS SHO ARATA! YOU SHOULD PUNISH HIM!
IGNORE HIM.
THAT WEAKLING CAN DO NOTHING.
IN ANY WORLD, POWER IS EVERY-THING.
KRK
IF HE MAKES IT HERE, PER-HAPS I'LL HAVE HIM SUBMIT.
ALL RIGHT...
ZOKU-SHO, TAKE YOUR POSI-TIONS!

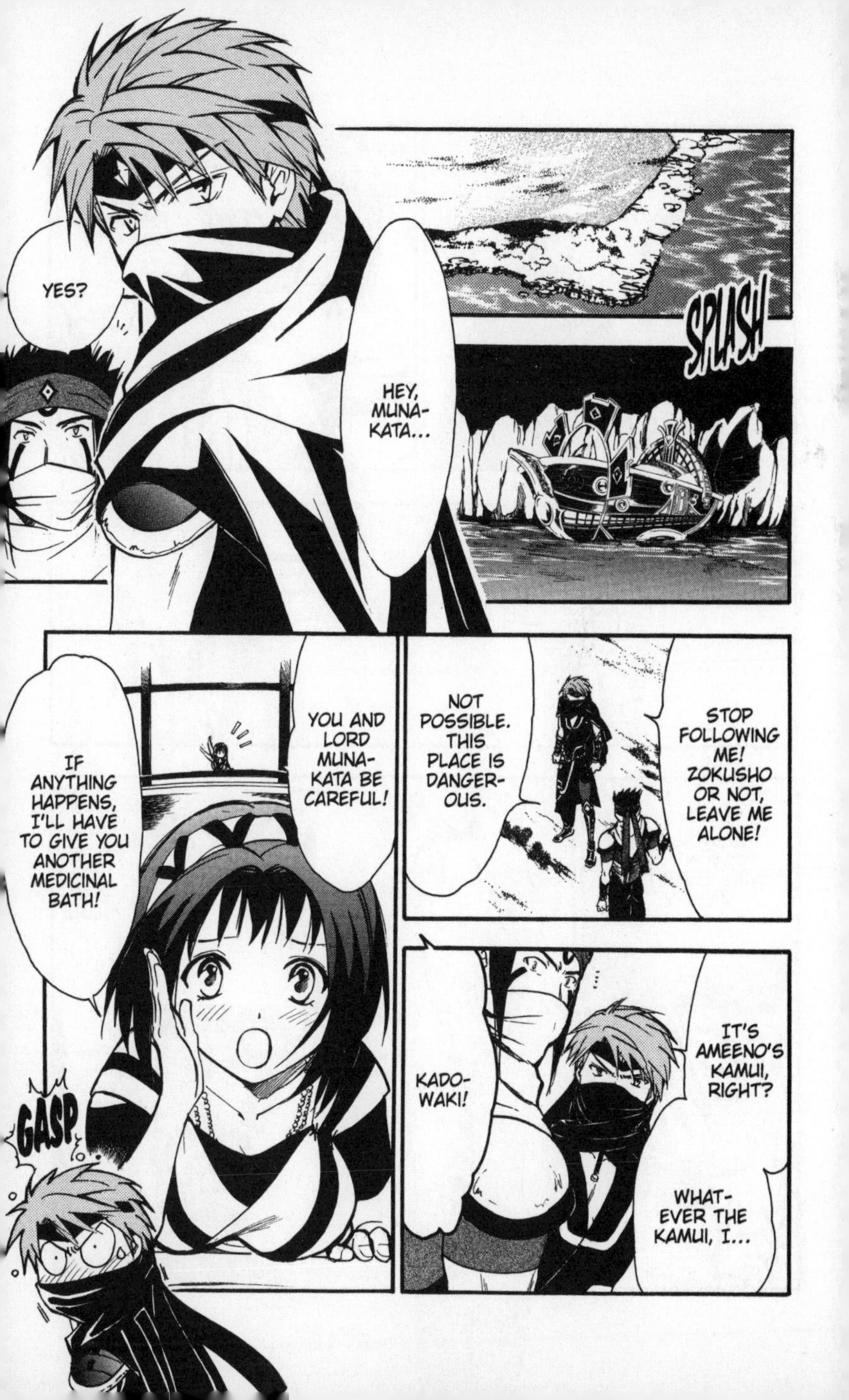
SPLASH
HEY, MUNA-KATA...
YES?
STOP FOLLOWING ME! ZOKUSHO OR NOT, LEAVE ME ALONE!
NOT POSSIBLE. THIS PLACE IS DANGER-OUS.
IT'S AMEENO'S KAMUI, RIGHT?
KADO-WAKI!
WHAT-EVER THE KAMUI, I...
YOU AND LORD MUNA-KATA BE CAREFUL!
IF ANYTHING HAPPENS, I'LL HAVE TO GIVE YOU ANOTHER MEDICINAL BATH!
GASP

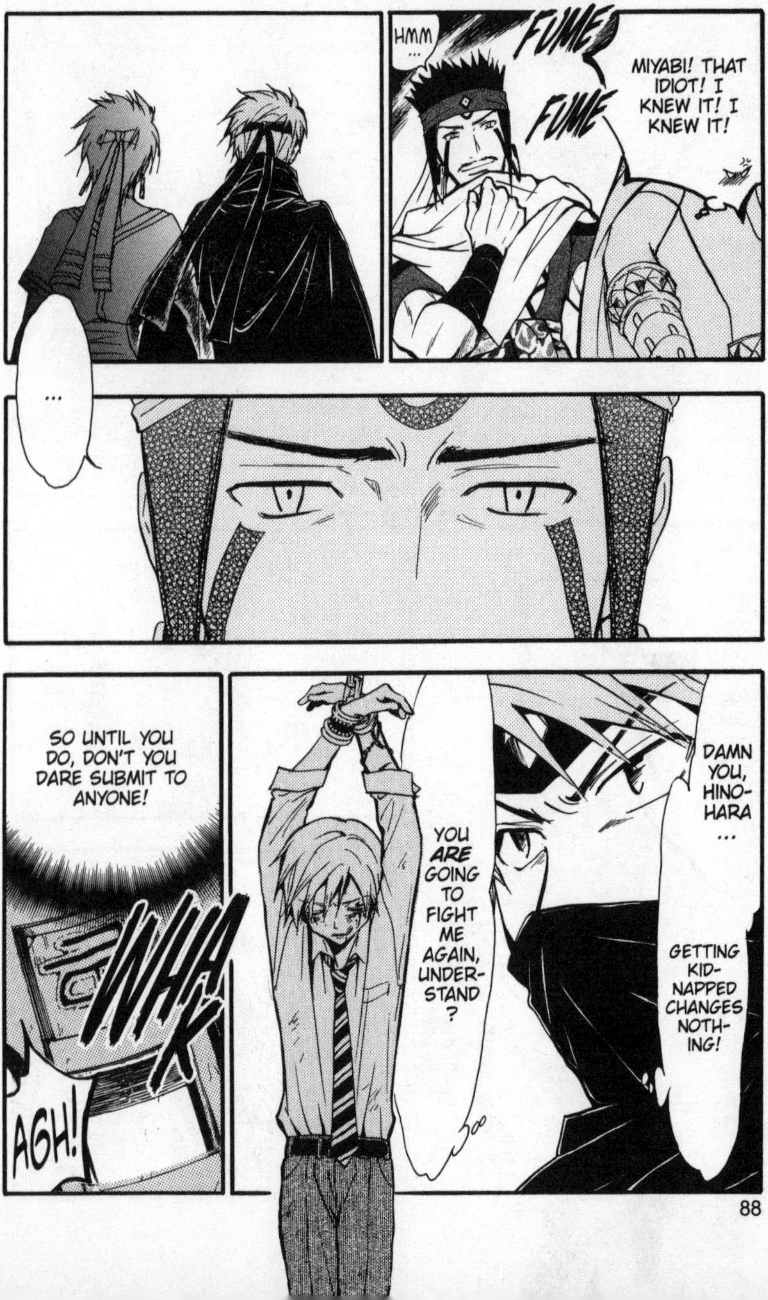
MIYABI! THAT IDIOT! I KNEW IT! I KNEW IT!
FUME
FUME
HMM ...
...
DAMN YOU, HINO-HARA ...
GETTING KID-NAPPED CHANGES NOTH-ING!
YOU ARE GOING TO FIGHT ME AGAIN, UNDER-STAND ?
SO UNTIL YOU DO, DON'T YOU DARE SUBMIT TO ANYONE!
WHA
AGH!

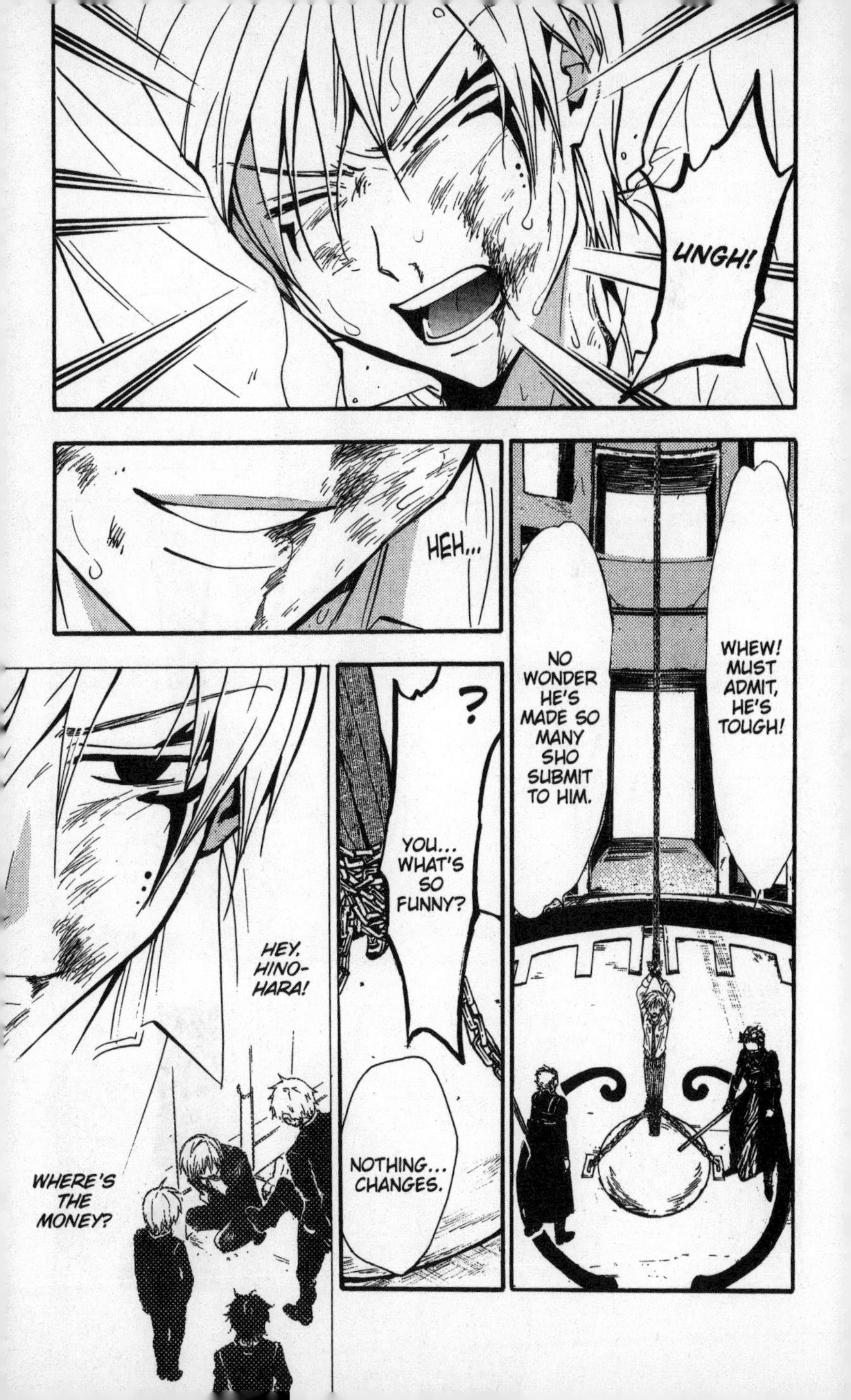
UNGH!
WHEW! MUST ADMIT, HE'S TOUGH!
NO WONDER HE'S MADE SO MANY SHO SUBMIT TO HIM.
HEH...
?
YOU... WHAT'S SO FUNNY?
NOTHING... CHANGES.
HEY, HINO-HARA!
WHERE'S THE MONEY?

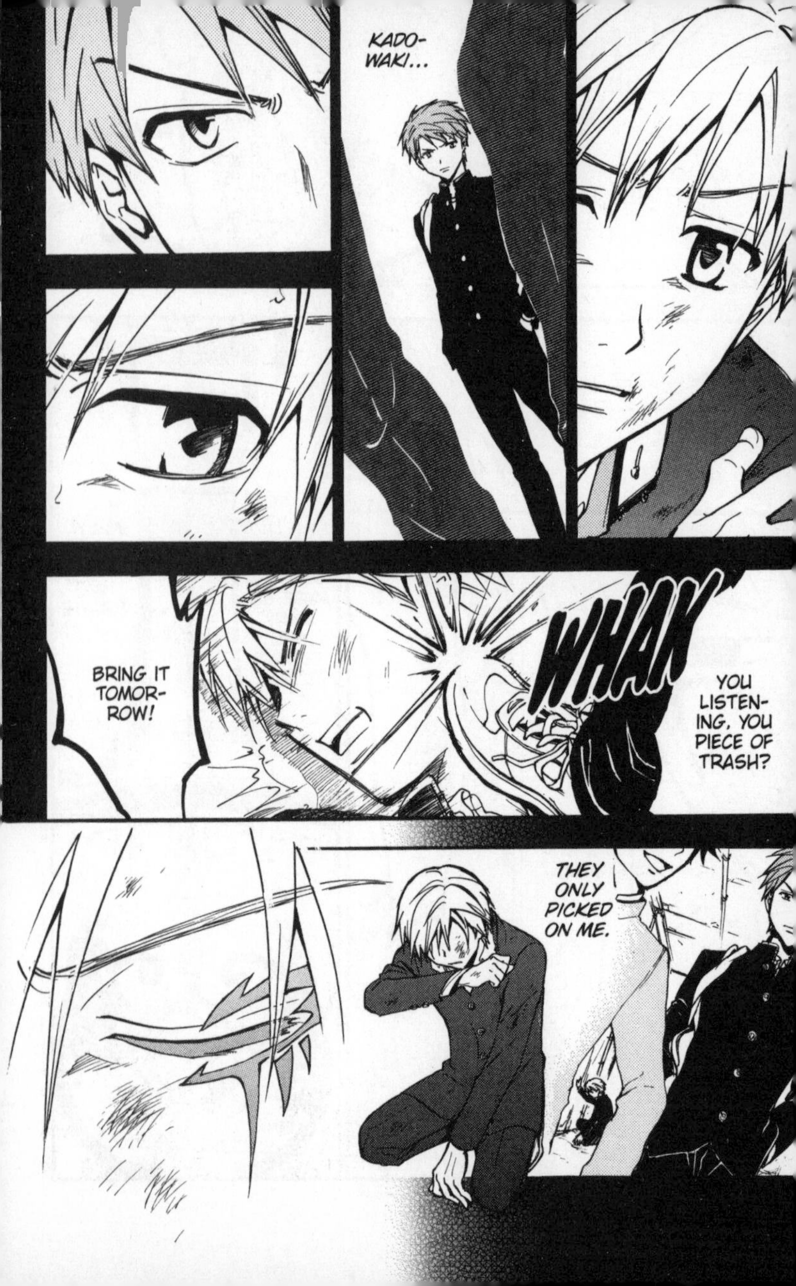
KADO-WAKI...
WHAK
YOU LISTENING, YOU PIECE OF TRASH?
BRING IT TOMORROW!
THEY ONLY PICKED ON ME.

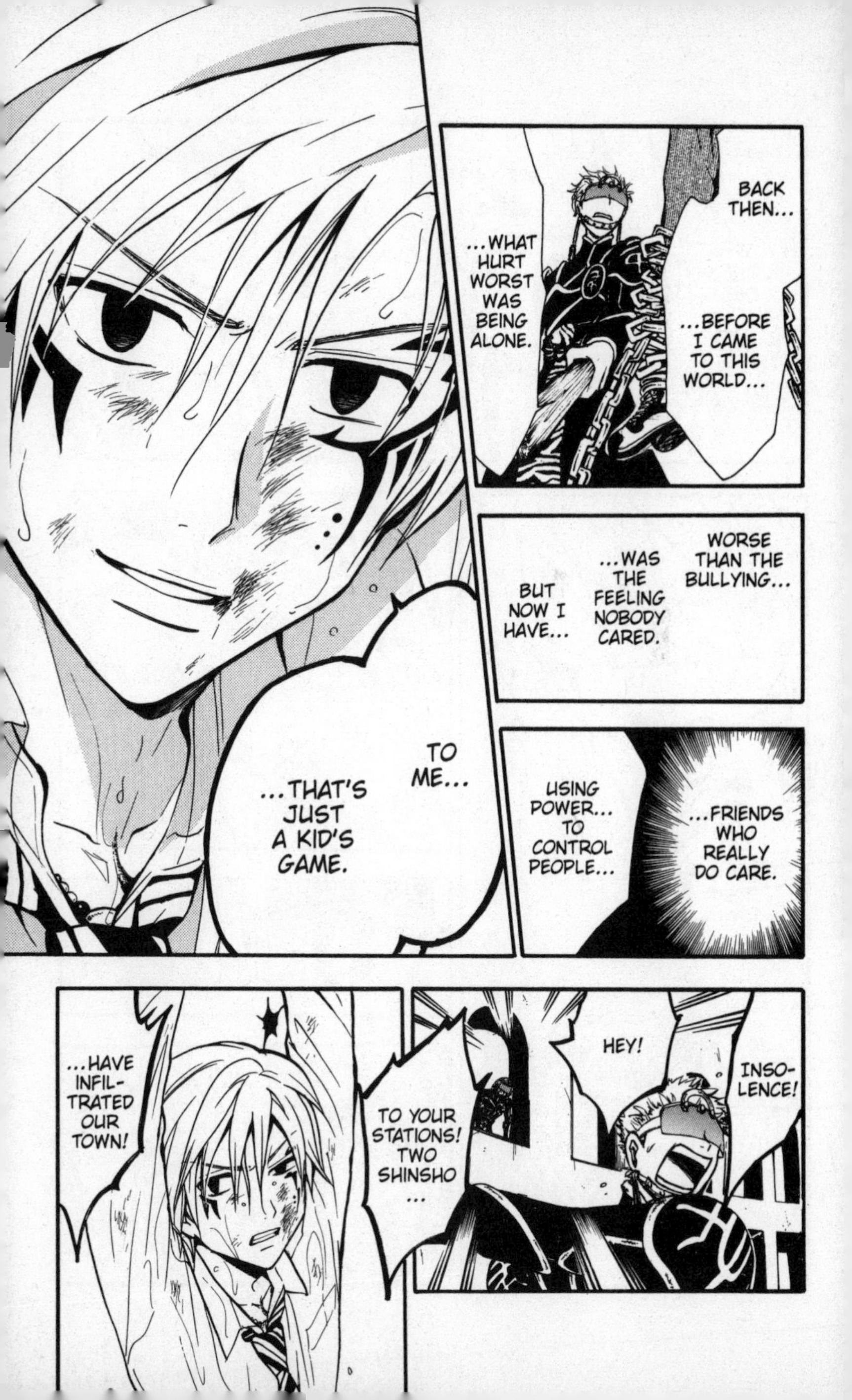
BACK THEN...
...BEFORE I CAME TO THIS WORLD...
...WHAT HURT WORST WAS BEING ALONE.
WORSE THAN THE BULLYING...
...WAS THE FEELING NOBODY CARED.
BUT NOW I HAVE...
...FRIENDS WHO REALLY DO CARE.
USING POWER... TO CONTROL PEOPLE...
TO ME...
...THAT'S JUST A KID'S GAME.
INSO-LENCE!
HEY!
TO YOUR STATIONS! TWO SHINSHO ...
...HAVE INFIL-TRATED OUR TOWN!

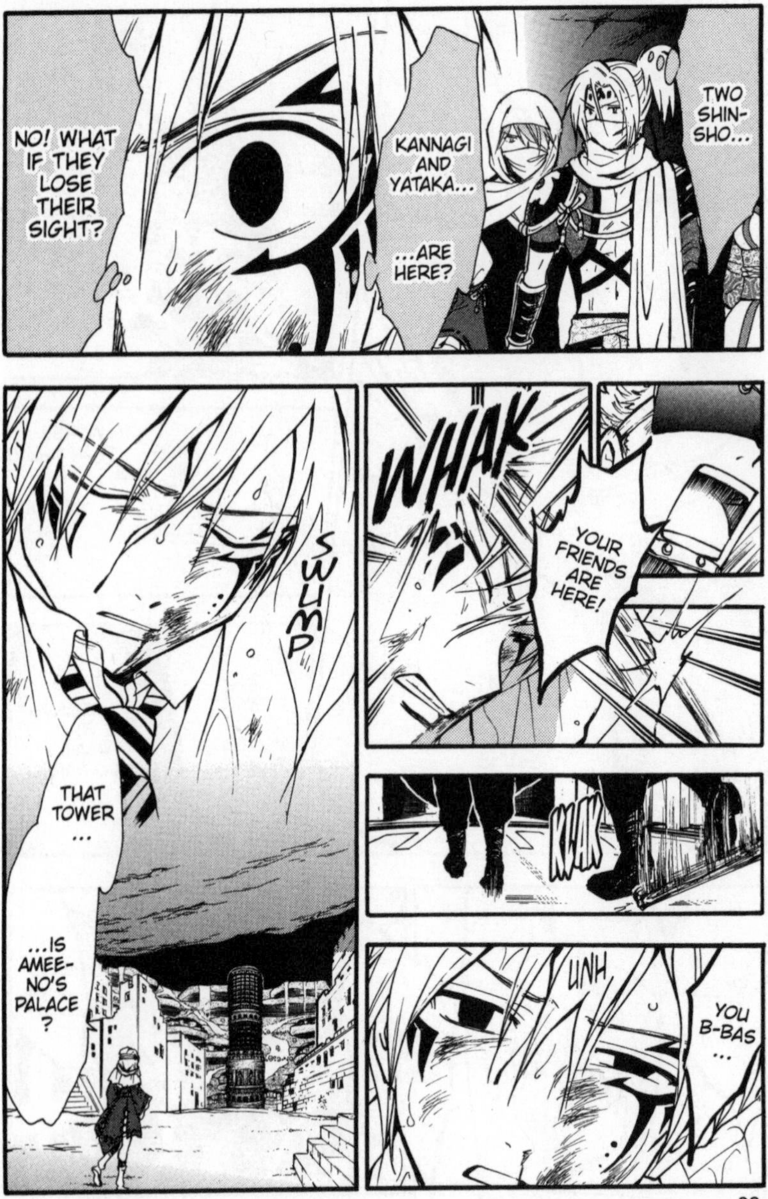
TWO SHIN-SHO...
KANNAGI AND YATAKA...
...ARE HERE?
NO! WHAT IF THEY LOSE THEIR SIGHT?
WHAK
YOUR FRIENDS ARE HERE!
KLAK
UNH
YOU B-BAS...
SWUMP
THAT TOWER...
...IS AMEE-NO'S PALACE?

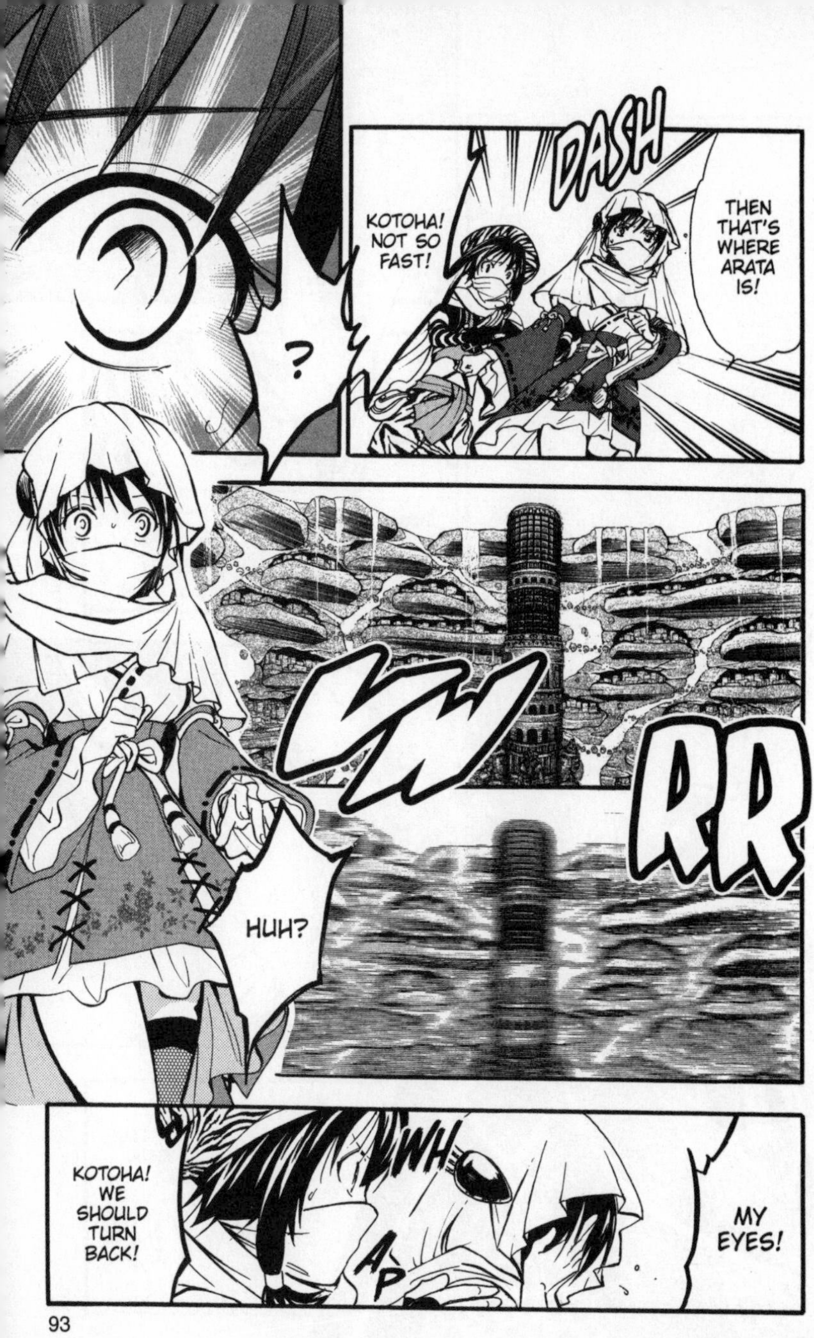
DASH
THEN THAT'S WHERE ARATA IS!
KOTOHA! NOT SO FAST!
?
RR
HUH?
MY EYES!
WHAP
KOTOHA! WE SHOULD TURN BACK!

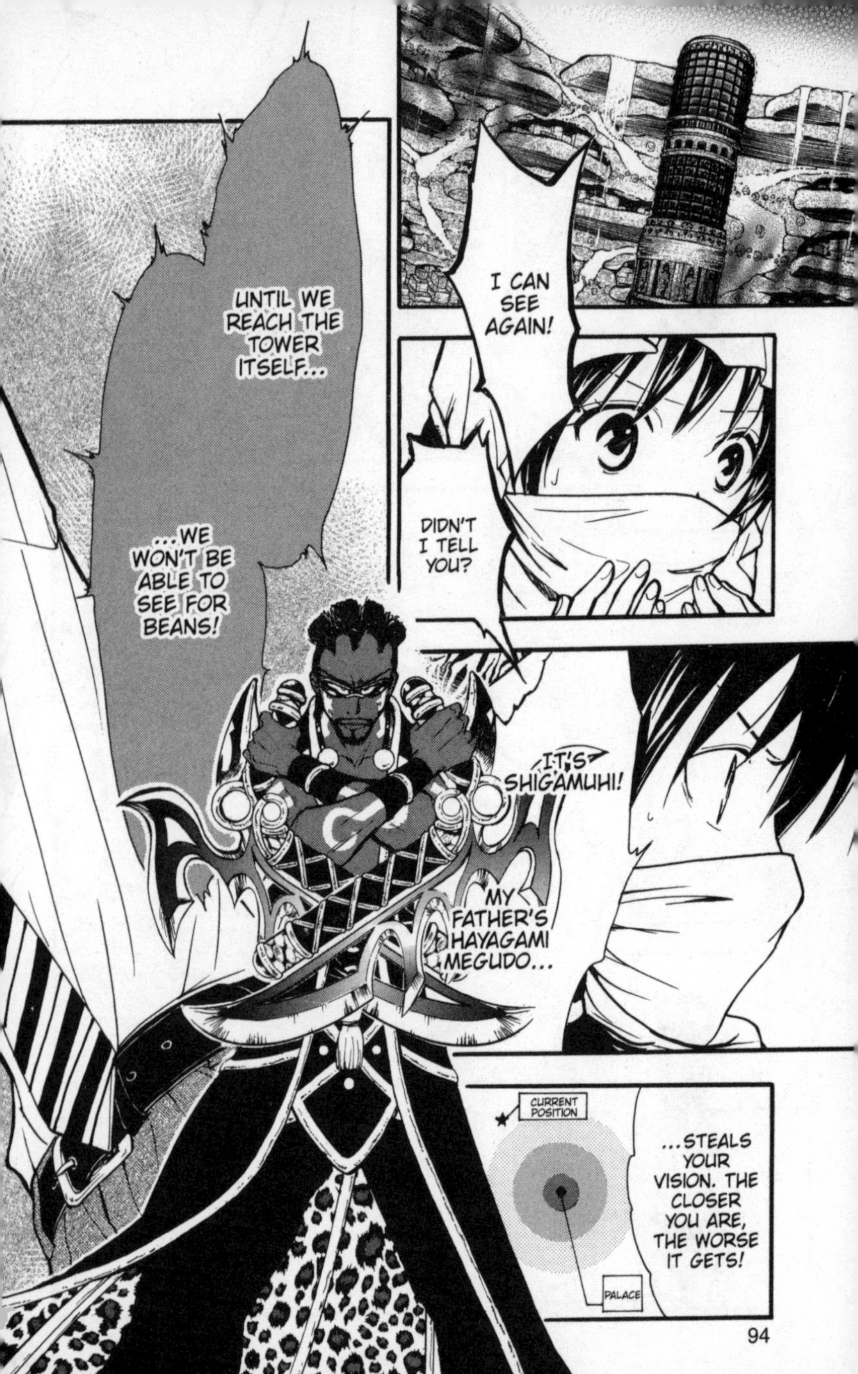
I CAN SEE AGAIN!
DIDN'T I TELL YOU?
IT'S SHIGAMUHI!
MY FATHER'S HAYAGAMI MEGUDO...
...STEALS YOUR VISION. THE CLOSER YOU ARE, THE WORSE IT GETS!
CURRENT POSITION
PALACE
UNTIL WE REACH THE TOWER ITSELF...
...WE WON'T BE ABLE TO SEE FOR BEANS!

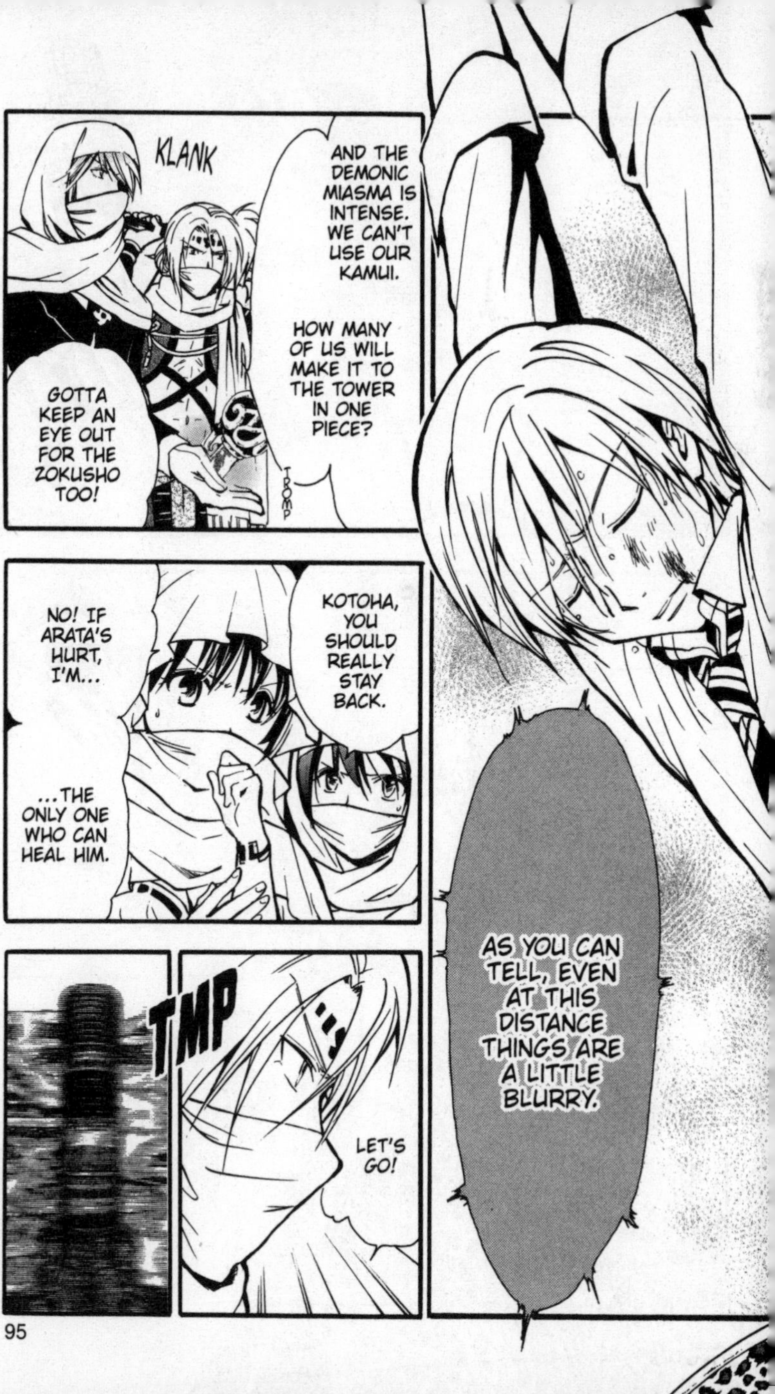
AS YOU CAN TELL, EVEN AT THIS DISTANCE THINGS ARE A LITTLE BLURRY.
AND THE DEMONIC MIASMA IS INTENSE. WE CAN'T USE OUR KAMUI.
KLANK
HOW MANY OF US WILL MAKE IT TO THE TOWER IN ONE PIECE?
TROMP
GOTTA KEEP AN EYE OUT FOR THE ZOKUSHO TOO!
KOTOHA, YOU SHOULD REALLY STAY BACK.
NO! IF ARATA'S HURT, I'M...
...THE ONLY ONE WHO CAN HEAL HIM.
TMP
LET'S GO!

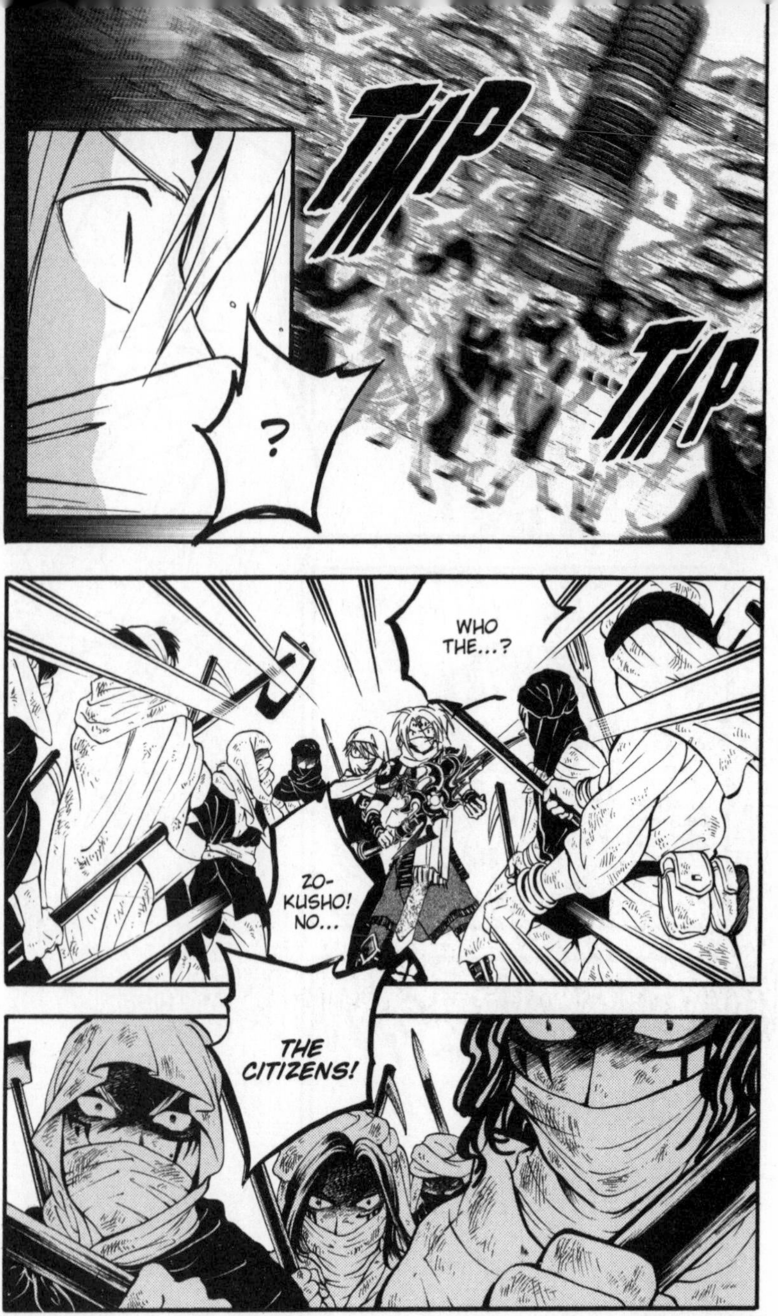
TIP
TIP
?
WHO THE...?
ZO-KUSHO! NO...
THE CITIZENS!

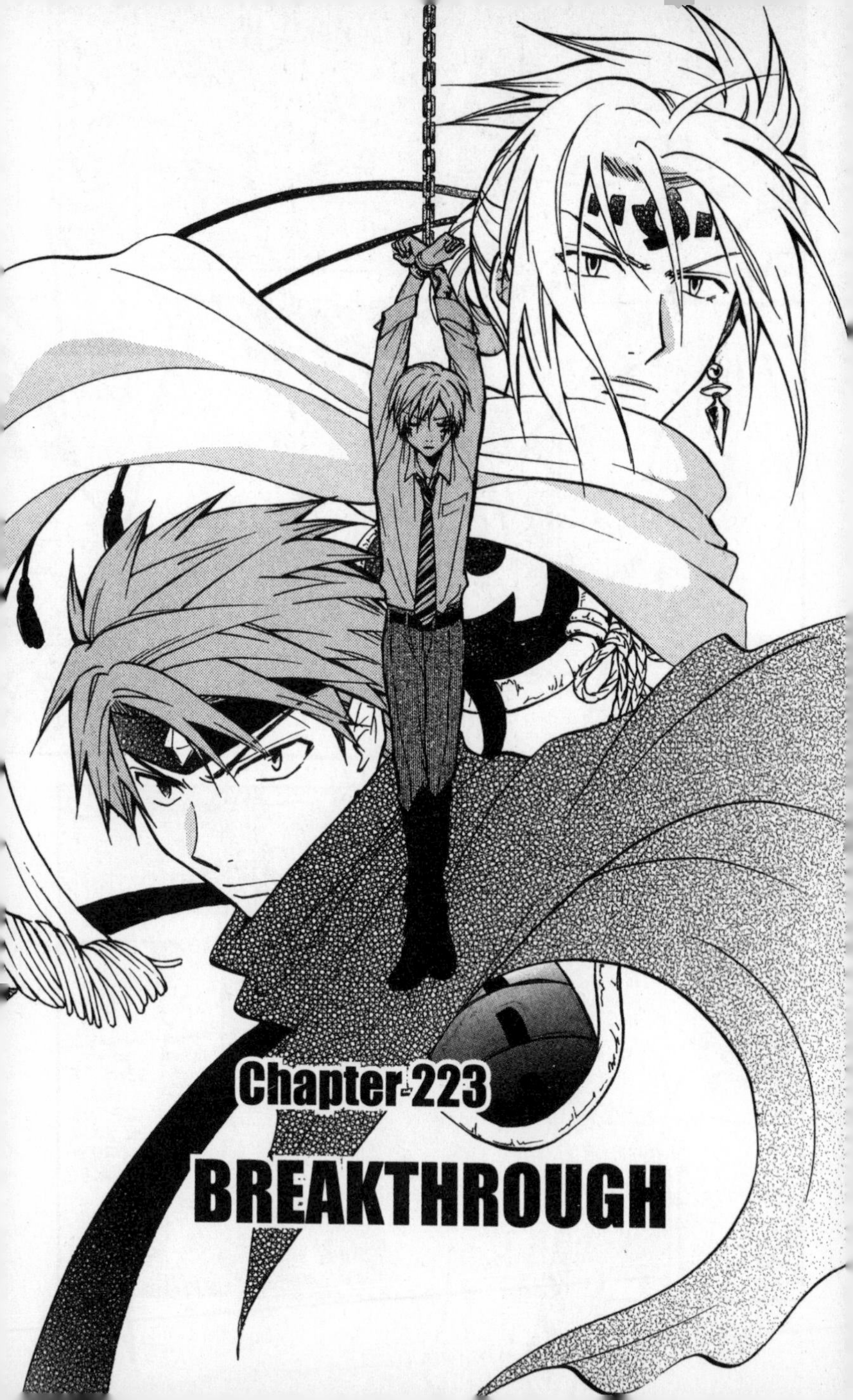
Chapter 223
BREAKTHROUGH

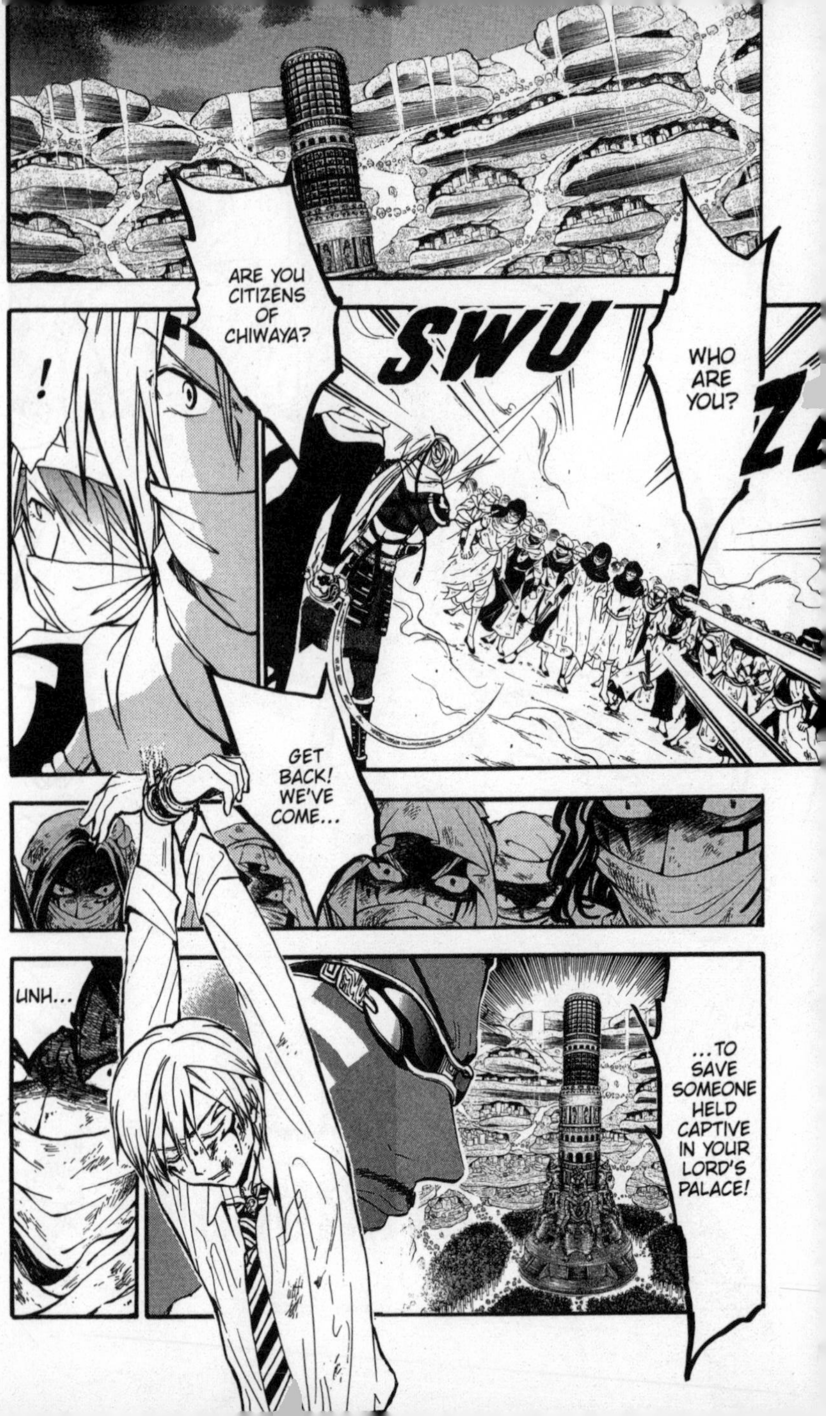
ARE YOU CITIZENS OF CHIWAYA?
WHO ARE YOU?
SWU
ZZ
!
GET BACK! WE'VE COME...
...TO SAVE SOMEONE HELD CAPTIVE IN YOUR LORD'S PALACE!
UNH...

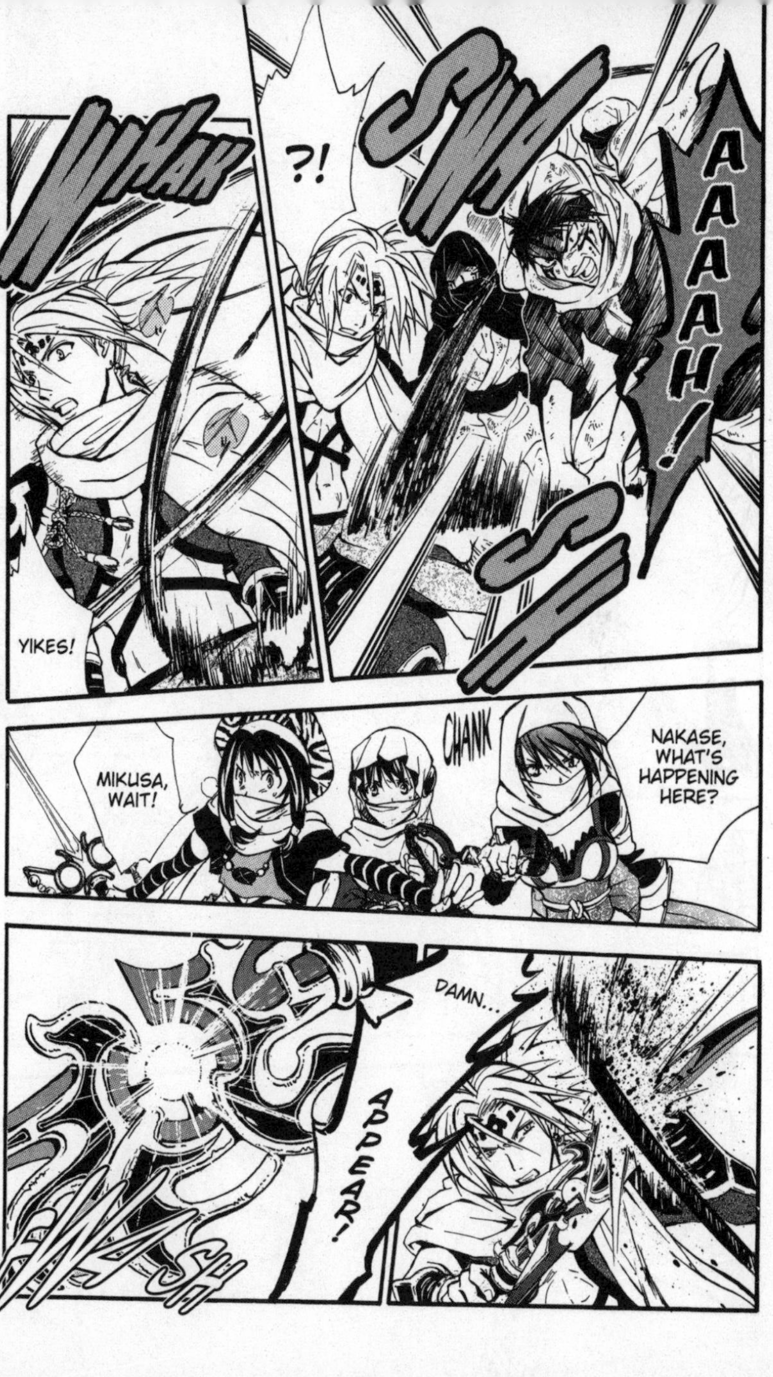
AAAAAH!
SH
?!
WHAK
YIKES!
NAKASE, WHAT'S HAPPENING HERE?
CHANK
MIKUSA, WAIT!
DAMN...
APPEAR!

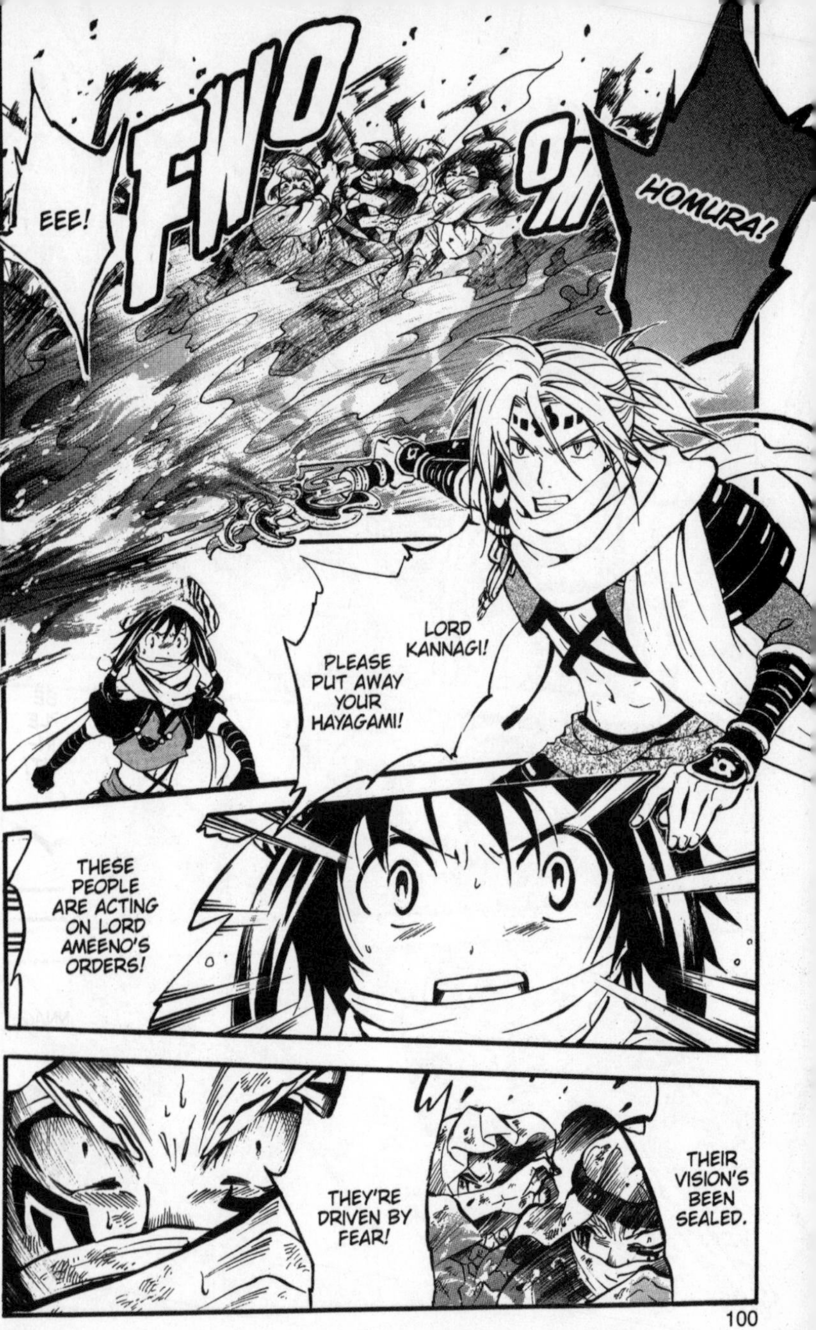
HOMURA!
FWOOM
EEE!
LORD KANNAGI!
PLEASE PUT AWAY YOUR HAYAGAMI!
THESE PEOPLE ARE ACTING ON LORD AMEENO'S ORDERS!
THEIR VISION'S BEEN SEALED.
THEY'RE DRIVEN BY FEAR!

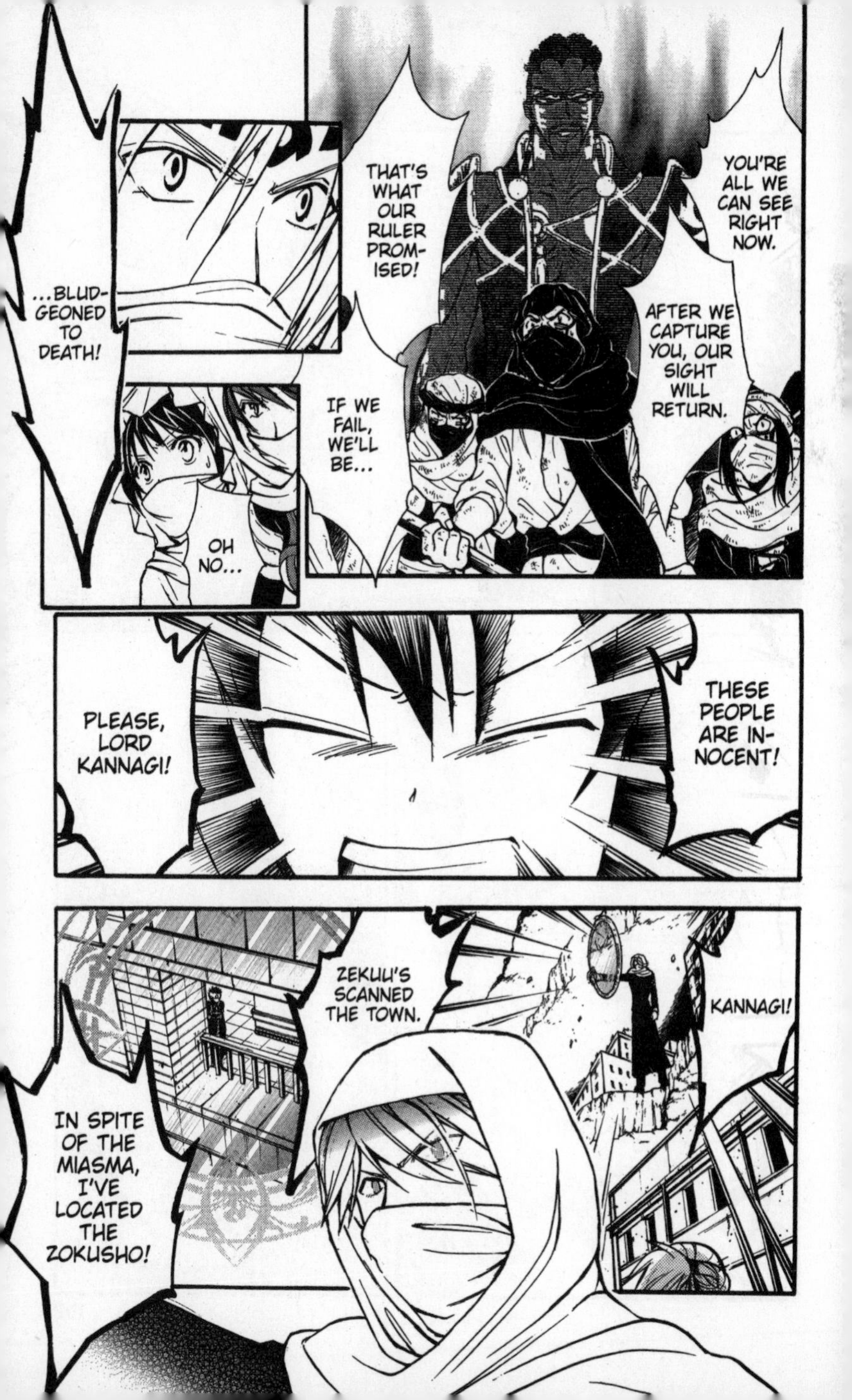
YOU'RE ALL WE CAN SEE RIGHT NOW.
AFTER WE CAPTURE YOU, OUR SIGHT WILL RETURN.
THAT'S WHAT OUR RULER PROMISED!
IF WE FAIL, WE'LL BE...
...BLUDGEONED TO DEATH!
OH NO...
THESE PEOPLE ARE INNOCENT!
PLEASE, LORD KANNAGI!
KANNAGI!
ZEKUU'S SCANNED THE TOWN.
IN SPITE OF THE MIASMA, I'VE LOCATED THE ZOKUSHO!

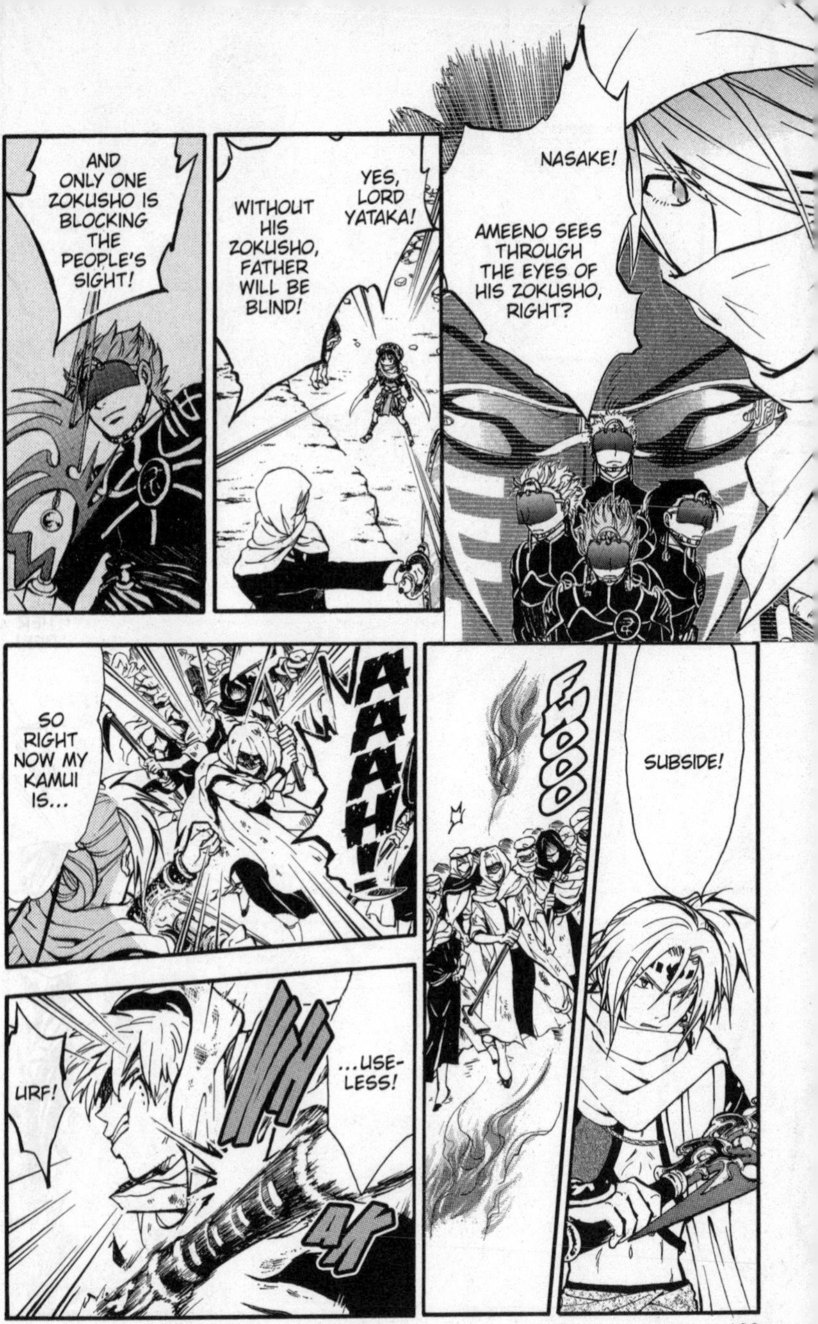
NASAKE!
AMEENO SEES THROUGH THE EYES OF HIS ZOKUSHO, RIGHT?
YES, LORD YATAKA!
WITHOUT HIS ZOKUSHO, FATHER WILL BE BLIND!
AND ONLY ONE ZOKUSHO IS BLOCKING THE PEOPLE'S SIGHT!
SUBSIDE!
FWOOO
AAAH!
SO RIGHT NOW MY KAMUI IS...
...USE-LESS!
WH
URF!
AK

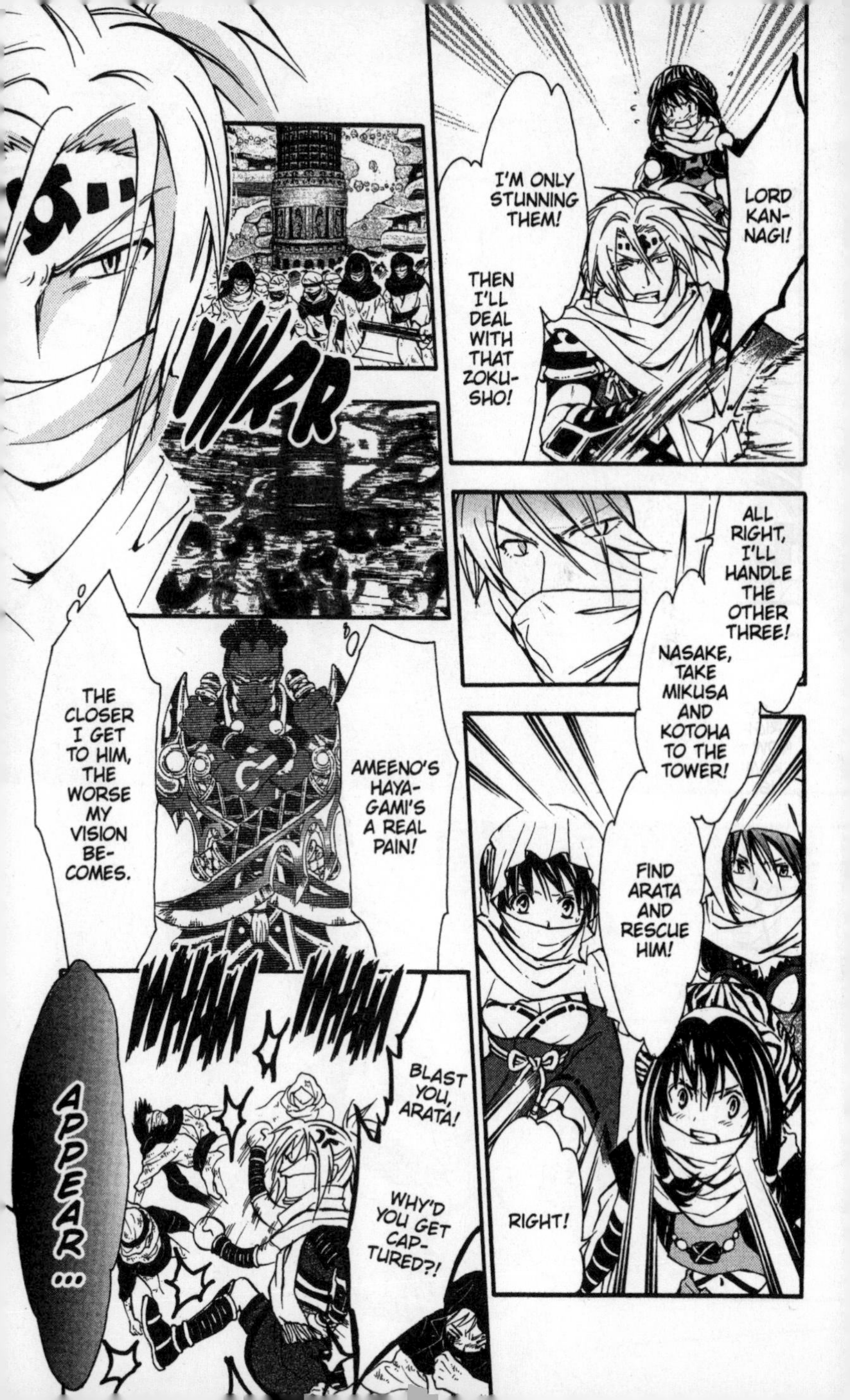
LORD KAN-NAGI!
I'M ONLY STUNNING THEM!
THEN I'LL DEAL WITH THAT ZOKU-SHO!
VWRR
ALL RIGHT, I'LL HANDLE THE OTHER THREE!
AMEENO'S HAYA-GAMI'S A REAL PAIN!
THE CLOSER I GET TO HIM, THE WORSE MY VISION BE-COMES.
NASAKE, TAKE MIKUSA AND KOTOHA TO THE TOWER!
FIND ARATA AND RESCUE HIM!
RIGHT!
BLAST YOU, ARATA!
WHY'D YOU GET CAP-TURED?!
APPEAR...

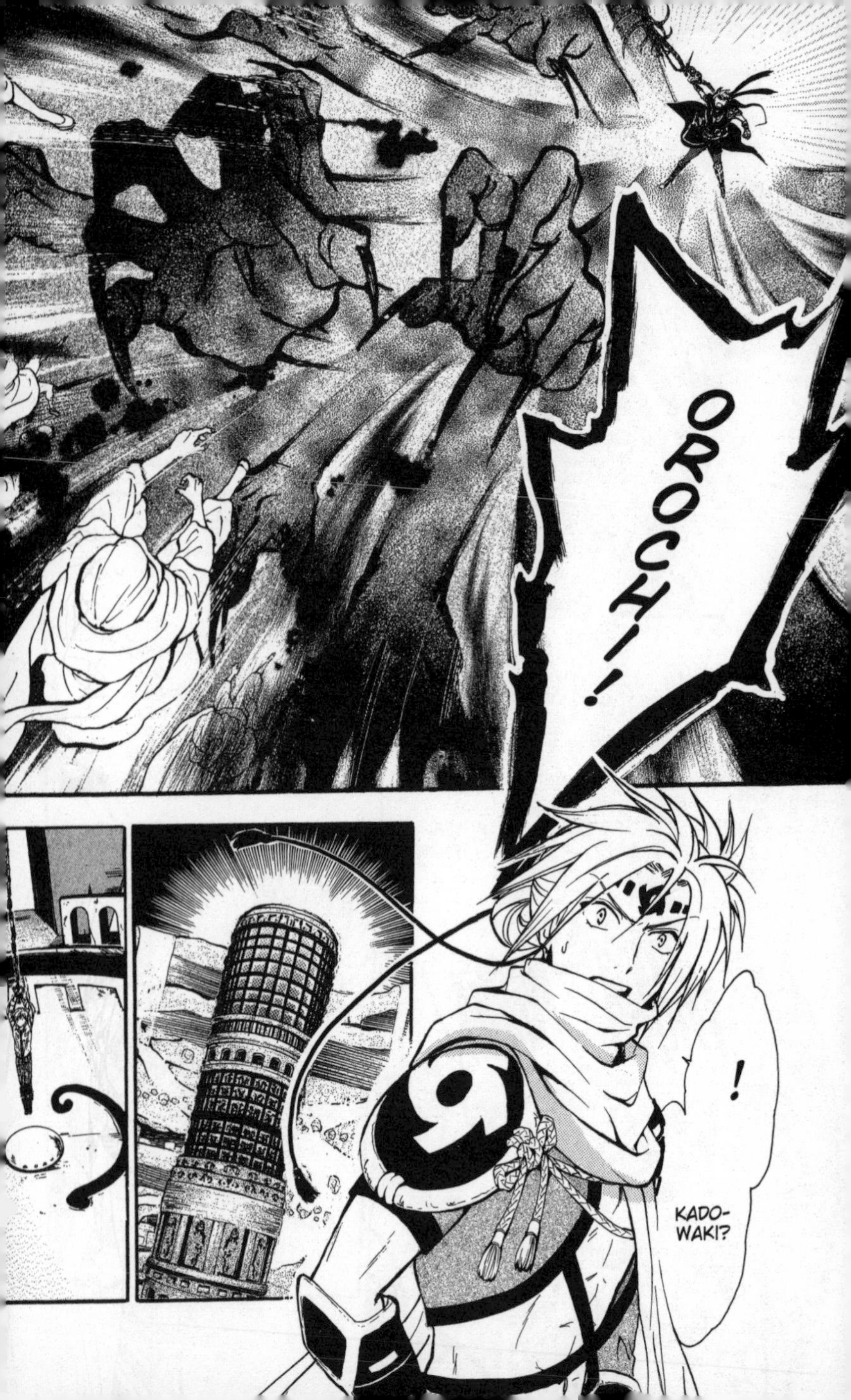
OROCHI!!
!
KADO-
WAKI?

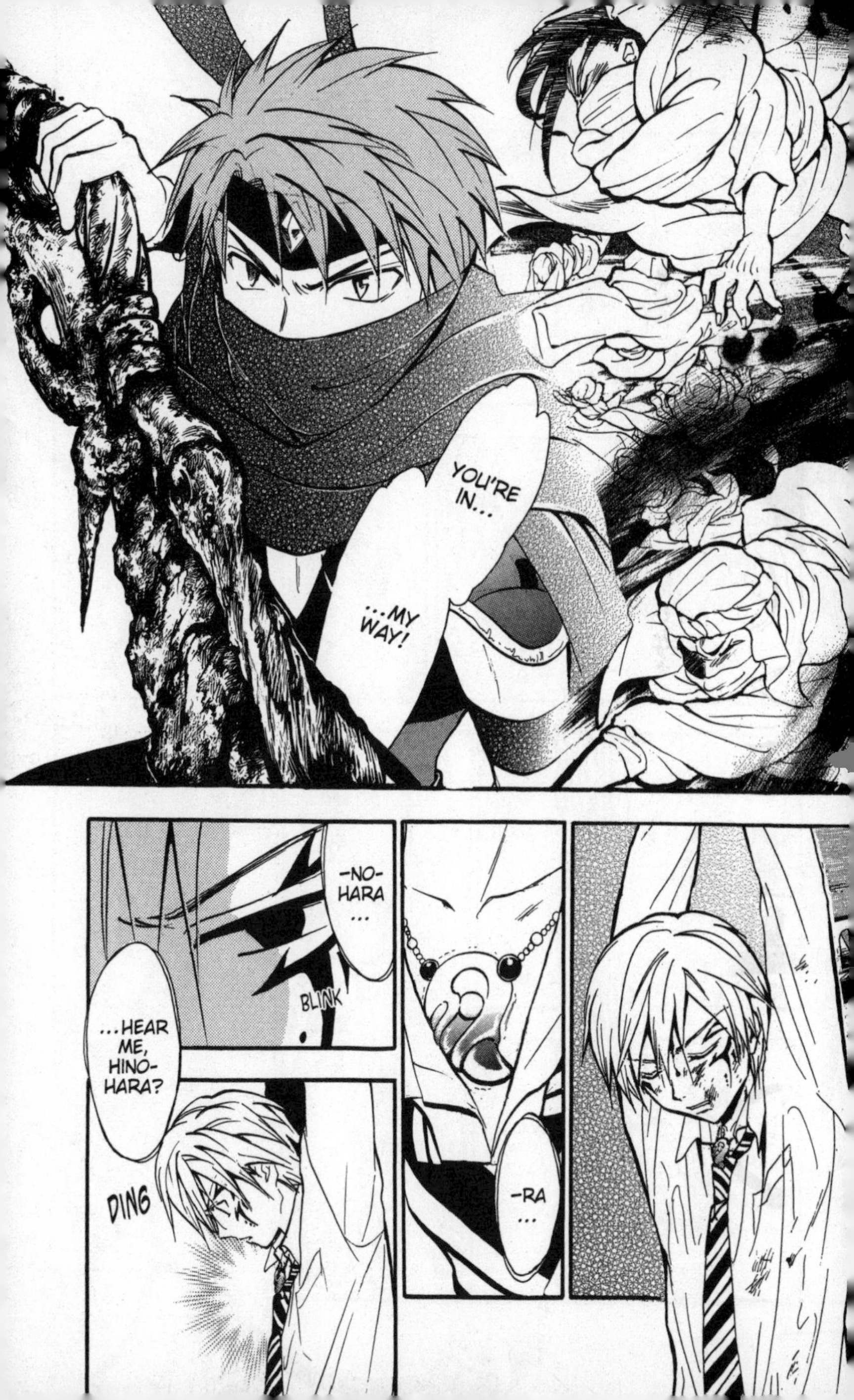

YOU'RE IN...
...MY WAY!
...
-RA ...
-NO-HARA ...
BLINK
...HEAR ME, HINO-HARA?
DING

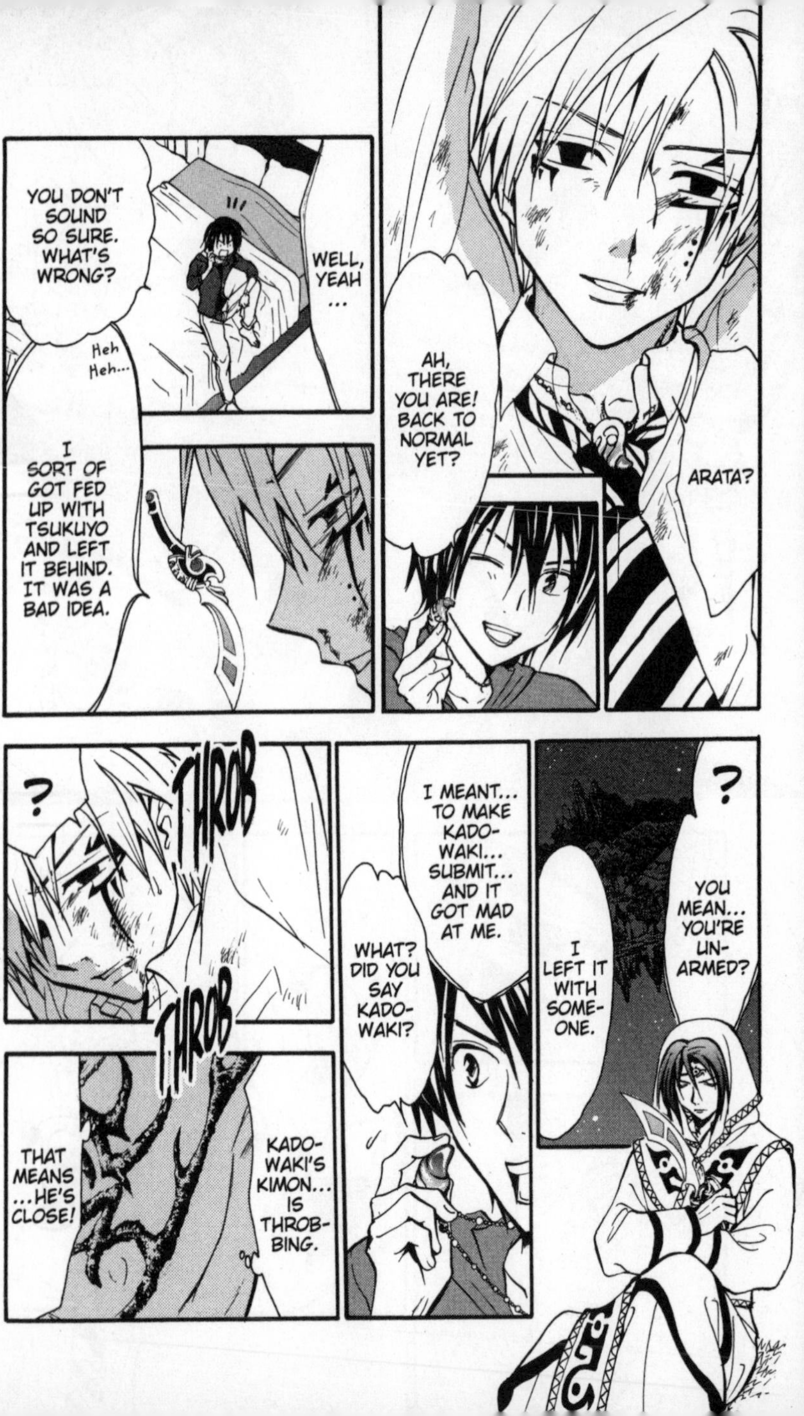
ARATA?
AH, THERE YOU ARE! BACK TO NORMAL YET?
WELL, YEAH ...
YOU DON'T SOUND SO SURE. WHAT'S WRONG?
Heh Heh...
I SORT OF GOT FED UP WITH TSUKUYO AND LEFT IT BEHIND. IT WAS A BAD IDEA.
?
YOU MEAN... YOU'RE UN-ARMED?
I LEFT IT WITH SOME-ONE.
I MEANT... TO MAKE KADO-WAKI... SUBMIT... AND IT GOT MAD AT ME.
WHAT? DID YOU SAY KADO-WAKI?
?
THROB
THROB
KADO-WAKI'S KIMON... IS THROB-BING.
THAT MEANS ...HE'S CLOSE!

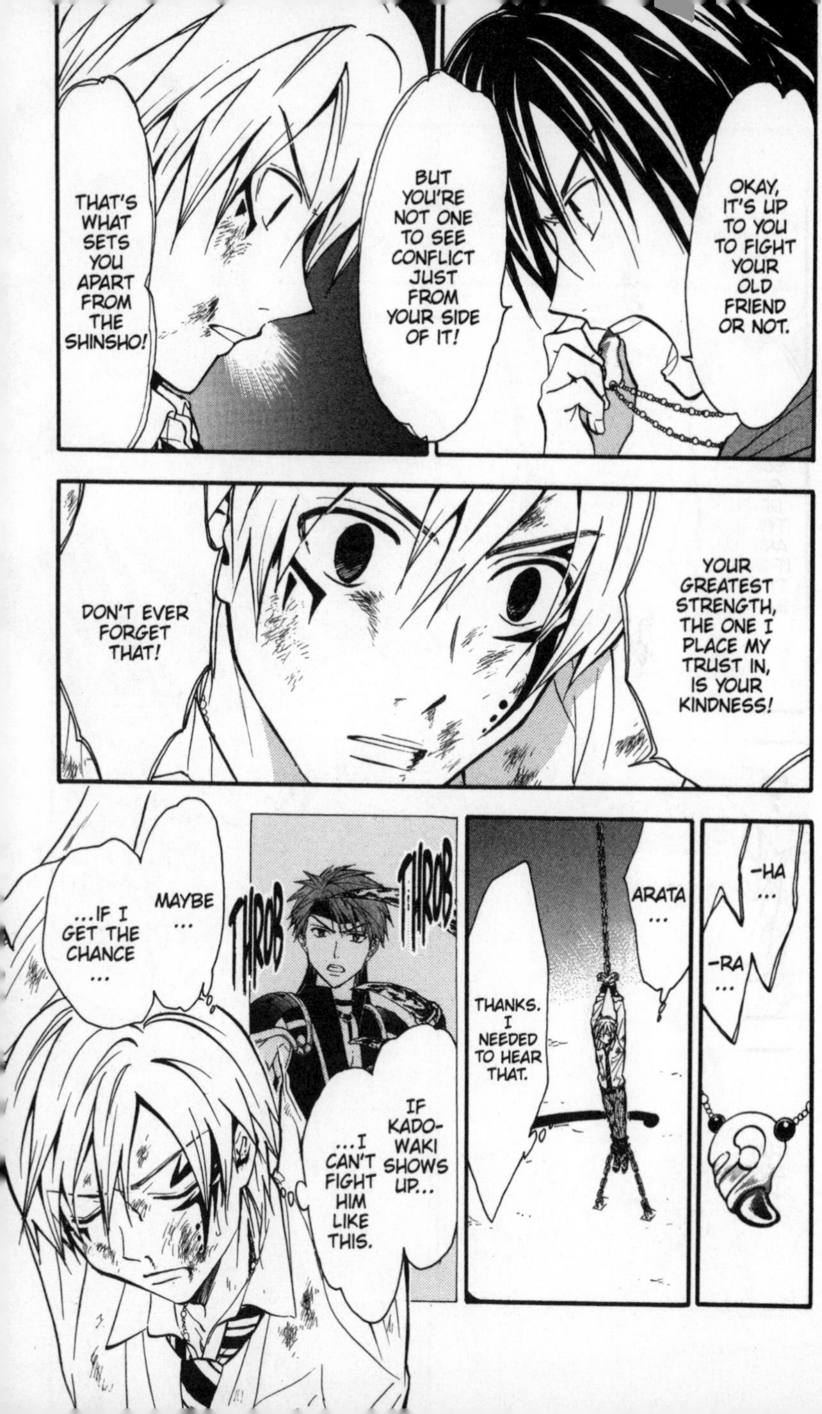
OKAY, IT'S UP TO YOU TO FIGHT YOUR OLD FRIEND OR NOT.
BUT YOU'RE NOT ONE TO SEE CONFLICT JUST FROM YOUR SIDE OF IT!
THAT'S WHAT SETS YOU APART FROM THE SHINSHO!
YOUR GREATEST STRENGTH, THE ONE I PLACE MY TRUST IN, IS YOUR KINDNESS!
DON'T EVER FORGET THAT!
-HA ...
-RA ...
ARATA ...
THANKS. I NEEDED TO HEAR THAT.
THROB
THROB
IF KADO-WAKI SHOWS UP...
...I CAN'T FIGHT HIM LIKE THIS.
MAYBE ...
...IF I GET THE CHANCE ...

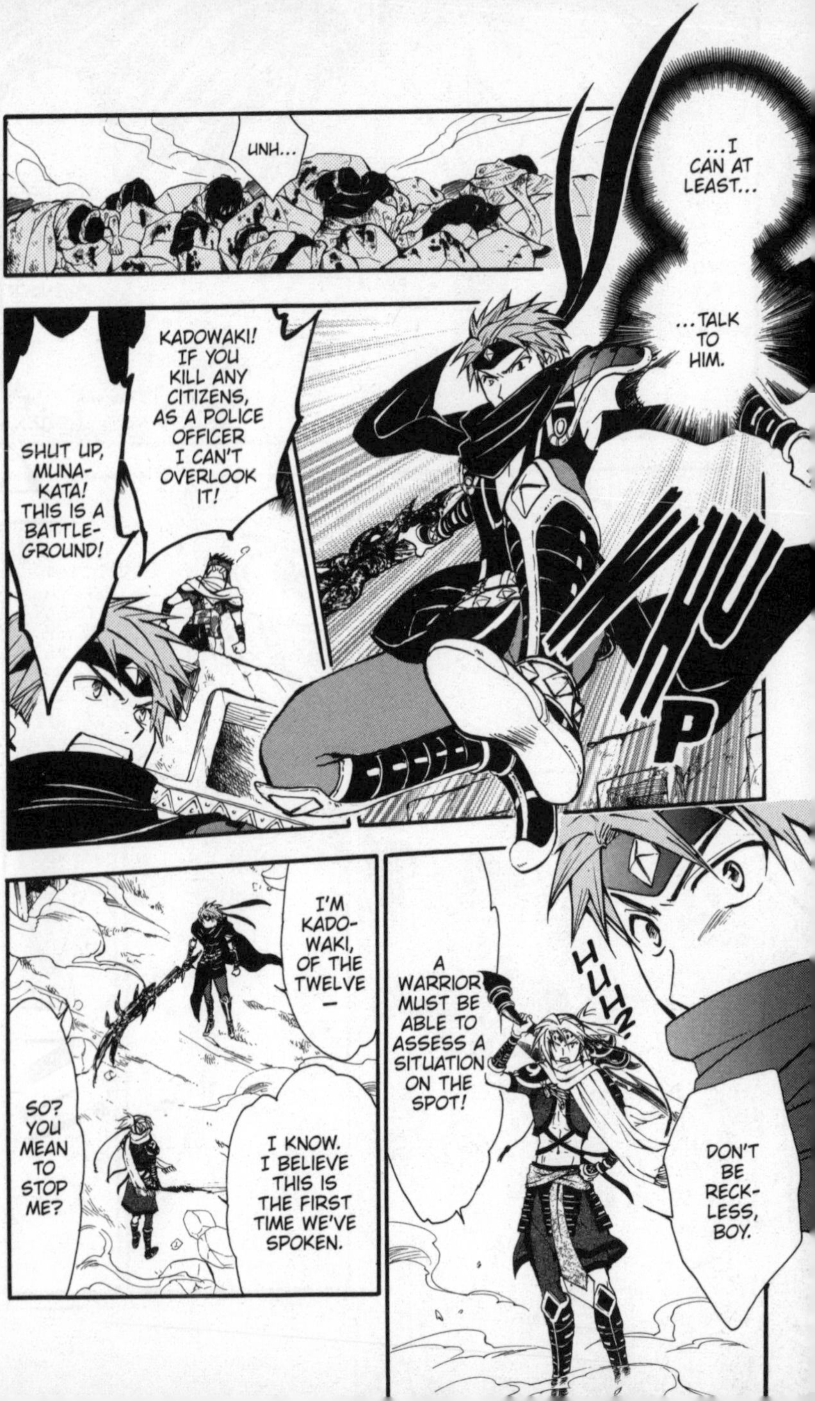
...I CAN AT LEAST...
...TALK TO HIM.
WHUMP
UNH...
KADOWAKI! IF YOU KILL ANY CITIZENS, AS A POLICE OFFICER I CAN'T OVERLOOK IT!
SHUT UP, MUNA-KATA! THIS IS A BATTLE-GROUND!
HUHN!
DON'T BE RECK-LESS, BOY.
A WARRIOR MUST BE ABLE TO ASSESS A SITUATION ON THE SPOT!
I'M KADO-WAKI, OF THE TWELVE —
I KNOW. I BELIEVE THIS IS THE FIRST TIME WE'VE SPOKEN.
SO? YOU MEAN TO STOP ME?

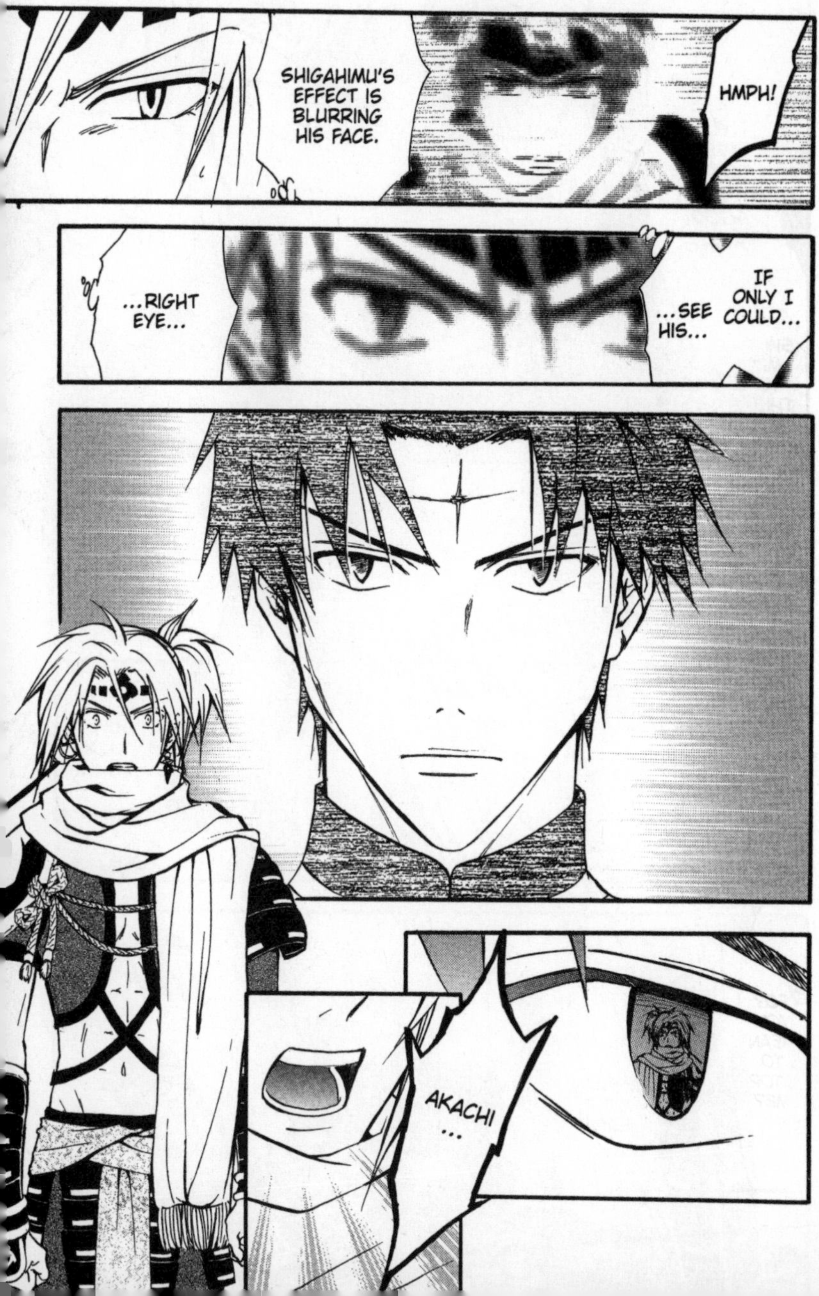
HMPH!
SHIGAHIMU'S EFFECT IS BLURRING HIS FACE.
IF ONLY I COULD...
...SEE HIS...
...RIGHT EYE...
AKACHI ...

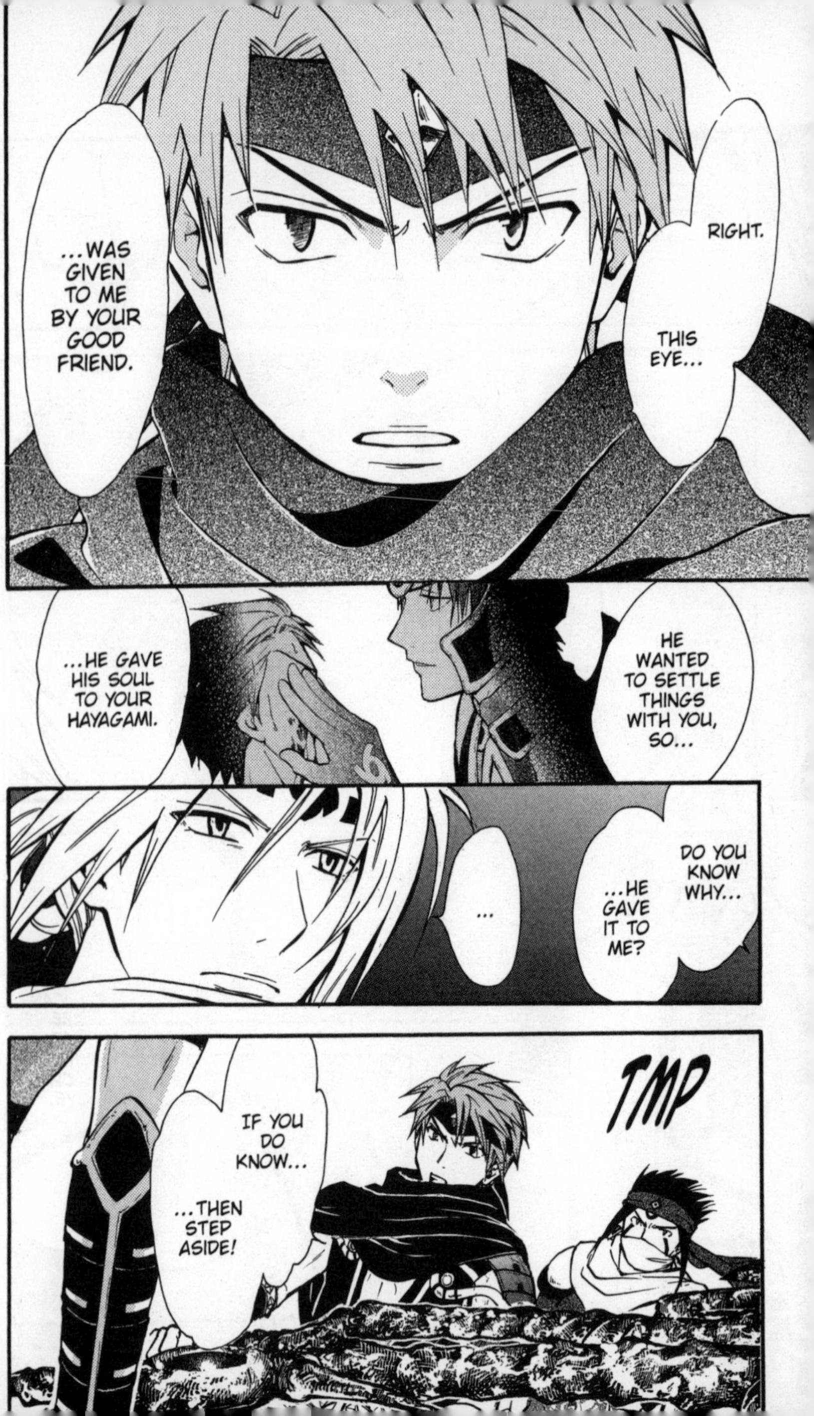
RIGHT. THIS EYE...
...WAS GIVEN TO ME BY YOUR GOOD FRIEND.
HE WANTED TO SETTLE THINGS WITH YOU, SO...
...HE GAVE HIS SOUL TO YOUR HAYAGAMI.
DO YOU KNOW WHY...
...HE GAVE IT TO ME?
...
TMP
IF YOU DO KNOW...
...THEN STEP ASIDE!

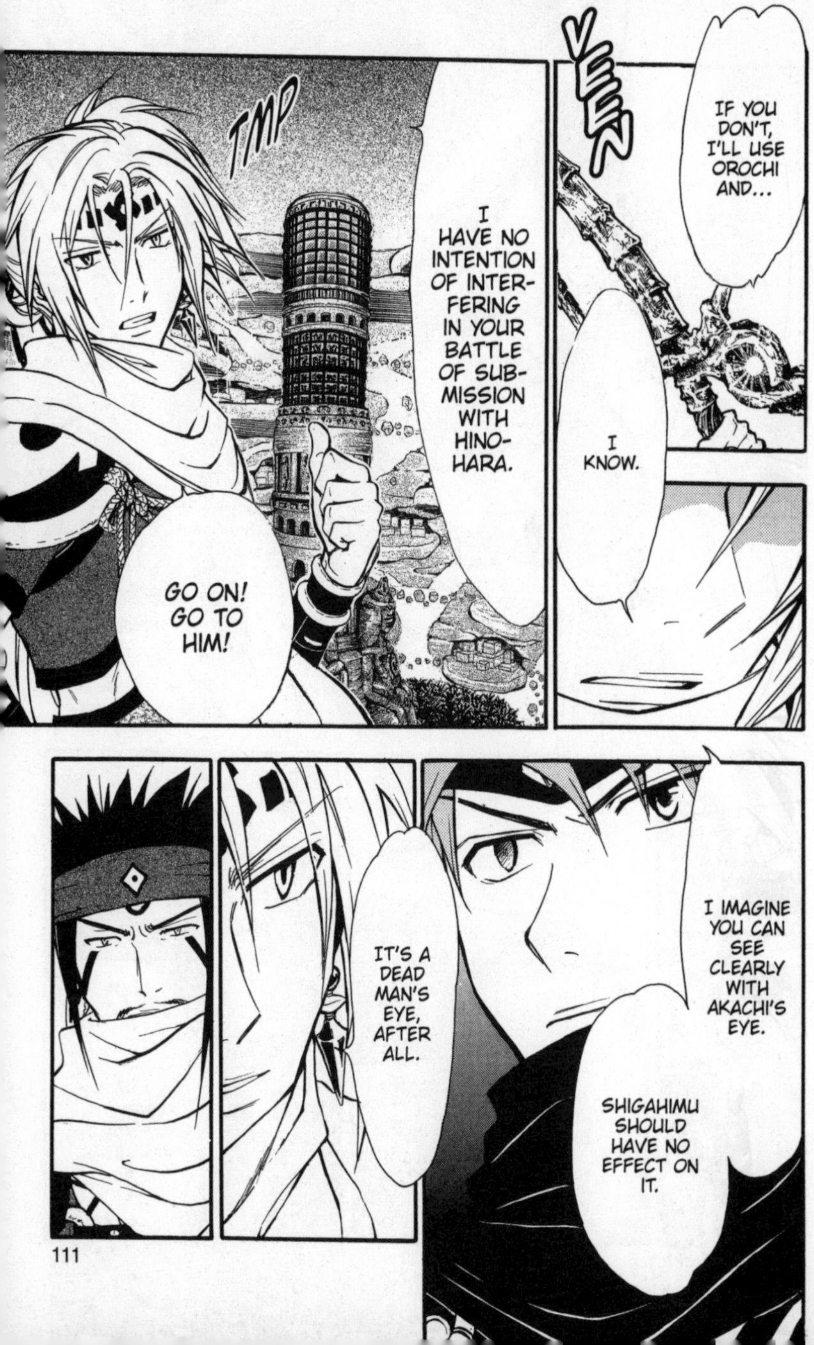
VEEN
IF YOU DON'T, I'LL USE OROCHI AND...
I KNOW.
I HAVE NO INTENTION OF INTER-FERING IN YOUR BATTLE OF SUB-MISSION WITH HINO-HARA.
TMP
GO ON! GO TO HIM!
I IMAGINE YOU CAN SEE CLEARLY WITH AKACHI'S EYE.
SHIGAHIMU SHOULD HAVE NO EFFECT ON IT.
IT'S A DEAD MAN'S EYE, AFTER ALL.

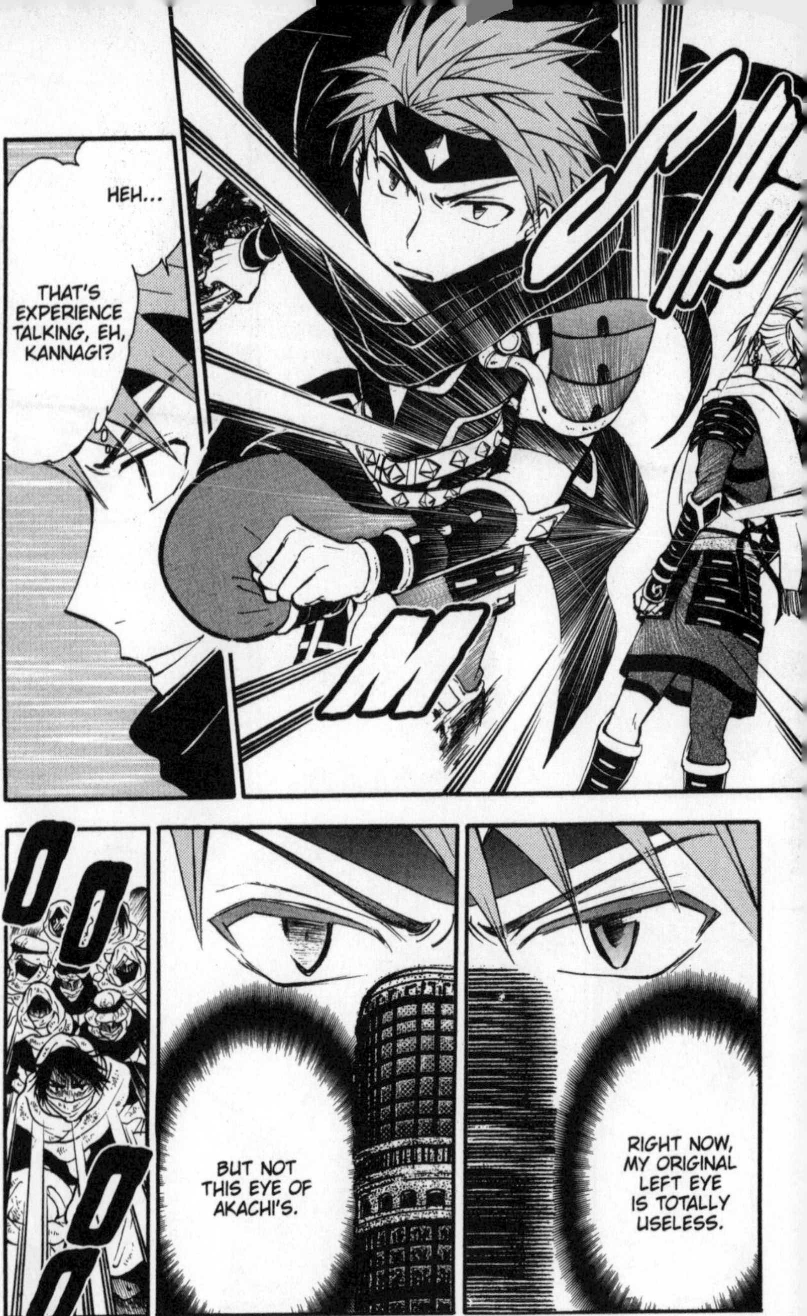
HEH...
THAT'S EXPERIENCE TALKING, EH, KANNAGI?
RIGHT NOW, MY ORIGINAL LEFT EYE IS TOTALLY USELESS.
BUT NOT THIS EYE OF AKACHI'S.

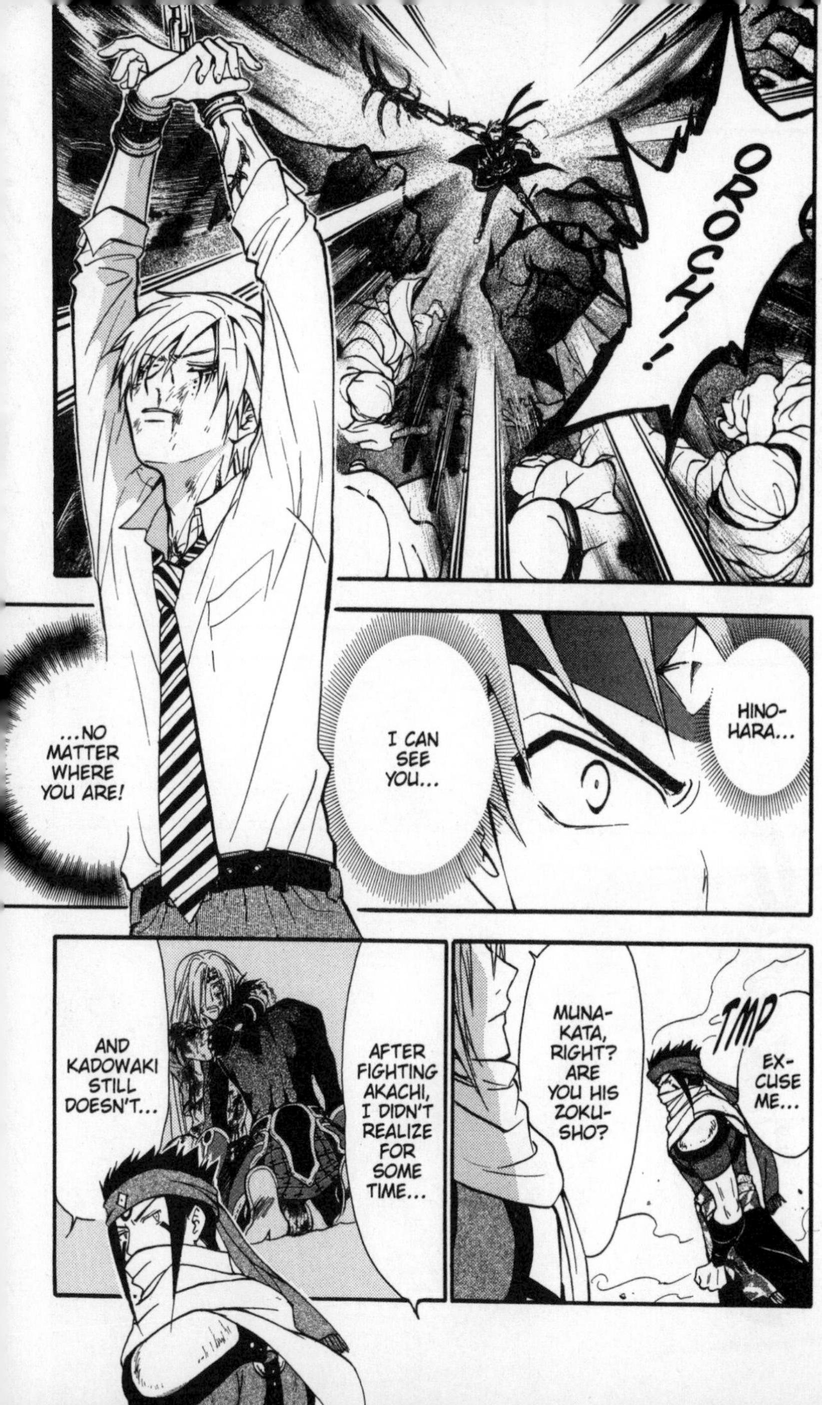
OROCH—!!
HINO-HARA...
I CAN SEE YOU...
...NO MATTER WHERE YOU ARE!
TMP
EX-CUSE ME...
MUNA-KATA, RIGHT? ARE YOU HIS ZOKU-SHO?
AFTER FIGHTING AKACHI, I DIDN'T REALIZE FOR SOME TIME...
AND KADOWAKI STILL DOESN'T...

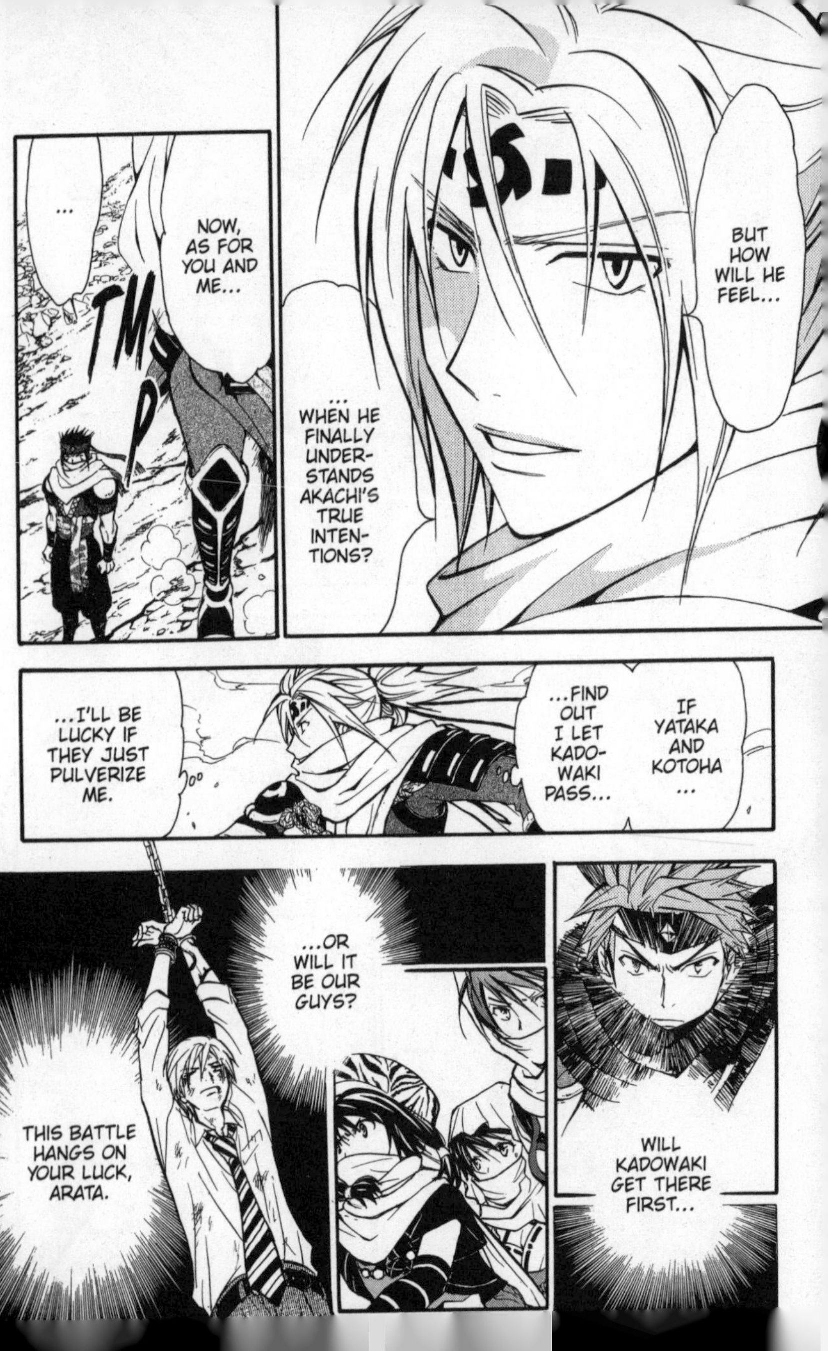
BUT HOW WILL HE FEEL...
...WHEN HE FINALLY UNDERSTANDS AKACHI'S TRUE INTENTIONS?
NOW, AS FOR YOU AND ME...
...
TMP
IF YATAKA AND KOTOHA...
...FIND OUT I LET KADOWAKI PASS...
...I'LL BE LUCKY IF THEY JUST PULVERIZE ME.
WILL KADOWAKI GET THERE FIRST...
...OR WILL IT BE OUR GUYS?
THIS BATTLE HANGS ON YOUR LUCK, ARATA.

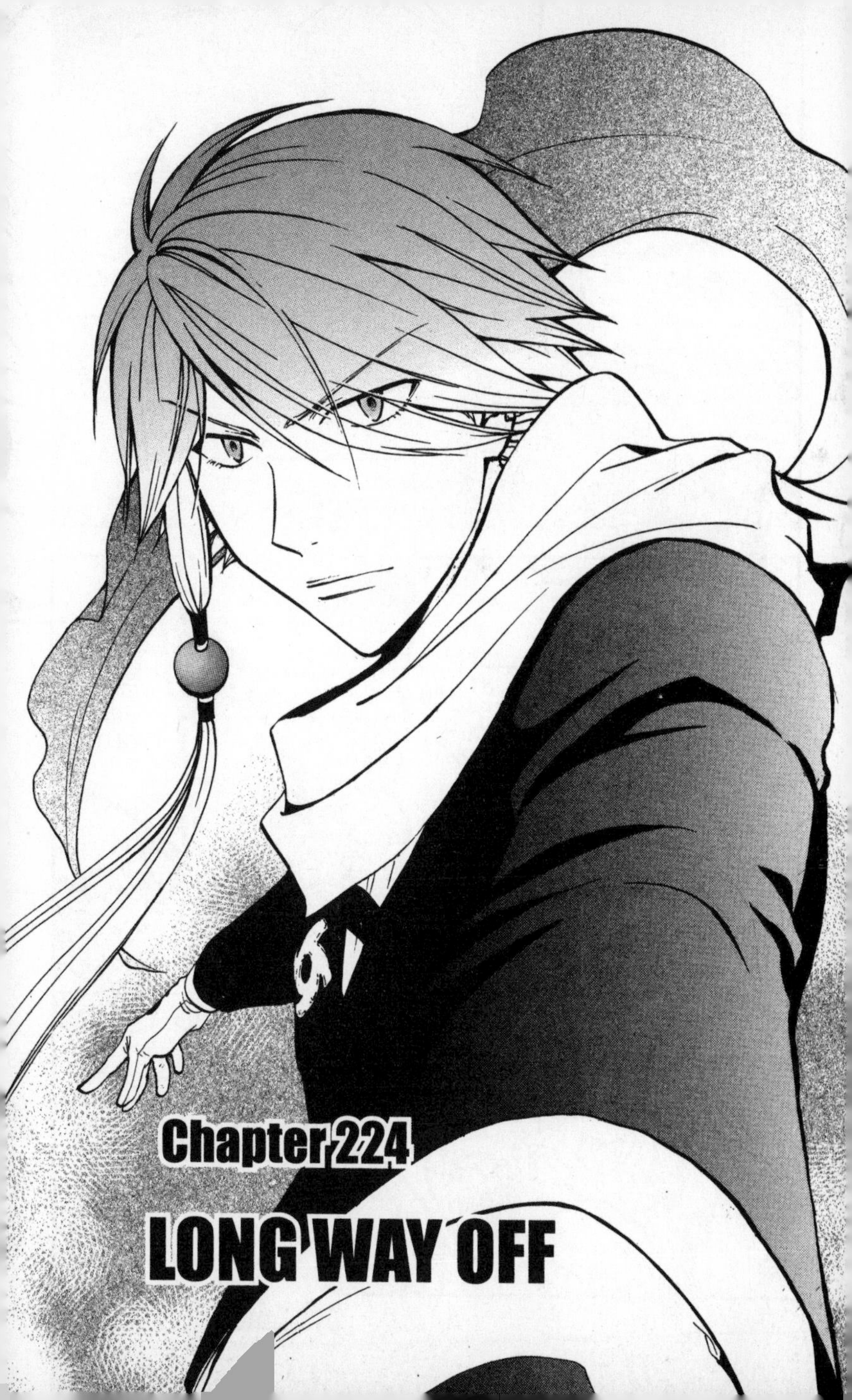
Chapter 224
LONG WAY OFF

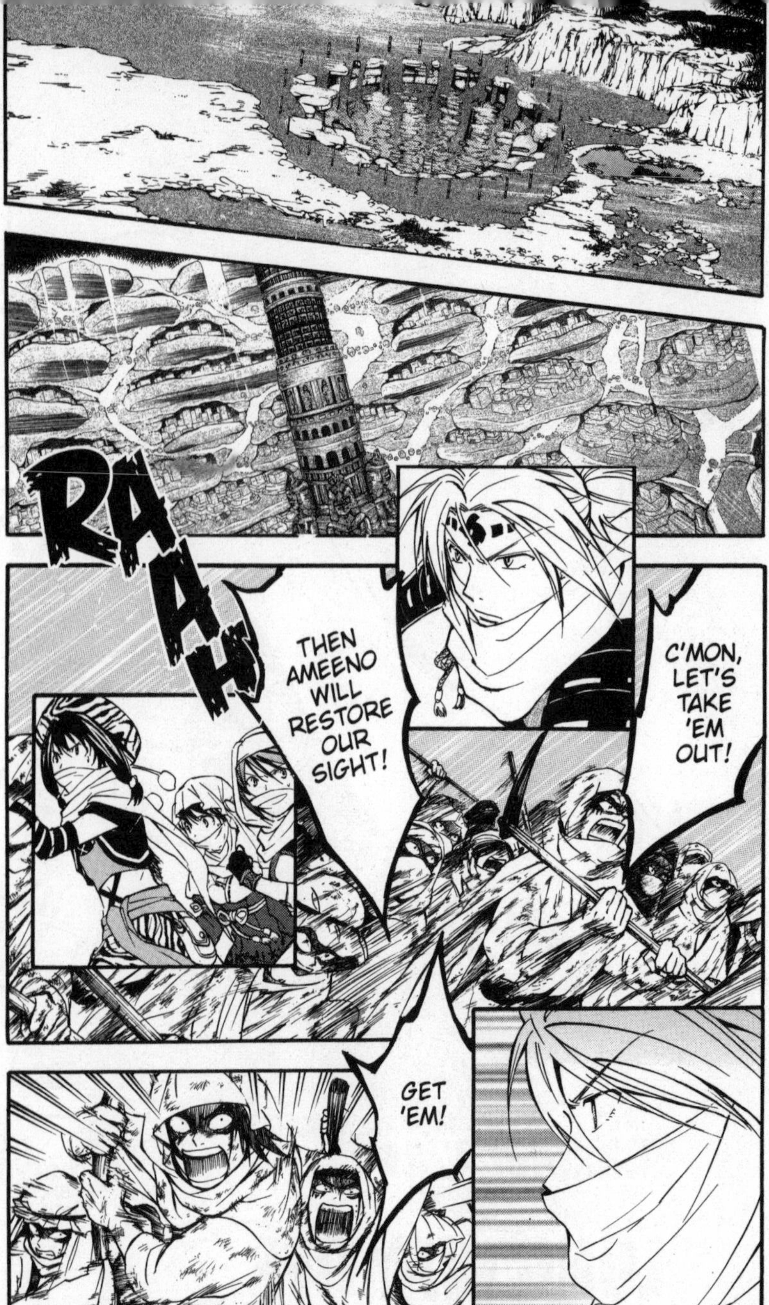
C'MON, LET'S TAKE 'EM OUT!
THEN AMEENO WILL RESTORE OUR SIGHT!
RAAAH
GET 'EM!

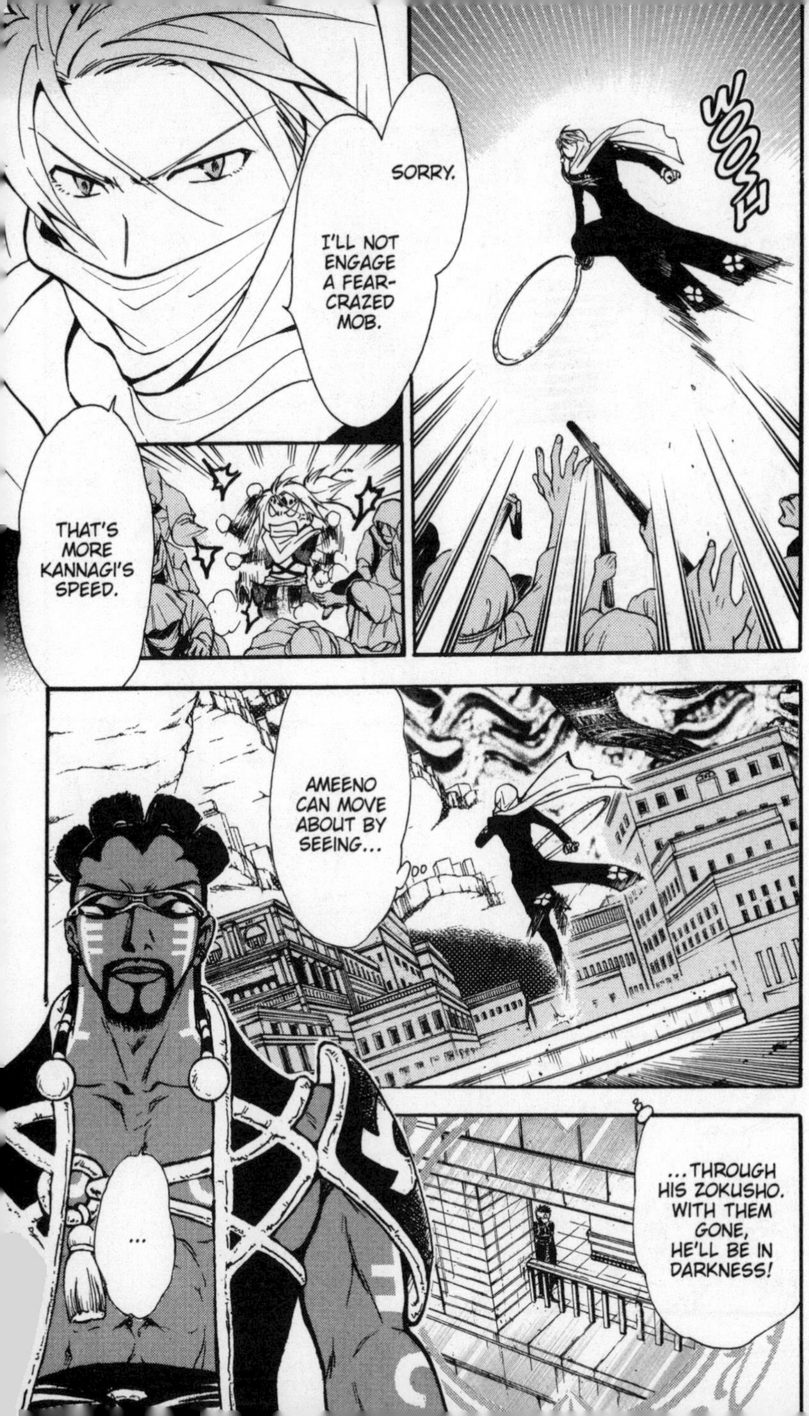
WOOM!
SORRY.
I'LL NOT ENGAGE A FEAR-CRAZED MOB.
THAT'S MORE KANNAGI'S SPEED.
AMEENO CAN MOVE ABOUT BY SEEING...
...THROUGH HIS ZOKUSHO. WITH THEM GONE, HE'LL BE IN DARKNESS!
...

YES, LORD AMEENO!

HEY...

YATAKA AND KANNAGI...

...SEEM INTENT ON GETTING IN MY WAY.

I'M SO SORRY ABOUT THIS.

PLEASE BE OKAY.

AND KOTOHA, MIKUSA, NASAKE...

OH...

KOTO-HA!

KAN-NAGI...

YATAKA...

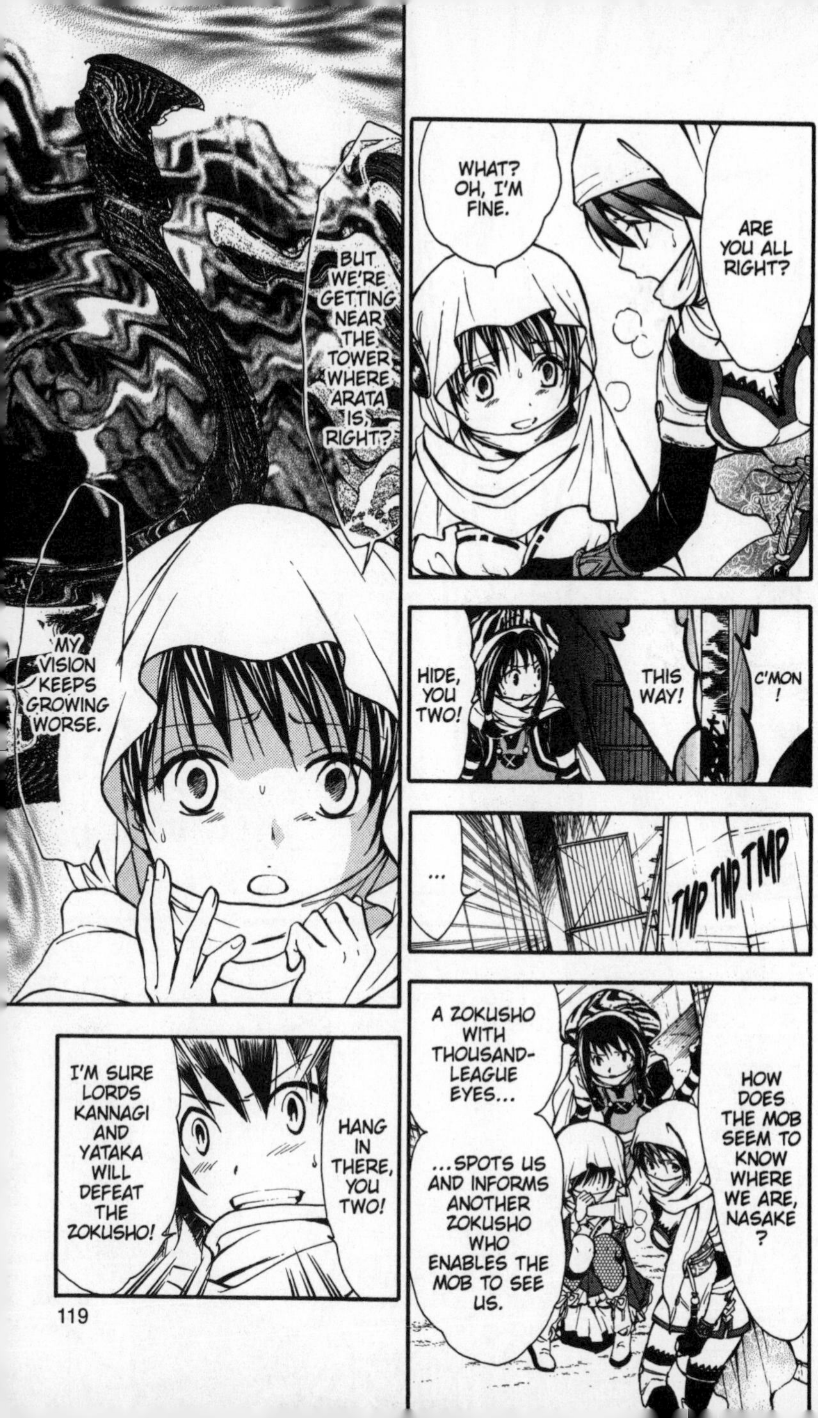
ARE YOU ALL RIGHT?
WHAT? OH, I'M FINE.
C'MON!
THIS WAY!
HIDE, YOU TWO!
...
TMP TMP TMP
BUT WE'RE GETTING NEAR THE TOWER WHERE ARATA IS, RIGHT?
MY VISION KEEPS GROWING WORSE.
HOW DOES THE MOB SEEM TO KNOW WHERE WE ARE, NASAKE?
A ZOKUSHO WITH THOUSAND-LEAGUE EYES...
...SPOTS US AND INFORMS ANOTHER ZOKUSHO WHO ENABLES THE MOB TO SEE US.
HANG IN THERE, YOU TWO!
I'M SURE LORDS KANNAGI AND YATAKA WILL DEFEAT THE ZOKUSHO!

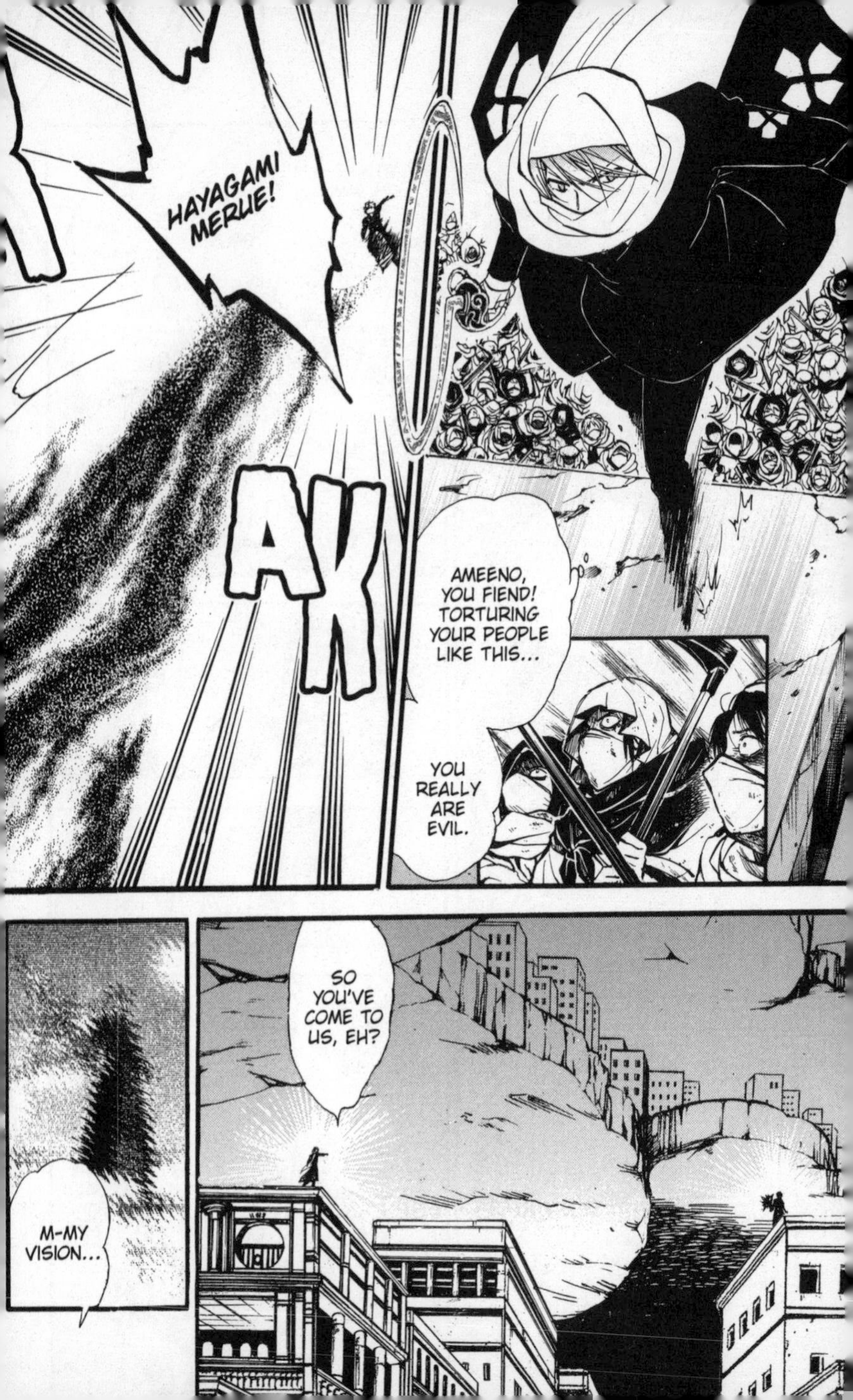
AMEENO, YOU FIEND! TORTURING YOUR PEOPLE LIKE THIS...
YOU REALLY ARE EVIL.
HAYAGAMI MERUE!
AK
SO YOU'VE COME TO US, EH?
M-MY VISION...

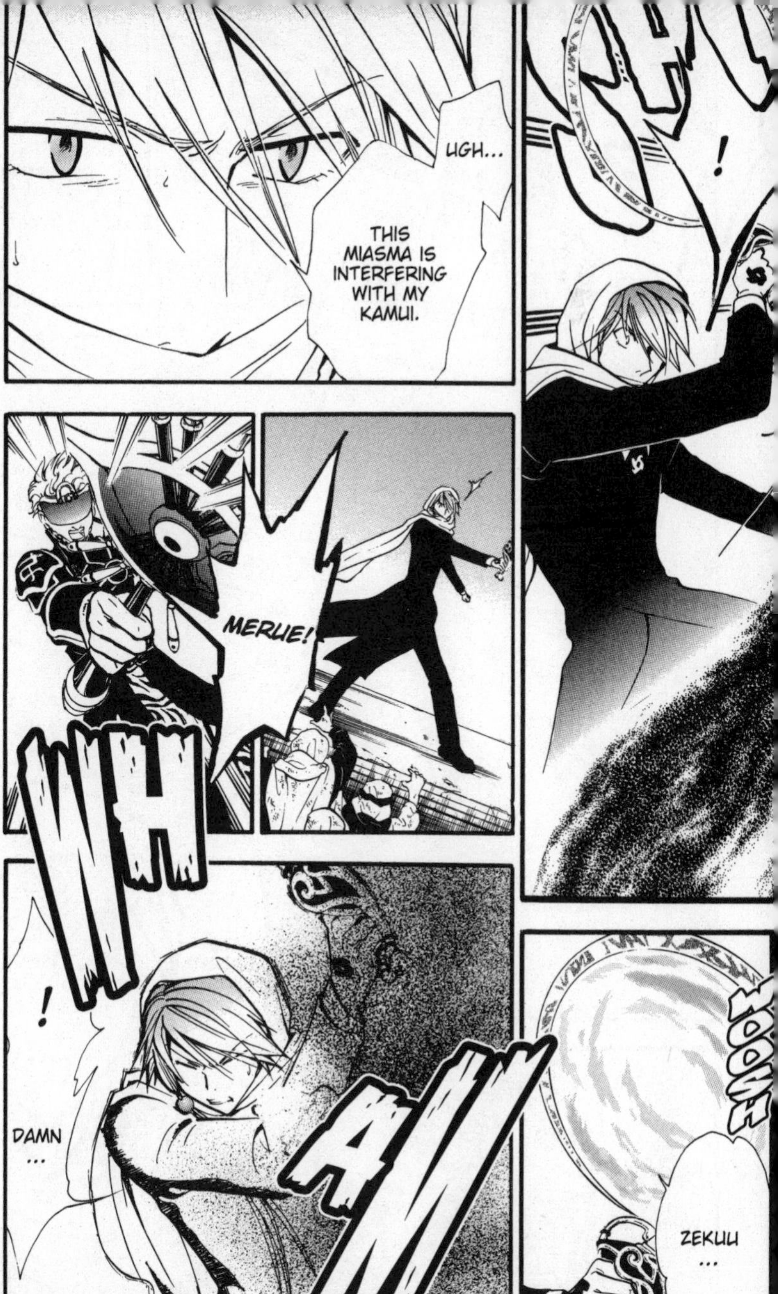
!
UGH...
THIS MIASMA IS INTERFERING WITH MY KAMUI.
MERUE!
WOOSH
ZEKUU ...
!
DAMN ...
WHAM

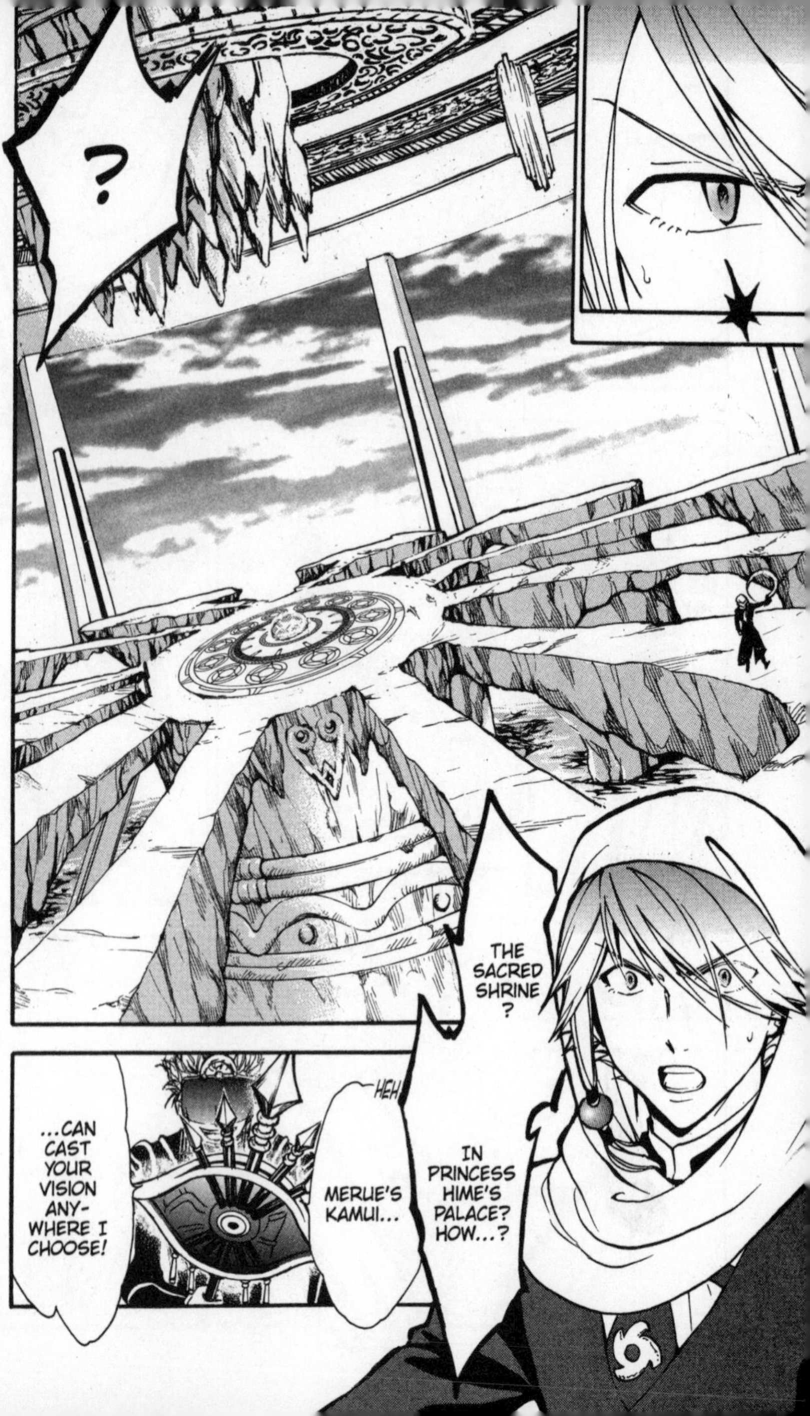
?
THE SACRED SHRINE?
IN PRINCESS HIME'S PALACE? HOW...?
HEH
MERUE'S KAMUI...
...CAN CAST YOUR VISION ANY-WHERE I CHOOSE!

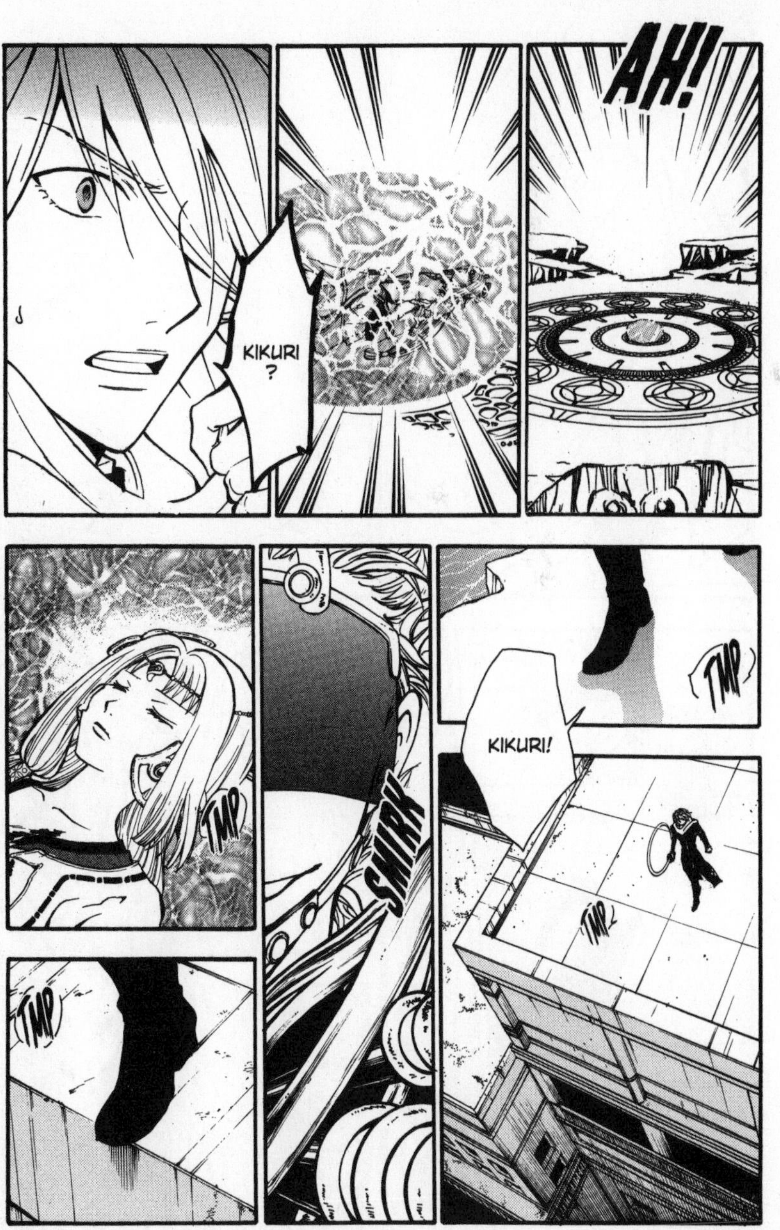
AH!
KIKURI ?
TMP
KIKURI!
TMP
SMIRK
TMP
TMP

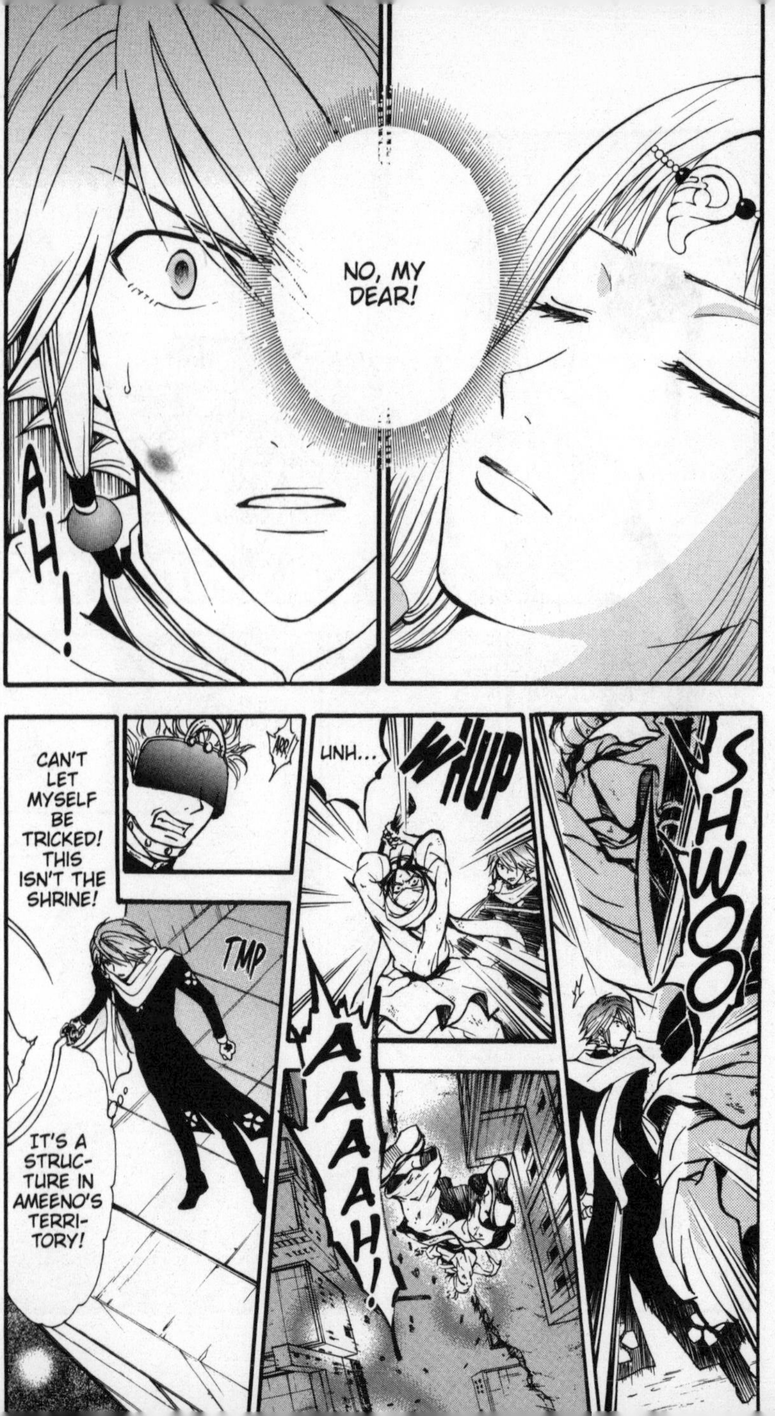
NO, MY DEAR!
AH!
SHWOOO
UNH...
WHUP
ARR!
CAN'T LET MYSELF BE TRICKED! THIS ISN'T THE SHRINE!
AAAAH!
TMP
IT'S A STRUC-TURE IN AMEENO'S TERRI-TORY!

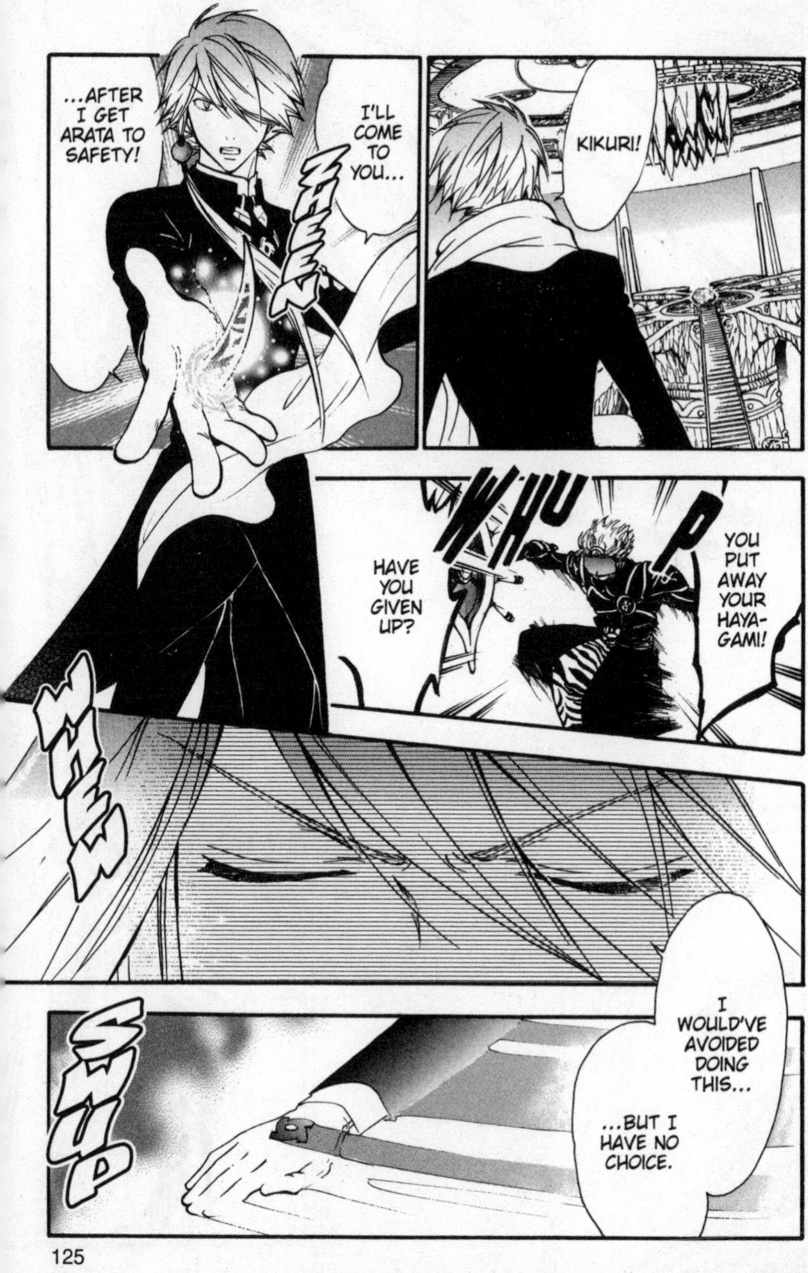
KIKURI!
I'LL COME TO YOU...
...AFTER I GET ARATA TO SAFETY!
YOU PUT AWAY YOUR HAYA-GAMI!
WHUP
HAVE YOU GIVEN UP?
I WOULD'VE AVOIDED DOING THIS...
...BUT I HAVE NO CHOICE.
SWUP

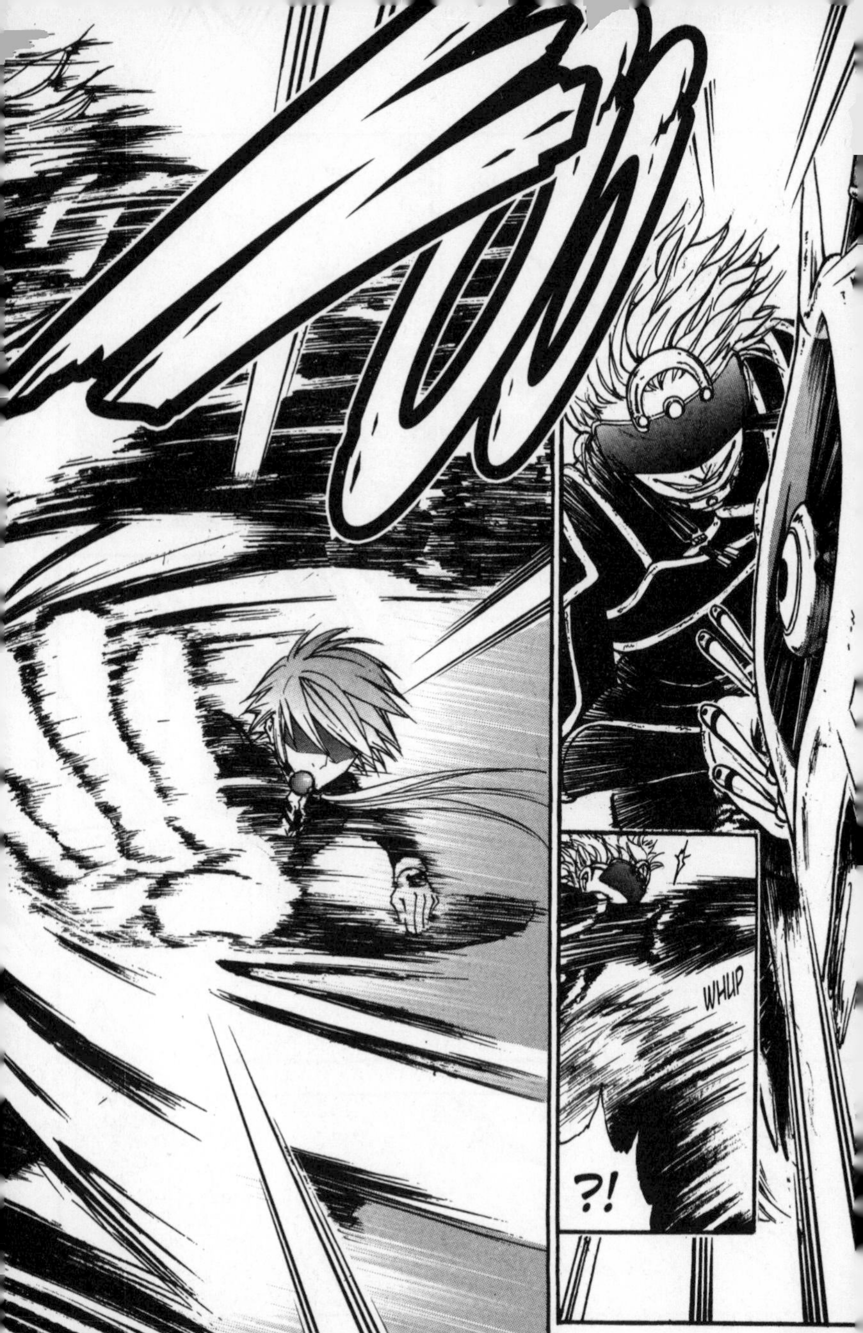
WHUP
?!

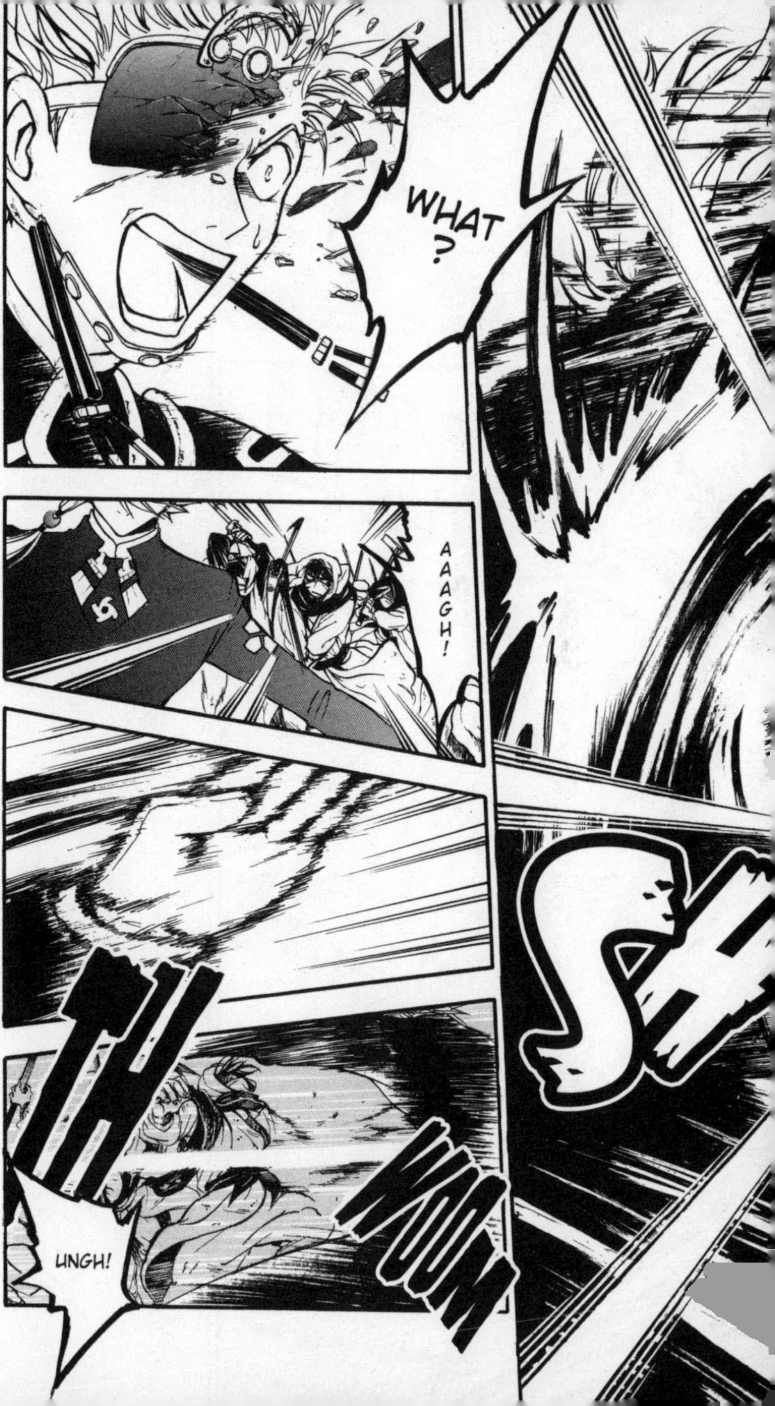
WHAT?
AAAAGH!
THWOOM
UNGH!

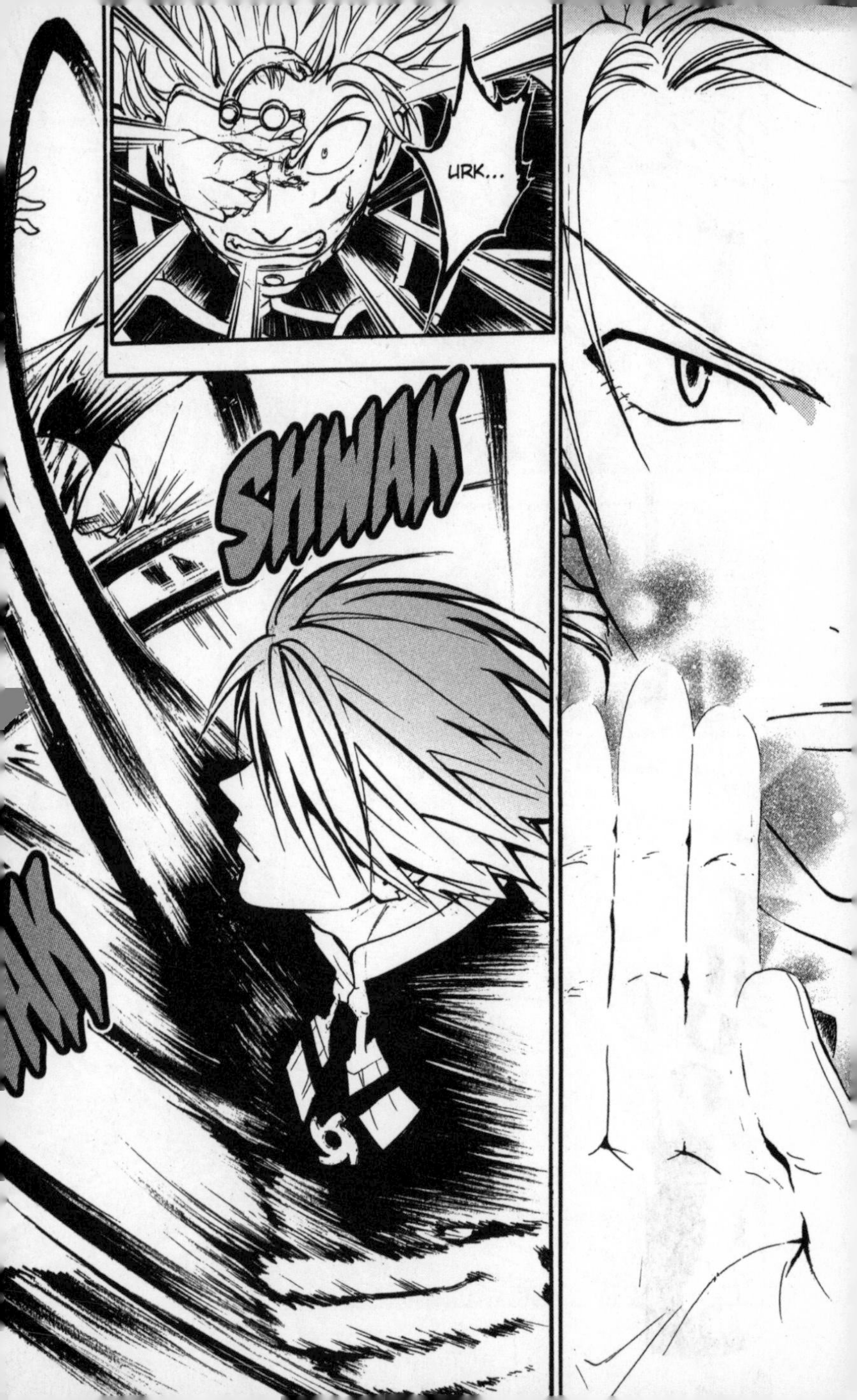
URK...
SHWAK

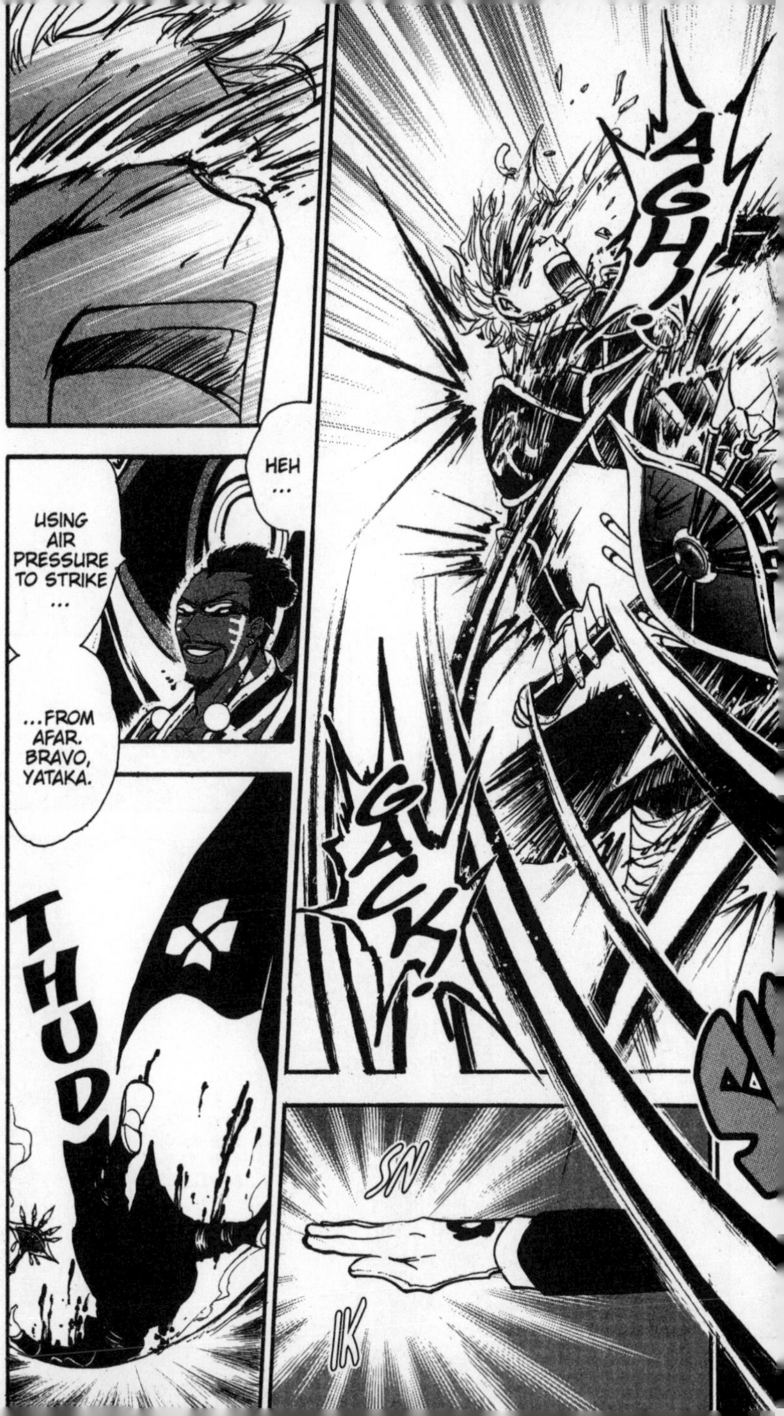
AGH!
GACK!
SN
IK
HEH...
USING AIR PRESSURE TO STRIKE...
...FROM AFAR. BRAVO, YATAKA.
THUD

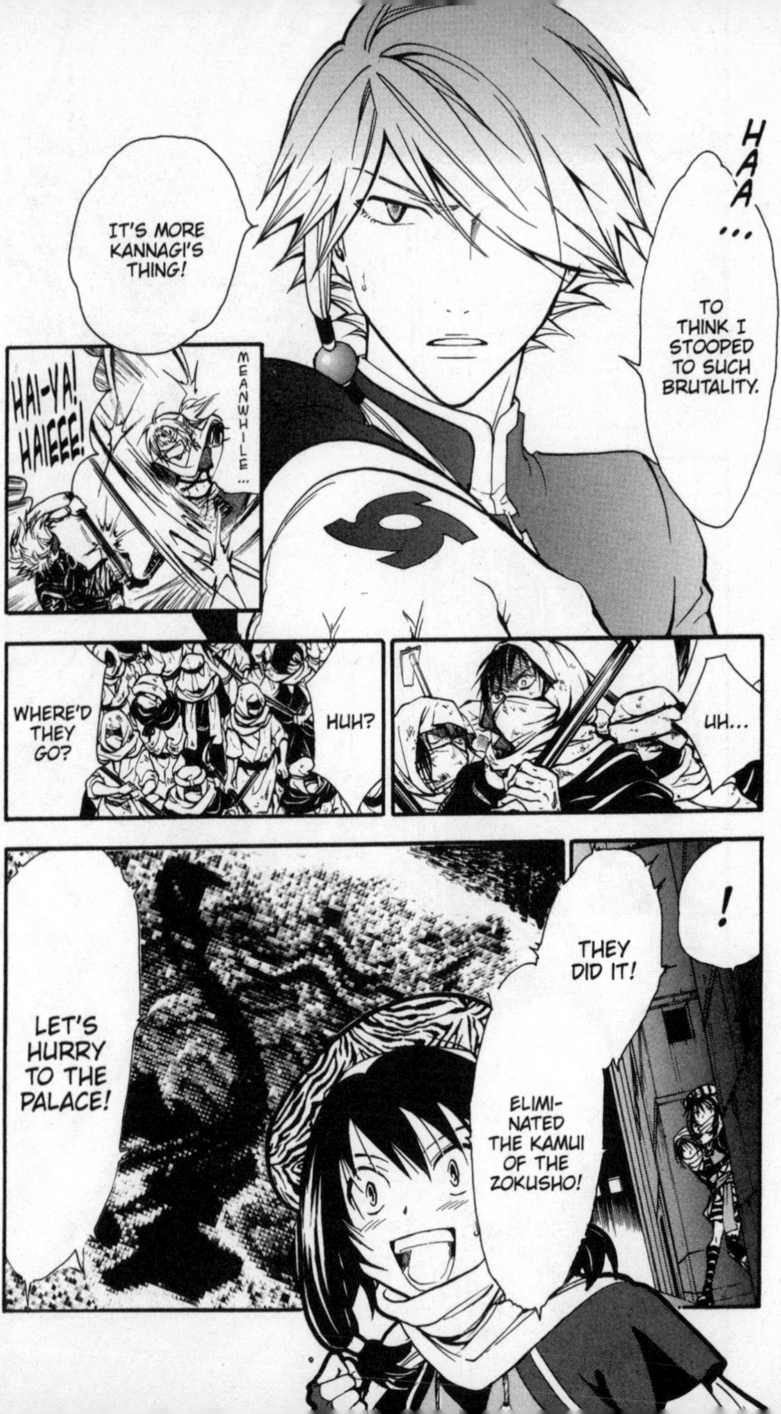
HAA...
TO THINK I STOOPED TO SUCH BRUTALITY.
IT'S MORE KANNAGI'S THING!
MEANWHILE...
HAI-YA! HAIEEE!
UH...
HUH?
WHERE'D THEY GO?
!
THEY DID IT!
ELIMI-NATED THE KAMUI OF THE ZOKUSHO!
LET'S HURRY TO THE PALACE!

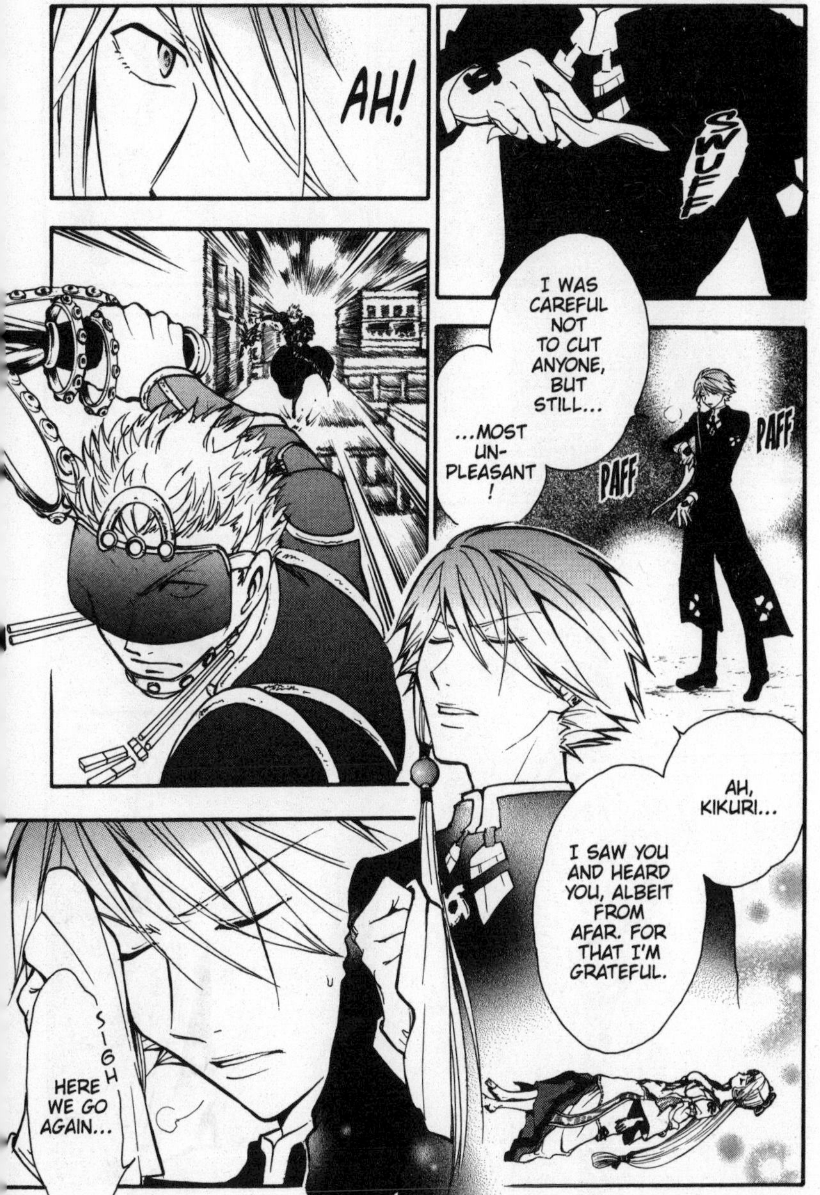
SWUFF
AH!
I WAS CAREFUL NOT TO CUT ANYONE, BUT STILL...
...MOST UN-PLEASANT!
PAFF
PAFF
AH, KIKURI...
I SAW YOU AND HEARD YOU, ALBEIT FROM AFAR. FOR THAT I'M GRATEFUL.
SIGH
HERE WE GO AGAIN...

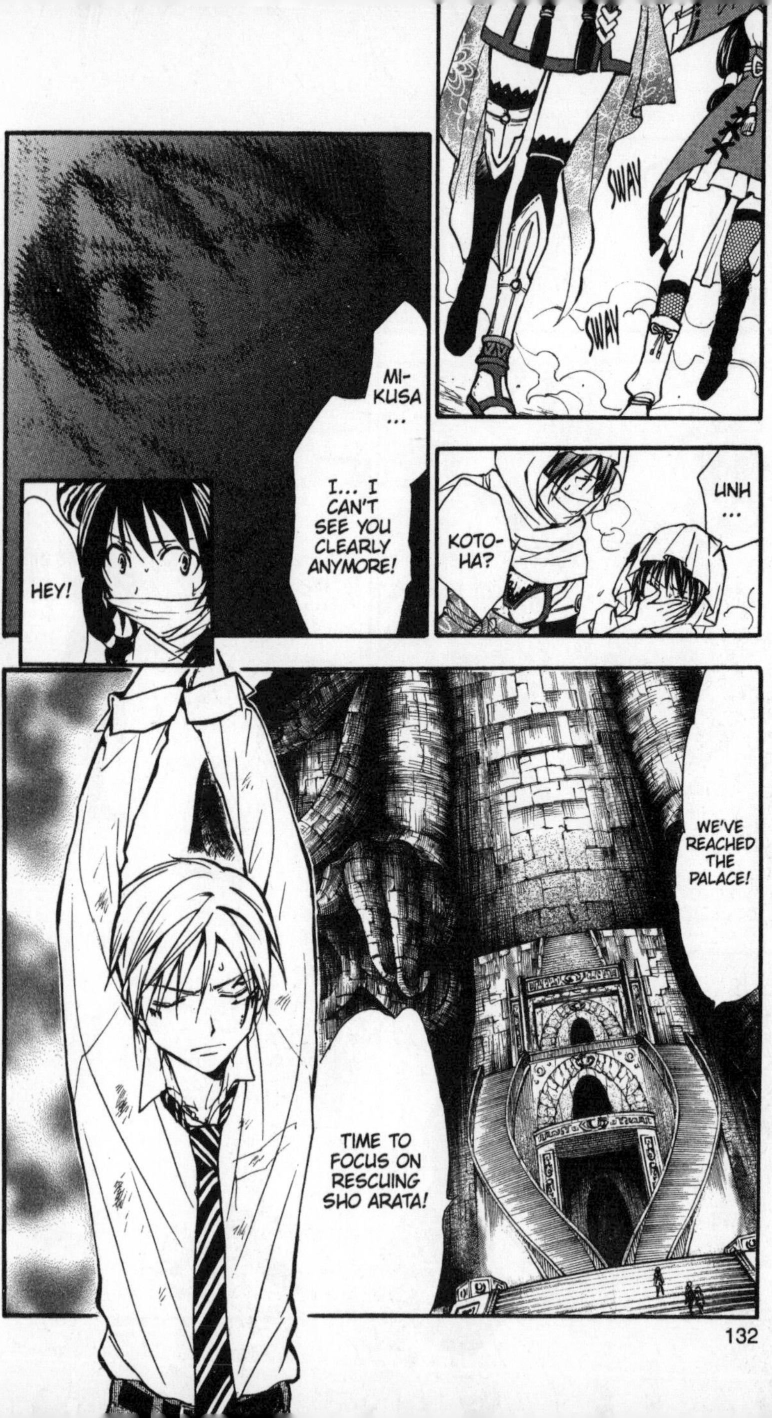
SWAY
SWAY
UNH ...
KOTO-HA?
MI-KUSA ...
I... I CAN'T SEE YOU CLEARLY ANYMORE!
HEY!
WE'VE REACHED THE PALACE!
TIME TO FOCUS ON RESCUING SHO ARATA!

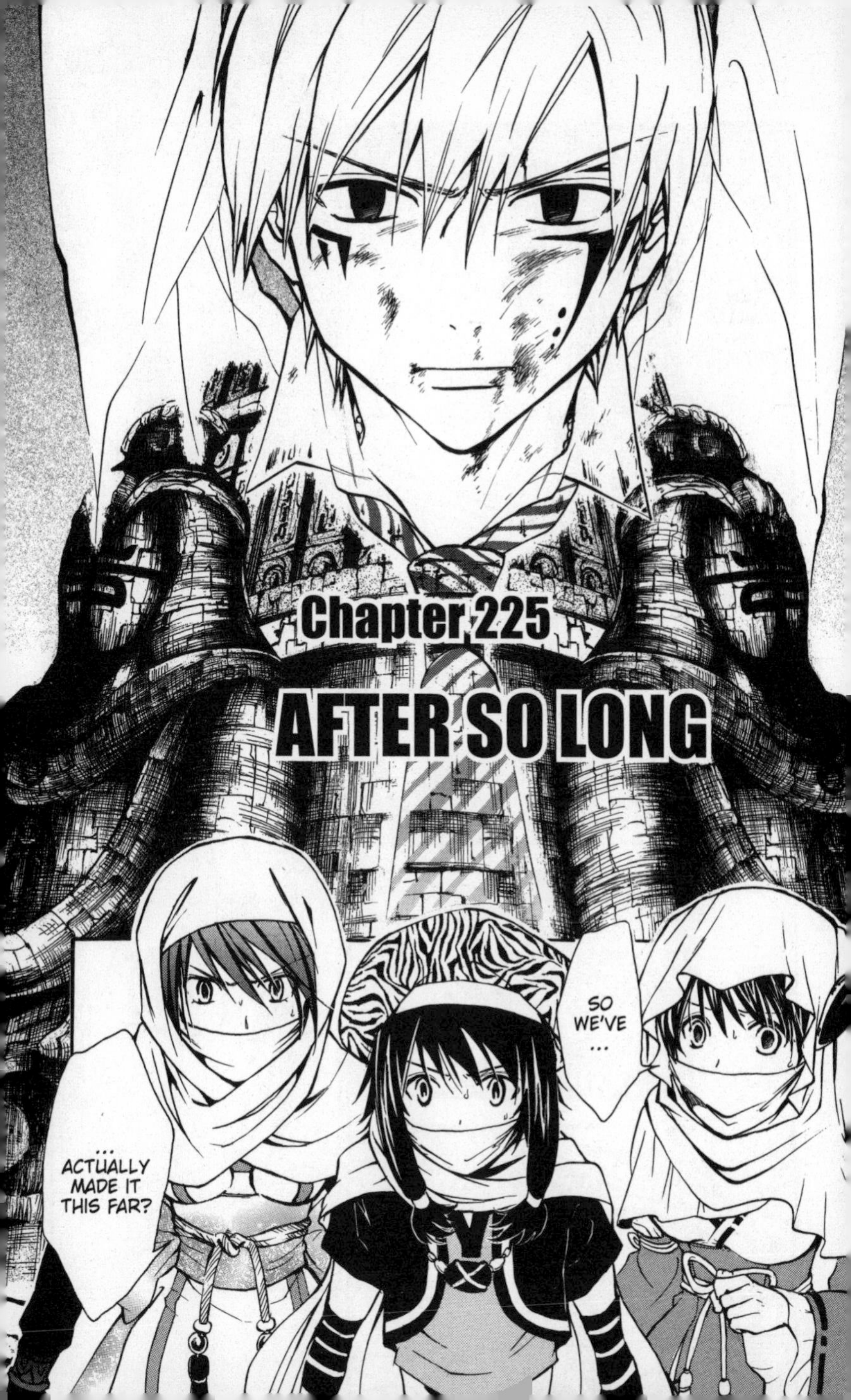
Chapter 225
AFTER SO LONG
SO WE'VE ...
... ACTUALLY MADE IT THIS FAR?

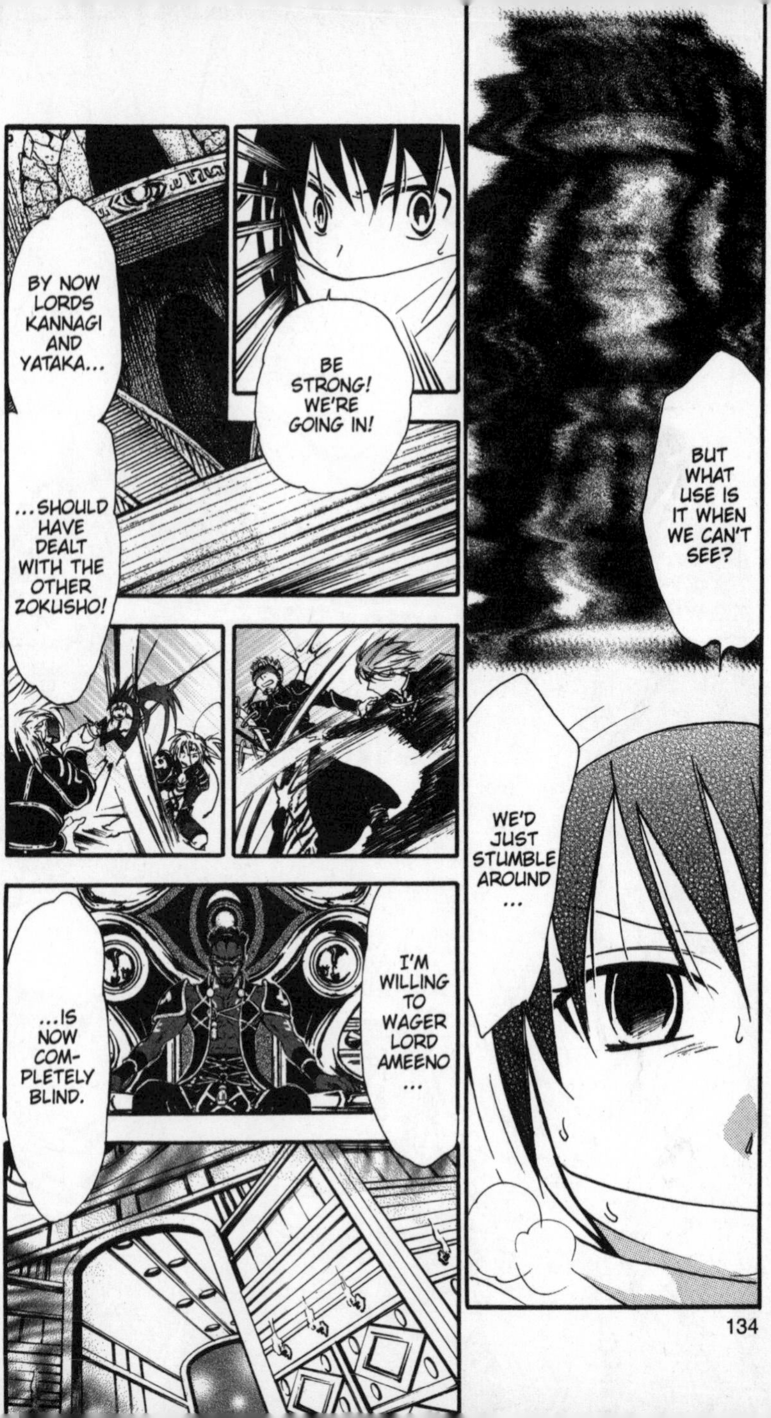
BUT WHAT USE IS IT WHEN WE CAN'T SEE?
WE'D JUST STUMBLE AROUND ...
BE STRONG! WE'RE GOING IN!
BY NOW LORDS KANNAGI AND YATAKA...
...SHOULD HAVE DEALT WITH THE OTHER ZOKUSHO!
I'M WILLING TO WAGER LORD AMEENO ...
...IS NOW COM-PLETELY BLIND.

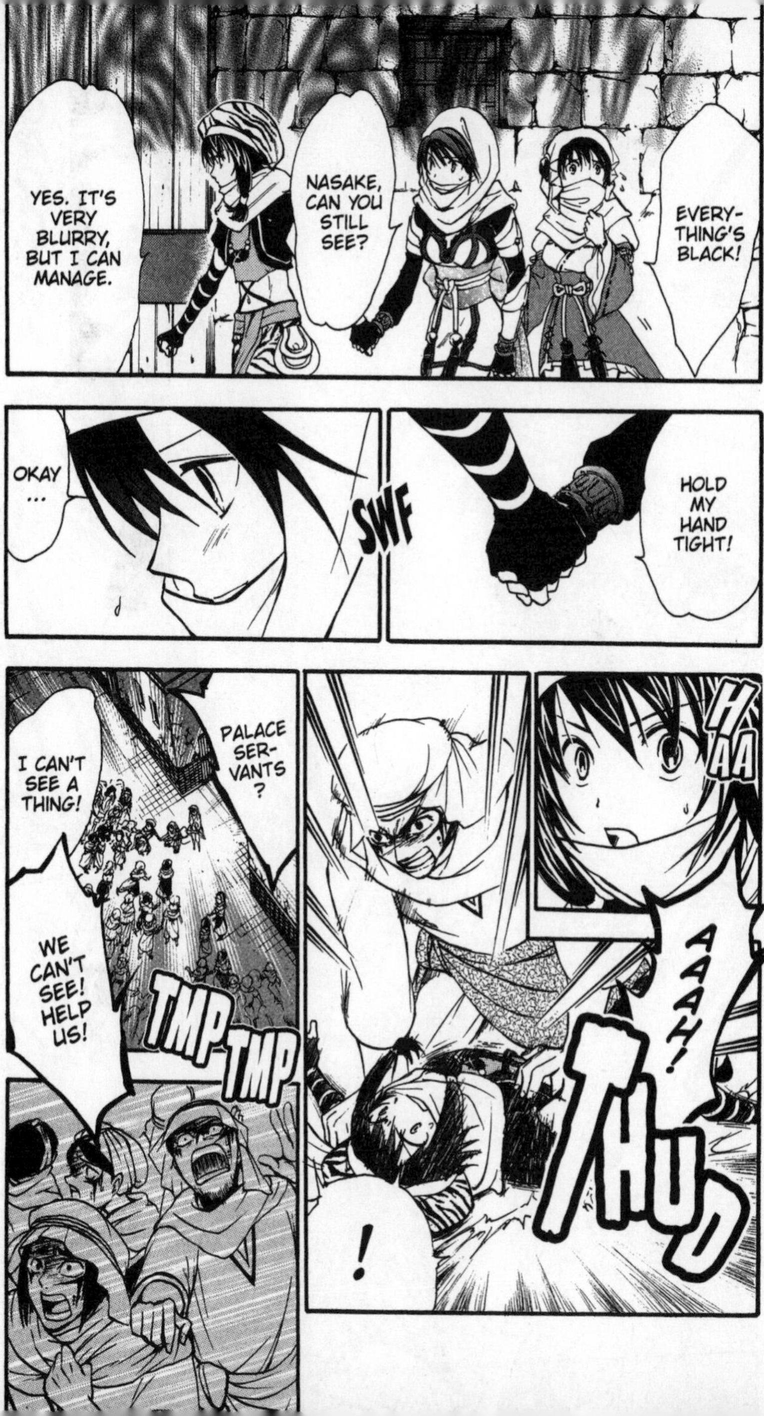
EVERY-THING'S BLACK!
NASAKE, CAN YOU STILL SEE?
YES. IT'S VERY BLURRY, BUT I CAN MANAGE.
HOLD MY HAND TIGHT!
SWF
OKAY ...
HAA
AAAAH!
THUD
!
PALACE SER-VANTS?
I CAN'T SEE A THING!
WE CAN'T SEE! HELP US!
TMP TMP

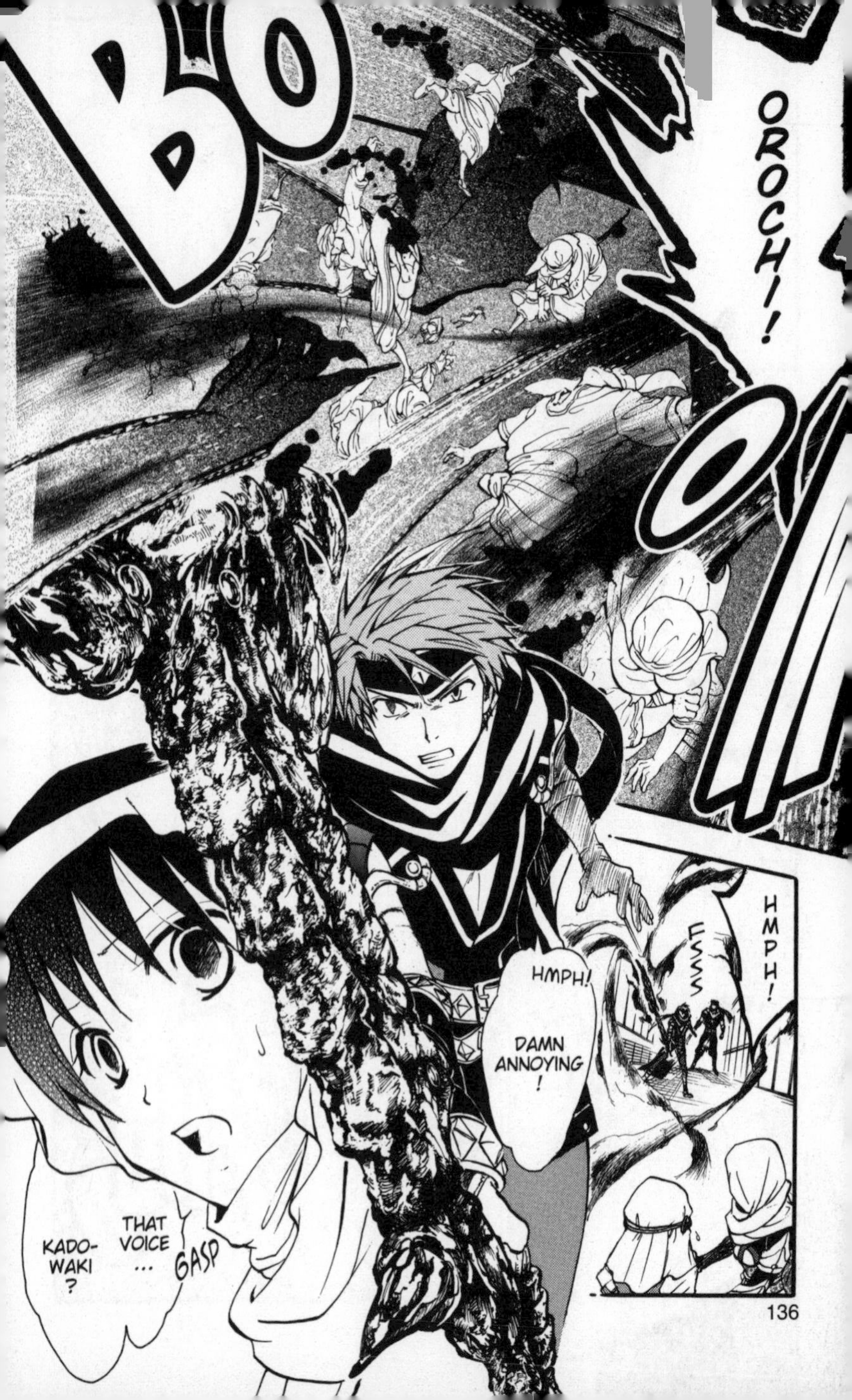
OROCHI!
BO
HMPH!
HMPH!
DAMN ANNOYING!
GASP
THAT VOICE ...
KADO-WAKI?

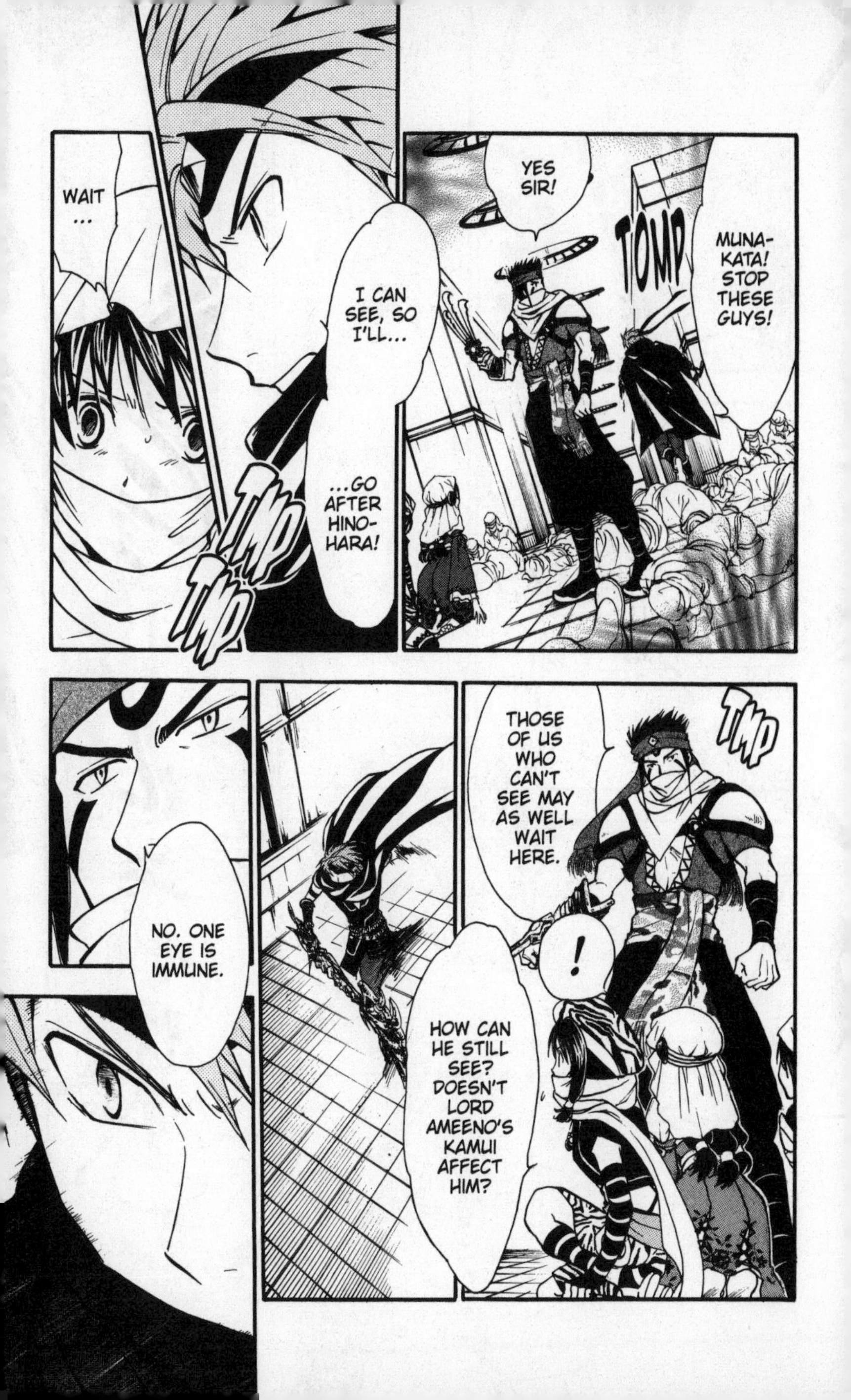
MUNA-KATA! STOP THESE GUYS!
TOMP
YES SIR!
I CAN SEE, SO I'LL...
...GO AFTER HINO-HARA!
TMP TMP
WAIT ...
TMP
THOSE OF US WHO CAN'T SEE MAY AS WELL WAIT HERE.
!
HOW CAN HE STILL SEE? DOESN'T LORD AMEENO'S KAMUI AFFECT HIM?
NO. ONE EYE IS IMMUNE.

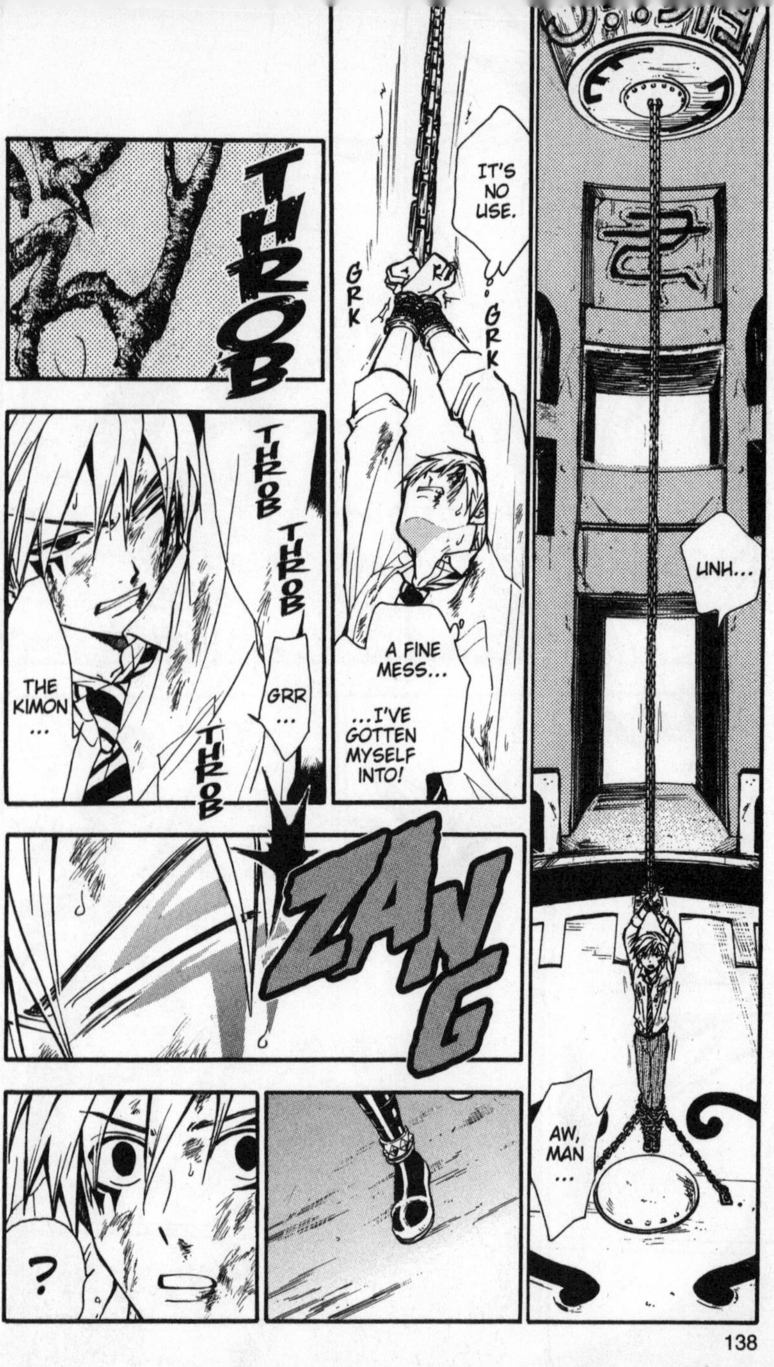
UNH...
AW, MAN ...
IT'S NO USE.
GRK GRK
A FINE MESS...
...I'VE GOTTEN MYSELF INTO!
THROB
THROB THROB
GRR ...
THE KIMON ...
THROB
ZANG
?

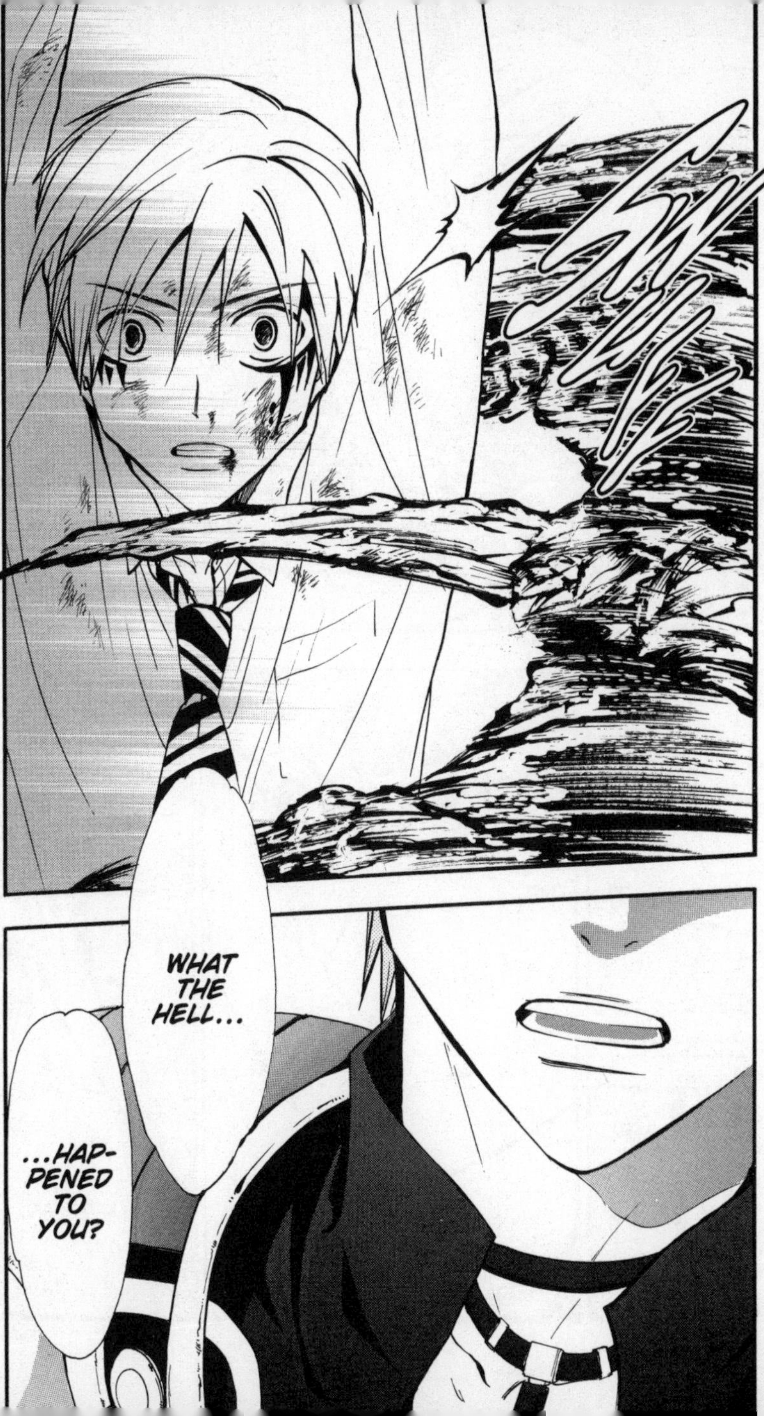
WHAT THE HELL...
...HAP-PENED TO YOU?

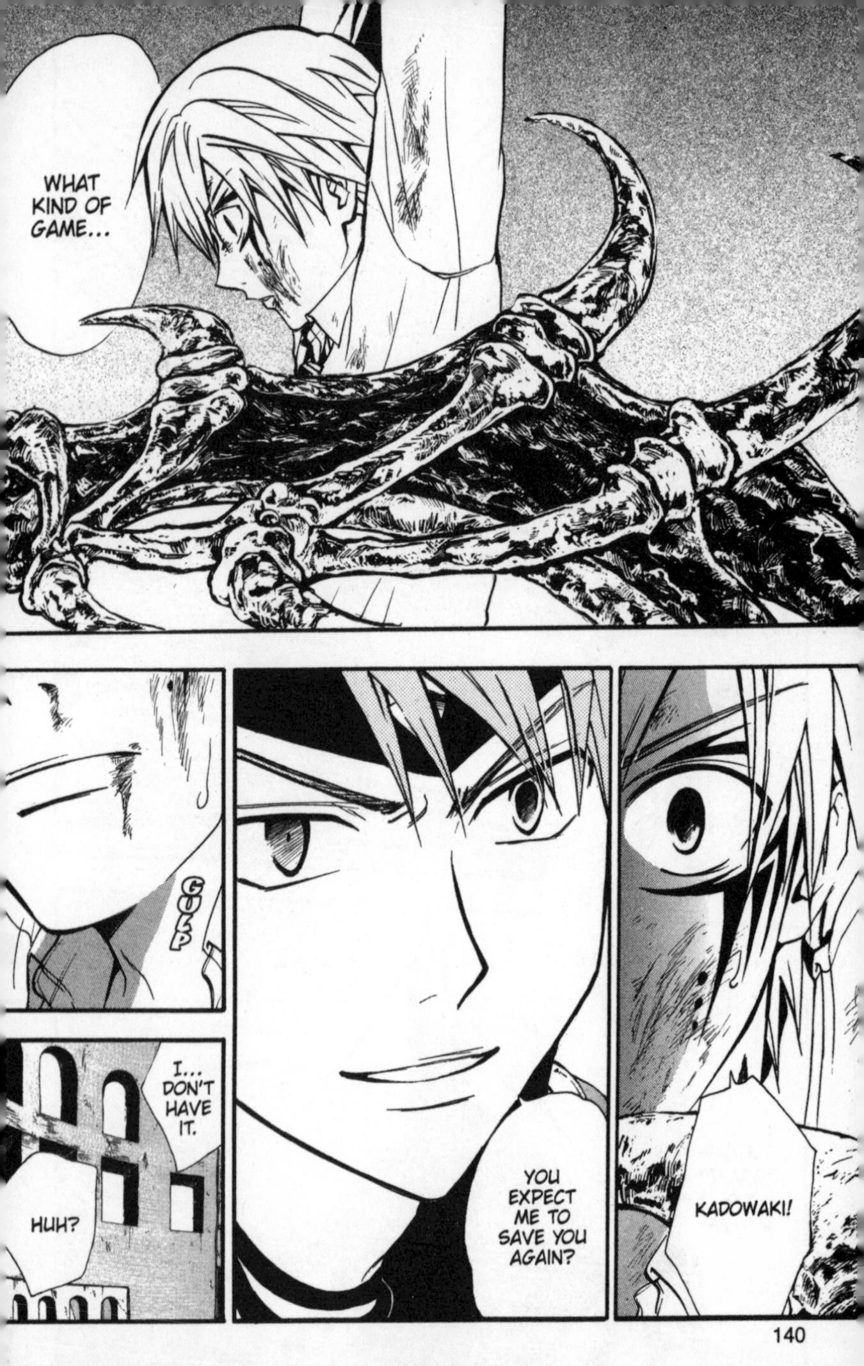
WHAT KIND OF GAME...
KADOWAKI!
YOU EXPECT ME TO SAVE YOU AGAIN?
GULP
I... DON'T HAVE IT.
HUH?

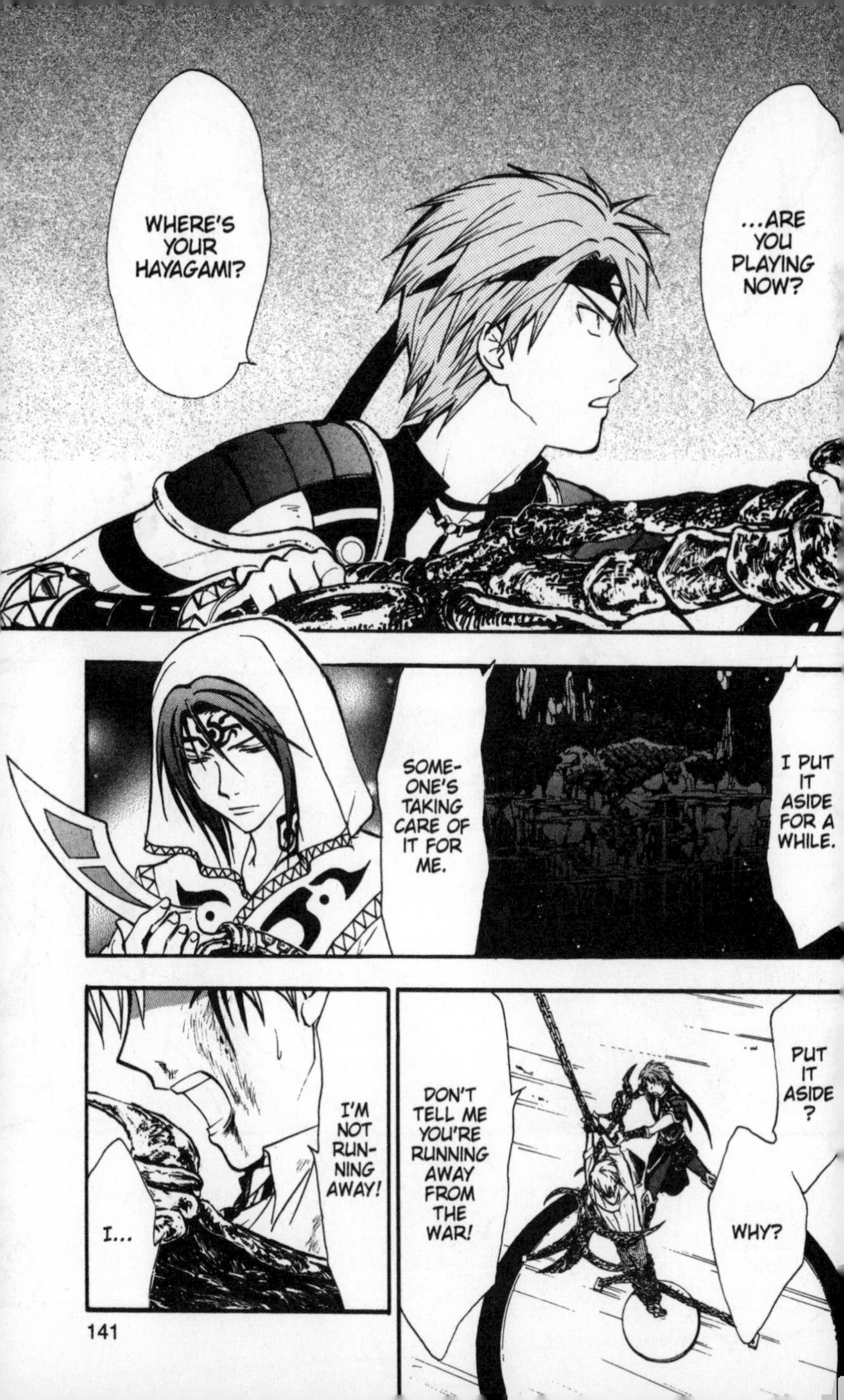
...ARE YOU PLAYING NOW?
WHERE'S YOUR HAYAGAMI?
I PUT IT ASIDE FOR A WHILE.
SOMEONE'S TAKING CARE OF IT FOR ME.
PUT IT ASIDE?
WHY?
DON'T TELL ME YOU'RE RUNNING AWAY FROM THE WAR!
I'M NOT RUNNING AWAY!
I...

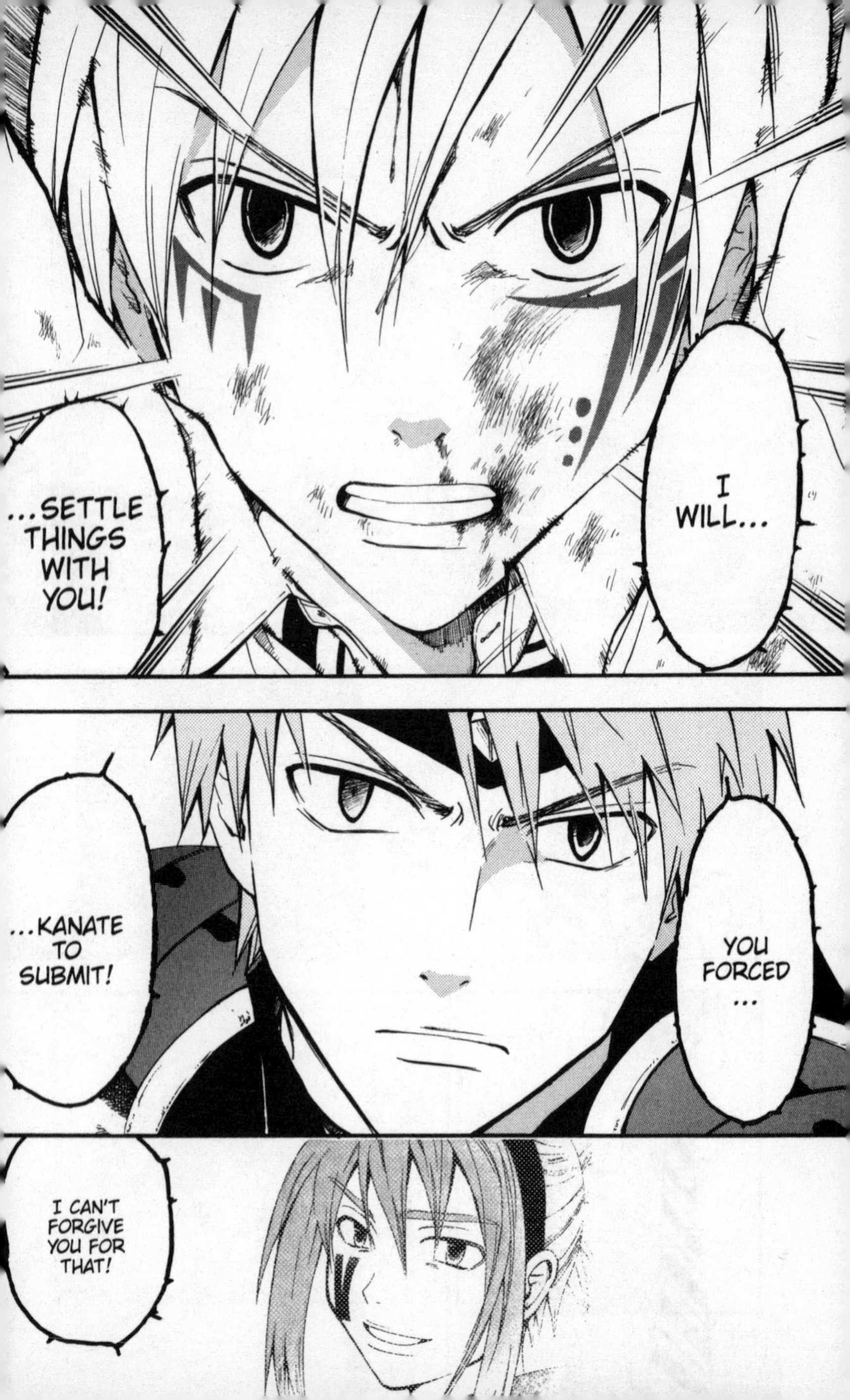
I WILL...
...SETTLE THINGS WITH YOU!
YOU FORCED ...
...KANATE TO SUBMIT!
I CAN'T FORGIVE YOU FOR THAT!

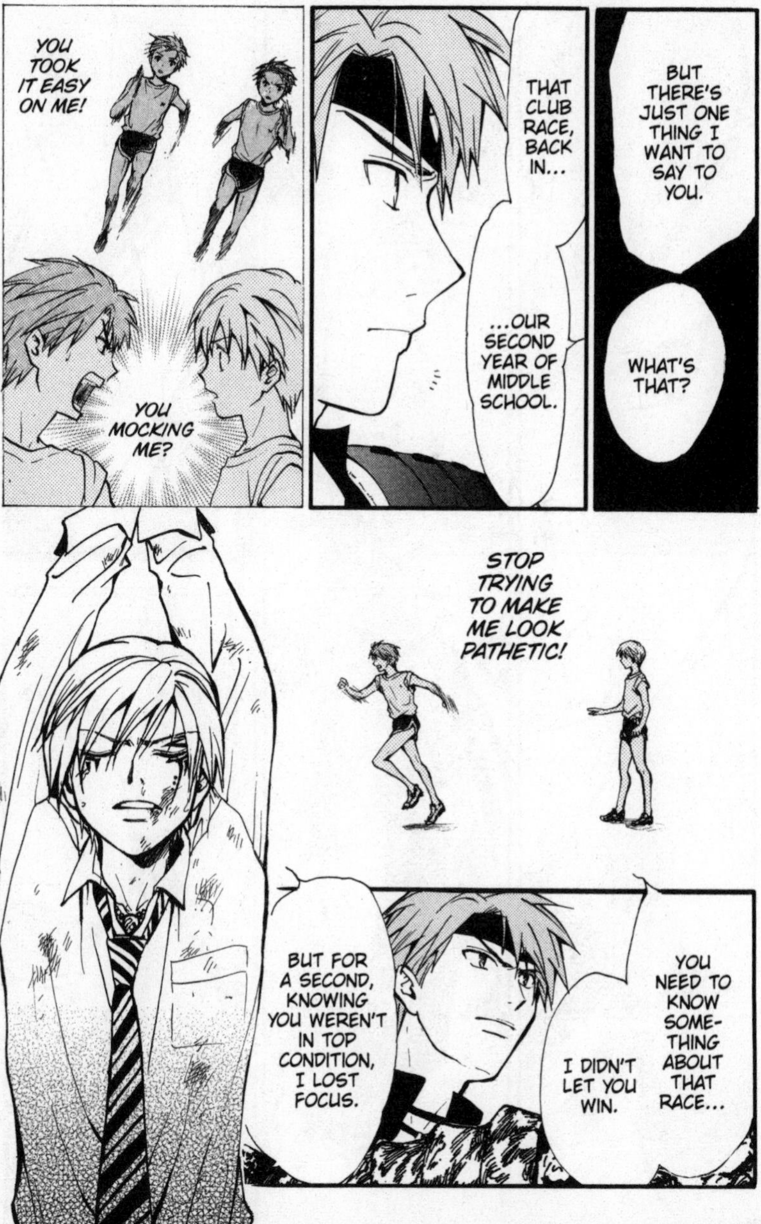
BUT THERE'S JUST ONE THING I WANT TO SAY TO YOU.
WHAT'S THAT?
THAT CLUB RACE, BACK IN...
...OUR SECOND YEAR OF MIDDLE SCHOOL.
YOU TOOK IT EASY ON ME!
YOU MOCKING ME?
STOP TRYING TO MAKE ME LOOK PATHETIC!
YOU NEED TO KNOW SOME-THING ABOUT THAT RACE...
I DIDN'T LET YOU WIN.
BUT FOR A SECOND, KNOWING YOU WEREN'T IN TOP CONDITION, I LOST FOCUS.

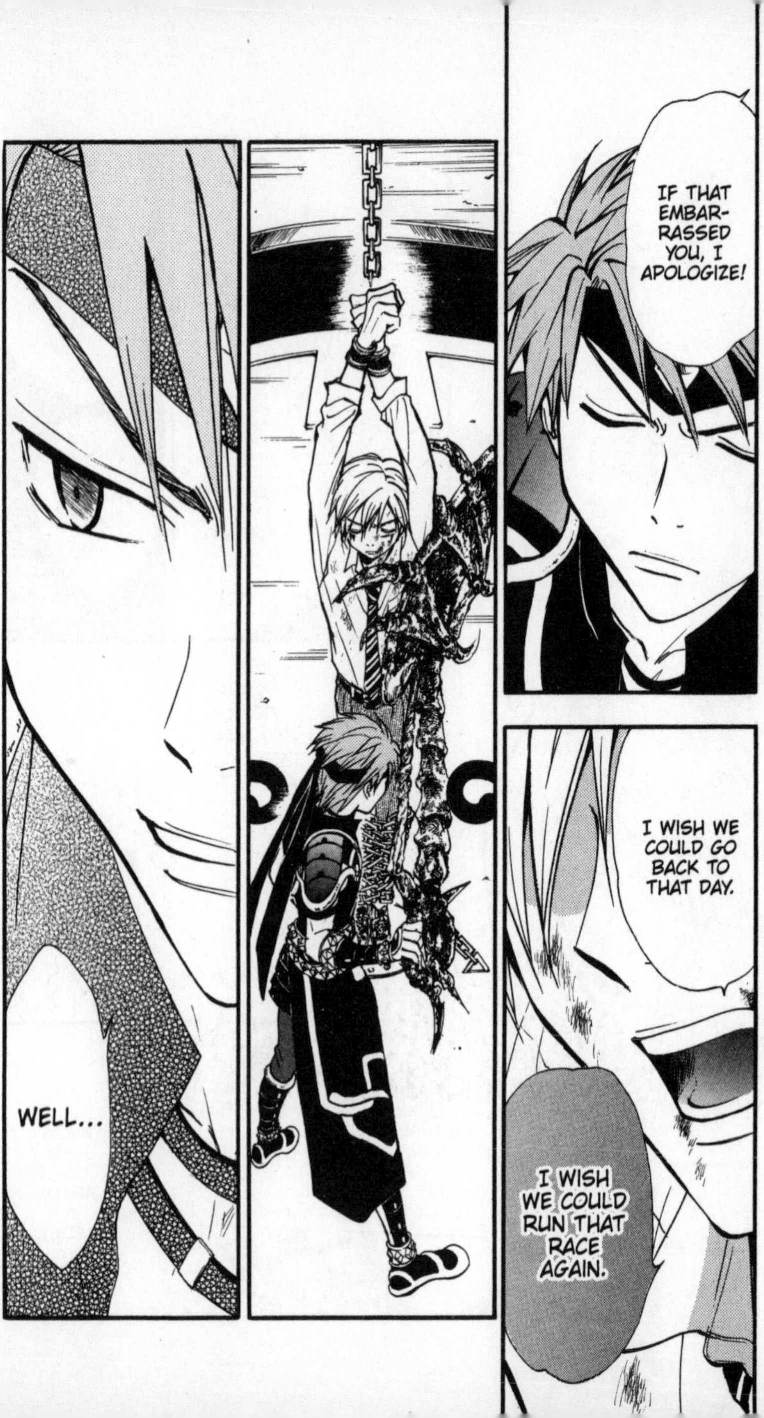
IF THAT EMBARRASSED YOU, I APOLOGIZE!
I WISH WE COULD GO BACK TO THAT DAY.
I WISH WE COULD RUN THAT RACE AGAIN.
WELL...

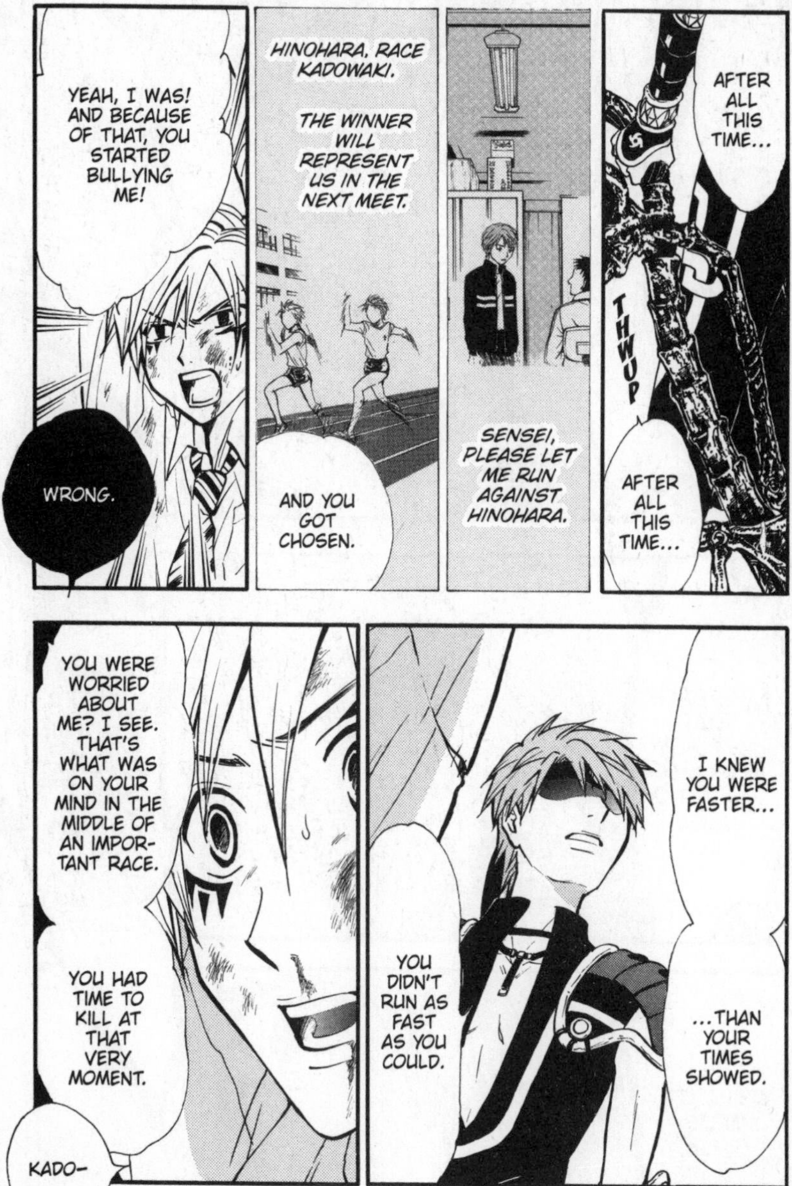
AFTER ALL THIS TIME...
THWUP
AFTER ALL THIS TIME...
SENSEI, PLEASE LET ME RUN AGAINST HINOHARA.
HINOHARA. RACE KADOWAKI.
THE WINNER WILL REPRESENT US IN THE NEXT MEET.
AND YOU GOT CHOSEN.
YEAH, I WAS! AND BECAUSE OF THAT, YOU STARTED BULLYING ME!
WRONG.
I KNEW YOU WERE FASTER...
...THAN YOUR TIMES SHOWED.
YOU DIDN'T RUN AS FAST AS YOU COULD.
YOU WERE WORRIED ABOUT ME? I SEE. THAT'S WHAT WAS ON YOUR MIND IN THE MIDDLE OF AN IMPORTANT RACE.
YOU HAD TIME TO KILL AT THAT VERY MOMENT.
KADO-

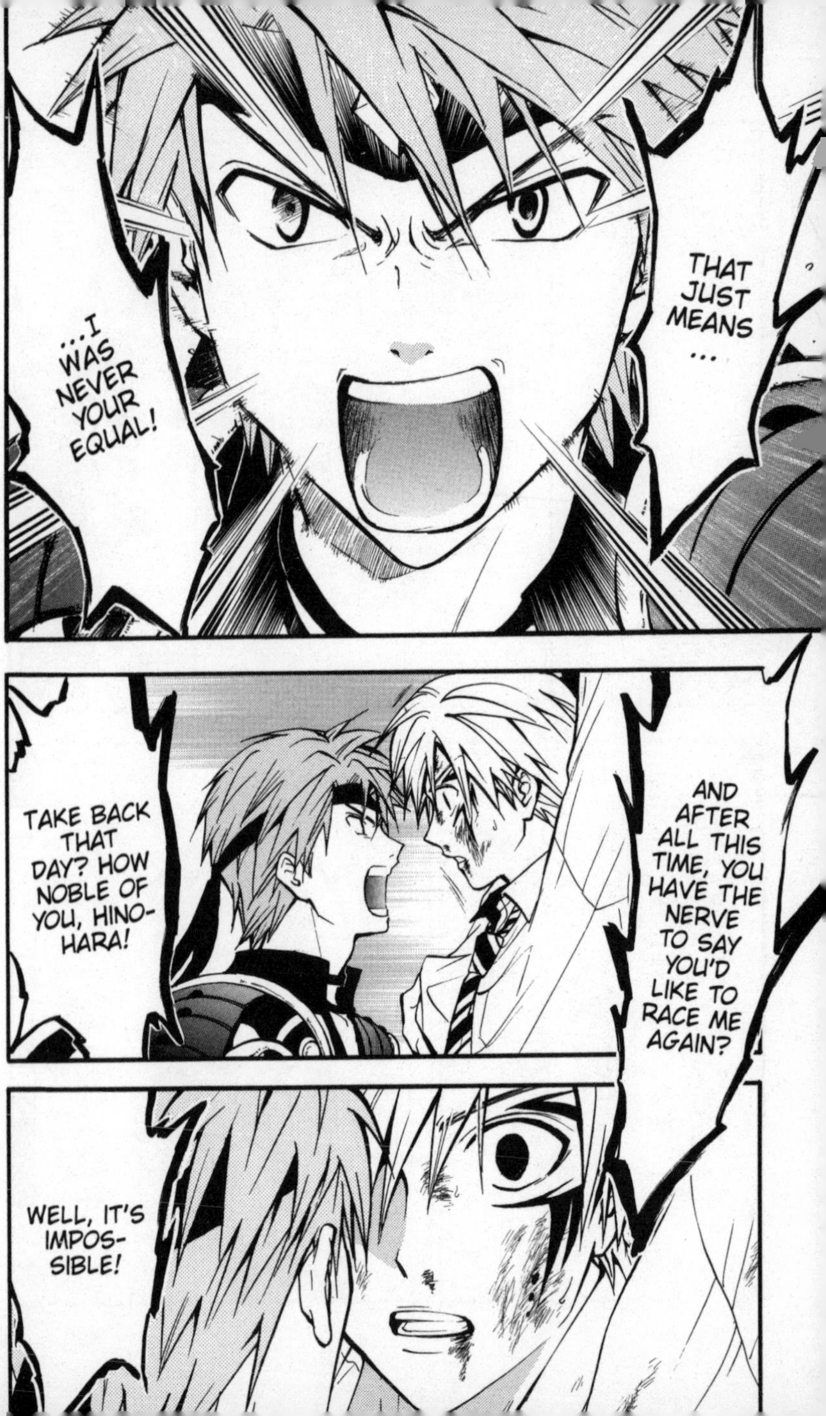
THAT JUST MEANS...
...I WAS NEVER YOUR EQUAL!
AND AFTER ALL THIS TIME, YOU HAVE THE NERVE TO SAY YOU'D LIKE TO RACE ME AGAIN?
TAKE BACK THAT DAY? HOW NOBLE OF YOU, HINO-HARA!
WELL, IT'S IMPOS-SIBLE!

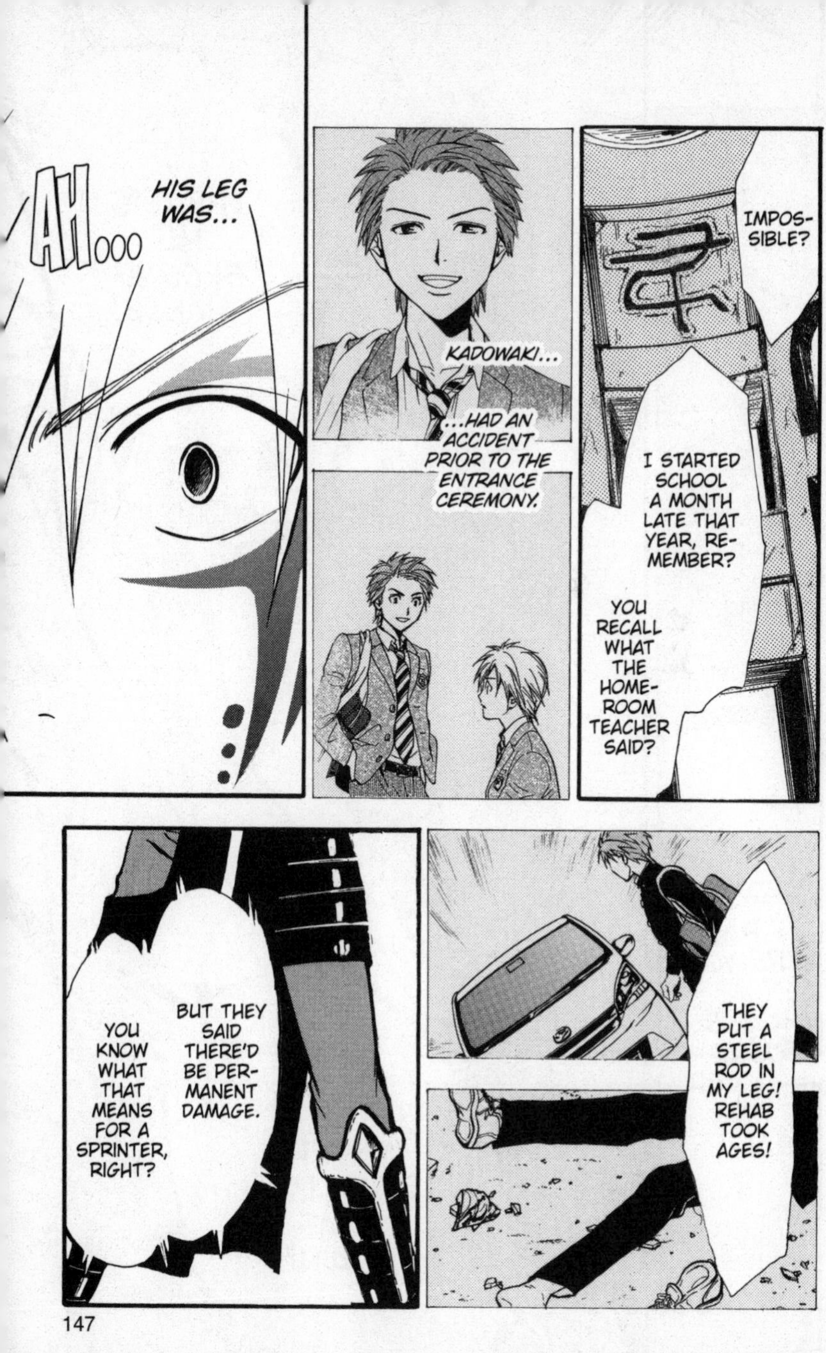
IMPOSSIBLE?
I STARTED SCHOOL A MONTH LATE THAT YEAR, REMEMBER?
YOU RECALL WHAT THE HOMEROOM TEACHER SAID?
KADOWAKI...
...HAD AN ACCIDENT PRIOR TO THE ENTRANCE CEREMONY.
HIS LEG WAS...
AHooo
THEY PUT A STEEL ROD IN MY LEG! REHAB TOOK AGES!
BUT THEY SAID THERE'D BE PERMANENT DAMAGE.
YOU KNOW WHAT THAT MEANS FOR A SPRINTER, RIGHT?

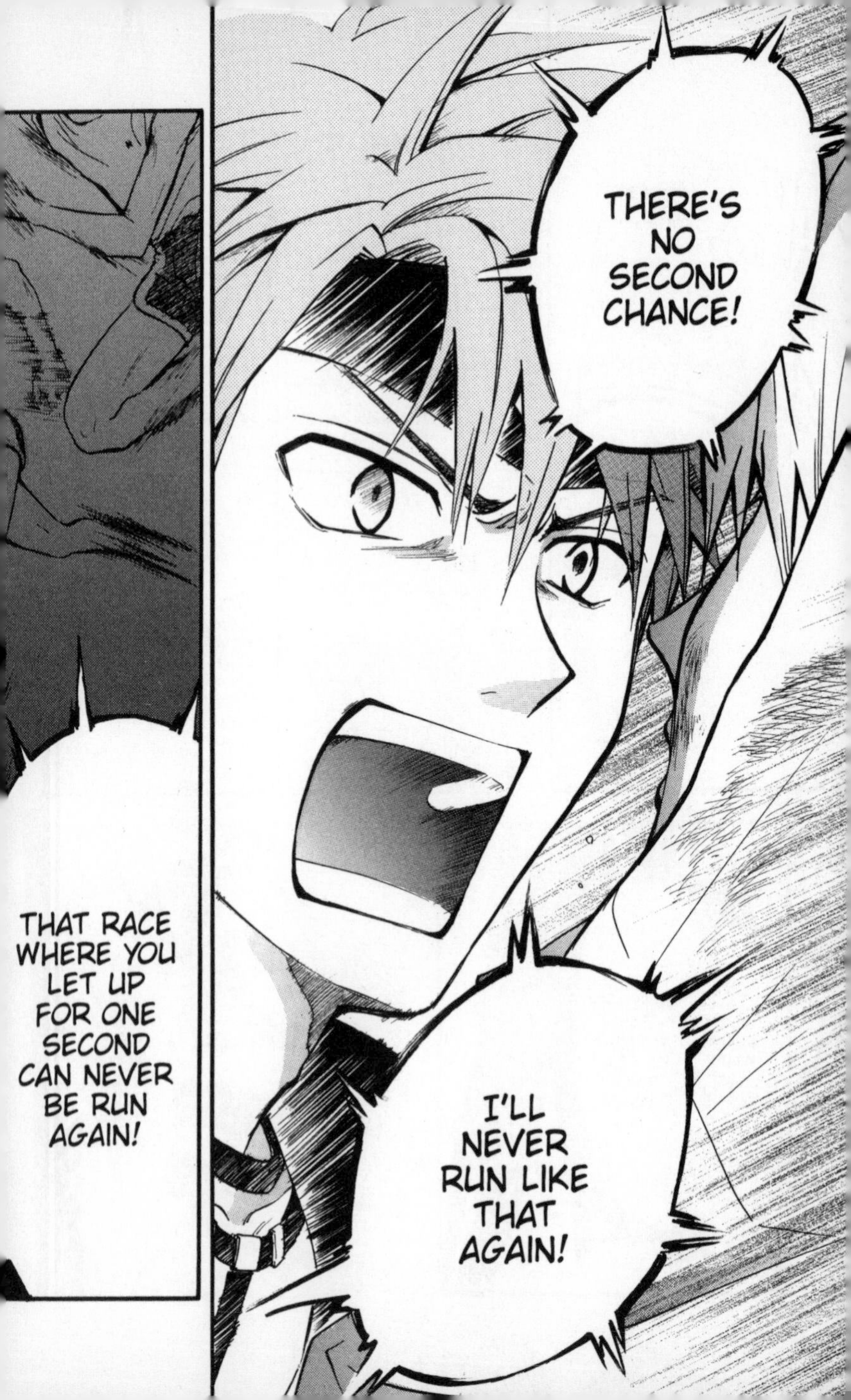
THERE'S NO SECOND CHANCE!
I'LL NEVER RUN LIKE THAT AGAIN!
THAT RACE WHERE YOU LET UP FOR ONE SECOND CAN NEVER BE RUN AGAIN!

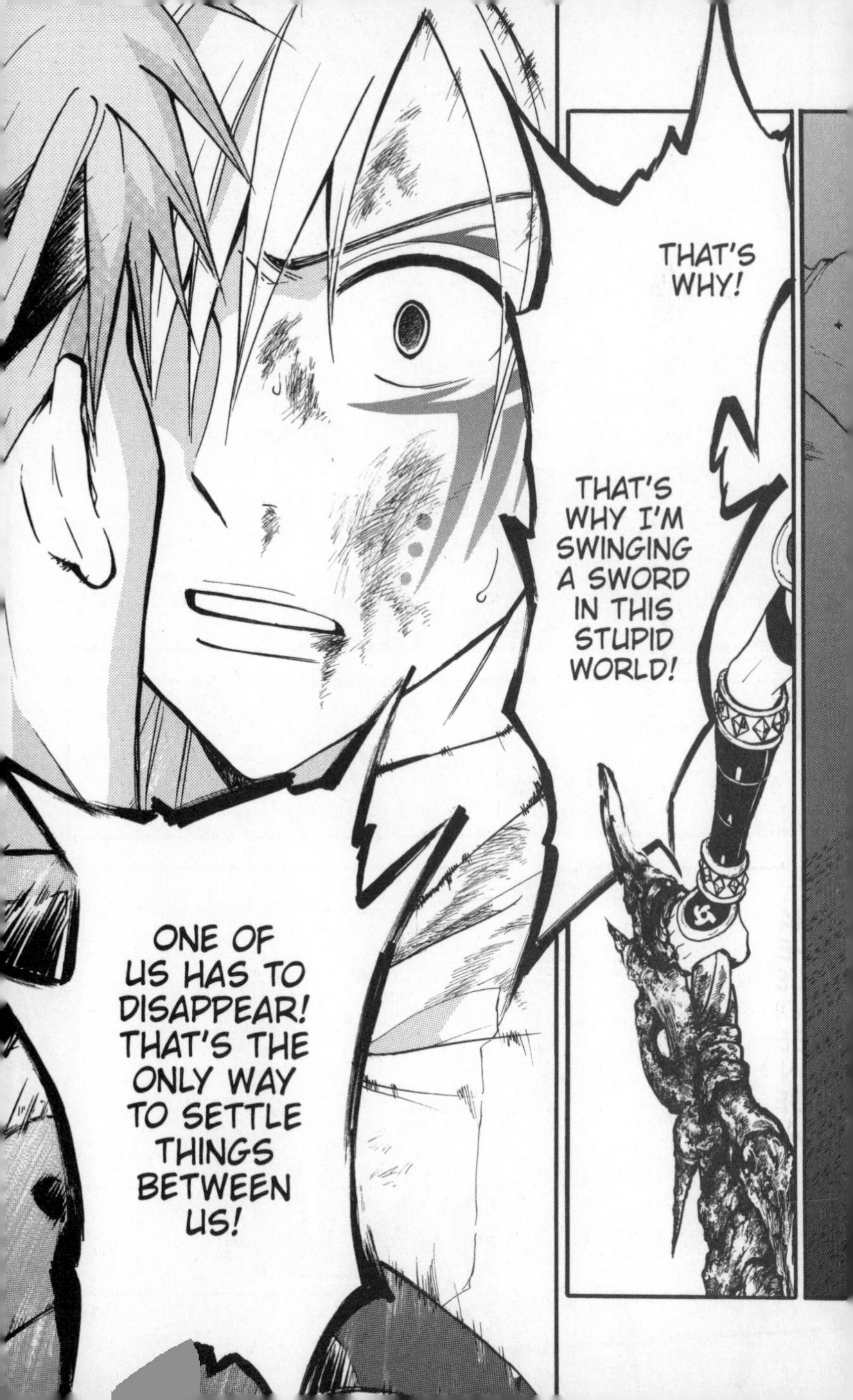
THAT'S WHY!
THAT'S WHY I'M SWINGING A SWORD IN THIS STUPID WORLD!
ONE OF US HAS TO DISAPPEAR! THAT'S THE ONLY WAY TO SETTLE THINGS BETWEEN US!

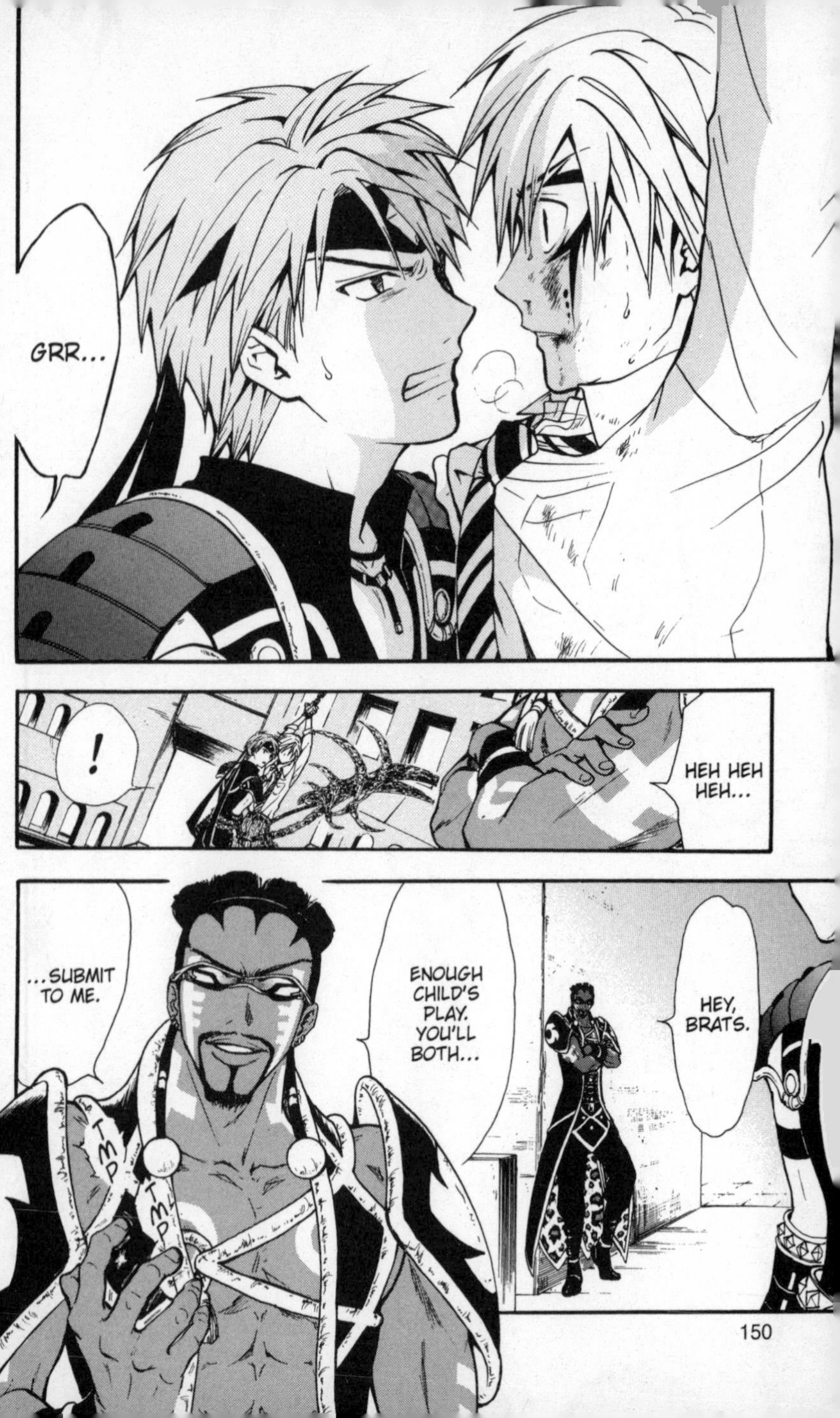
GRR...
HEH HEH HEH...
!
HEY, BRATS.
ENOUGH CHILD'S PLAY. YOU'LL BOTH...
...SUBMIT TO ME.
TMP
TMP

Chapter 226
VICTORY OR DEFEAT

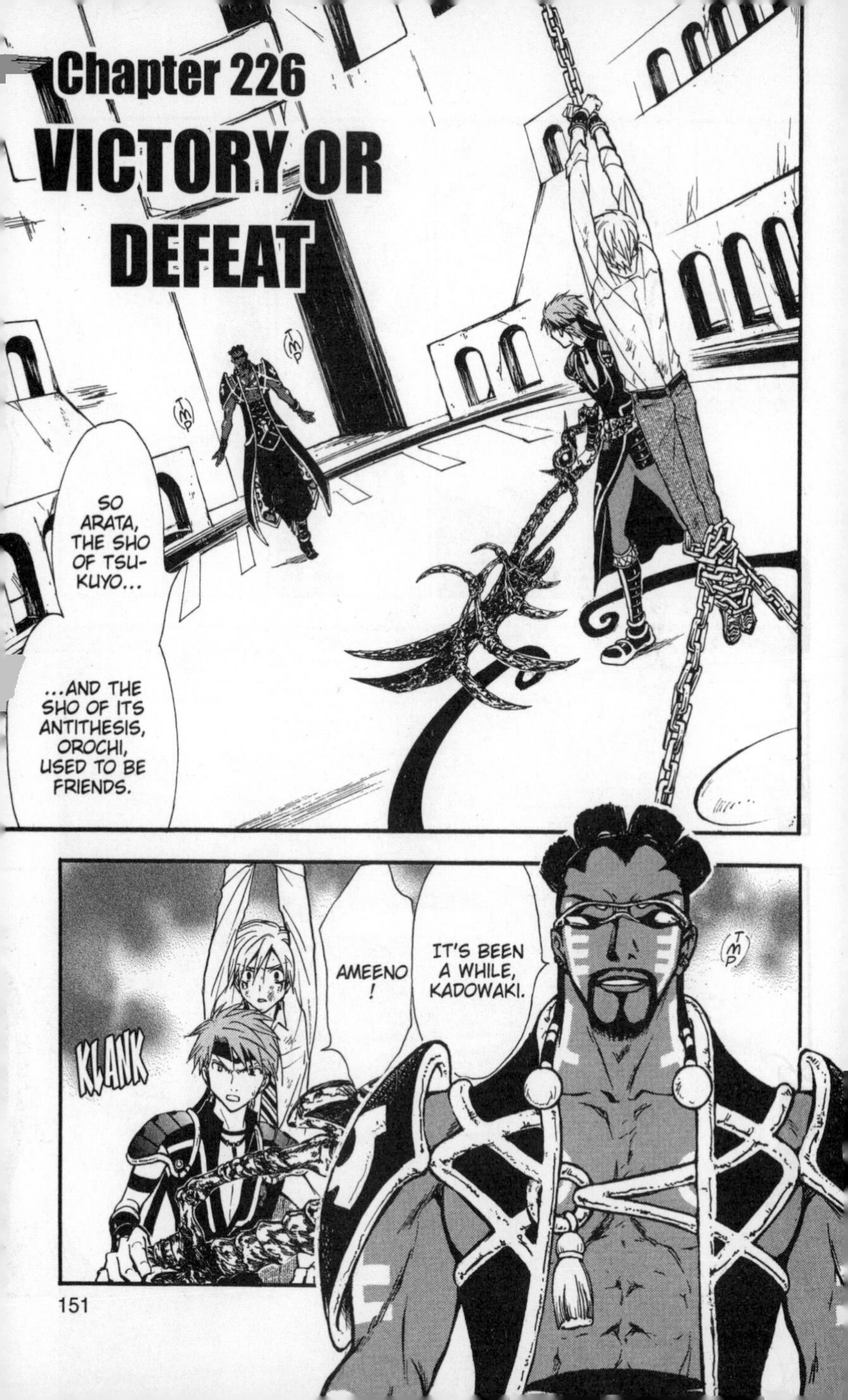
TMP
TMP
SO ARATA, THE SHO OF TSUKUYO...
...AND THE SHO OF ITS ANTITHESIS, OROCHI, USED TO BE FRIENDS.
TMP
IT'S BEEN A WHILE, KADOWAKI.
AMEENO!
KLANK

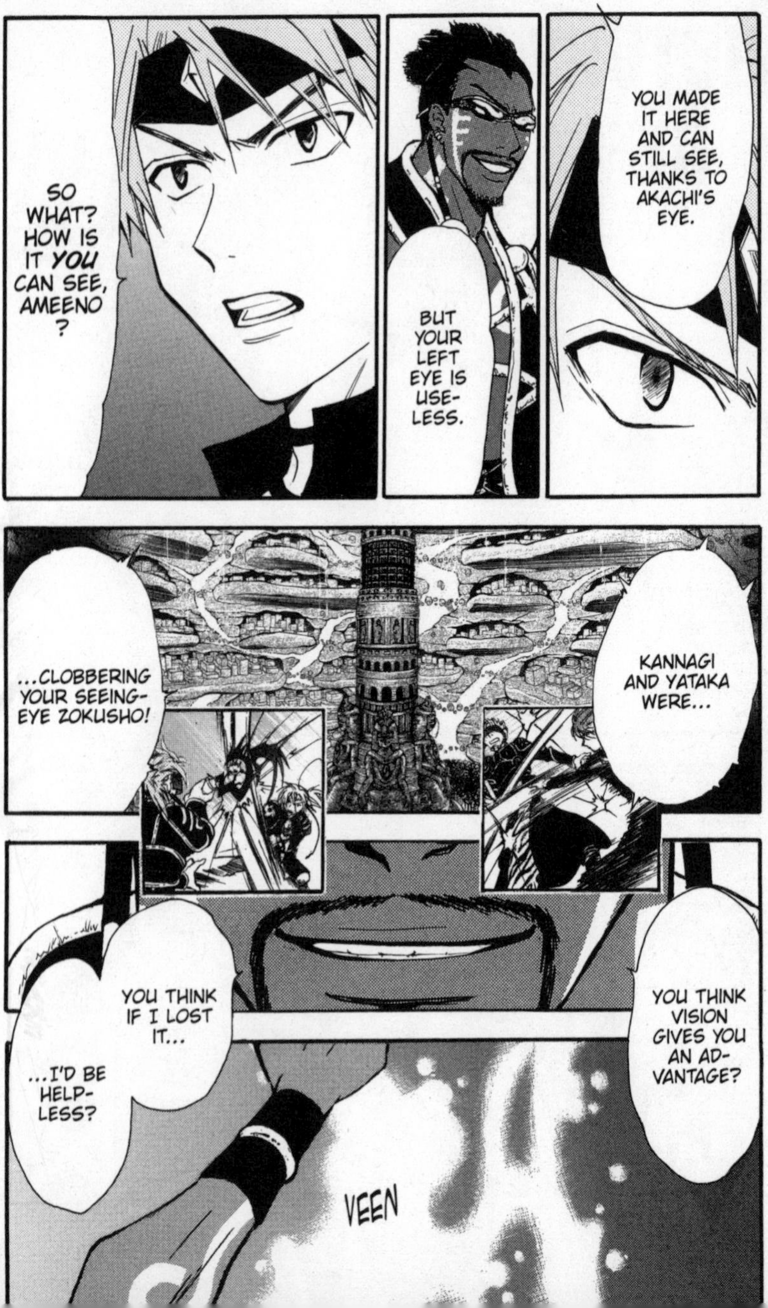
YOU MADE IT HERE AND CAN STILL SEE, THANKS TO AKACHI'S EYE.
BUT YOUR LEFT EYE IS USELESS.
SO WHAT? HOW IS IT *YOU* CAN SEE, AMEENO?
KANNAGI AND YATAKA WERE...
...CLOBBERING YOUR SEEING-EYE ZOKUSHO!
YOU THINK VISION GIVES YOU AN AD-VANTAGE?
YOU THINK IF I LOST IT...
...I'D BE HELP-LESS?
VEEN

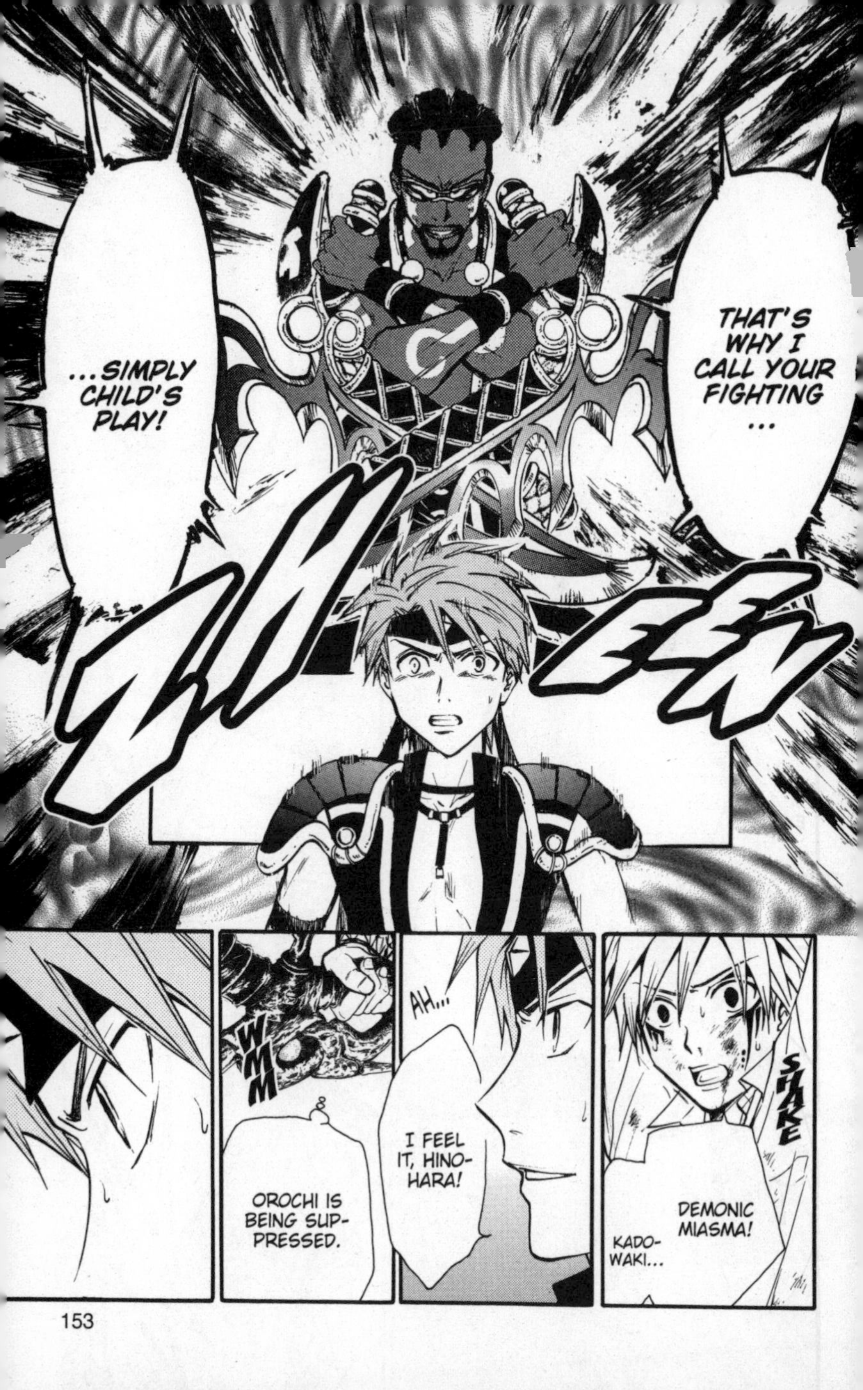
THAT'S WHY I CALL YOUR FIGHTING ...
...SIMPLY CHILD'S PLAY!
SHAKE
DEMONIC MIASMA!
KADO-WAKI...
AH...
I FEEL IT, HINO-HARA!
WMM
OROCHI IS BEING SUP-PRESSED.

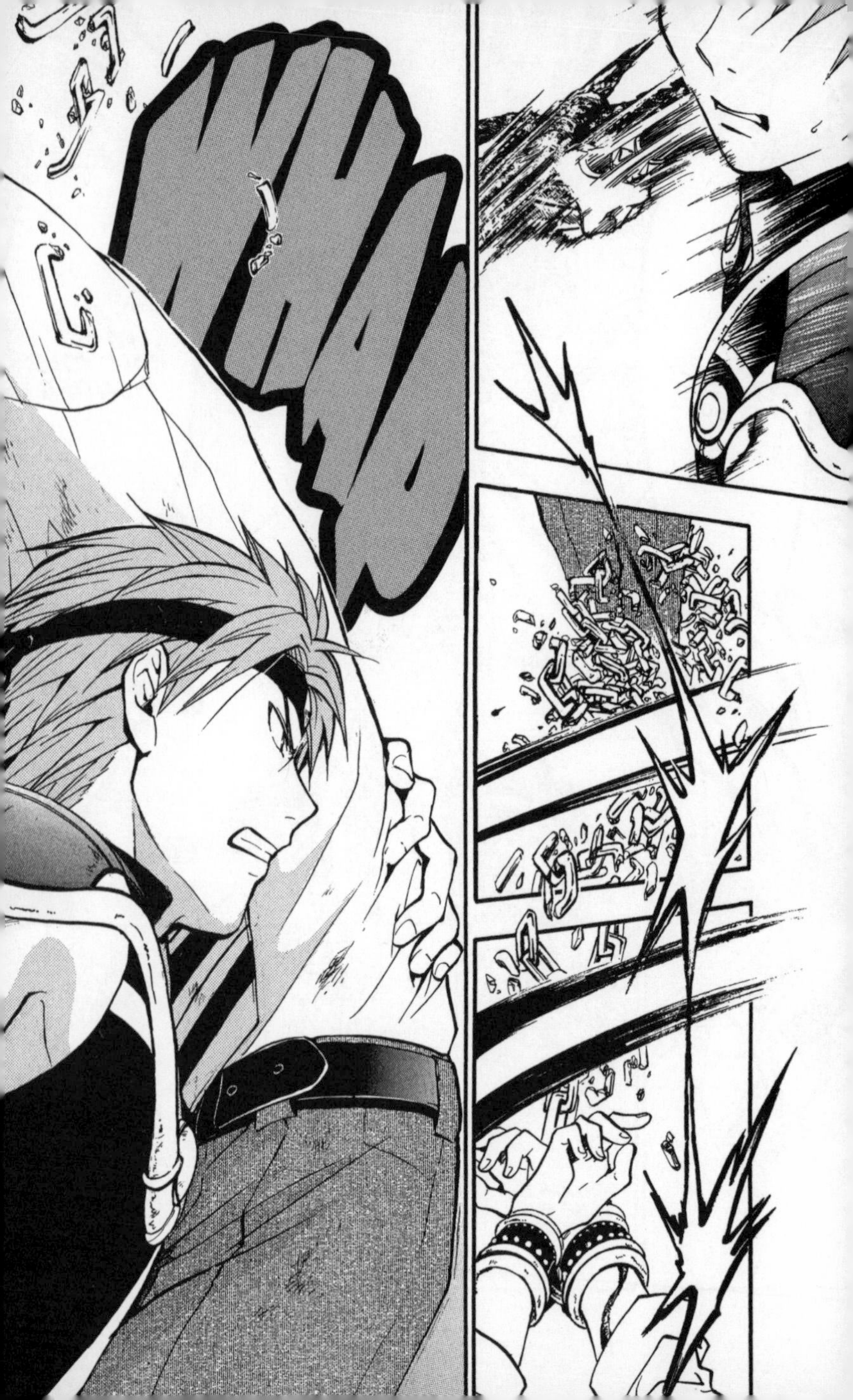
WHAP

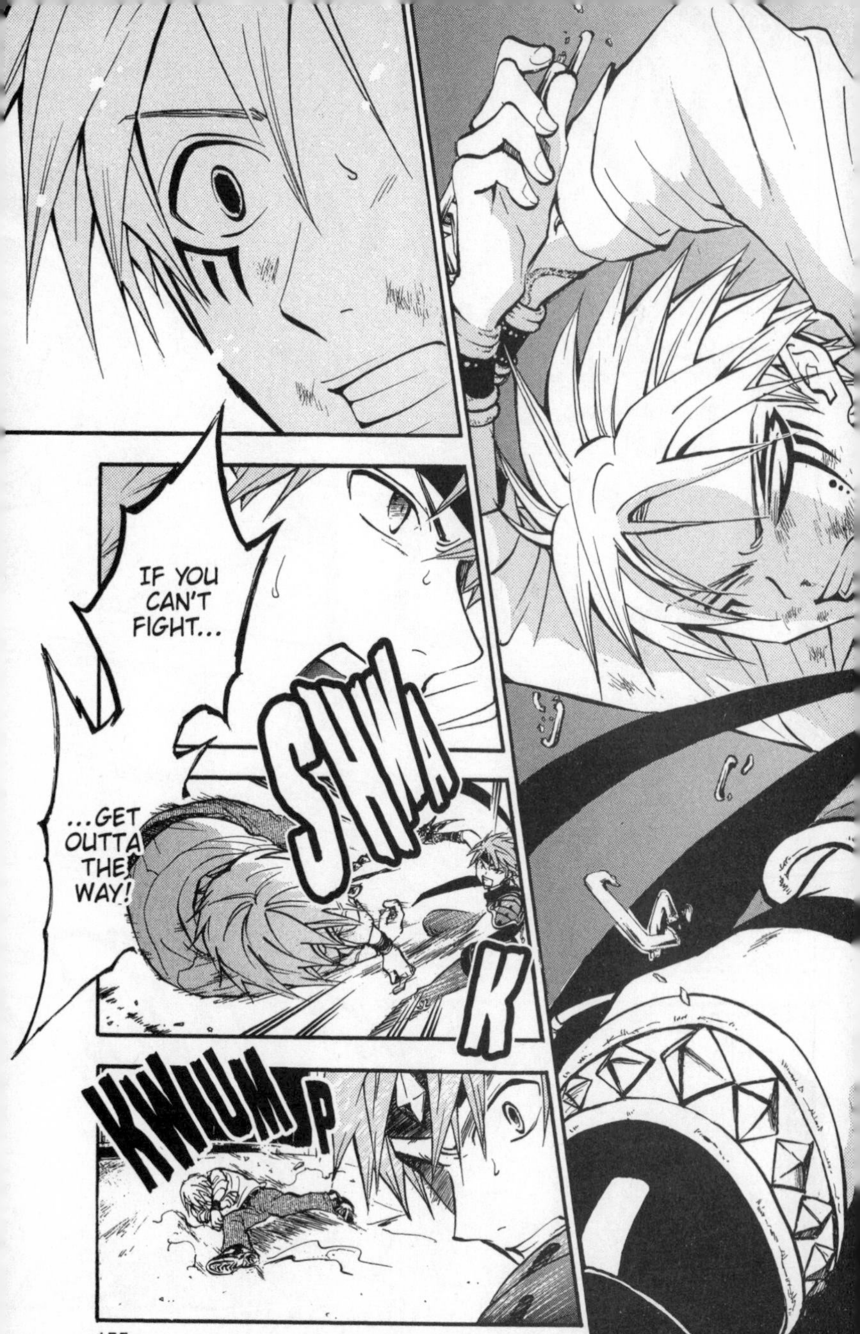
IF YOU CAN'T FIGHT...
...GET OUTTA THE WAY!
SHWAK
KWHUMP

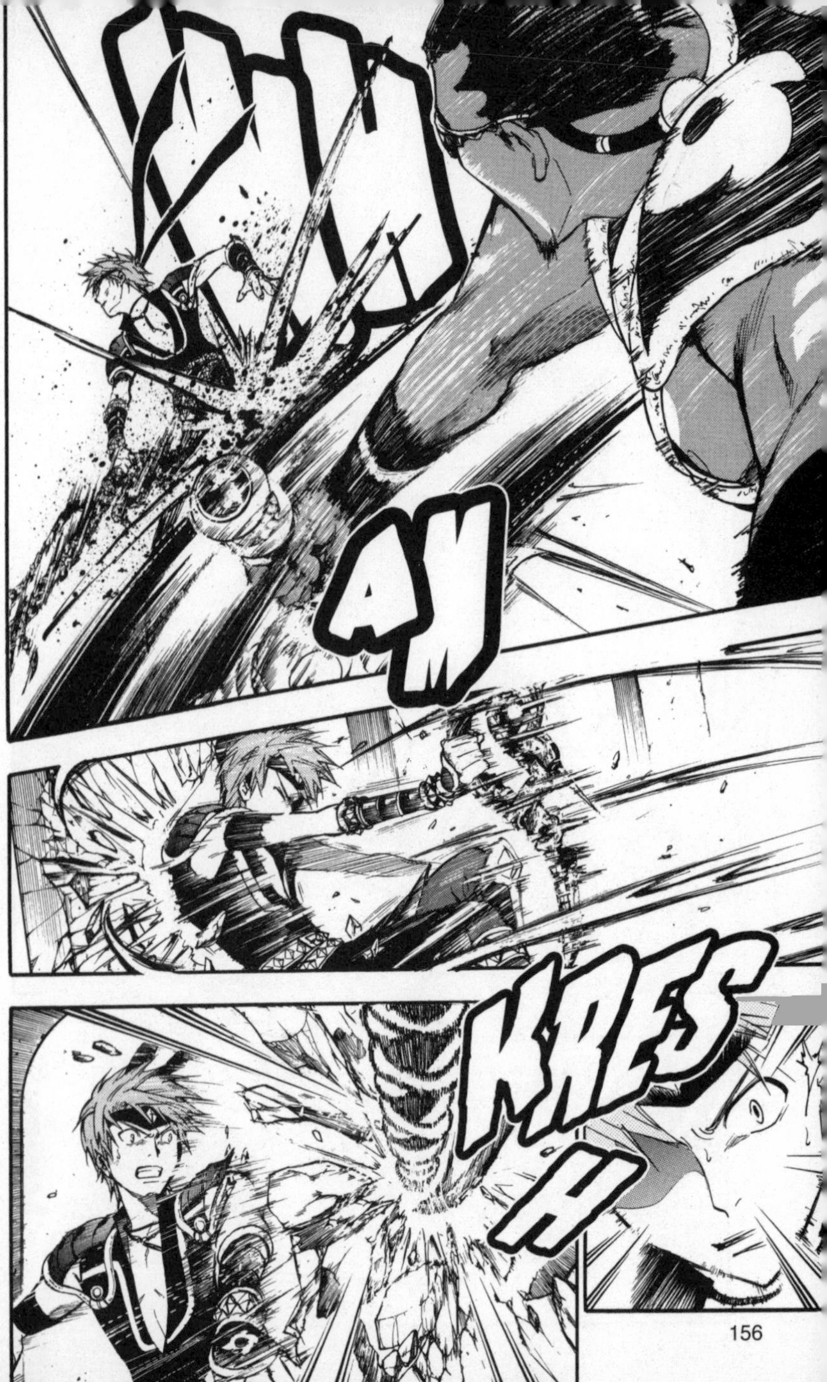
KRESH

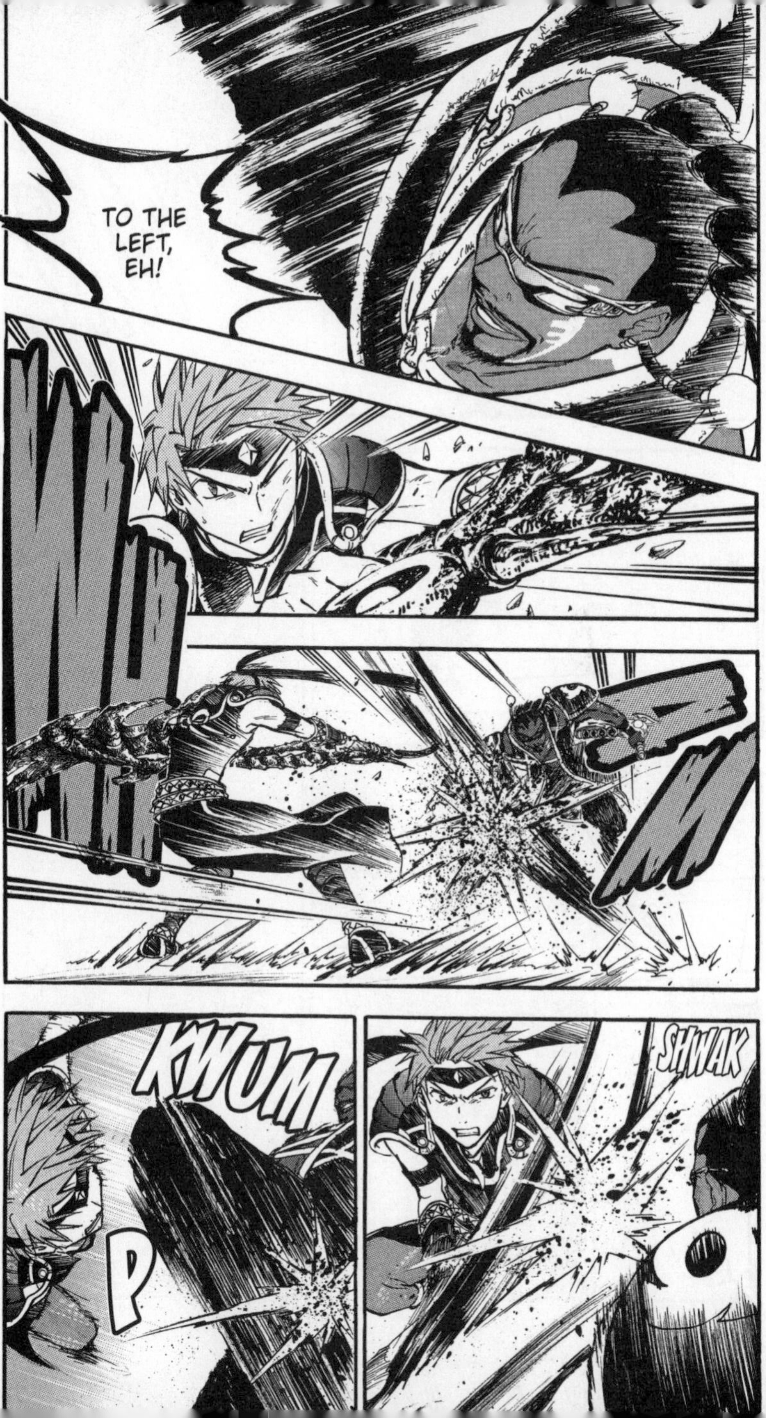
TO THE LEFT, EH!
SHWAK
KWUM
P

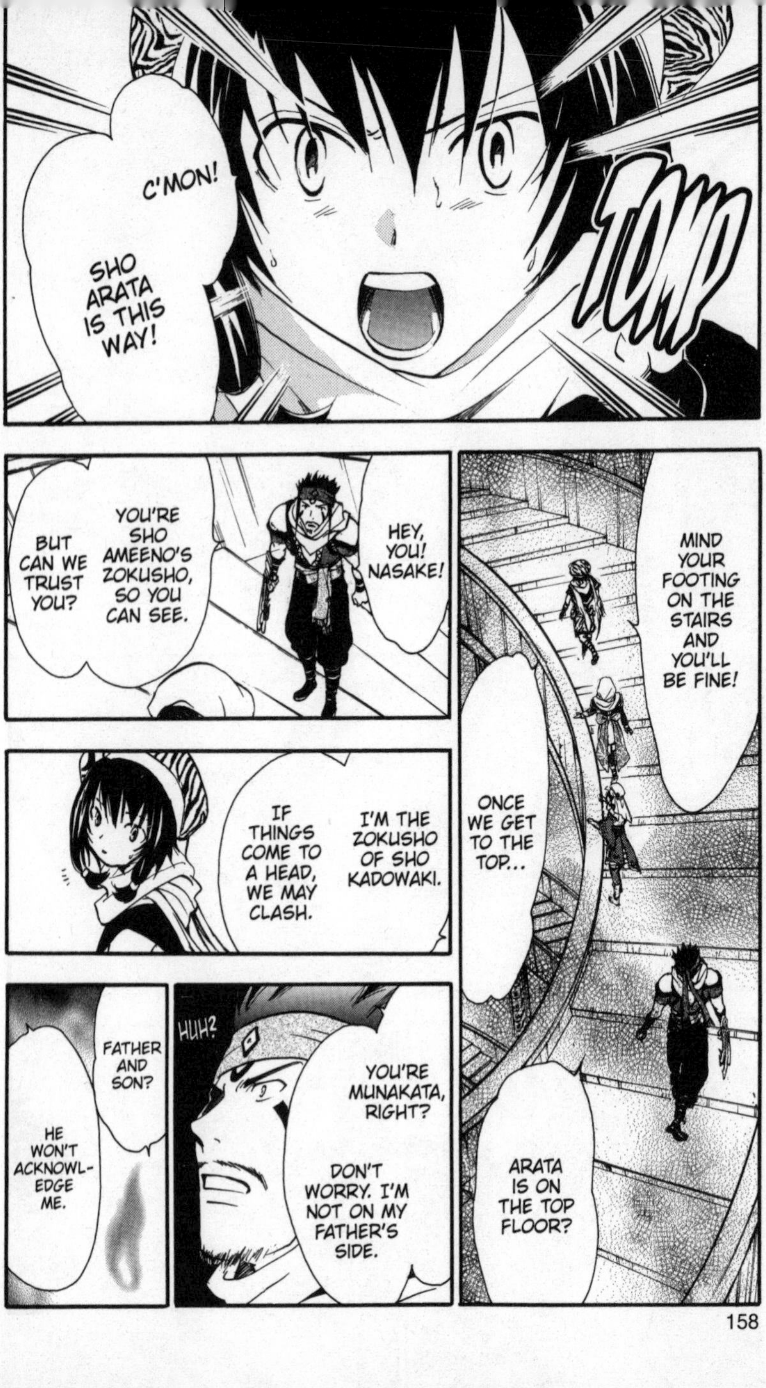
C'MON!
SHO ARATA IS THIS WAY!
TOMP
MIND YOUR FOOTING ON THE STAIRS AND YOU'LL BE FINE!
ONCE WE GET TO THE TOP...
ARATA IS ON THE TOP FLOOR?
HEY, YOU! NASAKE!
YOU'RE SHO AMEENO'S ZOKUSHO, SO YOU CAN SEE.
BUT CAN WE TRUST YOU?
I'M THE ZOKUSHO OF SHO KADOWAKI.
IF THINGS COME TO A HEAD, WE MAY CLASH.
HUH?
YOU'RE MUNAKATA, RIGHT?
DON'T WORRY. I'M NOT ON MY FATHER'S SIDE.
FATHER AND SON?
HE WON'T ACKNOWL-EDGE ME.

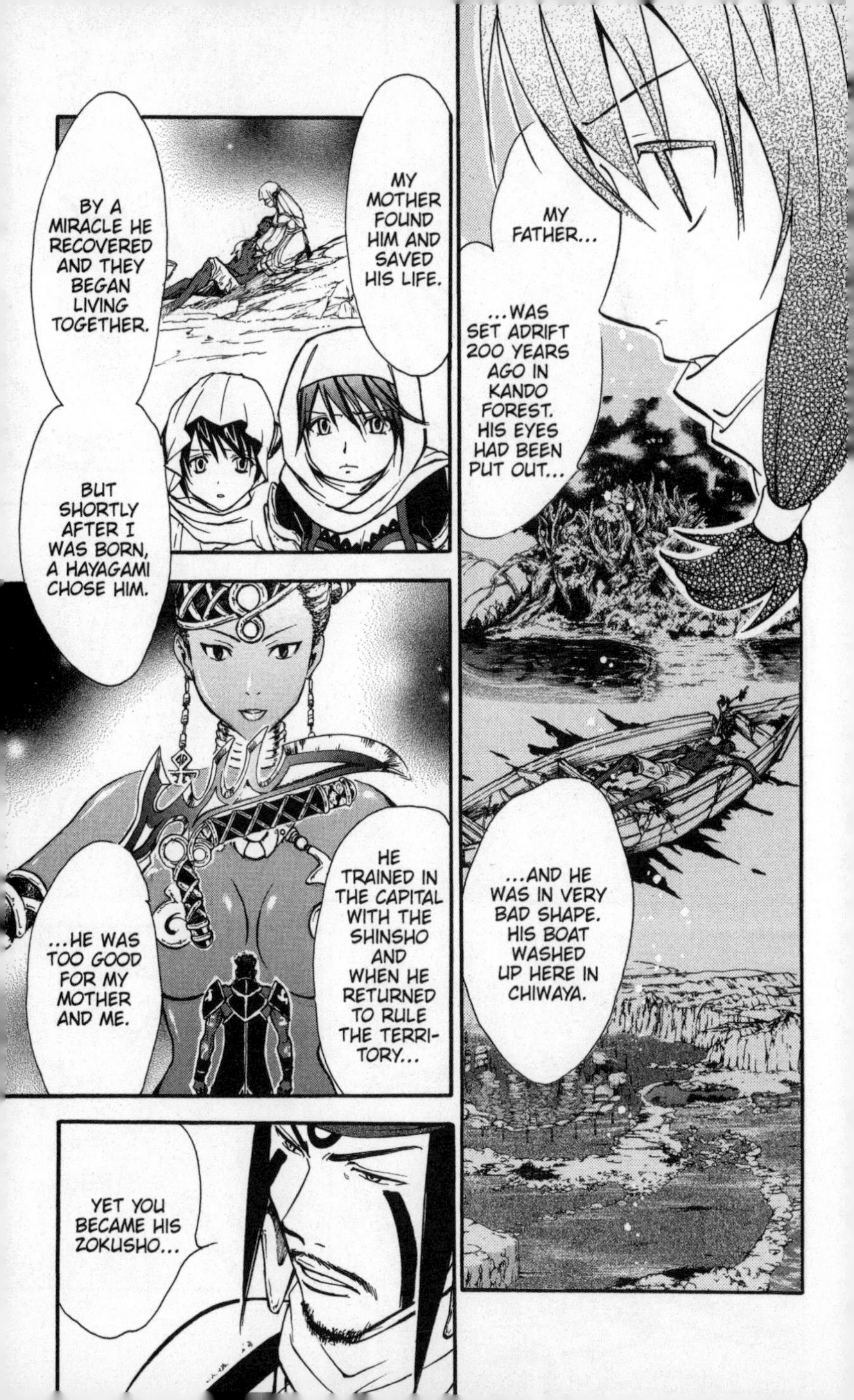
MY FATHER...
...WAS SET ADRIFT 200 YEARS AGO IN KANDO FOREST. HIS EYES HAD BEEN PUT OUT...
...AND HE WAS IN VERY BAD SHAPE. HIS BOAT WASHED UP HERE IN CHIWAYA.
MY MOTHER FOUND HIM AND SAVED HIS LIFE.
BY A MIRACLE HE RECOVERED AND THEY BEGAN LIVING TOGETHER.
BUT SHORTLY AFTER I WAS BORN, A HAYAGAMI CHOSE HIM.
HE TRAINED IN THE CAPITAL WITH THE SHINSHO AND WHEN HE RETURNED TO RULE THE TERRITORY...
...HE WAS TOO GOOD FOR MY MOTHER AND ME.
YET YOU BECAME HIS ZOKUSHO...

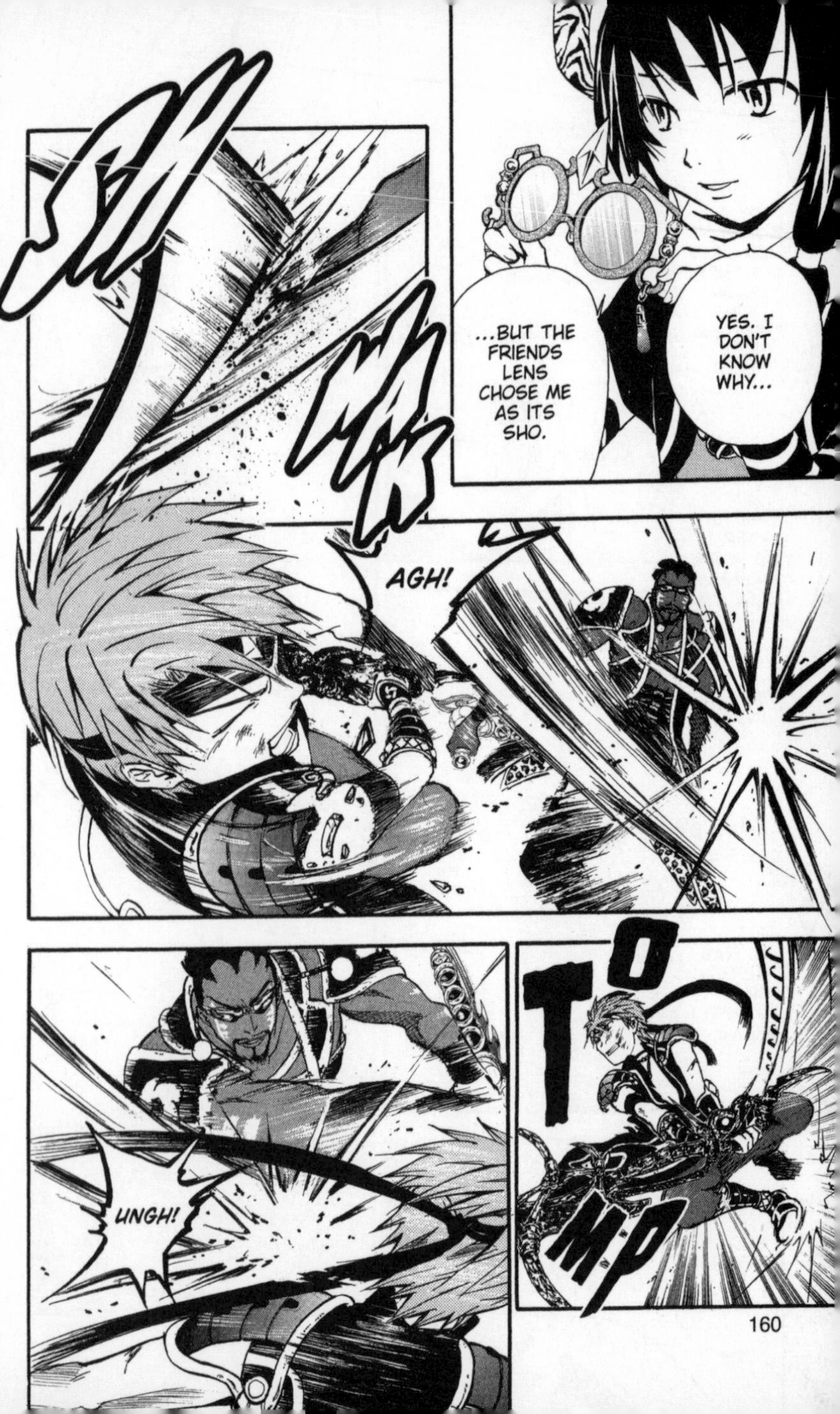
YES. I DON'T KNOW WHY...
...BUT THE FRIENDS LENS CHOSE ME AS ITS SHO.
AGH!
TOMP
UNGH!

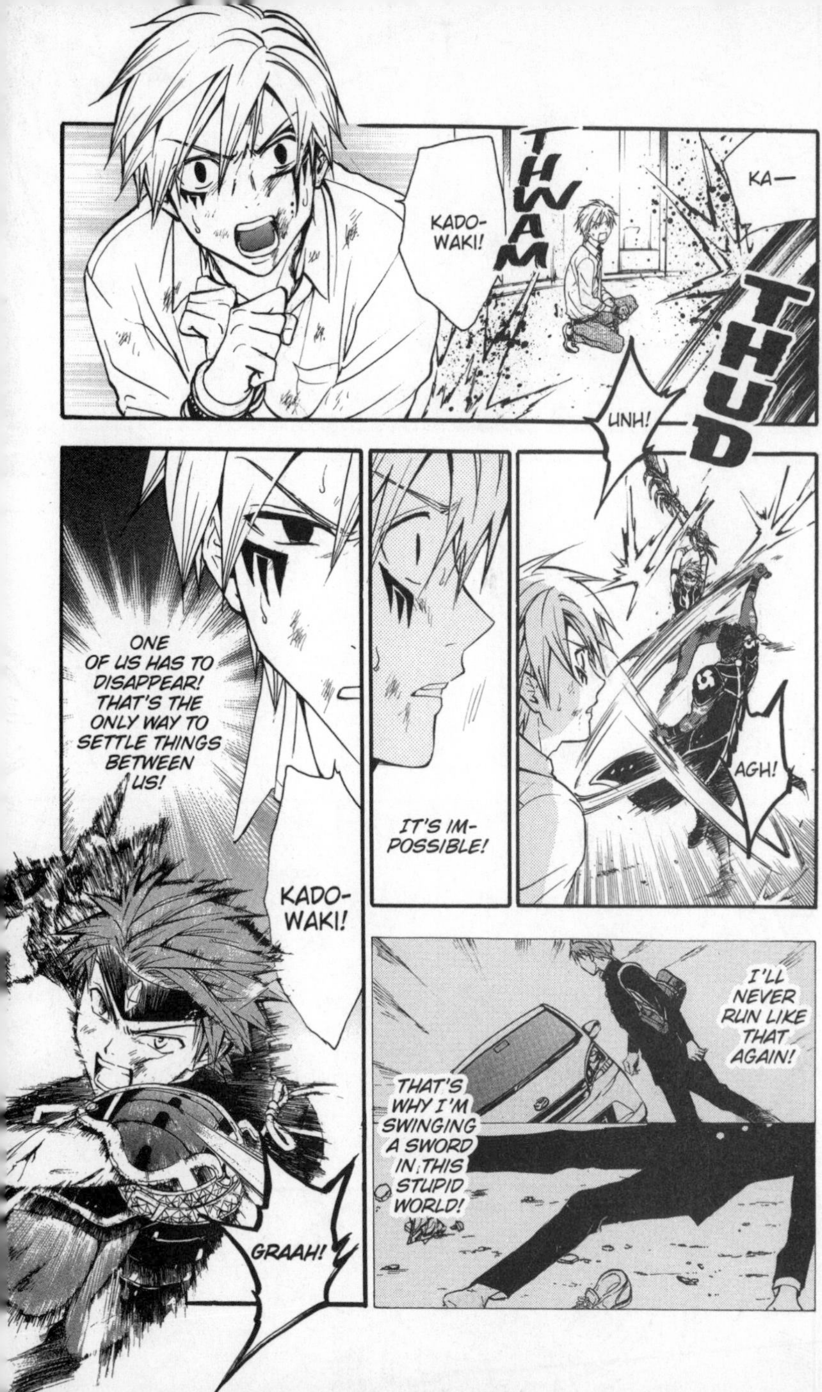
KA—
THUD
THWAM
KADO-WAKI!
UNH!
AGH!
IT'S IM-POSSIBLE!
I'LL NEVER RUN LIKE THAT AGAIN!
THAT'S WHY I'M SWINGING A SWORD IN THIS STUPID WORLD!
ONE OF US HAS TO DISAPPEAR! THAT'S THE ONLY WAY TO SETTLE THINGS BETWEEN US!
KADO-WAKI!
GRAAH!

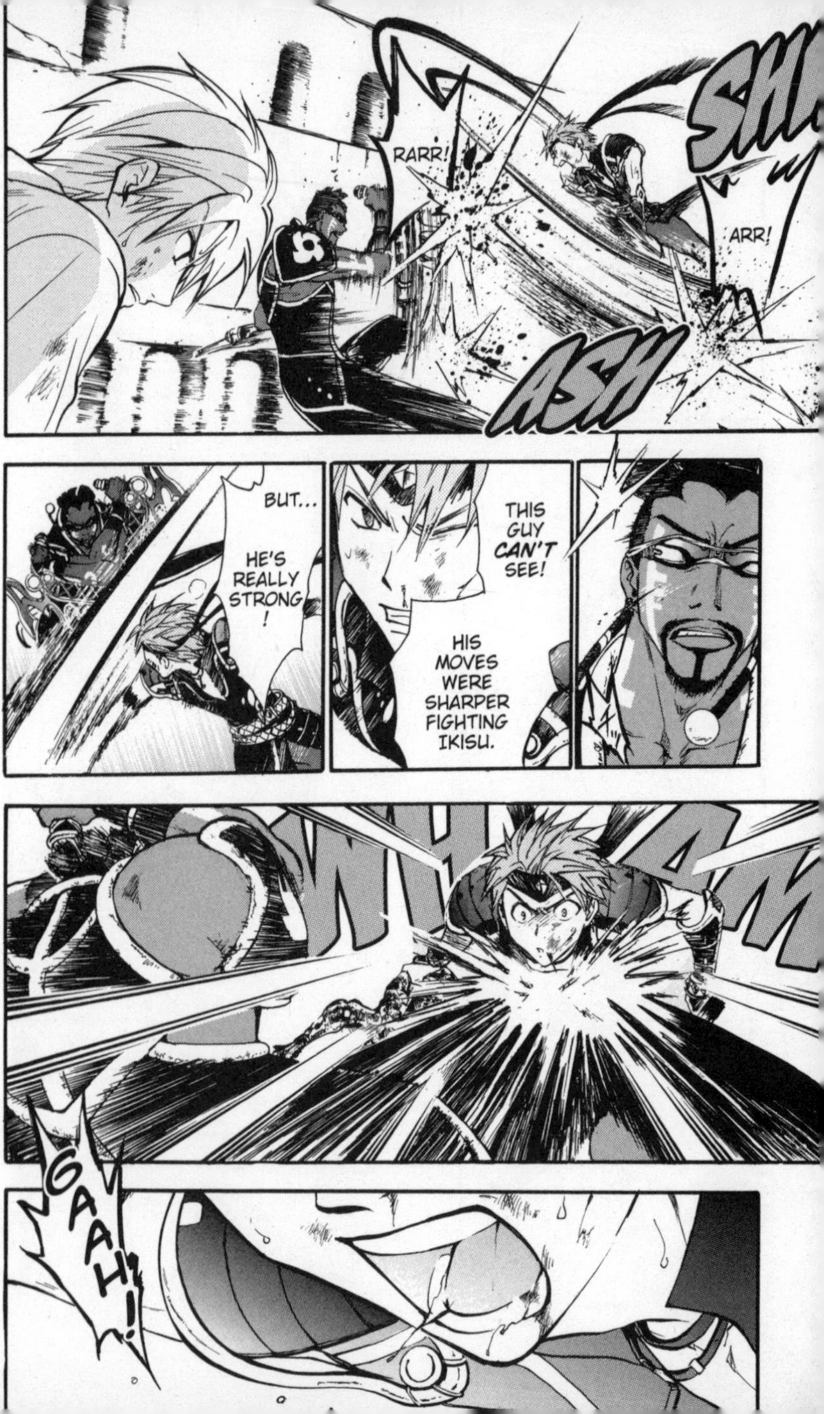
SH
ARR!
RARR!
ASH
THIS GUY *CAN'T* SEE!
HIS MOVES WERE SHARPER FIGHTING IKISU.
BUT...
HE'S REALLY STRONG!
WHAM
GAAH!

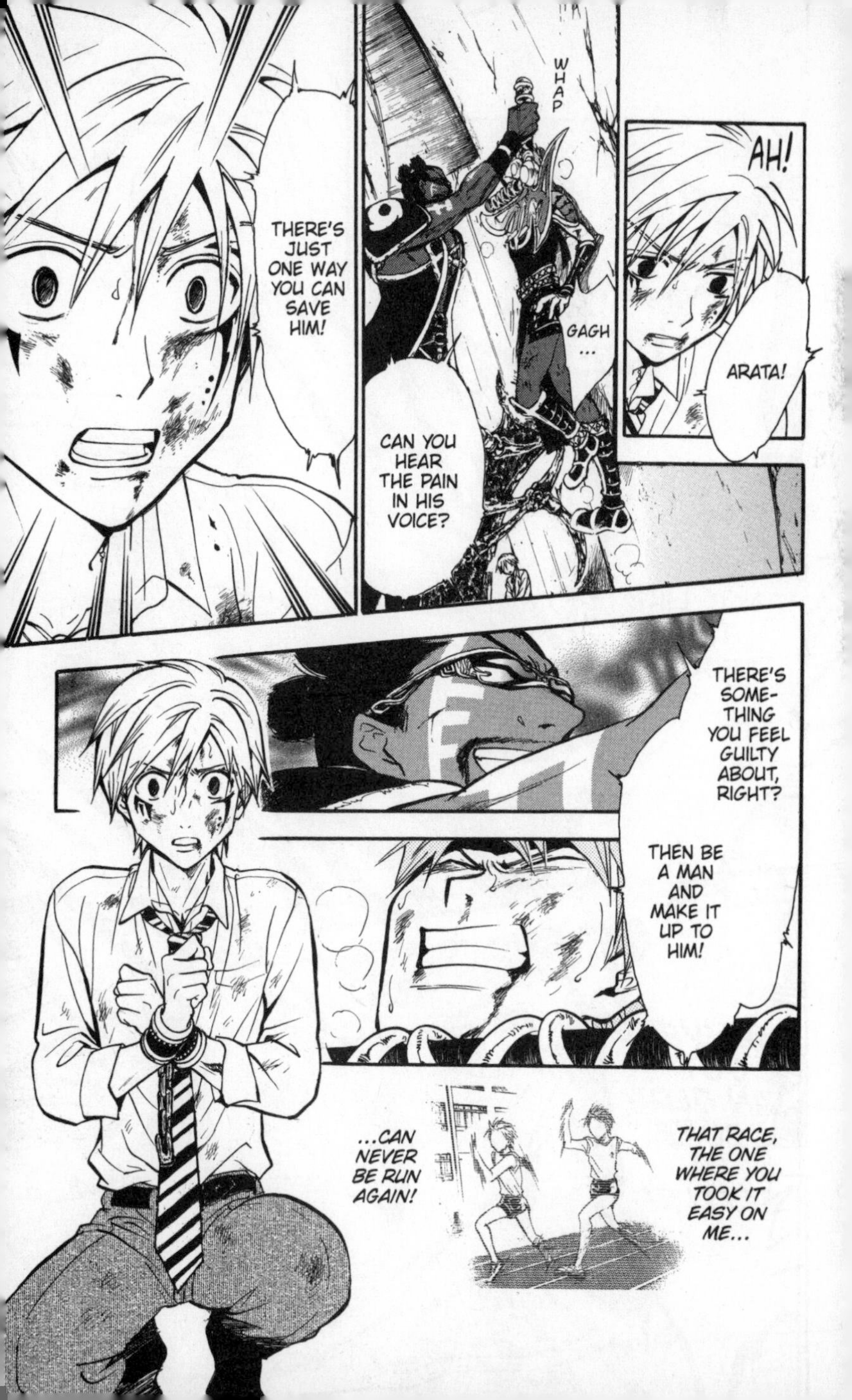
AH!
ARATA!
WHAP
GAGH...
CAN YOU HEAR THE PAIN IN HIS VOICE?
THERE'S JUST ONE WAY YOU CAN SAVE HIM!
THERE'S SOME-THING YOU FEEL GUILTY ABOUT, RIGHT?
THEN BE A MAN AND MAKE IT UP TO HIM!
THAT RACE, THE ONE WHERE YOU TOOK IT EASY ON ME...
...CAN NEVER BE RUN AGAIN!

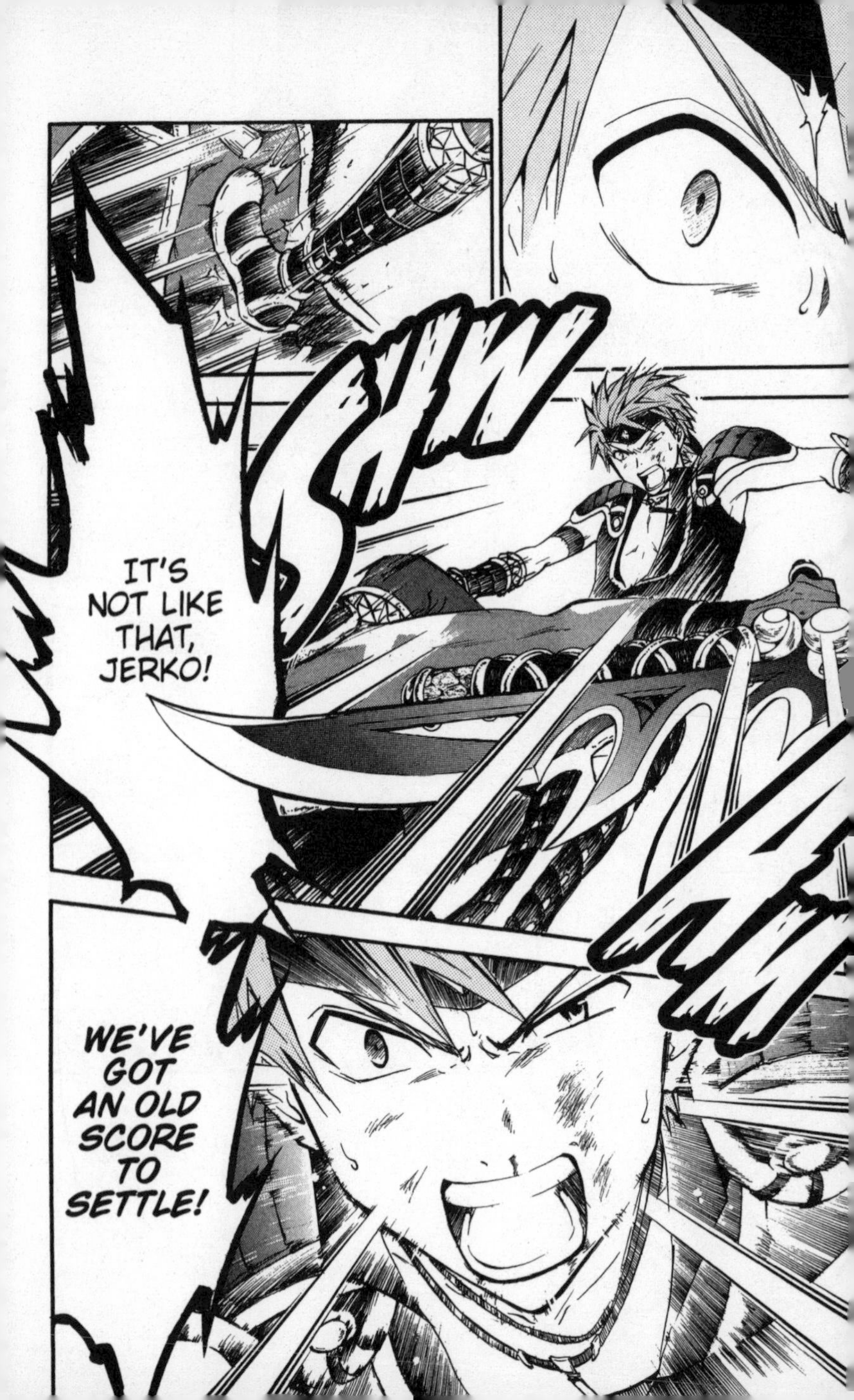
IT'S NOT LIKE THAT, JERKO!
WE'VE GOT AN OLD SCORE TO SETTLE!

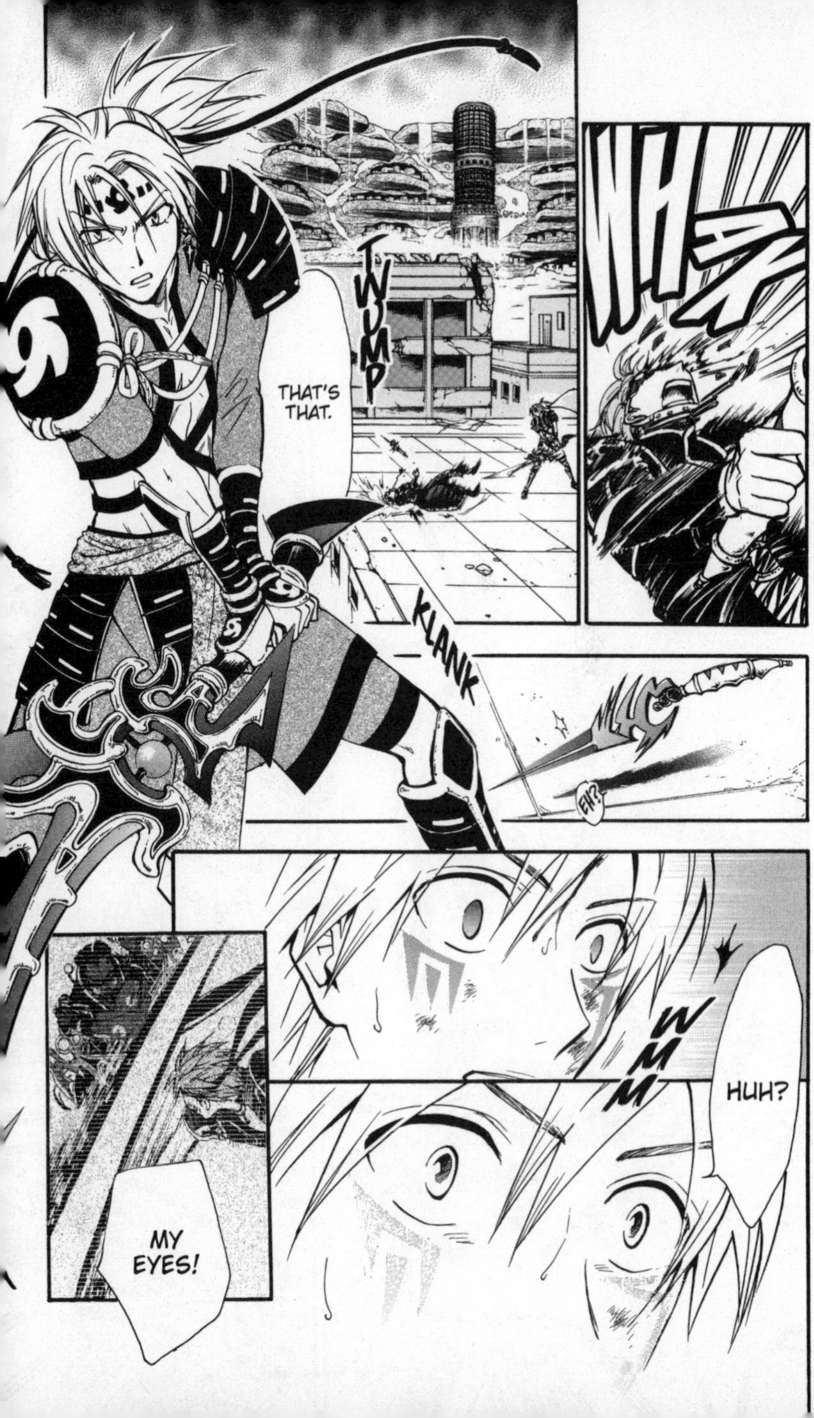
WHAM
TWUMP
THAT'S THAT.
KLANK
EH?
WUMM
HUH?
MY EYES!

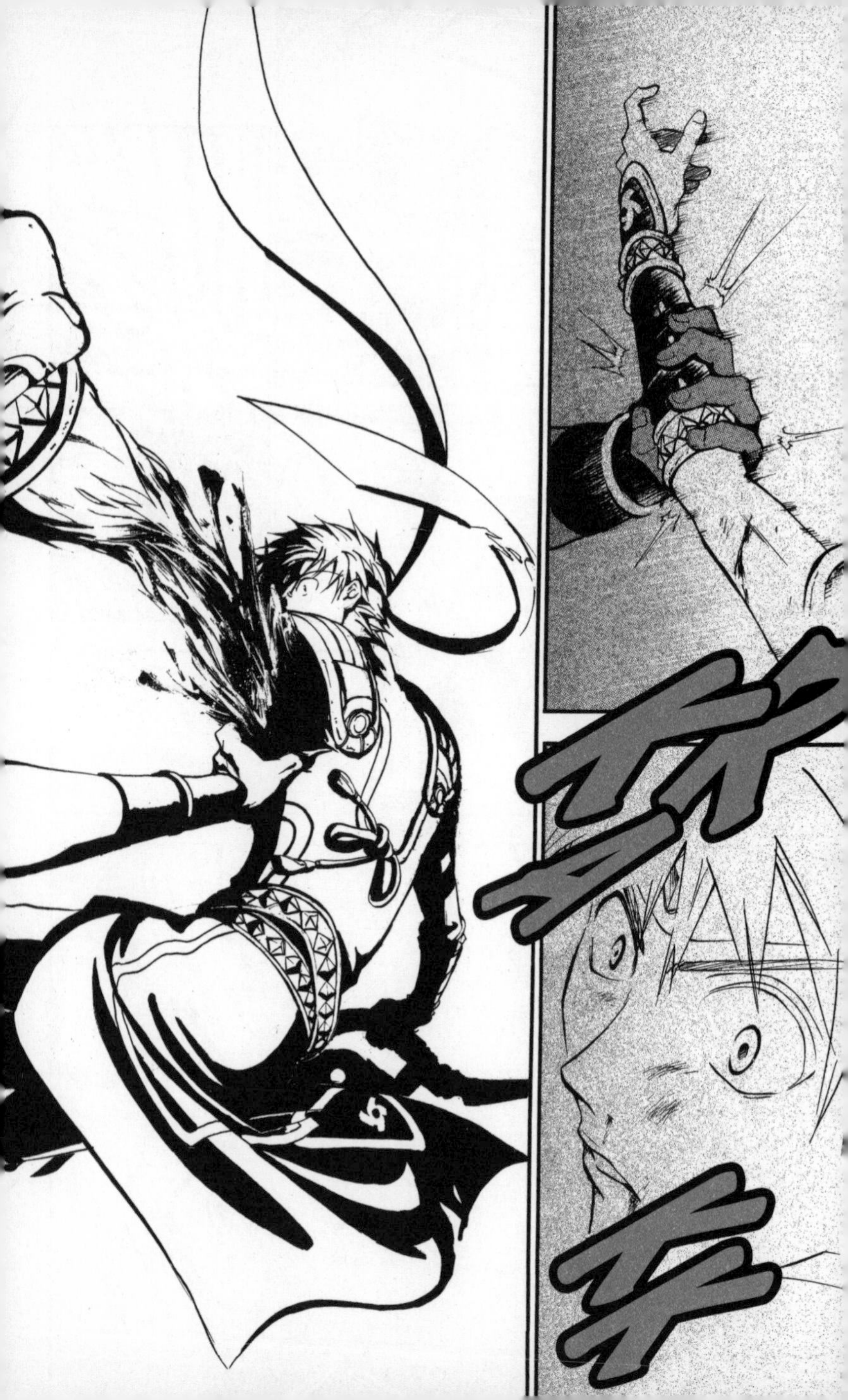

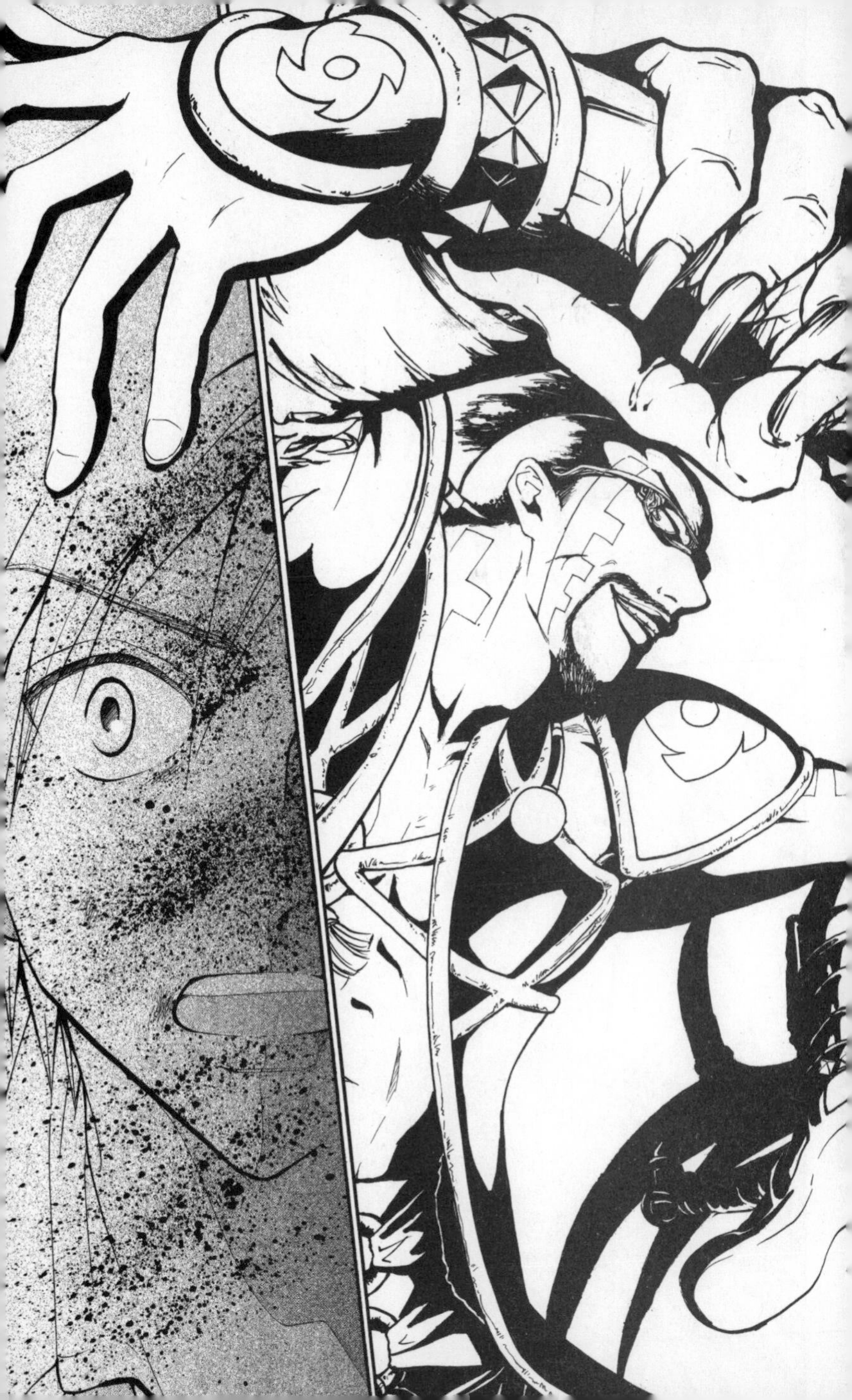

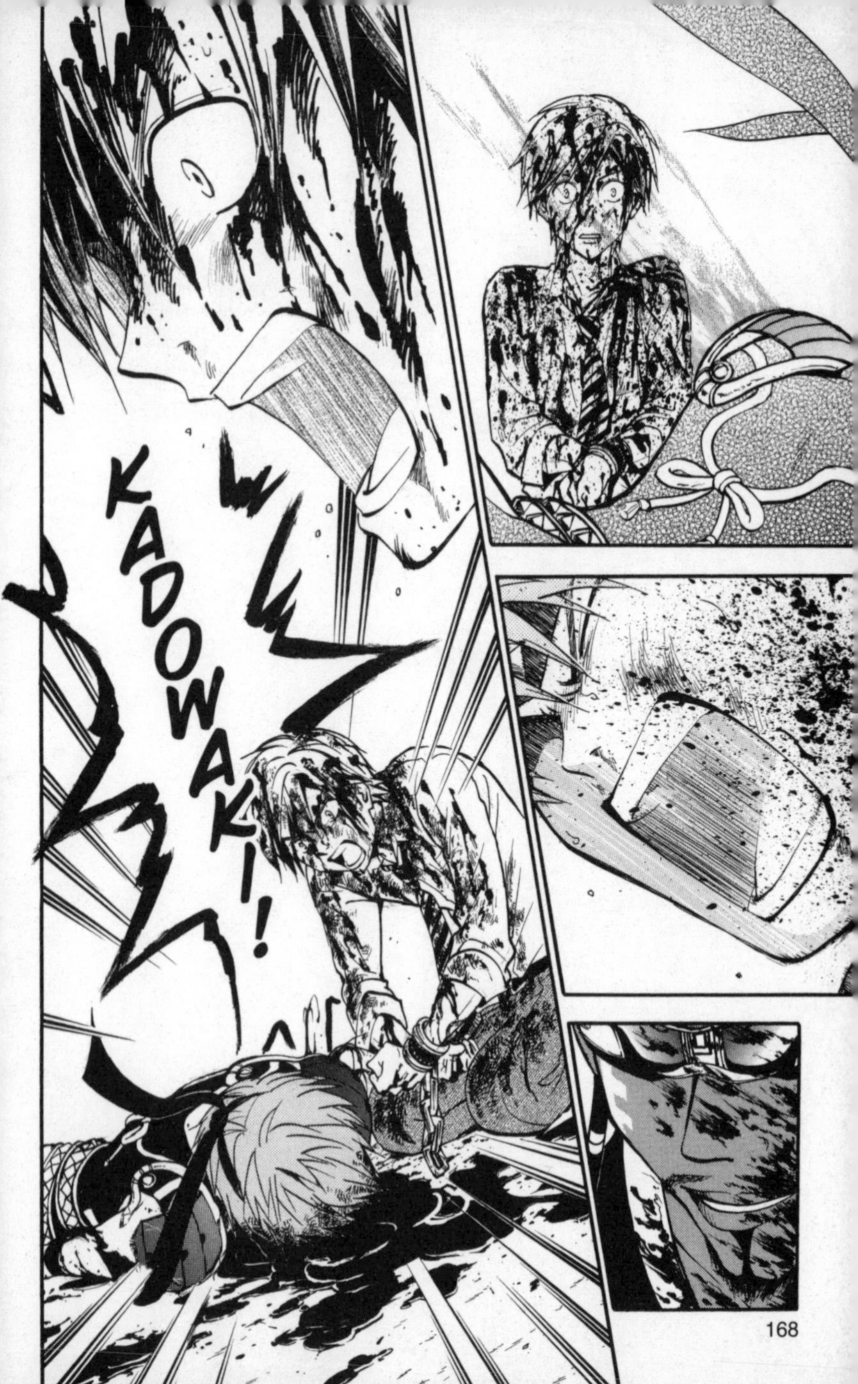
KADOWAKI!!

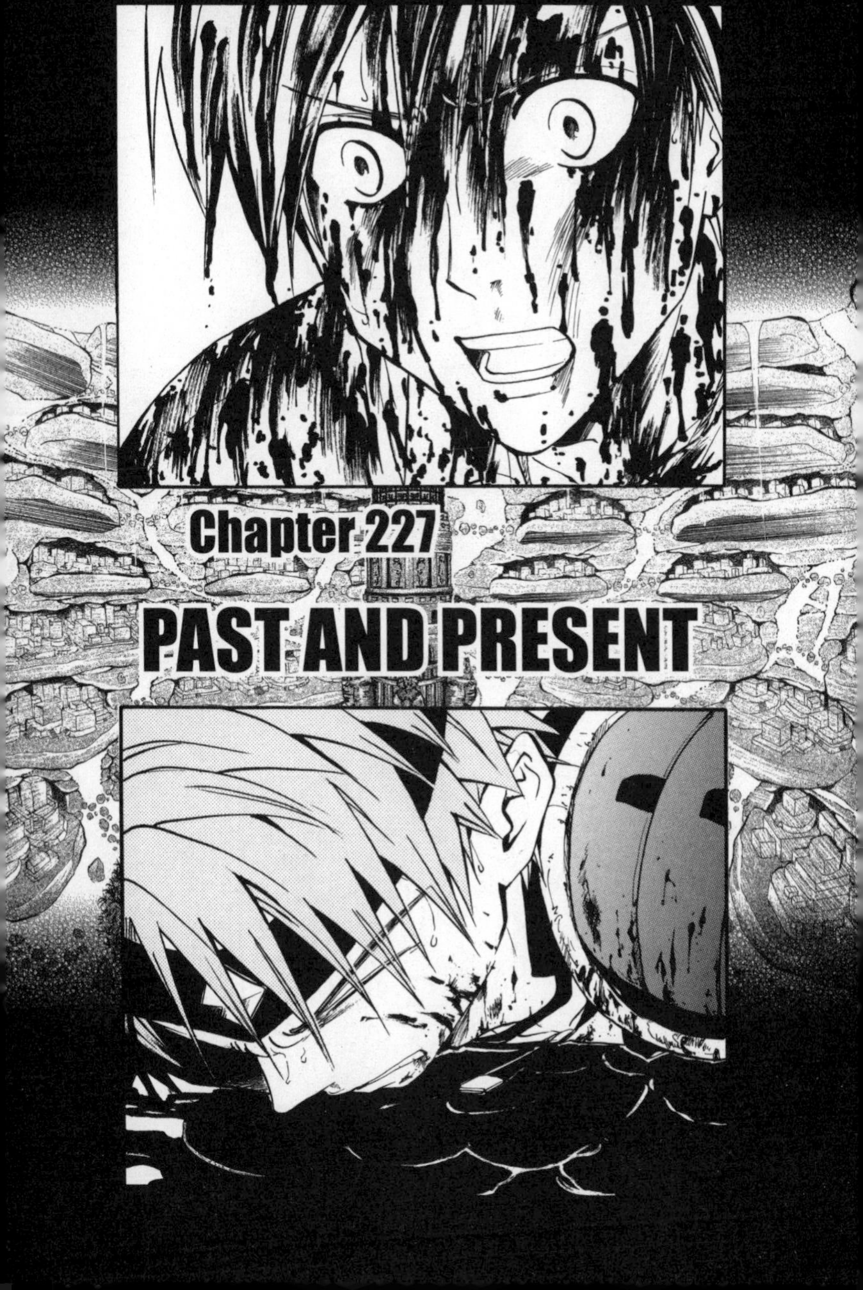
Chapter 227
PAST AND PRESENT

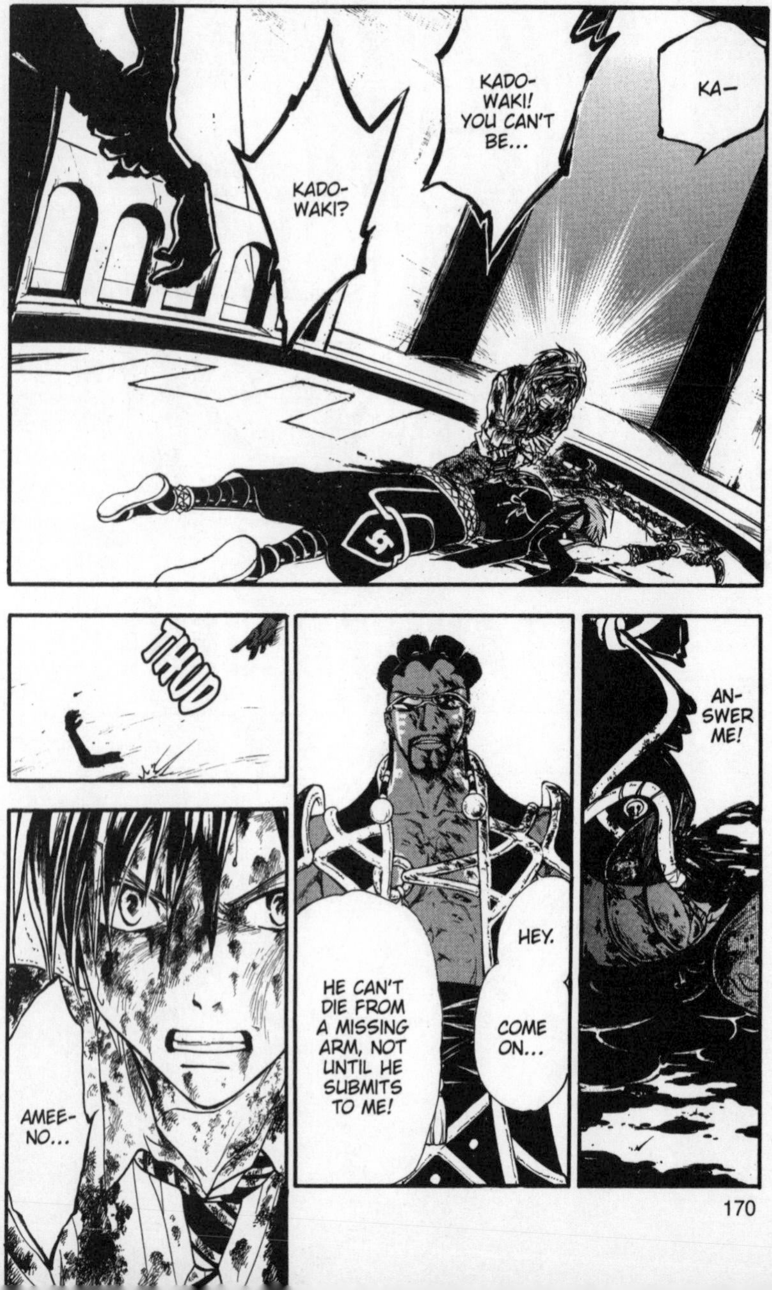
KA—
KADO-WAKI! YOU CAN'T BE...
KADO-WAKI?
AN-SWER ME!
HEY.
COME ON...
HE CAN'T DIE FROM A MISSING ARM, NOT UNTIL HE SUBMITS TO ME!
THUD
AMEE-NO...

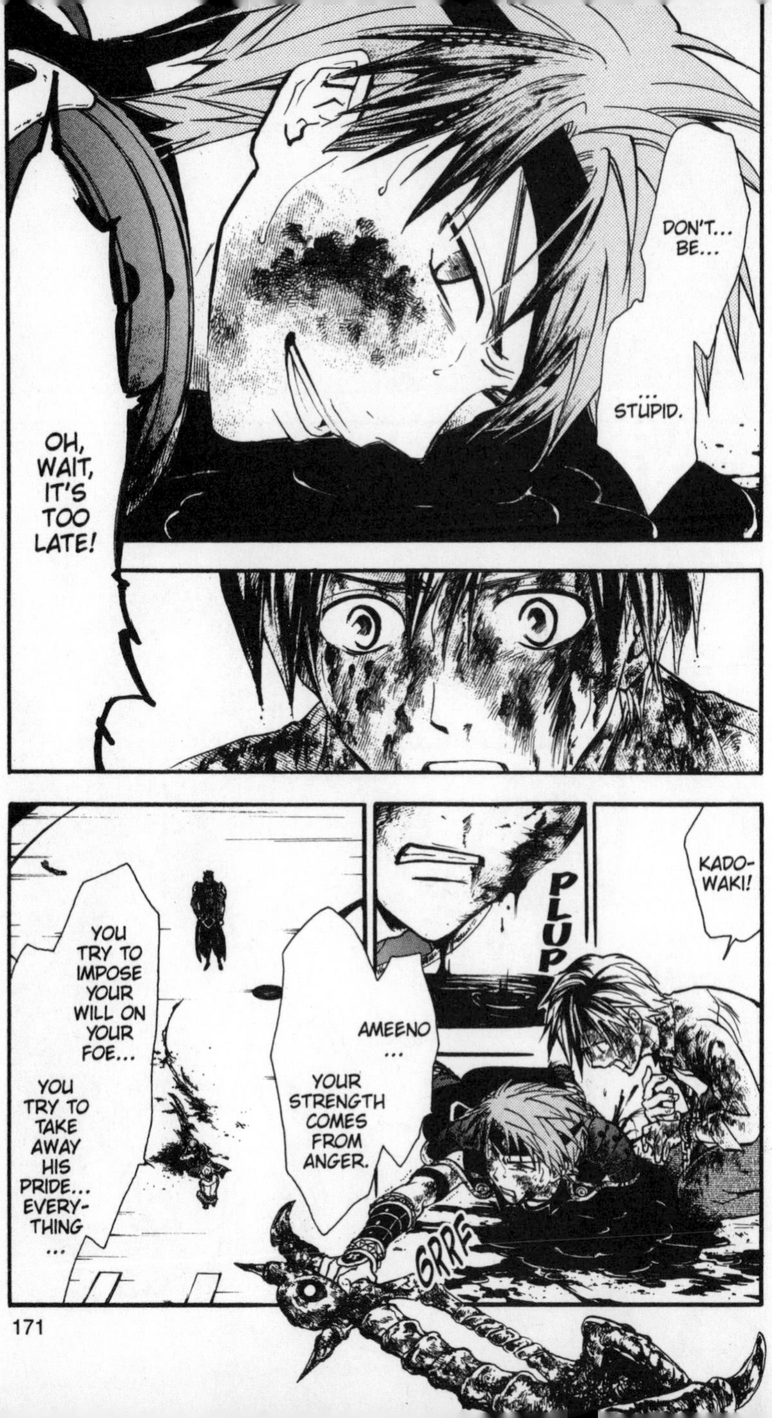
DON'T... BE...
...STUPID.
OH, WAIT, IT'S TOO LATE!
KADO-WAKI!
PLUP
AMEENO...
YOUR STRENGTH COMES FROM ANGER.
GRRF
YOU TRY TO IMPOSE YOUR WILL ON YOUR FOE...
YOU TRY TO TAKE AWAY HIS PRIDE... EVERYTHING...

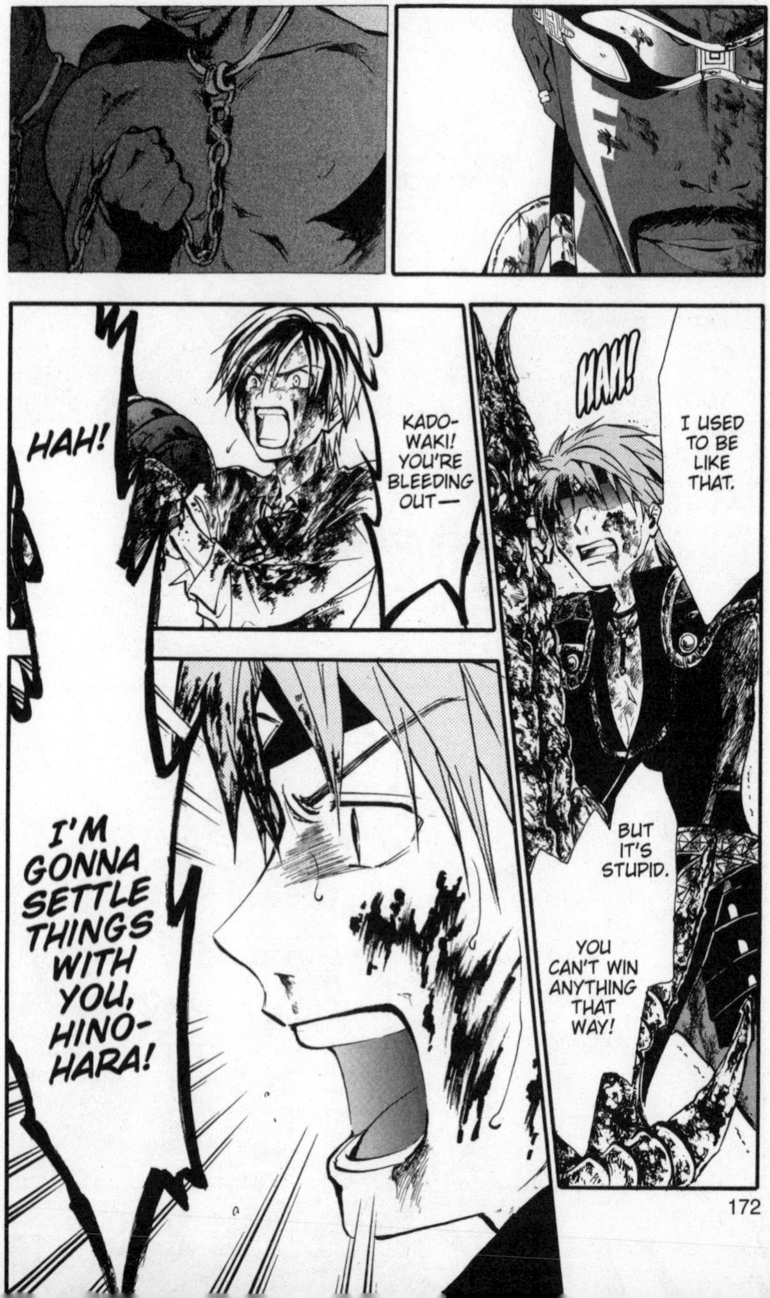
HAH!
I USED TO BE LIKE THAT.
BUT IT'S STUPID.
YOU CAN'T WIN ANYTHING THAT WAY!
KADO-WAKI! YOU'RE BLEEDING OUT—
HAH!
I'M GONNA SETTLE THINGS WITH YOU, HINO-HARA!

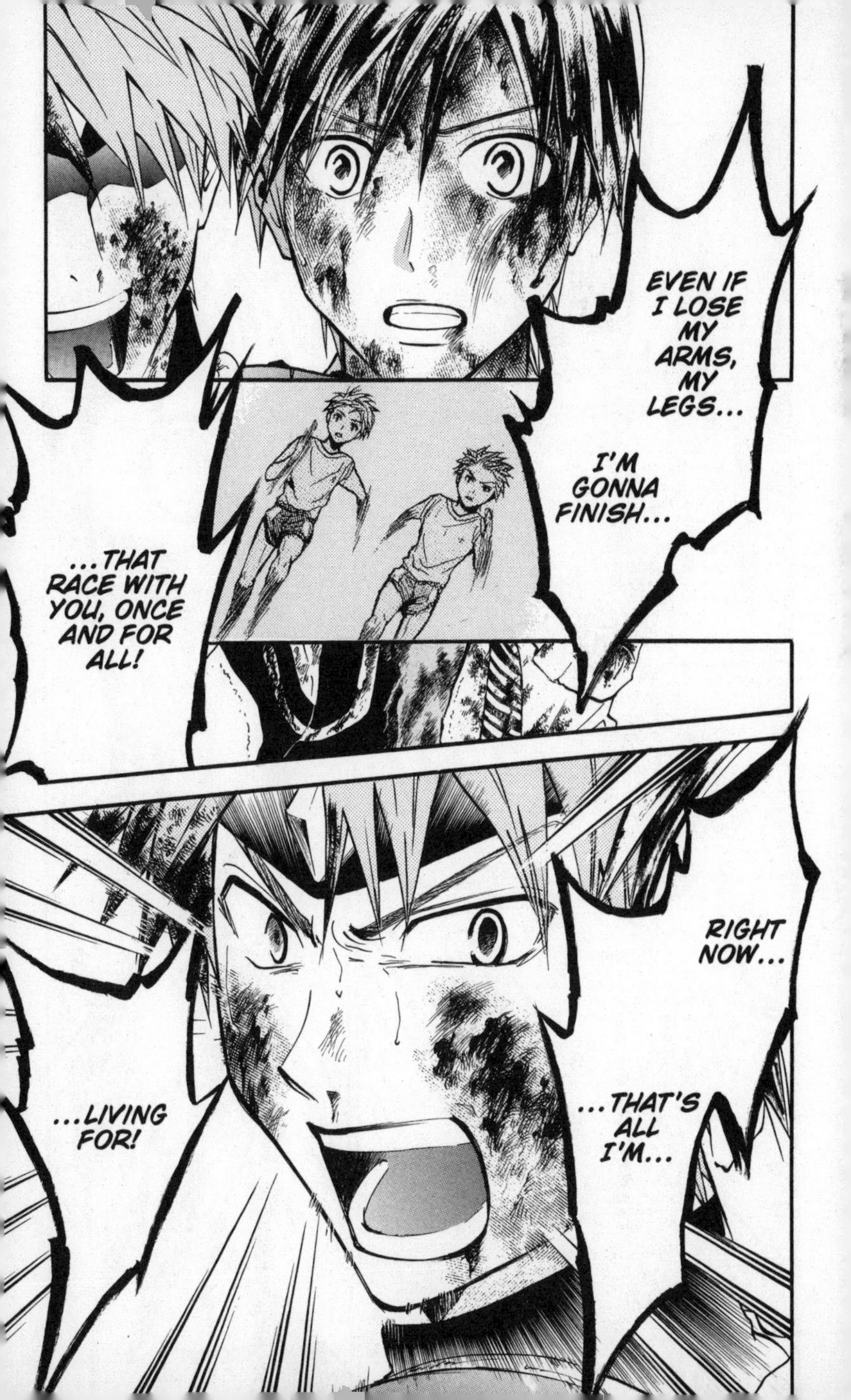
EVEN IF I LOSE MY ARMS, MY LEGS...
I'M GONNA FINISH...
...THAT RACE WITH YOU, ONCE AND FOR ALL!
RIGHT NOW...
...THAT'S ALL I'M...
...LIVING FOR!

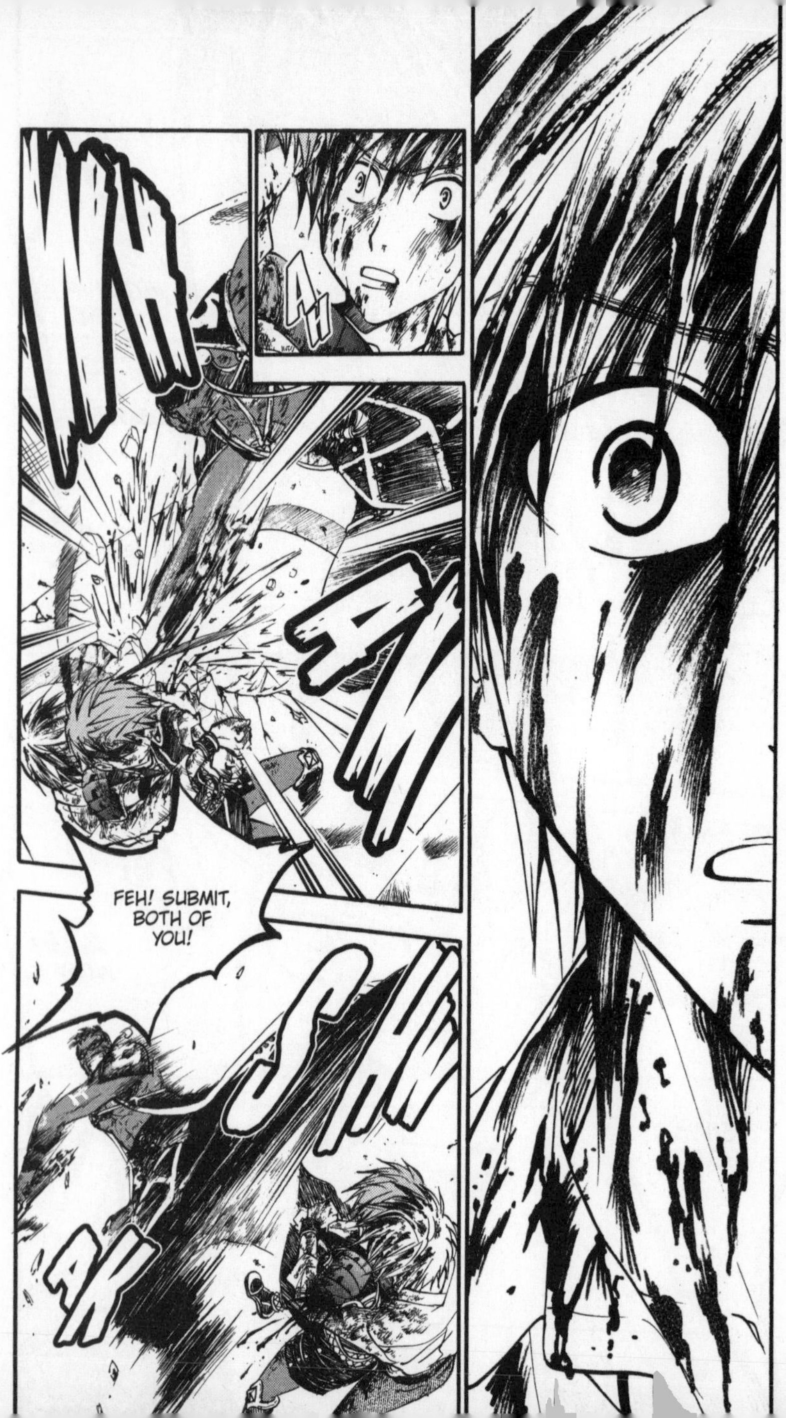
AH
FEH! SUBMIT, BOTH OF YOU!

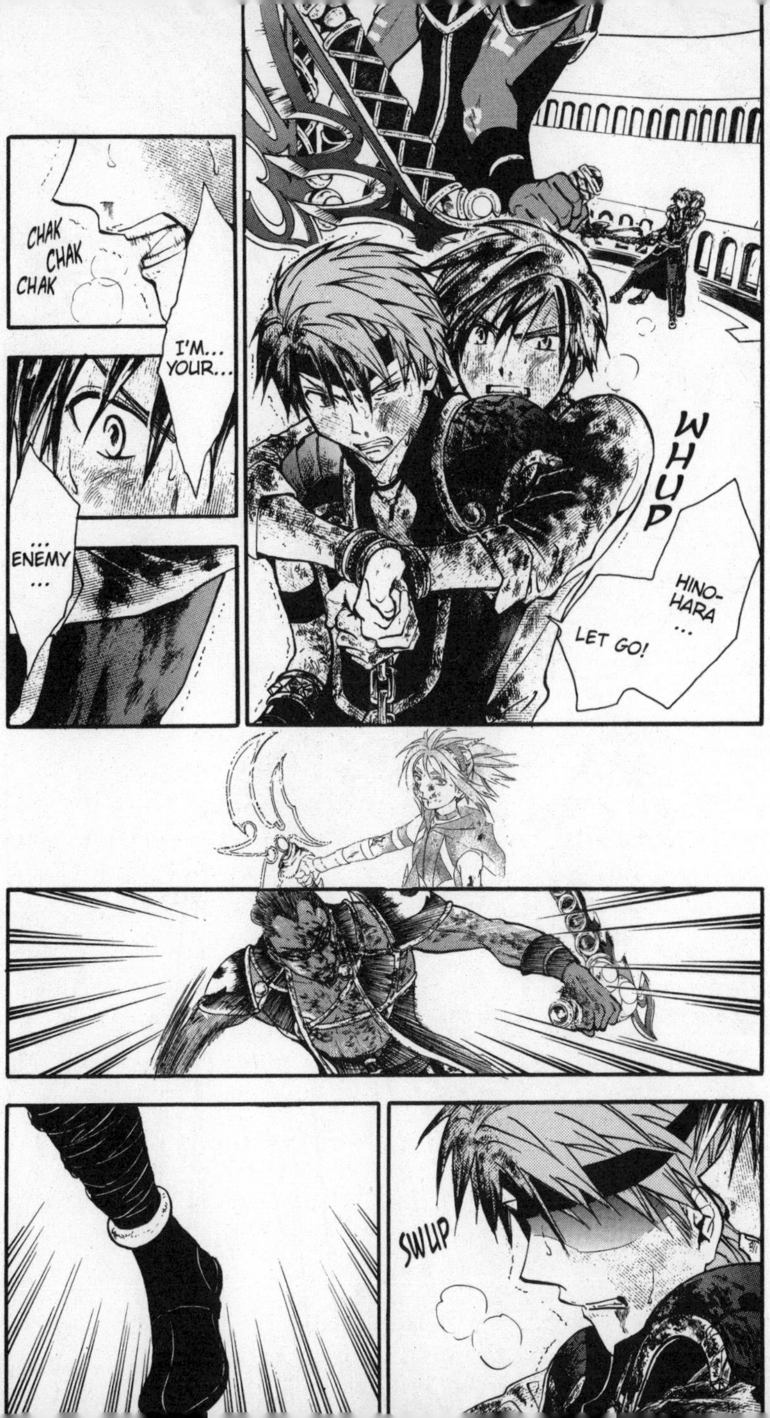
WHUP
HINO-HARA...
LET GO!
CHAK CHAK CHAK
I'M... YOUR...
...ENEMY...
SWUP

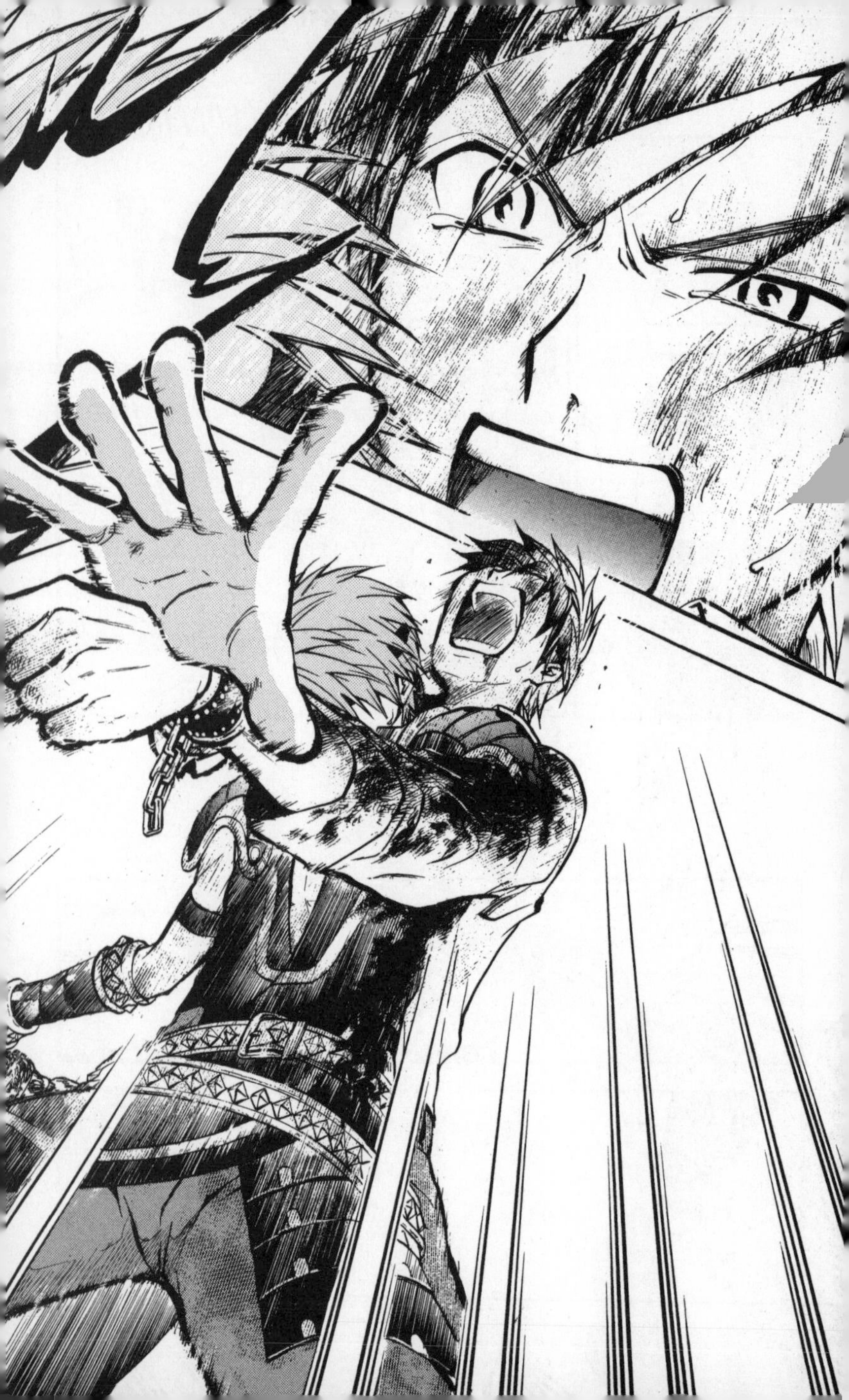

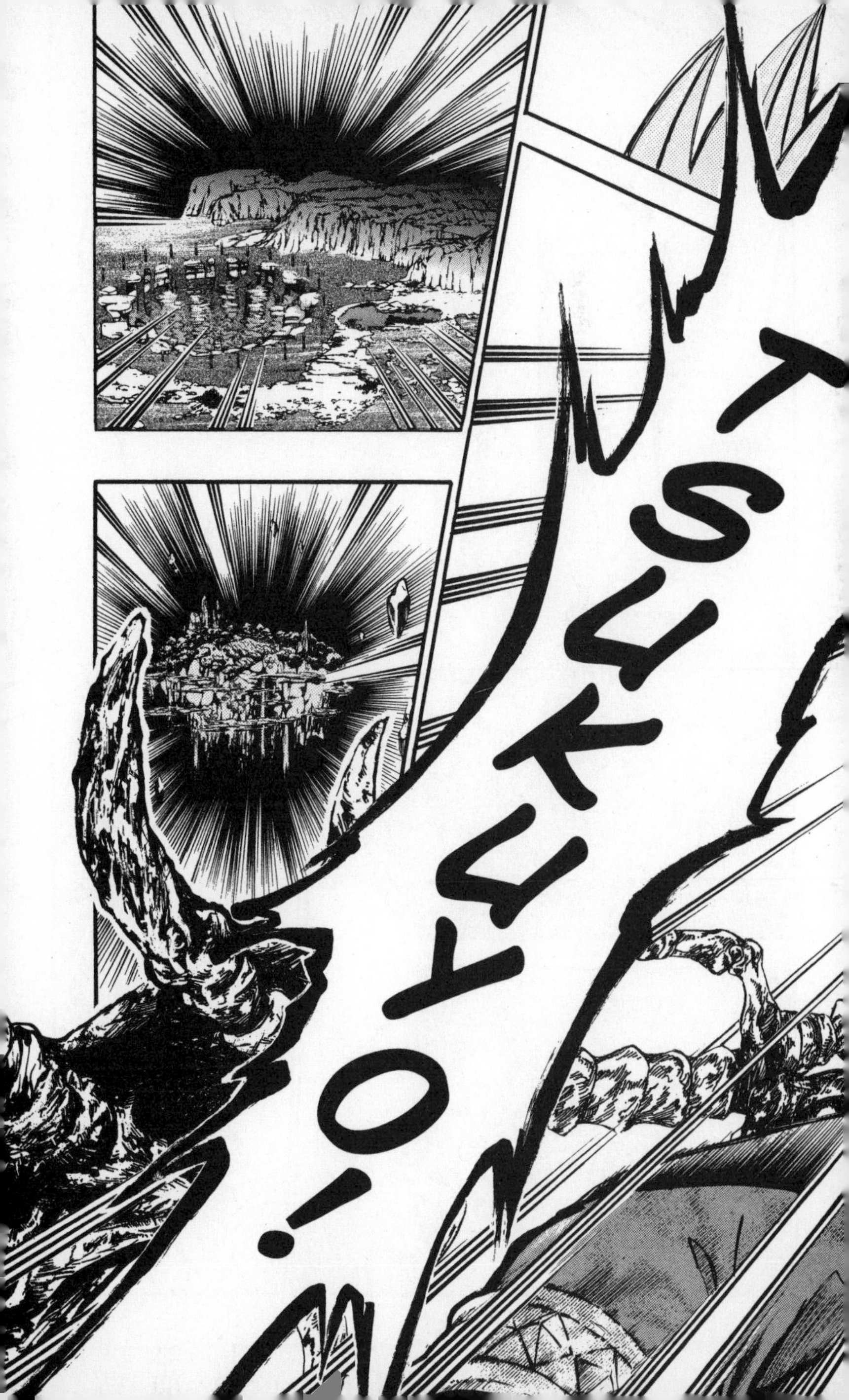
TSUKUYO!

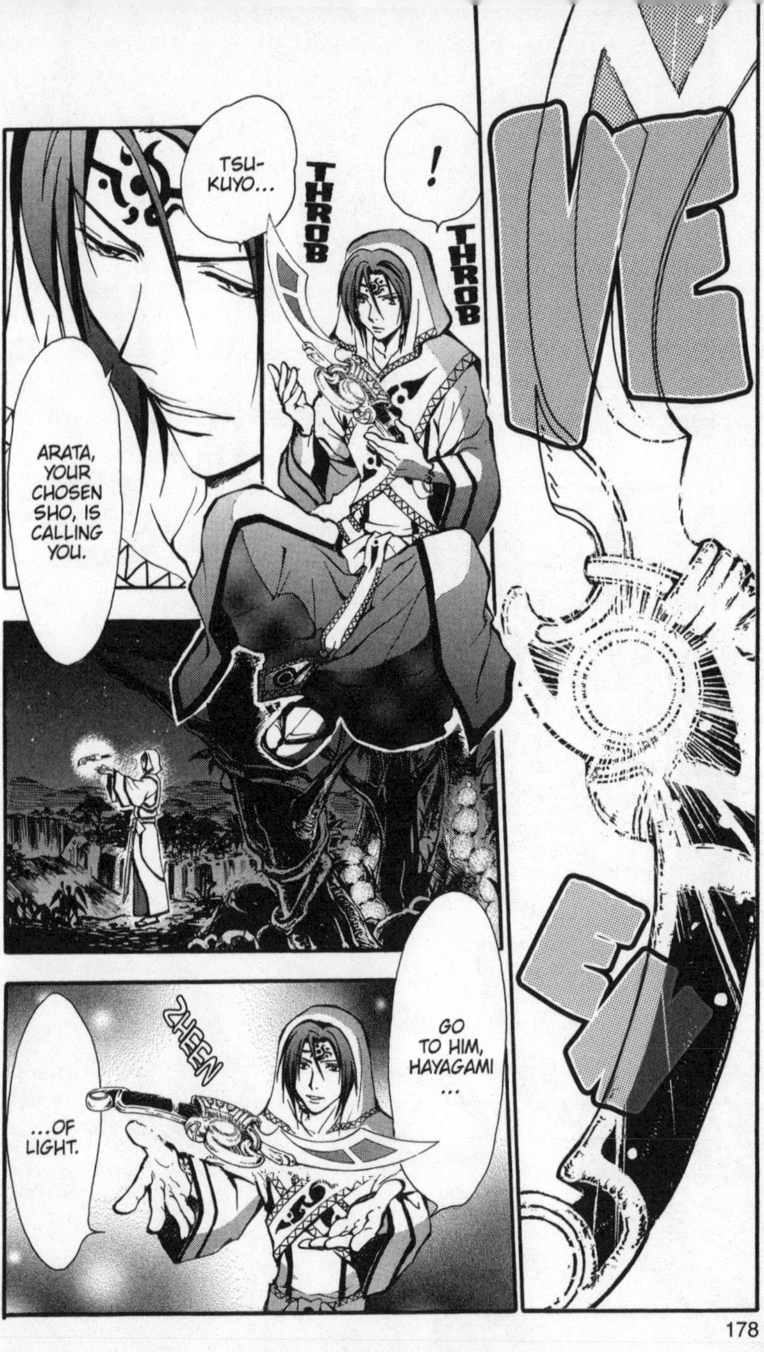
!
THROB
TSU-KUYO...
THROB
ARATA, YOUR CHOSEN SHO, IS CALLING YOU.
GO TO HIM, HAYAGAMI ...
ZHEEN
...OF LIGHT.

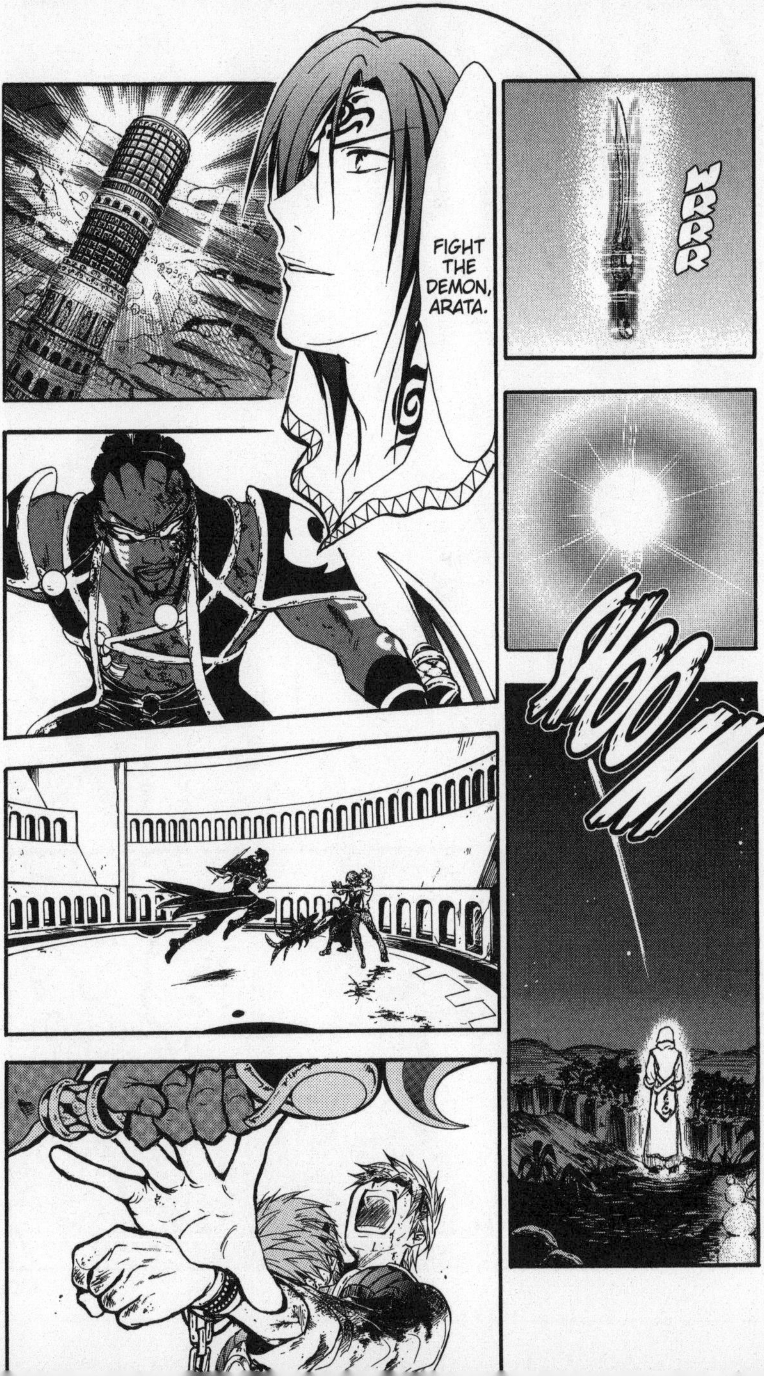
WRRR
FIGHT THE DEMON, ARATA.
SHOOM

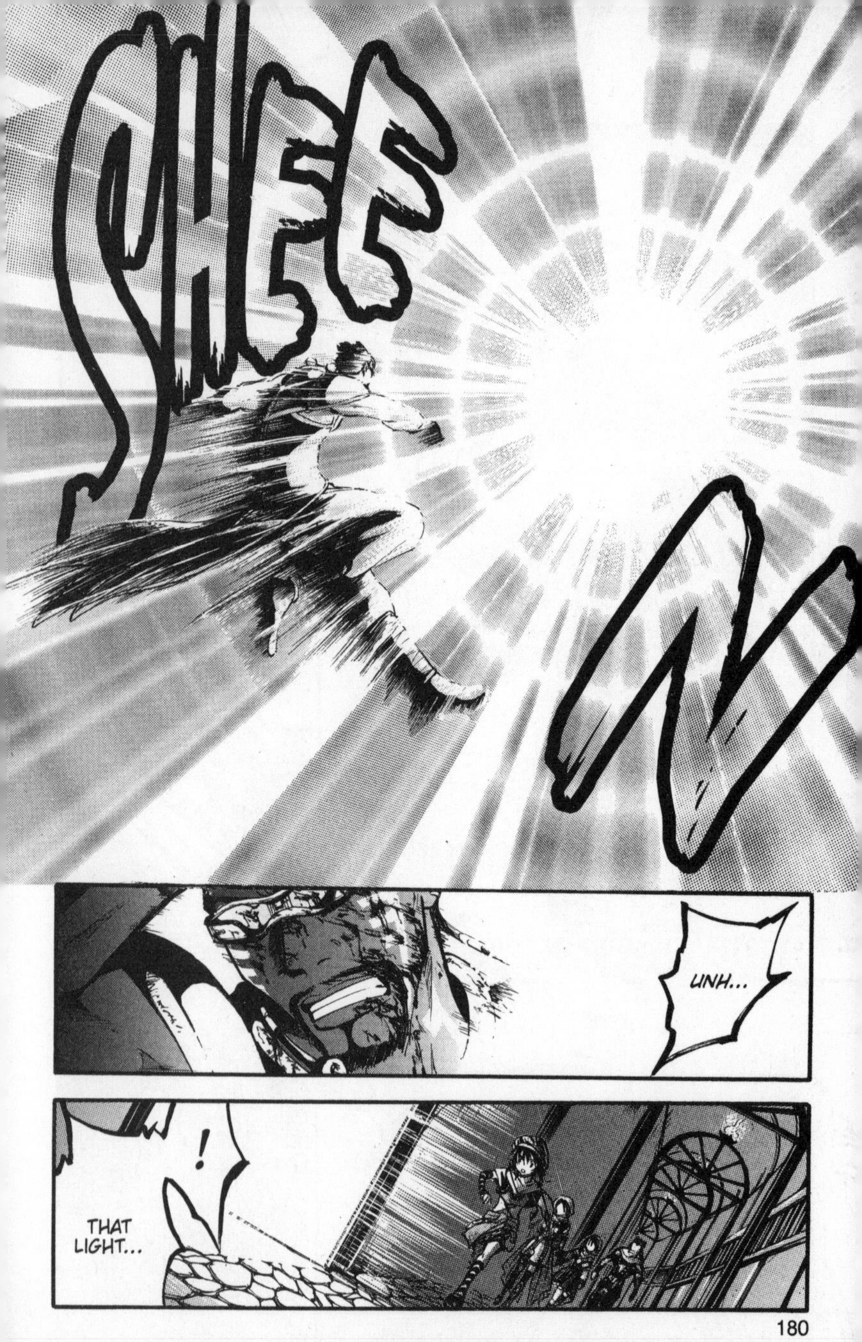
SHEEN
UNH...
!
THAT LIGHT...

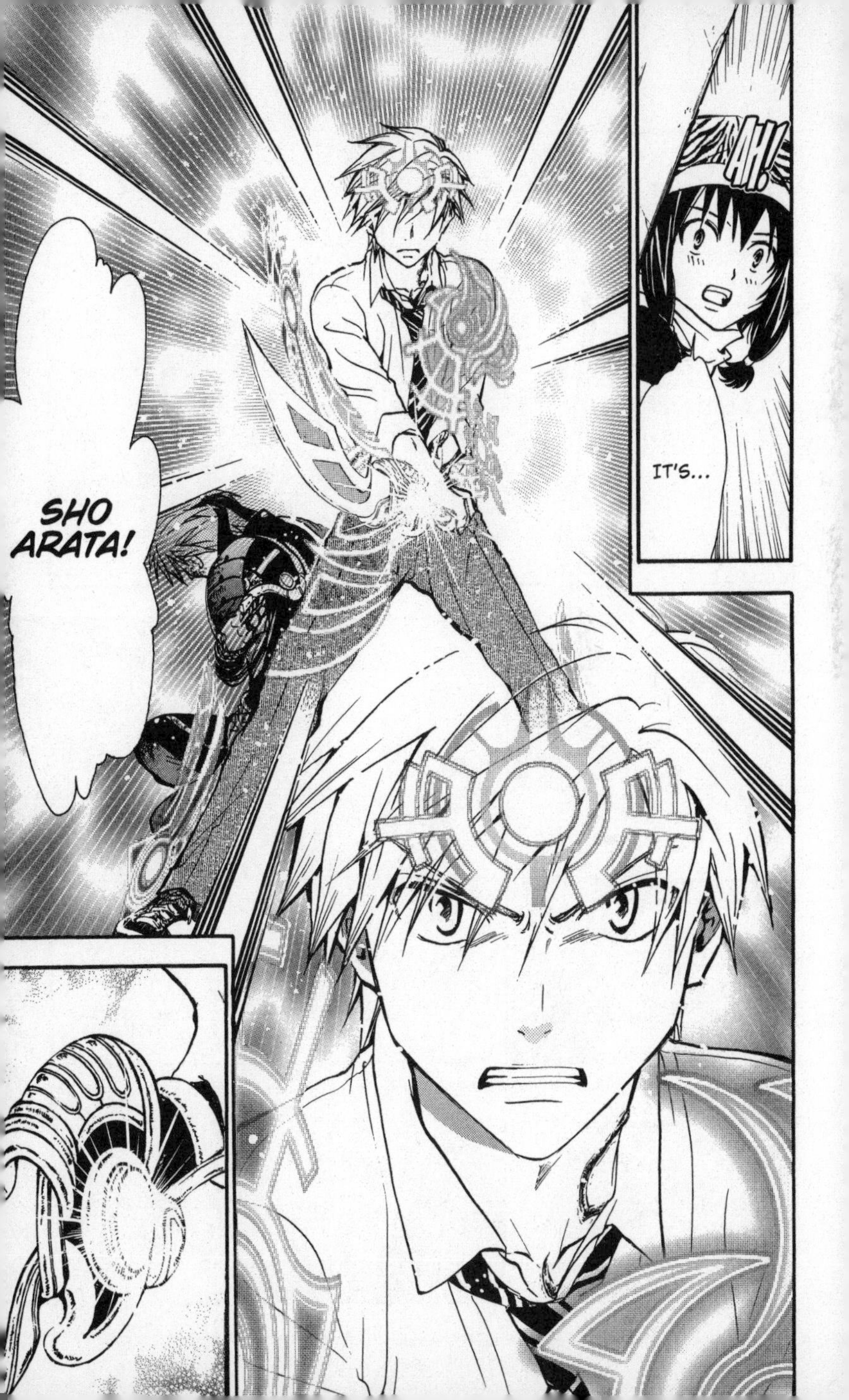
AH!
IT'S...
SHO ARATA!

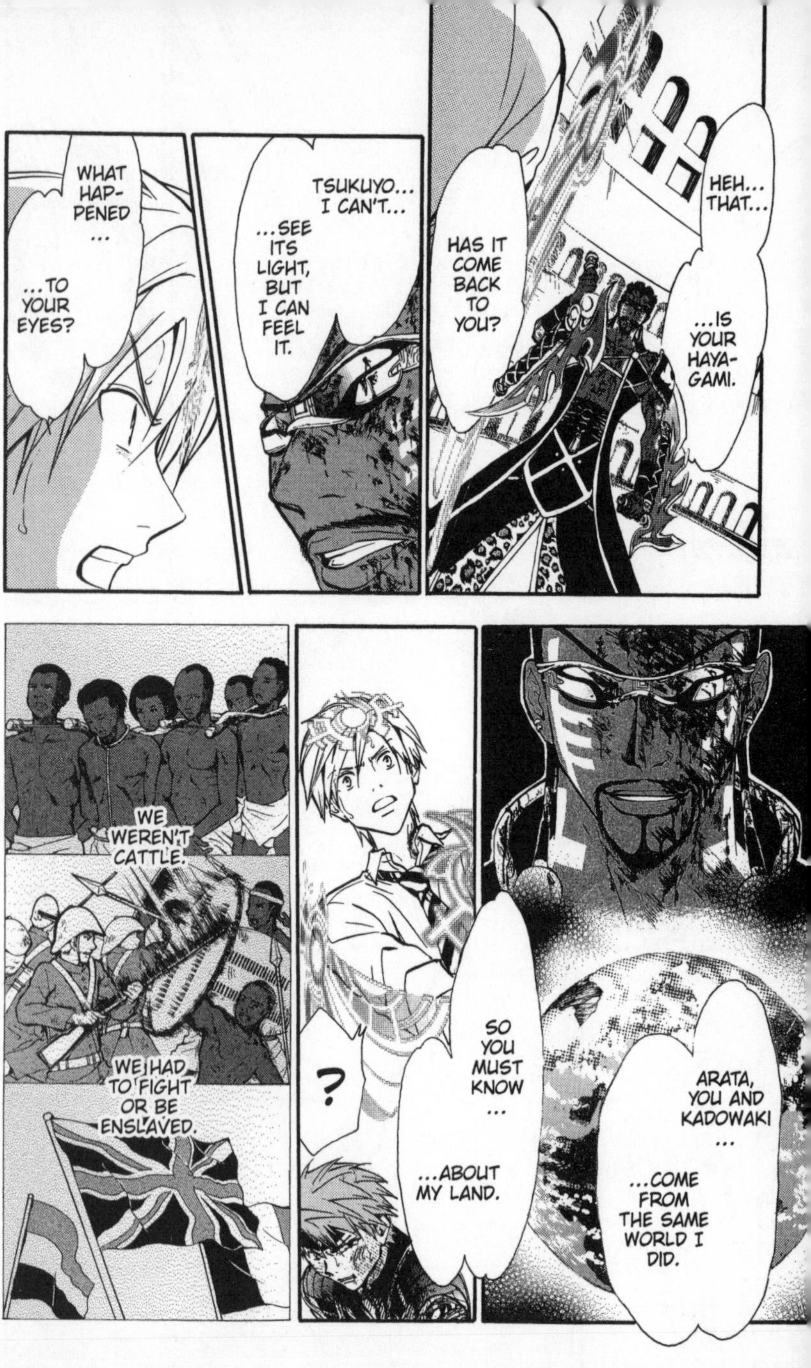
HEH... THAT...
...IS YOUR HAYA-GAMI.
HAS IT COME BACK TO YOU?
TSUKUYO... I CAN'T...
...SEE ITS LIGHT, BUT I CAN FEEL IT.
WHAT HAP-PENED ...
...TO YOUR EYES?
ARATA, YOU AND KADOWAKI ...
...COME FROM THE SAME WORLD I DID.
?
SO YOU MUST KNOW ...
...ABOUT MY LAND.
WE WEREN'T CATTLE.
WE HAD TO FIGHT OR BE ENSLAVED.

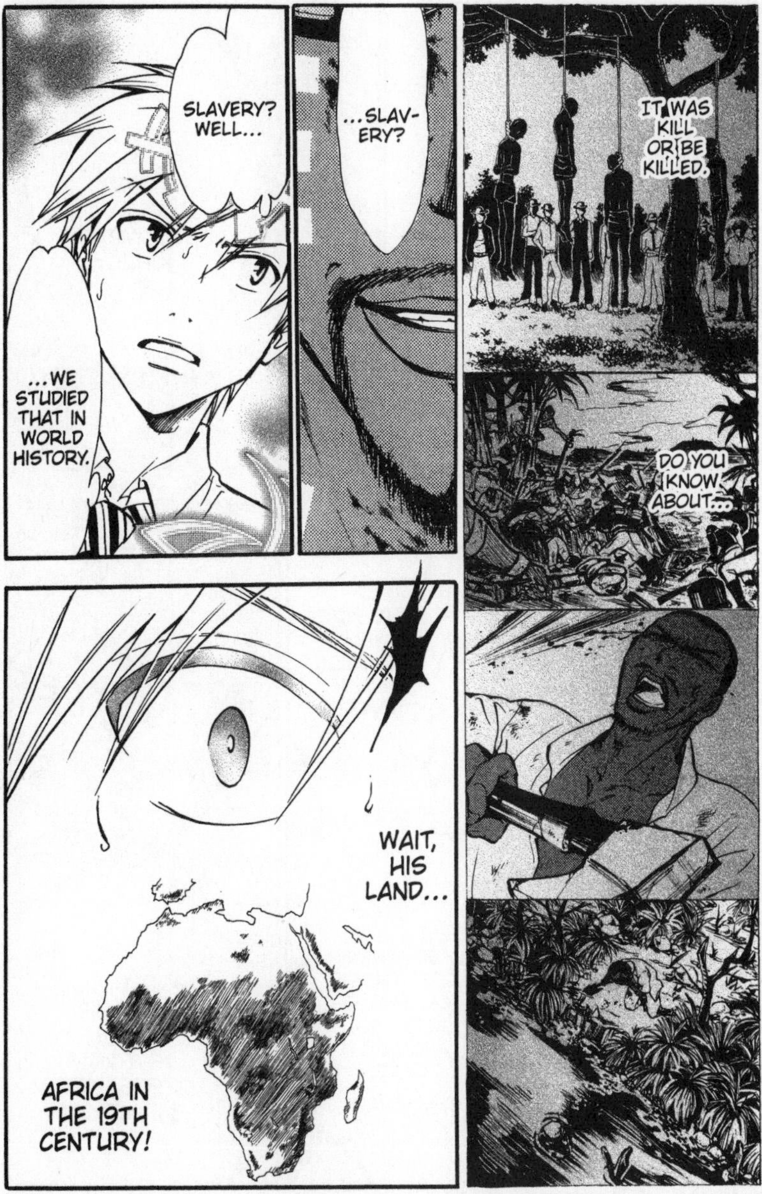
IT WAS KILL OR BE KILLED.
DO YOU KNOW ABOUT...
...SLAVERY?
SLAVERY? WELL...
...WE STUDIED THAT IN WORLD HISTORY.
WAIT, HIS LAND...
AFRICA IN THE 19TH CENTURY!

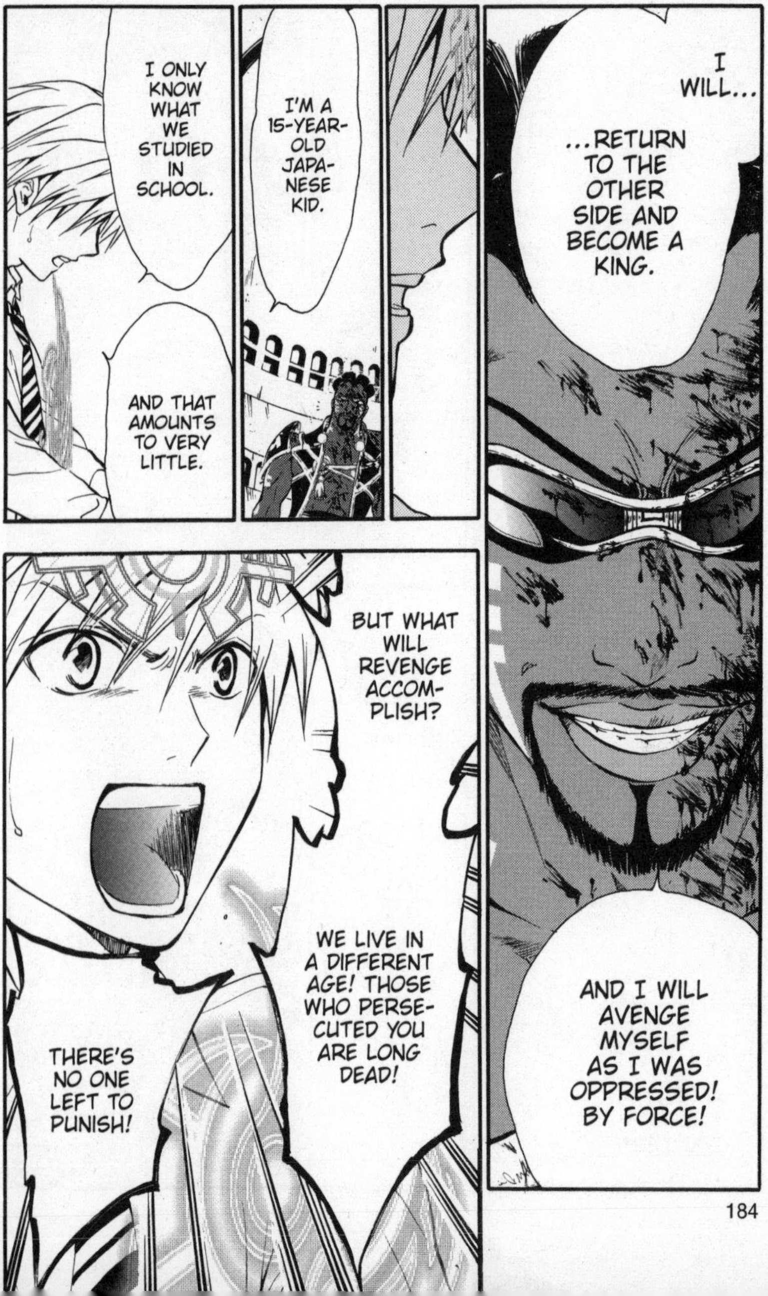
I WILL...
...RETURN TO THE OTHER SIDE AND BECOME A KING.
AND I WILL AVENGE MYSELF AS I WAS OPPRESSED! BY FORCE!
I'M A 15-YEAR-OLD JAPANESE KID.
I ONLY KNOW WHAT WE STUDIED IN SCHOOL.
AND THAT AMOUNTS TO VERY LITTLE.
BUT WHAT WILL REVENGE ACCOMPLISH?
WE LIVE IN A DIFFERENT AGE! THOSE WHO PERSECUTED YOU ARE LONG DEAD!
THERE'S NO ONE LEFT TO PUNISH!

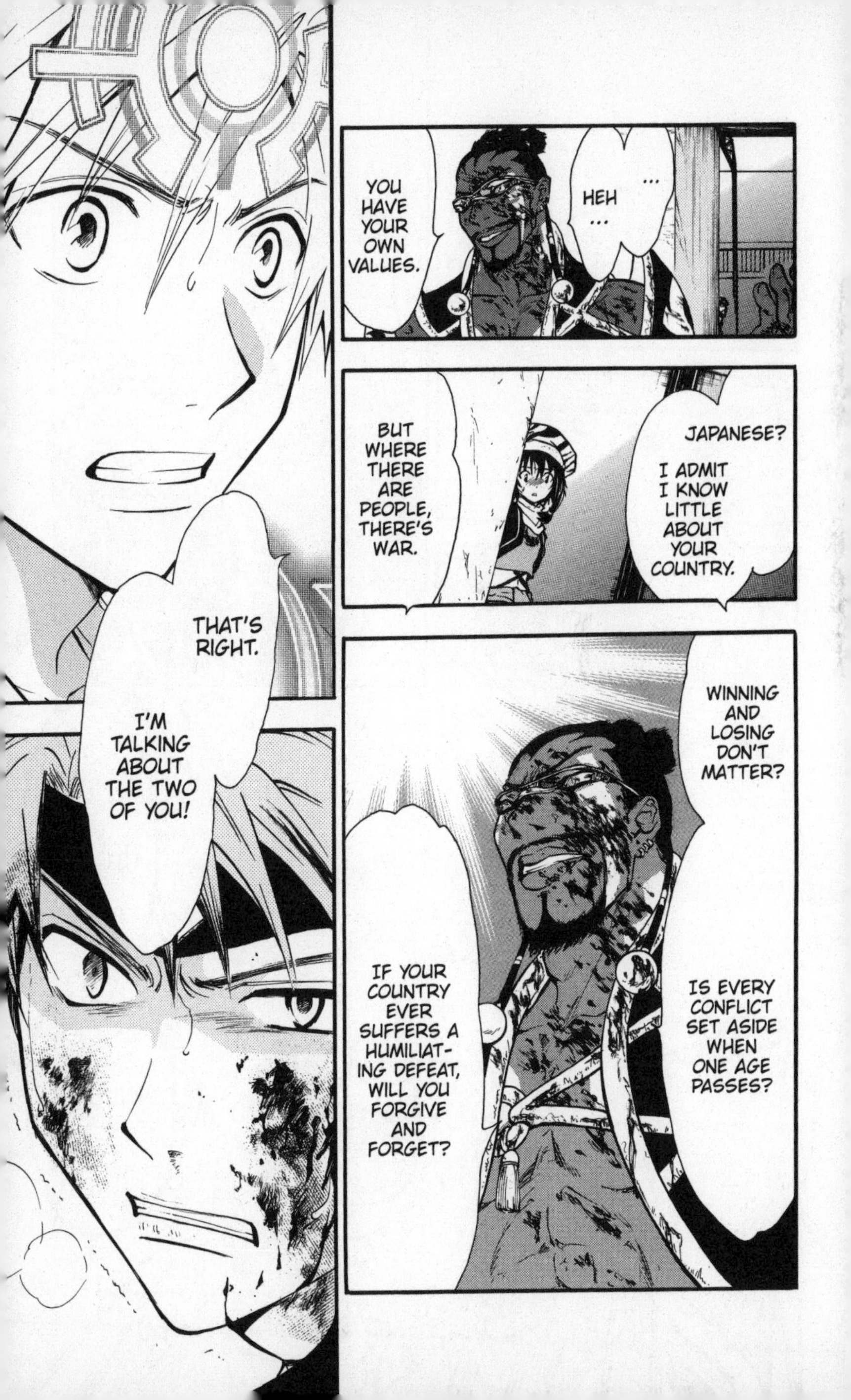
... HEH ...
YOU HAVE YOUR OWN VALUES.
JAPANESE?
I ADMIT I KNOW LITTLE ABOUT YOUR COUNTRY.
BUT WHERE THERE ARE PEOPLE, THERE'S WAR.
WINNING AND LOSING DON'T MATTER?
IS EVERY CONFLICT SET ASIDE WHEN ONE AGE PASSES?
IF YOUR COUNTRY EVER SUFFERS A HUMILIAT-ING DEFEAT, WILL YOU FORGIVE AND FORGET?
THAT'S RIGHT.
I'M TALKING ABOUT THE TWO OF YOU!

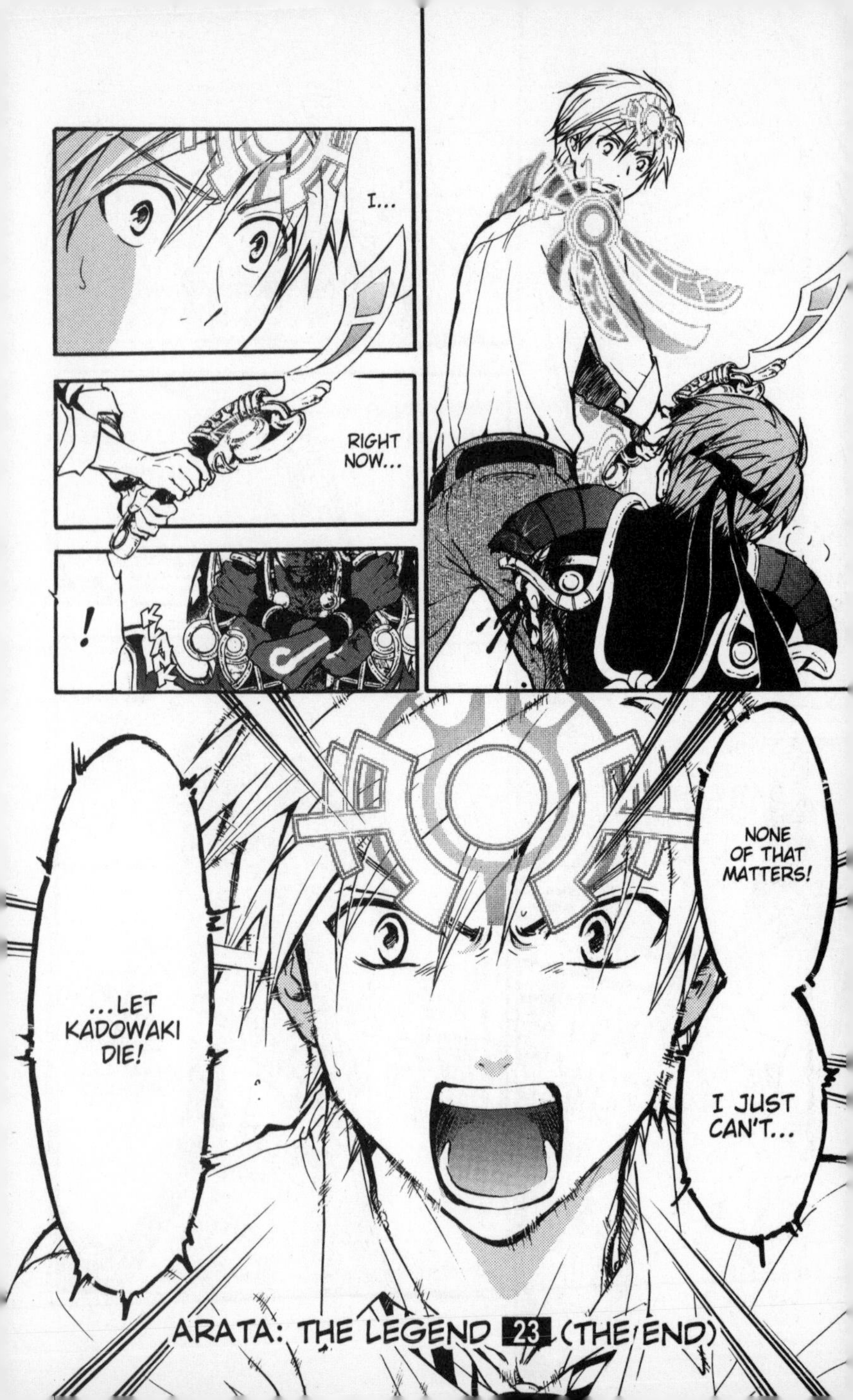
I...
RIGHT NOW...
!
KLANK
NONE OF THAT MATTERS!
I JUST CAN'T...
...LET KADOWAKI DIE!

ARATA: THE LEGEND 23 (THE END)

KIKUTSUNE KANGATARI

BY S-SAN

OUT OF THE BLUE...

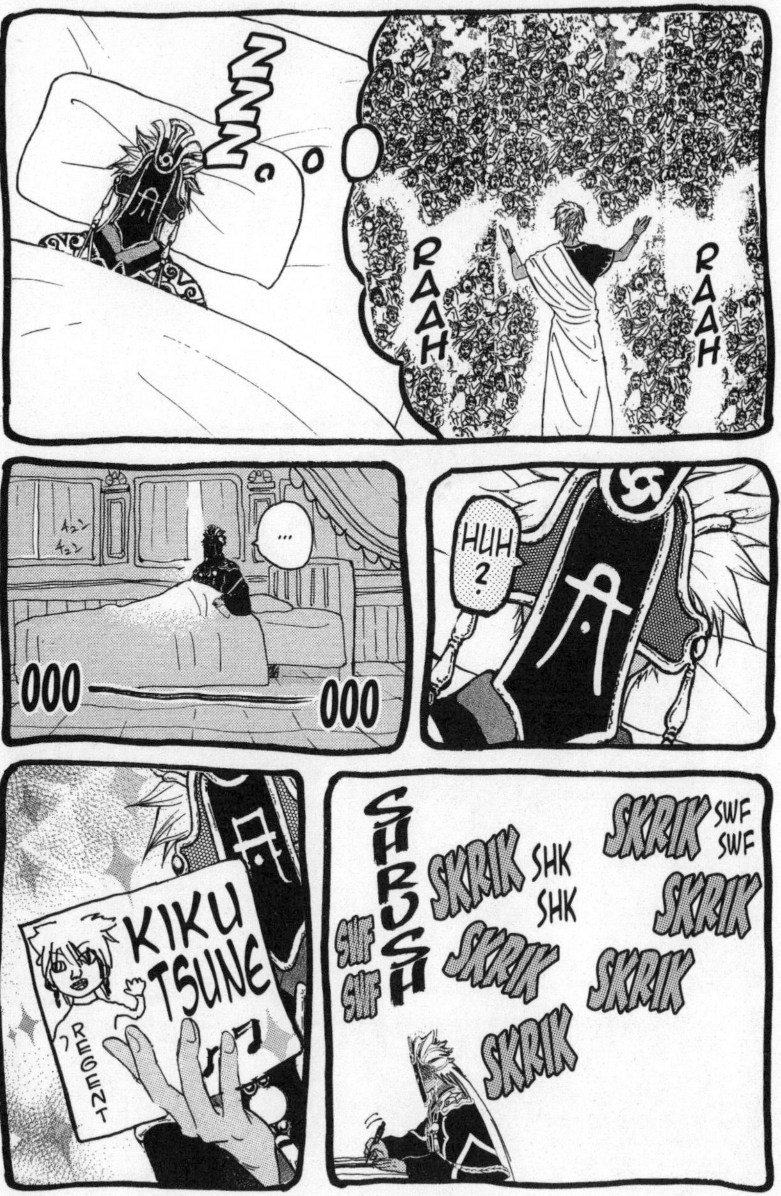
ZZZ
RAAH
RAAH
HUH ?
...
OOO
OOO
SHRUSH
SKRIK
SHK SHK
SKRIK
SWF SWF
SKRIK
SKRIK
SKRIK
SKRIK
SWF SWF
SKRIK
KIKU TSUNE
REGENT

WANT AN AUTOGRAPH?
HE GOES INTO ORO-CHI.
WOW ...
!
...
WANT AN AUTOGRAPH?
SEVERAL WEEKS LATER... ISORA?
WOW ...
SHRSHH

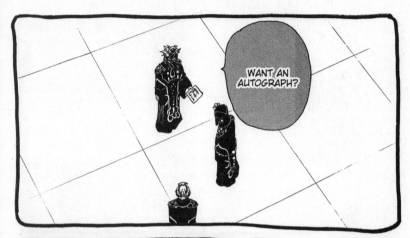

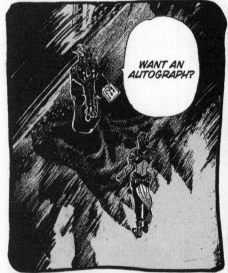

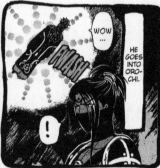

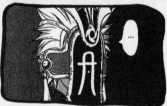

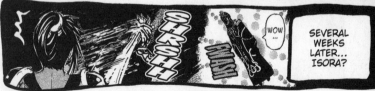

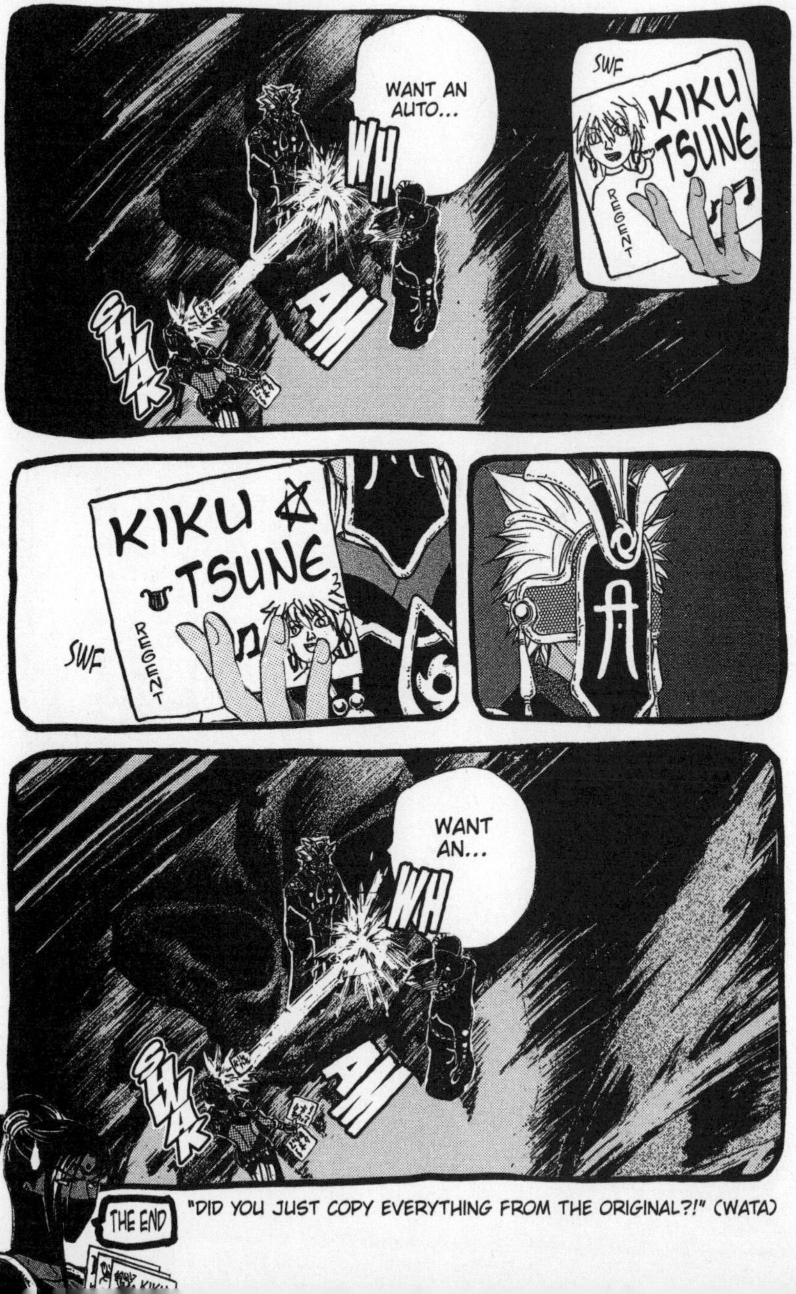
SWF
KIKU TSUNE
REGENT
WANT AN AUTO...
WHAM
SHWAK
KIKU TSUNE
REGENT
SWF
WANT AN...
WHAM
SHWAK
THE END
"DID YOU JUST COPY EVERYTHING FROM THE ORIGINAL?!" (WATA)

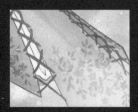

It's widely known (among my readers) that I love cherry blossoms, but in reality, I've never gone "flower viewing."

I've been to the Sakura Festival in Hirosaki in Aomori Prefecture though...but when I mention that, I'm told, "That's not flower viewing." Or, "I mean the kind where you spread out a mat and eat box lunches and drink sake!" Or, "That's not a real party!"

Oh right, a party!

Well, I've never partied under the cherry trees.

I have viewed flowers, but once in my life I'd like to make merry in the way that people mean!

I told my assistants, "Let's go this year!" and we were all so excited.

And here it's March and I'm so overworked! (*crying*) I guess I can take comfort in the fact that every year, there's at least a chance that we'll go.

–YUU WATASE

AUTHOR BIO

Born March 5 in Osaka, Yuu Watase debuted in the *Shôjo Comic* manga anthology in 1989. She won the 43rd Shogakukan Manga Award with *Ceres: Celestial Legend*. One of her most famous works is *Fushigi Yûgi*, a series that has inspired the prequel *Fushigi Yûgi: Genbu Kaiden*. In 2008, *Arata: The Legend* started serialization in *Shonen Sunday*.

ARATA: THE LEGEND

Volume 23
Shonen Sunday Edition

Story and Art by YUU WATASE

ARATA KANGATARI Vol. 23
by Yuu WATASE

Original Japanese edition published by SHOGAKUKAN.
English translation rights in the United States of America, Canada, the United Kingdom and Ireland arranged with SHOGAKUKAN.

English Adaptation: Lance Caselman
Translation: JN Productions
Touch-up Art & Lettering: Rina Mapa
Design: Veronica Casson
Editor: Gary Leach

Printed in the U.S.A.

Published by VIZ Media, LLC
P.O. Box 77010
San Francisco, CA 94107

10 9 8 7 6 5 4 3 2 1
First printing, September 2015

RATED T FOR TEEN

PARENTAL ADVISORY
ARATA: THE LEGEND is rated T for Teen and is recommended for ages 13 and up. This volume contains fantasy violence.
ratings.viz.com

www.viz.com

MANGA STARTS ON SUNDAY

WWW.SHONENSUNDAY.COM

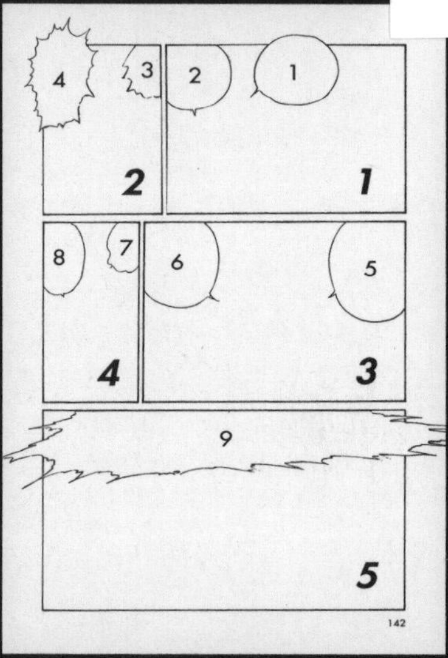
1
2
1
3
4
2
5
6
3
7
8
4
9
5
142

← Follow the action this way.

THIS IS THE LAST PAGE

Arata: The Legend has been printed in the original Japanese format in order to preserve the orientation of the original artwork.

Please turn it around and begin reading from right to left. Unlike English, Japanese is read right to left, so Japanese comics are read in reverse order from the way English comics are typically read. Have fun with it!